Religion, Rights and Secular Society

Religion, Rights and Secular Society

European Perspectives

Edited by

Peter Cumper

University of Leicester, UK

Tom Lewis

Nottingham Trent University, UK

Edward Elgar

Cheltenham, UK • Northampton, MA, USA

Published by
Edward Elgar Publishing Limited
The Lypiatts
15 Lansdown Road
Cheltenham
Glos GL50 2JA
UK

Edward Elgar Publishing, Inc.
William Pratt House
9 Dewey Court
Northampton
Massachusetts 01060
USA

A catalogue record for this book
is available from the British Library

Library of Congress Control Number: 2012944444

ISBN 978 1 84980 367 0

Typeset by Servis Filmsetting Ltd, Stockport, Cheshire
Printed and bound by MPG Books Group, UK

Contents

Contributors

Sylvie Bacquet is a Senior Lecturer in Law at the University of Westminster, UK. Much of her research to date has focused on Law and Religion, including religious discrimination and religious symbols at school. Her recent publications include 'Manifestation of belief and religious symbols at schools: setting boundaries in English courts', (2009) (4) *Religion and Human Rights* 121, and 'School uniforms, religious symbols and the Human Rights Act 1998: the "Purity Ring" case', (2008) *Education Law Journal* 11.

Marjolein van den Brink is a Lecturer in Law in the Netherlands Institute of Human Rights (SIM), in the Law School at Utrecht University, the Netherlands. Between 2001 and 2010 she combined this position with membership of the Dutch national equal opportunities body (*Commissie gelijke behandeling*). She has published on a variety of issues, which include human rights, the (ir)relevance of sex as a legal category, daily care as a legal issue, the accommodation of religious practices and a gender analysis of the concept of state sovereignty.

Peter Cumper is a Senior Lecturer in Law at the University of Leicester, UK. He undertakes research in the field of law and religion, with particular reference to domestic and European human rights law.

Eoin Daly is a Lecturer in Law at the School of Law, University College Dublin, Ireland. He lectures on constitutional law, legal theory and comparative law. His main research interests lie in the area of religious freedom in constitutional law, as well as in liberal and republican theories of justice, particularly Rawls's social contract.

Grace Davie is Professor Emerita in the Sociology of Religion at the University of Exeter, UK. She is a past President of the American Association for the Sociology of Religion (2003) and of the Research Committee 22 (Sociology of Religion) of the International Sociological Association (2002–6). In 2000–01 she was the Kerstin-Hesselgren Professor at the University of Uppsala, where she returned for extended visits in 2006–7, 2010 and 2012. In January 2008 she received an honorary degree from Uppsala. In addition to numerous chapters and articles, she is the author of *Religion in Britain since 1945* (Blackwell, 1994), *Religion in Modern Europe* (Oxford University Press, 2000), *Europe: the Exceptional Case* (Darton Longman and Todd, 2002) and *The Sociology of Religion* (SAGE, 2007), the second edition of which will be published in 2013. She is co-author of *Religious America, Secular Europe* (Ashgate, 2008) and co-editor of *Predicting Religion* (Ashgate, 2003) and *Welfare and Religion in 21st Century Europe* (2 vols) (Ashgate, 2010 and 2011).

Peter W Edge is Professor of Law at Oxford Brookes School of Law, Oxford, UK. He currently leads the Applied Study of Law and Religion Group. Recent publications include 'Believer beware: the challenges of commercial religion' in *Legal Studies* (2012), and 'Determining religion in 21st century England and Wales in the *Oxford Journal of Law and Religion* (2012).

Achilles C Emilianides is an Associate Professor of Law and Head of the Department of Law at the University of Nicosia, Cyprus, and the Director of Cyprus Institute for Church and State Relations. His recent publications include *Law and Religion in Cyprus* (Kluwer, 2011), *Religious Freedom in the European Union* (Peeters, 2010) and *Welfare of the Child and Beliefs of the Parents* (University of Nicosia Press, 2010).

Tom Lewis is a Reader in Law at Nottingham Trent University, UK and is Director of the Centre for Conflict, Rights and Justice at Nottingham Law School. His research covers constitutional law and human rights, with a particular emphasis on freedom of expression and freedom of religion and belief.

Titia Loenen is Professor of Legal Theory, with special interest in gender and law, at Utrecht University, the Netherlands. Her research covers human rights, equality theory and international, European and Dutch non-discrimination law. It is now focusing on gender and multicultural/ religious issues.

Valerie A Lykes, MA is a Doctoral Student in the Interdisciplinary Social Psychology Programme at the University of Nevada, Reno, USA. Her main focus area is religion, with consideration of its influence on politics, ageing and the environment.

Julie Mertus is a Professor and Co-Director of the MA program in Ethics, Peace and Global Affairs at the American University, Washington DC, USA. She has over twenty years of experience working for a wide range of non-governmental and governmental human rights organisations in the human rights and peace-building field. Her book *Bait and Switch: Human Rights and US Foreign Policy* (1st edn, Routledge, 2004; 2nd edn, Routledge,

2009) was named 'human rights book of the year' by the American Political Science Association Human Rights Section in 2005. Her work has also appeared in law journals and leading multidisciplinary journals such as *Ethics and International Affairs*, *Global Governance*, *International Studies Perspectives*, *International Feminist Journal of Politics* and *The Harvard International Review*.

Michaela Moravčíková is Director of the Institute for Legal Aspects of Religious Freedom in the Faculty of Law at the University of Trnava, Slovakia. She obtained her doctoral degree at the Theological Faculty of the Palacký University, Olomouc, in the Czech Republic. She has published widely in the field of law and religion on issues including natural rights, conscientious objection, contractual relations between church and state, the position of Islam in Europe, new religious movements and matters relating to multiculturalism and human rights.

Jørgen S Nielsen is Professor of Islamic Studies in the Faculty of Theology at the University of Copenhagen, Denmark. He has previously held academic positions in Beirut, Birmingham (UK) and Damascus. His research is focused on the situation of Muslims in Europe, and his major recent publications include *Muslims in Western Europe* (3rd edn, Edinburgh University Press, 2004; Arabic translation, Saqi Press, 2006), *Shari'a as Discourse: Legal Traditions and the Encounter with Europe* (ed, with Lisbet Christoffersen), (Ashgate, 2010) and *Yearbook of Muslims in Europe* (chief ed), (Brill, 2009).

Eugenia Relaño Pastor works currently as a legal adviser to the Spanish Ombudsman, and is also an Assistant Professor of Law at University Complutense (Madrid), Spain. She was a Fulbright Fellow in Salzburg in 2001 on the topic of International Human Rights. She has previously held visiting positions at Harvard University, the University of California, Berkeley, the University of Oxford, the Norwegian Institute of Human Rights and the University of Ottawa (Canada). She has published widely in the fields of law, religion and international human rights, is a member of the Legal Working Group of the European Group of NHRIs (Council of Europe) and is also a member of the Minority Research Network.

James T Richardson is Foundation Professor of Sociology and Judicial Studies at the University of Nevada, Reno, USA, where he is director of the Grant Sawyer Center for Justice Studies and a member of the Sociology Department and the Social Psychology Doctoral Programme. He has undertaken research for several decades on new religious movements, as well as the use of social and behavioural scientific evidence in courts around the world. He has produced about 300 articles and chapters in books, as well as a dozen books, including *Regulating Religion: Case Studies from around the Globe* (Springer, 2004) and most recently (with Stuart Wright) *Saints under Siege: The Texas State Raid on the Fundamentalist Latter-Day Saints* (New York University Press, 2011).

Gerhard Robbers is Professor for Public Law at the University of Trier, Germany. He is Director of the Institute for European Constitutional Law and Director of the Institute for Legal Policy at Trier University. Since 2008 he has also served as a Judge at the Constitutional Court of Rhineland-Palatinate. In 2003–4 he was President of the European Consortium of Church and State Research, and he is also a member of the Advisory Council for Freedom of Religion at ODIHR/OSCE. His main areas of work are law and religion, constitutional law and international public law, and he has served as an advisor to several national governments and international organisations. His publications include *Encyclopedia of World Constitutions* (ed), (3 vols) (Facts on File, 2006), *An Introduction to German Law*, (5th edn, Nomos, 2012) and *State and Church in the European Union* (ed), (2nd edn, Nomos, 2005) and he has also published in the areas of public law, civil ecclesiastical law, legal philosophy, constitutional history and European Union law.

Renata Uitz is Professor of Law, Chair of the Comparative Constitutional Law Programme and Head of the Legal Studies Department at the Central European University, Budapest. Her teaching and research covers problems in transition to democracy and constitutional review, as well as questions of individual liberty, including freedom of religion.

Marco Ventura is a Full Professor in the Faculty of Law at the University of Siena, Italy, a Professor at the Faculty of Canon Law at the Katholieke Universiteit Leuven, Belgium and an Associate Researcher at the Centre 'Société, Droit et Religion en Europe' (National Research Council, University of Strasbourg, France). He has been an academic visitor at University College London, the University of Oxford, the University of Strasbourg, the University of Coimbra, the Free University of Bruxelles, the Centro de Formação Jurídica e Judiciária of Macau, the Indian Law Institute of New Delhi and the University of Cape Town. His recent publications include *Wie wirkt sich die europäische Integration auf die Religion aus?* in G E Rusconi (ed), *Der säkularisierte Staat im postsäkularen Zeitalter* (Duncker & Humblot, 2010), 281 and 'The changing civil religion of secular Europe' (2011) 41(4), *George Washington University International Law Review* 947.

Abbreviations

CEDAW	UN Women's Rights Committee
CIE	Islamic Commission of Spain
COE	Council of Europe
CONTEST	UK counter-terrorism strategy
ECFR	European Council for Fatwa and Research
ECHR	European Convention on Human Rights 1950
ECtHR	European Court of Human Rights
ETC	(Dutch) Equal Treatment Commission (Dutch abbreviation: CGB)
FBO	faith-based organisation
FCI	Federation of Israelite Communities of Spain
FEREDE	Federation of Evangelical Religious Entities of Spain
GG	(German) *Grundgesetz* (Basic Law)
HRA	(UK) Human Rights Act 1998
LOLR	(Spain) *Ley Orgánica de Libertad Religiosa* (Organic Law of Religious Freedom)
MINAB	(UK) Mosques and Imams National Advisory Board
NGO	non-govermental organisation
NRM	new religious movements
RS	Republika Srpska
UOIF	Union des Organisations Islamiques de France
WRV	Constitution of the Weimar Republic

1. Introduction: freedom of religion and belief – the contemporary context

Peter Cumper and Tom Lewis

Attempting to assess or measure the extent to which the disparate populations of Europe are currently committed to religious or equivalent forms
of belief is a challenging task. It is one that is compounded by the fact that
today, as a senior British judge has observed, 'we live in a society, which is at
one and the same time becoming both increasingly secular but also increasingly diverse in religious affiliation'[1] – a comment that seems applicable not
just to the UK, but to many other parts of the continent.[2] Given the long-
standing co-existence of strong faith and secular traditions in Europe, and
the arrival of a multitude of other religious and equivalent philosophical
beliefs more recently through immigration, it is perhaps hardly surprising
that one commentator has described Europe's current relationship with
religion as being a 'complicated matter'.[3] Thus, it remains unclear whether
contemporary Europe can be best described as a 'Christian', 'secular', or
even a 'post-secular' continent.

To the extent that it is possible to estimate the religious 'temperature'
of such a vast and religiously diverse area, there is plenty of evidence to
suggest that, in parts of Europe, organised religion is in retreat. For a start,
unlike the United States where church attendance has traditionally (by
Western standards) been high,[4] in recent decades mainstream churches in
many European states have not only experienced a significant decline in

---

[1] Munby LJ in *Singh v Entry Clearance Officer New Delhi* [2004] EWCA Civ
1075, [62].
[2] See for example Jürgen Habermas, 'Religion in the Public Sphere' (2006) 14
(1) *European Journal of Philosophy*, 1–25.
[3] Andrew M Greeley, *Religion in Europe at the End of the Second Millennium:
A Sociological Profile* (Transaction, 2004) xii.
[4] See for example Howard M Bahr and Bruce A Chadwick, 'Religion and
family in Middletown, USA' (1985) 47(2) *Journal of Marriage and Family*, 407 and
C Kirk Hadaway, Penny Long Marler and Mark Chaves, 'What the polls don't

membership,[5] but have even struggled to recruit new priests or religious leaders.[6] Moreover, the growing influence of non-religious precepts in European public life is highlighted by the well-publicised concerns of some prominent religious leaders that Christianity is increasingly under threat from secular values.[7] Additional factors that have detrimentally affected the influence of religion in Europe in recent years include: the rise of militant Islam and other forms of religious extremism; high-profile terrorist acts in the name of a religion (for example '9/11' and the attacks on Madrid (2004) and London (2005)); child-sex scandals involving priests and claims of church cover-ups; an apparent conflict between science and the beliefs of some faith groups (for example the evolution and creationism debate); and even the publication of an unprecedented number of best-selling books on the perceived irrationality of religious belief.[8] Thus, at first sight, it might appear that Europe is today a decidedly 'secular' continent. However, on closer inspection, this is evidently not the case, and rumours of the demise of religion in Europe have, to paraphrase Mark Twain, been 'greatly exaggerated'.

In the last decade or so there has been a global resurgence of religion in international affairs, which has prompted claims of a 'desecularisation of the world'.[9] By the same token, a number of factors have contributed to a re-emergence of religion in the public sphere across much of Europe. These factors include: the revival of religious belief in some European

---

show: a closer look at US church attendance' (1993) 58(6) *American Sociological Review*, 741.

5   See for example Callum G Brown, *The Death of Christian Britain (Christianity and Society in the Modern World)* (Routledge, 2000) and Grace Davie, *Europe: The Exceptional Case* (Darton, Longman and Todd, 2002).

6   See for example José Pérez Vilariño and José L Sequeiros Tizón, 'The demographic transition of the Catholic priesthood and the end of clericalism in Spain', (1998) 59(1) *Sociology of Religion* 25.

7   See for example the comments of the former Archbishop of Canterbury, Lord Carey, who has accused the UK judiciary of having a 'disparaging attitude to the Christian faith and its values' and of having a 'clear *animus*' towards Christian beliefs: *McFarlane v Relate Avon Limited* [2010] EWCA Civ B1 at [17]; [2010] I.C.R. 507 (EAT).

8   See for example Richard Dawkins, *The God Delusion* (Houghton Mifflin, 2006); Christopher Hitchens, *God Is Not Great: How Religion Poisons Everything* (Twelve Books, 2007); Sam Harris, *The End of Faith: Religion, Terror, and the Future of Reason* (Free Press, 2006); and Daniel C Dennett, *Breaking the Spell: Religion as a Natural Phenomenon* (Penguin, 2007).

9   Peter L Berger (ed) *The Desecularisation of the World: Resurgent Religion in World Politics* (William B Eerdmans Publishing Co, 1999).

states;[10] a growth in 'alternative' forms of spirituality;[11] the proliferation of new religious movements;[12] the influence of religion in domestic political discourse;[13] the centrality of religion in the identity of many European minority faith communities;[14] and a rejection by some faith groups (particularly Muslims) of rigid public/private classifications in relation to the manifestation of religious belief.[15] These developments do not merely cast doubt on the view that religion in Europe is in terminal decline, but have even prompted some commentators to claim that 'God is back'.[16] The increasing influence of faith in European public life is also demonstrated by the fact that some of the continent's most influential scholars are now engaging in a constructive dialogue with religious leaders in a way that would have been almost unimaginable in an earlier age.[17] Accordingly, given what Karen Armstrong has termed a 'backlash against secularism' in the West,[18] few now dispute the potential impact of religion in the public sphere,[19] and even

---

[10] See Willfried Spohn, 'Multiple modernity, nationalism and religion: a global perspective' (2003) 51(3/4) *Current Sociology*, 265.

[11] See for example Cole Moreton, *Is God Still an Englishman?: How We Lost Our Faith (But Found New Soul)* (Little, Brown, 2010) and Grace Davie, *Religion in Britain Since 1945: Believing without Belonging (Making Contemporary Britain)* (Wiley Blackwell, 1994).

[12] See for example R Stark, 'Europe's receptivity to new religious movements: Round two (1993) 32 *Journal for the Scientific Study of Religion*, 389.

[13] See Martin Beckford, 'Gordon Brown insists Britain is still Christian country', *The Daily Telegraph* (London, 7 August 2009) available at http://www.telegraph.co.uk/news/politics/gordon-brown/5988706/Gordon-Brown-insists-Britain-is-still-Christian-country.html and Robert Marquand, 'With Pope's visit, Sarkozy challenges French secularism', *The Christian Science Monitor* (Boston, MA, 15 September 2008) available at http://www.csmonitor.com/World/Europe/2008/0915/p01s01-woeu.html.

[14] See for example Z Khan, 'Muslims' presence in Europe: the British dimension – identity, integration and community activism', (2000) 48(4) *Current Sociology*, 29.

[15] See for example David Harte, 'Defining the legal boundaries of orthodoxy for public and private religion in England' in R O'Dair and A Lewis (eds) *Law and Religion* (Oxford University Press, 2001) 471.

[16] John Micklethwait and Adrian Wooldridge, *God is Back: How the Global Rise of Faith is Changing the World* (Penguin, 2010).

[17] See for example Joseph Ratzinger and Jürgen Habermas, *The Dialectics of Secularization: On Reason and Religion* (Ignatius Press, 2007) and Jürgen Habermas, *An Awareness of What is Missing: Faith and Reason in a Post-secular Age* (Polity Press, 2010).

[18] See Karen Armstrong, 'Resisting modernity: the backlash against secularism', (2004) 25(4) *Harvard International Review*, 40.

[19] Judith Butler, Jürgen Habermas, Charles Taylor and Cornel West, *The Power of Religion in the Public Sphere* (Columbia University Press, 2011).

scholars that a decade ago referred to God as being 'dead' in the West now reflect changed perceptions by describing secularism as an 'unfashionable theory'.[20] Of course, one must acknowledge that secularism, in its many different forms, shows no sign of vacating the public stage in contemporary Europe,[21] but it is equally apposite to note that once commonly held assumptions that religion would in time become a spent force in European public life have proven to be ill-founded.

THE BOOK'S STRUCTURE AND THEMES

It is within the context of nations having to balance religious and secular values that this book examines a number of the ways in which religion and equivalent belief are currently protected in Europe. The structure of the book is as follows. Its initial focus is on western Europe. It starts by examining three nations (the Netherlands, the UK and Germany) that have been (at least in part) shaped by the Protestant tradition, before turning to four countries (Ireland, Spain, Italy and France), that have had historically close ties (at least in terms of the religious affiliation of their citizens) with the Roman Catholic Church. We then move eastwards and consider freedom of religious belief in a number of nations that have faced challenges of the kind that have not been experienced, in recent decades, by their western European counterparts. We begin with the Republic of Cyprus, the southern part of that divided island, before proceeding to focus on a number of states that, in the last half-century, suffered under the yoke of Communism. In this regard we examine Hungary, followed by a brief history of religious freedom in Slovakia, the Czech Republic and Poland, before finally considering the relevant position in Bosnia, Kosova and the Former Yugoslav Republic of Macedonia. In the last section of the book, our attention turns to three thematic chapters that consider, respectively, the changing patterns of religion and belief in Europe; the status of Islam and Europe's Muslims; and finally, the protection of new religious movements and other minority faith groups in Europe.

Whilst a range of very different constitutional models and arrangements can be found today in Europe, a number of common themes pervade many of the chapters in this book. The first of these is that the very *existence*

---

[20]   See for example Steve Bruce, *Secularization: In Defence of an Unfashionable Theory* (Oxford University Press, 2011) and Steve Bruce, *God is Dead: Secularism in the West* (Blackwell, 2002).

[21]   See for example Craig Calhoun, Mark Juergensmeyer and Jonathan Van Antwerpen (eds) *Rethinking Secularism* (Oxford University Press, 2011).

of some European states can be traced back to violent conflicts that once had their origins in religious enmity. From the Great Schism between the Eastern Orthodox and Roman Catholic Churches in 1054 to the Protestant Reformation in the sixteenth century, events with a religious dimension have helped to shape the spiritual *and* political maps of Europe. Secondly, a distinctive religious identity has often been regarded as a key marker of national affiliation in Europe, as witnessed by the doctrine of *cuius regio eius religio* (whose region, his religion) established at the Peace of Augsburg in 1555, or more recent constitutional arrangements under which certain religions are afforded a unique and privileged status. A third common theme is that whilst religion itself has been a formative element in the creation of the national identities of European states, the struggles *between* religious groups have often been the catalyst for constitutional 'compromises' (often tortuously reached) ensuring de facto (though not always de jure) state neutrality on matters of faith. Fourthly, there seems little doubt that Christianity has had a considerable impact on European public life, as illustrated by the fact that Europe's working week and public holidays tend to be reflective of the Christian calendar. And finally, as the book makes clear, a salient truth about the role and status of religious belief across Europe is that there exists a kaleidoscope of diversity on the status of religion in European societies, and the methods/means by which religious freedom (for both individuals and groups) can be most appropriately secured. So deeply engrained is this view that the European Court of Human Rights has consistently used it to justify the granting of a wide margin of appreciation to states in cases involving religion, belief and secular values.[22]

THE RELATIONSHIP BETWEEN RELIGIOUS AND SECULAR VALUES

At the heart of the relationship between religious and secular values in contemporary Europe lies a paradox. As noted above, the values of European liberal democracies in the twenty-first century – de facto state neutrality, and the protection of human rights, tolerance, 'liberty, equality, fraternity' – often lead to religious and social pluralism, as individuals and groups exercise their liberty and pursue their own paths in matters of

---

[22] See for example *Şahin v Turkey* (App no 44774/98) (10 November 2005) (GC) (2007) 44 EHRR 5 at [109]; *Otto-Preminger-Institut v Austria* (App no 13470/87) (20 September 1994) (1994) 19 EHRR 34 at [50]; and *Murphy v Ireland* (App no 44179/98) (10 July 2003) (2004) 38 EHRR 13 at [67].

faith. Yet, ironically, it appears that these paths are often at odds with the *secular* liberal values that have facilitated their very existence. This is most obviously the case in areas ranging from discrimination on the grounds of one's gender or sexuality to curbs on freedom of expression and blasphemy laws. This aforementioned paradox is also present in the secular tenet that a counterpart of state neutrality is that religion should be an essentially *private* matter. Of course, in many respects this tenet can protect freedom of religion, since it ensures that there is an equal footing between all different faiths – but it may also conflict with various elements of religious belief, such as where a 'believer' maintains that a particular conviction requires him/her, say, to wear a form of religious dress or display a certain religious symbol in public. As the following chapters make clear, this paradox has led to a number of related tensions in the nations under consideration.

The first such tension often occurs when religious groups are relatively new to a particular state, or their members were not involved in the crucial constitutional 'compromises' that were reached many years earlier between the dominant religion and the state's organs of government. This is most obviously the case in relation to immigrant minority faith communities (for example Muslims, Hindus, Sikhs, Buddhists) or groups that are often regarded as being new religious movements (for example Jehovah's Witnesses, Mormons, Scientologists). Many of the religious controversies of the last few decades have revolved, in different ways, around this tension, and range from the publication of allegedly blasphemous material (for example *The Satanic Verses* and the 'Danish cartoons' furores in 1988 and 2005 respectively) to the emotive Islamic 'headscarf' debates throughout much of Europe. A second related tension occurs when there is a conflict between the tenets of contemporary secular thought and long-standing religious precepts. A case in point is where national legislation outlaws discrimination on the grounds of sexuality or sexual orientation in a way that is contrary to the way in which some conservative religious organisations interpret their sacred texts. And a final tension that exists, particularly in the new democracies that have emerged in recent decades in central and eastern Europe, is where historically powerful churches seek to retain the residues of their hegemony, or further, wish to reassert it in areas such as education or church building, following the demise of repressive regimes. The resulting picture is that some citizens are left feeling isolated and marginalised, while others regret having lost the 'certainties' of previous generations. Thus, mindful of such tensions, this book will seek, at least in part, to explore some of the problems, challenges and opportunities facing law and policy makers in having to balance a myriad of Christian, secular and multi-faith values in a number of European states.

A SUMMARY OF THE CHAPTERS

In the first chapter on the Netherlands, Marjolein van den Brink and Titia Loenen explain how the Netherlands, whilst being a 'state that was basically founded on Protestantism', developed methods to avoid religious conflict. These started with the abolition of the 'preferred' status of the Protestant Reformed Church and thereafter the gradual severing of ties between church and state, which culminated in the 1983 Constitution that removed all religious provisions, other than those guaranteeing freedom of religion. Van den Brink and Loenen demonstrate how the modern Netherlands has adopted an approach of 'inclusive neutrality' in which the state itself is secular (in that it maintains an impartial stance towards many religions) but adopts a 'benevolent and accommodating' stance towards religion, and is 'not intent on banning religion from the public sphere'. The authors also discuss how the Dutch courts have tended to adopt a balanced approach in relation to issues such as the wearing of Islamic dress by public employees, the granting of religion-based exemptions for officials officiating at gay marriages, and the case of a religious political party that cited faith as the basis for its exclusion of women from full membership. However, they conclude that the country is now at a 'crossroads', and that there are signs that it may adopt a more exclusivist approach, especially with regard to Islam, in the future.

The United Kingdom (UK) experiences many challenges similar to those faced by the Netherlands, as Peter Edge explains. The constitutional structure of the UK is 'distinctive, although not quite unique' in that there is no single, codified, constitutional instrument that affords protection to freedom of religion or equivalent belief. The UK is also in an unusual position in that, whilst it is an 'assertively secular state', it is also the home of an Established Church (the Church of England). In considering the consequences of Establishment, Edge observes that the monarch is the Supreme Governor of the Church of England, and that 26 Church of England Bishops (the Lords Spiritual) still retain seats in the House of Lords, the second chamber of the UK's Parliament. This formal legal position, however, belies the fact that over the centuries the UK has become increasingly tolerant of religious difference, at least in practice. In particular, the Human Rights Act 1998 has incorporated the bulk of the European Convention on Human Rights (ECHR) 1950 into UK law, and these rights have been supplemented by more recently enacted equalities legislation, outlawing discrimination on a range of grounds, including religion and belief. Notwithstanding some recent controversies in regard to discrimination on grounds of sexual orientation and religious freedom, the UK model is today synonymous with a 'confident assertion of state values', and a modern secular constitutional order, despite traditional constitutional arrangements that are 'anything but secular'.

In Germany, according to Gerhard Robbers, the relationship between law and religion has been strongly influenced by the 'complete moral and legal breakdown under National Socialism'. Other relevant factors in this regard include the bloody sixteenth-century religious wars between Catholics and Protestants, and, more recently, the traumatic division of Germany between East and West that followed the Second World War and lasted until 1990. Today the German Constitution begins with an *invocatio dei* – not a reference to a Christian God (which would have been inconceivable after the Holocaust) but rather a nod in the direction of transcendence and a reminder that there 'is more and other than the state and its constitution, something that goes beyond what is made by human kind'. Robbers suggests that the German position is not one of 'secularism', at least in the *laicist* sense of implying hostility towards religion. Instead, the constitutional position is one of 'neutrality' in that the state does not base its legitimacy on religious assumptions yet nevertheless has a 'responsibility to make religious life possible'. Key constitutional principles, in addition to neutrality, include tolerance, parity, pluralism and an 'openness to religion'. According to Robbers, Germany's difficult recent past has 'deeply affected' the constitutional order, and has allowed for the mitigation of many of the current tensions facing the nation, especially in relation to how it responds to the religious practices of its immigrant communities.

The Republic of Ireland, which is next examined, is unlike many of its 'northern' European neighbours in that it is a country that has traditionally been (and arguably still continues to be) significantly influenced by Roman Catholicism. In his chapter on Ireland, Eoin Daly explains how the relevant Irish constitutional arrangements are associated with two competing narratives. Liberal secular-republican values have to be balanced against a 'romantic-Gaelic nationalism' that emphasises a 'shared religious identity' as one of the 'anchoring points of national identity'. Daly suggests that the 'distinctiveness of the role of religion in Ireland's constitutional order lies primarily in the oscillation between the[se] competing narratives'. This tension is evident in several areas that include the 1937 Constitution itself (which 'embraces a specifically religious dimension' in its preamble); church–state relations in regard to Ireland's denominational (Roman Catholic) schools; and the difficult question of balancing religious freedom and the principle of non-discrimination. Whilst Daly observes that the religious ethos of the broader constitutional order has dissipated in recent decades, along with a weakening of the grasp of religion on the public sphere, the constitutional provisions addressing religion still remain 'poised between a liberal requirement of state neutrality . . . and a recognition of the centrality of religion to national identity'.

Spain, like Ireland, is a nation in which the Catholic Church has played a very important role in shaping national identity. Traditionally, as Eugenia Relaño Pastor points out, 'to be a Spaniard and to be a Catholic were understood as being equivalent – two sides of a single national identity', which gives Catholicism a 'fundamental role in the national consciousness'. For much of the twentieth century Spain alternated between two extremes: on one hand, under the Second Republic of 1931-6, there was an anti-clerical reaction to the centuries of Catholic domination at the heart of Spain's body politic; and, on the other, under General Franco, a confessional state existed that had strong links to the Roman Catholic Church. Pastor explains how the 1978 Constitution, together with the Organic Law on Religious Freedom (1980), improved the position greatly by proclaiming that Spain had no official religion, which helped to enshrine religious liberty, and thereby establish a framework for religious pluralism and tolerance. However, she maintains that the current system is far from perfect when it comes to protecting the religious freedom of minority faiths – and that the present arrangements need 'fine-tuning', especially because of the continued privileged position of the Catholic church within the state, as well as the requirement for minority religions to be granted official recognition. What is needed, argues Pastor, is the creation of a 'third way' that is sensitive to 'the public promotion of the greatest level of diversity compatible with harmonious coexistence', and she is hopeful that this may be provided by recently proposed legal reforms.

In Italy, as in Spain, the national sense of identity or self-conception has historically been inextricably linked to Roman Catholicism. However, as Marco Ventura explains, unlike some other European nations (for example Spain) this phenomenon has strongly re-emerged in recent years. In tracing the influence of Catholicism and *laicità* in Italy, Ventura points out that the Constitutional Court stated in 1989 that *laicità* was the 'supreme constitutional principle', and in 1997 it was said that this principle implied 'the equidistance and the impartiality of the law with regard to all religious denominations'. However, factors from the early 1990s that led to a retreat of *laicità* and the growth of what Ventura terms 'Christian secular Italy' include the effects of 'rapid and massive immigration'; the impact of Italian bishops becoming more active in the public sphere in promoting the role of Italy as a 'bulwark against the spreading in Europe of social secularization and political and legal secularism'; and the influence of Silvio Berlusconi who, eager to please the Catholic church, objected to several liberalising measures in the fields of equality and family law. Ventura also comments on the important case of *Lautsi v Italy*, in which the Grand Chamber of

the European Court of Human Rights in 2011 held that the requirement
for the crucifix to be displayed in the classrooms of Italian schools does
not violate the ECHR. Ventura concludes that, against the background of
a heavily secularised and increasingly multi-religious Italian society, Italy
is indisputably a *stato laico*, but acknowledges that the exact meaning of
laicità is highly contested.

Just as the debate on the role of faith in public life in Italy has been associated in recent years with a religious symbol (the crucifix), so too has the
debate in France centred upon a religious symbol, though in the French case
the emphasis has been on symbolism of a different kind – religious dress.
In her chapter on France Sylvie Bacquet explains how *läicité* has become
the very 'cornerstone of French republicanism', emerging 'as a reaction to
the church at a time when France was overwhelmingly Catholic'. A central
trope of this republicanism – which goes back to the 1789 revolution and
the Enlightenment, and crystallised in the 1905 settlement that separates
church and state – is a 'universalist' view that 'purports to establish French
identity, and requires that the individual transcends any cultural, social or
religious belonging in order to achieve individual autonomy . . .'. Bacquet
explains how the immigration of Muslims from France's former colonies in
the last half-century has posed a serious challenge to the French conception
of *läicité,* not least because the 'goal of creating a universal community of
citizens' sharing a single culture 'sits uneasily with the diverse French social
reality'. Bacquet also traces the debates over the legal bans on headscarves
and *burqas*, and concludes that if the condition of being seen as a French
citizen is to 'detach oneself from any religious and cultural background',
then there is a risk that this 'may lead to ignorance and segregation rather
than integration'.

Notions of citizenship and religion are also considered by Achilles
Emilianides in the context of Cyprus, which has been divided on religious
lines since the Turkish invasion of the north of the island in 1974. In his
chapter, Emilianides gives an account of the majority Orthodox Christian
south, in which religious organisations and individual freedom of religion
and belief are afforded strong constitutional protection, notwithstanding the fact that the overwhelming majority of people there belong to the
Autocephalous Cypriot Orthodox church. What is more, the five constitutionally recognised religious groupings enjoy considerable autonomy
with regard to their internal affairs and administration of property. As
Emilianides points out, this autonomy has its roots in Ottoman law that
preceded Cypriot independence. Emilianides characterises the model
prevailing in Cyprus as essentially 'pluralistic', with the state recognising
and embracing the 'public dimension to religion, while at the same time
attempting cooperation with all religions'. However, tensions nevertheless

arise, since the 'lofty constitutional declarations about the intended equal standing of all religions before the law' often do not accord with 'social reality', as illustrated by the fact that the 'Archbishop's standing, as the leader of the Orthodox Church . . . rivals, in stature and importance, the President of the Republic' – a position with which other faiths are not able to compete. These tensions have arisen in areas such as the provision of education, the allocation of public space for worship and the funding of projects by the state more generally. As Emilianides concludes, 'it is only by putting the legal principles into actual practice and by taking into account the social realities in a never-ending quest for reform, that the Cypriot legal system might live up to its characterisation as "pluralistic"'.

We now turn to a number of countries in central and eastern Europe that, during the last half-century, have been transformed (to varying degrees) from avowedly Communist states to emerging democracies, in which religious identities been permitted to re-emerge within the parameters of new constitutional settlements. A nation in point is Hungary, which is examined by Renata Uitz. In her chapter Uitz suggests that Hungary has avoided some of the causes of tension currently present in other European states because it has not been 'a primary target for immigration', and 'still does not have a very visible or sizeable Muslim community'. In reviewing Hungary's history of religious freedom Uitz observes that, since the Reformation, it has swung on a 'pendulum', alternating between tolerant and restrictive regimes – for example, ranging from a 'wave of religious toleration' in the early seventeenth century to an 'aggressive Counter-Reformation' late in that century. A similar swing was also evident in the second half of the twentieth century. Curbs on religious freedom under Communism were replaced by the enactment of the (post-Soviet) democratic Hungarian constitution, and with a new Act guaranteeing freedom of conscience and religion (1990), a permissive system for the registration of churches was established that allowed 'for unprecedented religious diversity and opportunities for new faith-based initiatives'. Very recently, however, the pendulum has swung back with the new constitution of 2011. This, Uitz observes, reads in parts like an 'ode to Christianity', in that it explicitly refers to the 'role of Christianity in the preservation of nationhood'. Furthermore, in 2011, following accusations that some small religious organisations were nothing more than 'business sects' used for money-laundering purposes, the liberal 1990 regime on the registration of religious denominations has been tightened up, with the result that Uitz describes it as 'highly problematic from a human rights perspective'. In her conclusion Uitz expresses the hope that the pendulum will swing back, as has been the case before in Hungarian history.

In the next chapter Michaela Moravčíková sketches the history of religious freedom in three countries that also suffered under the yoke of totalitarianism for much of the twentieth century: Slovakia, the Czech Republic and Poland. She observes that, whilst all three nations continue to bear the legacy of their post-war Communist past, there are significant differences between these states – not least in the religious affiliations of their populations – with Poland and Slovakia being considered to be Roman Catholic, while the Czech Republic (which was conjoined with Slovakia as a single state until 1993) is now generally regarded 'as being one of Europe's most atheistic countries'. Moravčíková also points out that there are striking differences in relation to the constitutional status of religion in the respective states. For example, the preamble to Poland's constitution of 1997 contains both an *invocatio dei* and an acknowledgement that it is a 'culture rooted in the Christian heritage of the nation and in universal human values', whilst the preamble to the 1992 constitution of the Slovak Republic is more muted, in that it refers to the 'spiritual heritage' of Slovakia. In contrast, the preamble to the 1993 Czech constitution refers only to secular values such as human dignity, equality, democracy and respect for human rights. In spite of these differences of emphasis Moravčíková comments that important provisions guarantee freedom of religion and belief in the constitutions of Slovakia, the Czech Republic and Poland.

In the chapter that follows Julie Mertus focuses on Bosnia, Kosova and the Former Yugoslav Republic of Macedonia – parts of Europe in which religious, cultural and ethnic differences led to vicious and bloody conflicts a mere two decades ago. Mertus explains that during the Balkan war 'religion played a role in demarcating the enemy', and consequently the creation of democratic states respecting religious freedom has presented an 'incredible challenge'. In her chapter she chooses to focus, because of their 'illustrative nature', on three of the states that were parties to the conflict in the former Yugoslavia: Bosnia-Herzegovina ('Bosnia'), Kosova and the Former Yugoslav Republic of Macedonia ('Macedonia'). Since the breakup of Yugoslavia, the experience of each of these states, with regard to religious freedom, has been very different. In Bosnia, the most ethnically and religiously diverse of these states, there is a conflation of religion and national identity: 'to be Serb is to be Orthodox; to be Bosniak is to be Muslim; and to be Croat is to be Catholic'. Since peace is dependent on harmonious relations between these groups 'Bosnia has made religious freedom a central component of its new society', and the resulting constitutional protection certainly 'looks good on paper'. However, according to Mertus, the reality is that the 'degree to which one can enjoy religious freedom in Bosnia very much depends on whether one is of an ethno/religious minority in a particular region' – with 'police escorts often being the difference between life and death for ethno/religious minorities'.

Kosova, by contrast, is the least diverse of the states and, among Albanians in Kosova, 'religion has played a far less important role in forming national identity': 'the religion of Albanians is Albanianism'. However, Kosova is firmly divided on nationalist rather than religious lines, between the large Albanian majority and a small Serb minority − so much so that de facto parallel institutions and legal systems have arisen. Even though human rights are prominent in the nation's constitution, Mertus notes that the 'mechanisms for ensuring the implementation of those rights are not yet in place'. Finally Macedonia, with its overwhelmingly Macedonian Orthodox population, was not plagued by the conflicts of the rest of the Balkans, perhaps because the main struggle, dating back hundreds of years, was for Macedonia to establish its *own* identity − in particular that of the Macedonian Orthodox church against the Serbian Orthodox church. In Macedonia the debate over Orthodoxy 'does not pit the state against a minority group (as in Kosova), but rather it creates a bilateral struggle of state religion (Macedonian Orthodox) against its perennial enemy and powerful neighbour, the Serbian Orthodox church'.

The final three chapters of the book focus on some 'trans-national' themes that are of relevance to Europe today as a whole. In the first of these Grace Davie provides an overview of the position of faith in Europe. In particular, she examines one of the key paradoxes that emerge from the chapters in this book: that 'on one hand [there] are the relatively high levels of secularity in most if not all of Europe, but on the other is the marked resurgence of religion in public debate'. Davie identifies and discusses six factors that help us understand this paradox and, with it, the place of religion in modern Europe. These are the role of historic churches in shaping European culture; an awareness that these churches still play a role at 'particular moments' in the lives of modern Europeans; a shift in the 'churchgoing constituencies of the continent which operate increasingly as a model of choice rather than . . . obligation or duty'; the arrival in Europe of groups of people from different parts of the world who have 'very different religious aspirations from those in host societies', especially in regard to the place of religion in the public sphere; the reactions of Europe's 'secular elites' to the increasing salience of religion in public and private life; and finally, a growing realisation that, in patterns of religious life, modern Europe is perhaps the exception when compared to the rest of the world. A critical issue here is the fact that Europeans are 'losing their knowledge of religion' at the *very time* that they most need it. As a result of this lack of knowledge, Davie observes, the debates surrounding religion are often both 'ill-informed and ill-mannered', as Europeans return to asking questions about issues that they had previously regarded as being closed.

The fact that these debates over the role of faith and the rights of believers are increasingly taking place in Europe is at least partly due to two interconnected and overlapping factors. First, with immigration, numerically significant Muslim populations have arrived that were not involved in the constitutional settlements of yesteryear, which expected faith to retreat into the private sphere. And secondly, religious minorities have emerged that differ from those long-established churches that were the key actors in the shaping of European history. It is these areas that form the subject matter of the final two chapters – by Jørgen Nielsen on Islam, and by James T Richardson and Valerie Lykes on minority religions.

In relation to high-profile controversies or well-publicised events concerning Islam, Jørgen Nielsen says that central to this 'process has been a strengthening of the tendency to treat Islam and Muslims in Europe as if they constitute an undifferentiated community'. However, he notes that Islam in Europe is far more diffuse than is commonly thought to be the case in contemporary debates. Nielsen also points out that, in much of Europe, a 'process of secularization, in its broadest sense, has been under way for two centuries or more', leading to the 'disappearance of shared authoritative references and discourses'. This development has led to 'an environment in which Muslims, especially those who have arrived since 1945, find a scope for reviewing what it means to be Muslim on a scale which is quite unfamiliar historically or in the countries of origin'. In essence the question for Muslims is: how is it possible to live a 'Muslim life in a modern, non-Muslim, urban environment'? Nielsen suggests that the fluidity and increasingly fragmentary nature of Islam in Europe means that the traditional legal 'recognition regimes' applied to religion, previously developed for a particular set of historical circumstances, to a great extent are no longer applicable to the 'realities on the ground'. They have become 'unsustainably brittle and will have to give way to something that makes space for the fluidity' of Islam on the European continent. Nielsen concludes that secularism is necessary to create space for participation and negotiation, but it must be a secularism that is conceived of and functions as a 'framework', and not as a competing ideology.

In the final chapter, sociologists James T Richardson and Valerie Lykes focus on another issue that has generated much controversy and debate: the emergence in recent decades of numerous minority faith groups in Europe. Richardson and Lykes examine the status of groups they characterise as new religious movements (NRMs) in six nations – Germany, France, the Netherlands, Hungary, Poland and Russia – as well as analysing the relevant jurisprudence of the European Court of Human Rights. They describe a picture of 'tremendous variability' in terms of the different ways that Europe's nations and institutions respond to minority religious groups. While some nations, such as Hungary and the Netherlands, are quite receptive to such religious difference, others, including France and Russia, are much less accommodating in this regard. Indeed, in parts of Europe, Richardson and Lykes point out that, in an effort to reassert their hegemony after the demise of Communism, some long-established religions have been in the vanguard of opposition to NRMs and minority religious groups – with examples of this being the role played by the Roman Catholic Church in Poland and the Russian Orthodox Church in Russia. The authors thus conclude that both national European courts and the European Court of Human Rights have afforded a degree of protection to minority religions that, on occasions, has been decidedly mixed.

CONCLUSION

In attempting to document the complex relationship between secular and religious values in twenty-first-century Europe the chapters in this book demonstrate that, when it comes to such matters, Europe is a continent in which a range of divergent constitutional structures, views and opinions can be found. Although the vast majority of the states considered in this book are viewed as functioning liberal democracies (albeit to varying degrees), the challenge of identifying a detailed list of common 'European' values for such nations in regard to religion and belief is nonetheless a difficult and daunting one. As noted above, this lack of pan-European consensus has been – and continues to remain – the rationale for the long-standing willingness of the European Court of Human Rights to grant states a wide margin of appreciation as regards the protection of religious and secular values. The margin of appreciation is doubtlessly a useful mechanism, in the sense that it enables the European Court to take account of local sensibilities when making rulings in particular cases – yet, as Richardson and Lykes point out, its use can also result in the impoverishment of protection for minority faiths, and may also mean that some of the more philosophically taxing questions about the accommodation of religious belief remain unanswered.

It is a truism that ready answers are not easily found to the problems of accommodating and reconciling secular and religious values in Europe. Yet, in a continent that has been powerfully shaped by religious difference throughout its history, and is now the home of European citizens who subscribe to a broad range of religious and equivalent secular forms of belief, the importance of continually striving to identify a number of common and workable standards cannot be overstated. With its contributors covering a range of disciplines, and providing insights from the perspective of many different nations, this edited collection aims to contribute, albeit in a modest way, to the debate on how the Europe of the *present* can best respond to the problems posed by the legacies of its religious and secular *past*.

2. The Netherlands: neutral but not indifferent

Marjolein van den Brink and Titia Loenen

1. INTRODUCTION

Should judges be allowed to wear a headscarf in the courtroom? Are face-covering veils to be banned from the streets? Should state officials be excused from performing same-sex marriages because of their Christian convictions? Can a municipal organisation turn away a Muslim applicant because he refuses to shake hands with colleagues or clients of the opposite sex? Should the government take action to stop an orthodox Christian party from excluding women from standing for election on religious grounds? These are just a small selection of issues involving religious values and practices that have given rise to extensive public debates in the Netherlands, where religion and the accommodation of religious practices are highly contested.

In this chapter we will explore the current state of affairs concerning this subject. We will start by briefly explaining the constitutional position of religion and religious freedom (section 2) and the way in which the relationship between church and state has developed over the centuries (section 3). To fully understand the current debates it is necessary to be aware of the peculiar way in which, historically, the Dutch have dealt with tensions stemming from religious pluralism. If anything, this system of 'pillarisation' gave a prominent and very visible place for religion and belief in the public sphere (section 4). The legacy of this system, however, is now under serious attack. The Dutch approach seems to be at a crossroads. Will the Dutch accommodationist legacy be continued or will we turn to a more 'French' policy that bans religion and religious manifestations from the public sphere? Alternatively, will we choose some other road? We then discuss the current state of affairs (section 5) and give an impression of where, so far, legal limits to the accommodation of religious practices have been drawn (section 6). As space does not allow for a comprehensive overview we have selected some topics that have been highly publicised in the media. The same constraint is responsible for our decision not to include a section on Dutch approaches to offensive or hate speech that is either inspired by religion and directed against certain groups, or is directed against religious groups.[1] We round off with a brief discussion of current developments and challenges for the Dutch position on the freedom of religion (section 7).

2. CONSTITUTIONAL PROTECTION OF RELIGION

In 1983, the Dutch Constitution was modified substantially. Whereas a specific part of the former constitution was devoted to religion, the 1983 version pays only scant attention to religion, including freedom of religion.[2]

The main provision concerning religion, Article 6, protects both religion and other convictions. It states the following:

1. Everyone shall have the right to profess freely his religion or belief, either individually or in community with others, without prejudice to his responsibility under the law.

---

[1]   Examples of the first category: statements by religious leaders or politicians insulting homosexuals in the media. Examples of the second category: offensive public statements by Dutch (former) politicians such as Ayaan Hirsi Ali and Geert Wilders against Islam. Generally speaking, so far free speech has been given priority. For a brief overview of the Dutch approach see JP Loof, 'Freedom of expression and religiously-based ideas on homosexuality: European and Dutch standards' in MLP Loenen & JE Goldschmidt (eds) *Religious Pluralism and Human Rights in Europe: Where to Draw the Line?* (Intersentia, 2007) 267. The criminal proceedings against Wilders raised tremendous debate. At first the Public Prosecutor decided against starting criminal proceedings against Wilders, but after a complaint by several interest groups a court order forced him do so all the same (Hof Amsterdam, 21 January 2010, LJN: BH0496). After a hectic and highly mediatised trial, Wilders was acquitted (Rechtbank Amsterdam 23 June 2012, LJN: BQ9001). All Dutch case law referred to with reference to an LJN number is available at http://www.rechtspraak.nl.

[2]   The short overviews in sections 1 and 2 of this chapter are largely derived from SC van Bijsterveld, *Godsdienstvrijheid in Europees perspectief* (Freedom of religion in a European perspective) (Tjeenk Willink, 1998); SC van Bijsterveld, 'Freedom of religion in the Netherlands' [1995] *Brigham Young University Law Review* 555; H Knippenberg, 'The changing relationship between state and church/religion in the Netherlands' (2006) 67 *GeoJournal* 317; T Loenen, *Geloof in het geding. Juridische grenzen van religieus pluralisme in het perspectief van de mensenrechten* (Religion contested. Legal limits to religious pluralism in a human rights perspective) (Sdu Uitgevers, 2006).

2. Rules concerning the exercise of this right other than in buildings and enclosed places may be laid down by Act of Parliament for protection of health, in the interest of traffic and to combat or prevent disorders.[3]

The right to profess a religion or belief as guaranteed in the first section is potentially broad in scope since it is considered to include the right to act according to one's religion or belief and may apply to groups and organisations, not just individuals. It is understood that any limitations to this right must be based on legislation stemming from the national Parliament. As the provision does not give any substantive criteria that have to be met to limit the right, the guarantee provided is only procedural.

The second section of Article 6 concerns a more specific aspect of the right to profess a religion or belief, that is its exercise outside buildings. This section should be read in its historical context. Since 1848, the Dutch Constitution has contained a provision which was known as 'the prohibition of processions'. This provision was a bone of contention from the start and was clearly directed at the Catholic practice of holding processions, Catholics constituting a large minority group. Only in 1983 was the prohibition of processions abolished and replaced by the current provision in the second section of Article 6. This also explains why the main justifications for the restrictions to religious manifestations relate to traffic and the prevention of disorder.

Other constitutional provisions bearing on religious freedom include the prohibition of discrimination on grounds of, among others, religion (Article 1), the right of all Dutch nationals to be eligible for public office (Article 3) and rights pertaining to freedom of association and expression. In education, specific constitutional protection has been afforded to denominational schools. They have to be funded by the state on an equal basis with public education (Article 23).

As Article 6 only provides procedural protection against limitations – for an act of Parliament is required – so complainants have, in practice, turned to Article 9 of the European Convention on Human Rights (ECHR) to seek protection of their religious freedom. Because the ECHR has direct effect in the Netherlands, Article 9 can be invoked by individual parties in national procedures. More importantly, in cases of conflict the ECHR takes priority over any Dutch legal provisions or measures, including acts of Parliament or even the Constitution itself.

The General Equal Treatment Act of 1994, which aims to specify and

---

[3] Translation is available from a website on the Dutch Constitution developed by Leiden University: http://www.denederlandsegrondwet.nl/9353000/1/j9vvihlf299q0sr/vgrnbhimm5zv.

elaborate the right to non-discrimination guaranteed in Article 1 of the Constitution, has turned out to be an important instrument in enforcing claims for accommodation of religion in many areas of social and economic life (see further sections 5.5 and 6.2).[4]

3. CHURCH–STATE RELATIONS

When discussing church–state relations it is important to distinguish between the institutional meaning of the term and the broader concept of the relationship between religion and state. In the Netherlands, the institutional separation of church and state was realised over a period extending back to the late eighteenth century. In 1795 a first major step was taken by abolishing the formal status of the Reformed Church as the 'preferred church'. The financial and other bonds between church and state were not severed completely, though. In compensation for declaring church funds 'national', the state was constitutionally required to subsidise the salaries paid to church officials. Although the amount reduced considerably over the years, these direct payments lasted until 1983. In addition, in many other respects the close connections between church and state did not disappear overnight, and the two parties retained considerable influence over one another. Thus, for instance, the king (who was installed by the conquerors at the end of the Napoleonic era) held a strong position in the Reformed Church and could exert his powers both ways. During the second half of the nineteenth century the bonds between the Reformed Church and the state further weakened. As of 1853 the state was formally prohibited from interfering in the internal functioning of churches. In addition, the large Catholic minority increasingly claimed and received equal treatment to the Reformed Church, and for a long time this approach became the dominant one instead of a full separation model. In many ways the state kept financially supporting churches and related religious organisations, and was constitutionally allowed to do so, if only on a basis of equality between different denominations (mainly Protestant and Catholic).[5]

---

[4] Wet van 2 maart 1994, houdende algemene regels ter bescherming tegen discriminatie op grond van godsdienst, levensovertuiging, politieke gezindheid, ras, geslacht, nationaliteit, hetero- of homoseksuele gerichtheid of burgerlijke staat, *Staatsblad* 1994, 230. An English translation of the Act, as well as the opinions of the Equal Treatment Commission (ETC) and other information is available at the website of the ETC: http://www.cgb.nl.

[5] This is not to say that, de facto, minority religions were indeed treated equally to the Protestant majority.

In a way this situation continues to this day. After the abolition of the direct contributions to the salaries of church officials, the constitutional provisions remaining (under the heading 'On religion') were removed, and since 1983 the Constitution has no longer referred to religion except in the context of the right to freedom of religion and several other rights as mentioned in section 2 of this chapter. In fact, the institutional separation of church(es) and state that has been realised and generally accepted as a guiding principle is not even explicitly formulated in it. It is considered to be implicitly included in other constitutional provisions, especially in the constitutional protection of religious freedom.

As stated above, institutional separation of church and state need not imply a separation of religion and state. Indeed, the Netherlands has a long tradition of funding denominational organisations, and of allowing manifestations of religion in the public domain. A clear choice has been made in favour of an inclusive view of state neutrality or secularism, broadly conceived, as opposed to an exclusive one.[6] That is, state neutrality is not sought in the guise of banning religion from the public sphere, but rather in equal treatment of different religions and beliefs. This allows room for the accommodation and support of religion, with religion being visible in the public sphere, provided the state does not favour one religion or belief over another. To fully understand this approach to the relationship between religion and state in the Netherlands, it is important to grasp the specific way in which religious pluralism was dealt with in the Netherlands in the nineteenth and twentieth centuries.

4. THE HISTORICAL, POLITICAL AND SOCIAL CONTEXT OF SECULARISM

Notwithstanding the general climate of religious tolerance today in the Netherlands, for a major part of its history as an independent nation Dutch society was confronted with serious tensions between social groups that were largely organised along religious lines: Protestant Christian groups, Catholics and those affiliated to neither, such as liberals and socialists. The way to curb the dangers stemming from this uneasy pluralism was found in a system of 'pillarisation' (*verzuiling*).

---

6   See W van den Burg, 'Het ideaal van de neutrale staat. Inclusieve, exclusieve en compenserende visies op godsdienst en cultuur (The neutral state as an ideal. Inclusive, exclusive and compensatory visions on religion and culture)', inaugural lecture, Erasmus University, Rotterdam (Boom, 2009).

Pillarisation developed over the nineteenth century, and was firmly established at the beginning of the twentieth century. It reached its height between 1920 and 1960 and then rather rapidly declined, no doubt under the influence of the watershed represented by 'the Sixties' more generally. Pillarisation entailed the organisation of almost all social, cultural and political life on the basis of religion and belief systems, in so-called 'pillars'. The two that developed most fully were the Protestant Christian and Catholic pillars. The third or 'general' pillar consisted of those who did not belong to the other two, and was much less homogeneous. It included as subgroups a socialist pillar and a liberal pillar.

Pillarisation had several important characteristics. First of all, it covered almost all areas of life. In social life, people would socialise with members of their own denominations and not with others. Intermarriage was deemed unacceptable. Within each pillar separate associations were set up for social activities such as football or scouting; but hospitals, schools, old age homes and welfare organisations and the like were also segregated along denominational lines. In cultural life, Catholics would typically join a Catholic choir or theatre group and be informed by Catholic radio and television broadcasting, read a Catholic newspaper and work for a Catholic employer. Protestant Christians would similarly live much of their lives within their own exclusive circles. Political life was organised along the same lines. Each pillar was affiliated with its own political parties, trade unions and other politically active associations.

This social organisation in fact resulted in a highly segregated society. Keeping the nation together, the pillar elites worked closely together at the top, providing a 'common national roof'. Another important characteristic of the system was that the state supported it: public money for all kinds of facilities (such as subsidies for welfare organisations, the media, political parties, and, most importantly perhaps, education) was funnelled on an equal basis through the pillar structure.

As early as 1920 equal treatment and equal state funding of public and denominational schools was constitutionally guaranteed. In fact this was the result of a package deal between the major groups involved, and can be seen as a historical example of the success of the pragmatic '*poldermodel*' type of decision making in the Netherlands. Protestant and Catholic groups realised their goal of receiving funding for their schools on a basis of equality with public schools, but in return gave up their resistance to universal suffrage, a long-standing goal of the socialists and liberals.

During and after the 1960s the pillar system quickly lost its grip on Dutch society. It did not withstand the tides of secularisation, individualisation and the sexual revolution, to name only three of the major developments in this period. However, some pockets of pillarisation have survived. Thus, a number of local communities – the so-called 'Bible belt' – have retained their orthodox Christian identity and still live largely within their own pillar. And in education nearly 70 per cent of the primary schools still are denominational, although in practice the religious or other identity of most schools has been watered down considerably.[7] Nevertheless, the continuing existence of the system in education has provided new religious groups with the opportunity to claim the establishment of schools of their own denomination. So far over 40 Islamic primary schools have been founded, but there have also been several new Hindu schools.[8]

5. HOW THE STATE PROTECTS ITS NEUTRALITY IN THE FACE OF THE FREEDOM OF RELIGION OF ITS CITIZENS

5.1 Inclusive Neutrality and Generous Accommodations

As previously discussed, the position of the Dutch state regarding religion may be characterised as one of 'inclusive neutrality': neutral because the state itself is secular and maintains an impartial stance towards the many religious and other convictions held in the Netherlands;[9] inclusive because the state is not intent on banning religion from the public sphere. On the contrary, the state's stance towards religion is generally benevolent and accommodating.

---

[7] Denominational schools are privately run and can refuse admittance to pupils whose parents do not subscribe to the belief or ideology of the school. (See section 5.5 for some case law on this issue.) They are subject to private law and generally are government-funded on an equal basis with public schools. Private schools are governed by the board of the founding association. Teaching is based on religious or ideological beliefs and this category includes Catholic, Protestant, Jewish, Muslim, Hindu and anthroposophic schools. Freedom to organise teaching means that private schools can decide what they teach and how. The Ministry of Education, Culture and Science sets quality standards that apply to both public and private education.

[8] 'CBS statistiek basisonderwijs (2005/2006)' in *CBS – Onderwijsjaarboek* (Central Bureau for Statistics – Education Yearbook, 2007) 155, available at http://www.cbs.nl/NR/rdonlyres/7776AD12-1045-4177-9423-1201982C8 247/0/2007f162pub.pdf. On the issue of Islamic schools see Geert Driessen and Michael S Merry, 'Islamic schools in the Netherlands: expansion or marginalization?' (2006) 37 *Interchange* 201–23.

[9] Generally speaking, religion is not entirely absent from state actions. The preamble to statutory acts, for example, always opens with reference to 'the grace of God'.

Freedom of religion is, at its core, an individual right.[10] Individuals have the right to believe what they want, as well as the right to live according to the commands of their faith. That freedom includes the rights to associate with fellow believers and to found organisations such as schools, political parties, associations, churches, etc.

In the first part of this section, the Dutch state's position regarding religion is outlined and illustrated with examples. Space restrictions do not allow for a comprehensive overview. The generous approach as to what counts as a religion or a manifestation thereof is discussed first (5.2), followed by an overview of the policy and practice that are traditional to the Netherlands regarding religions and their manifestations (5.3), and those that are new (5.4). The scope of freedom of religion in horizontal relationships is then discussed (5.5).

The most important legal restrictions that have been drawn to accommodate religious practices (that is, the preservation of state neutrality and the protection of the rights and freedoms of others) are discussed in section 6.

5.2   Determining What Counts as Religion

The Dutch position regarding the relationship between religion and the state entails that neither the government nor the judiciary should interfere in theological disputes.[11] The approach taken by the Dutch Equal Treatment Commission (ETC) to the question whether a specific belief or manifestation thereof counts as religious is illustrative in this regard.[12] The mere claim that a specific manifestation is based on religion is generally sufficient, provided that the manifestation at issue is not completely unknown. For a Muslim woman, for instance, it suffices to state that she

---

[10]   See Hof Arnhem, 24 June 2008, LJN: BF3815, para 5.2.3: 'The right to freedom of religion is in the end focused on the freedom of individuals to manifest their religious convictions.'

[11]   See Bijsterveld 1995 (note 2 above), 565.

[12]   The ETC can hear claims of discrimination on grounds of, *inter alia*, religion, race and sex that fall under the scope of application of the General Equal Treatment Act. The Act covers a wide area, such as employment and the supply of goods and services. Though the ETC cannot give legally binding decisions, its judgments are adhered to in the majority of cases. As access to the ETC is easy and inexpensive, it handles several hundred equal treatment and non-discrimination claims each year and has built up a considerable jurisprudence. Owing to the foundation of the College voor de rechten van de mens (a national institute for human rights) in 2012 the ETC will cease to exist as such, and all its tasks will be integrated in the new institute.

covers for religious reasons, even though not all women adhering to Islam cover their heads.[13]

Claims are never rejected at first instance, even though they may seem clearly unfounded. An example (albeit a rare one) from the case law of the ETC is that of a self-proclaimed Nazirite.[14] This man was asked to leave a diner because customers complained that he smelled and looked unsavoury. He sued the diner on grounds of (indirect) discrimination on the basis of religion and explained that he abstained from washing, cutting hair and nails, etc because of his religion. As Nazirites, and in particular this far-reaching interpretation, are virtually unknown in the Netherlands, the applicant was asked to explain a bit more about his belief, to allow the Commission to establish whether his habits could be regarded as a manifestation of religion. The claimant failed to provide more information, whereupon the Commission turned down his claim.

The Dutch courts apply the same marginal approach and generally do not reject claims unless they are clearly unlikely. A well-known example is the Supreme Court (Hoge Raad) case of the 'Sisters of Saint Walburga'.[15] This 'satanic church' was subject to strict control by the police, who considered the establishment to be a sex club. Had the court accepted the claim that it was a house of worship, the police would not have been allowed to enter during the hours of worship. However, the court found that 'the activities of Saint Walburga could not be distinguished from those in a regular sex club. Moreover, the police had not noticed anything that looked like a religious experience among either the performing women, or the paying (male) visitors' (translation from Dutch by the authors).

5.3 Accommodation of 'Old' Religions and their Manifestations

As will be clear by now, generous accommodation of religious minority groups has a long history in the Netherlands. Examples of accommodation of traditional religious minority groups include exemptions from child vaccination programmes, and special facilities in tax law. Article 64(1)(a) of the Act on the funding of social insurance, for instance, provides that those

---

[13] See for instance ETC decision 2010-105 on the dress code of a fitness centre that did not allow any form of headwear in the gym.

[14] ETC decision 2005-28. Another example of a claim turned down is case 2007-53: the father of a little girl refused to let his daughter take a shower at school after sports. His claim that this was based on Islam was not accepted because he failed (marginally) to substantiate this claim.

[15] Hoge Raad, 31 October 1986, LJN: AC9553, *Nederlandse Jurisprudentie* (NJ) 1987, 173, comment ThWvV.

who have scruples regarding insurance may be exempted from the obligation to contribute to such funding.[16] Another example is the stance of
subsequent governments that marriage officials should be allowed to refuse
to officiate at same-sex marriages because of their religious conviction,
after marriage was opened up to same-sex couples in 2001.[17] Recently this
position has changed. This issue is discussed in more detail in section 6.2.

Traditionally, the Dutch political sphere has also respected freedom of
religion. As is the case in many other European countries (but not in the
USA, for instance), there exist several political parties with a religious
foundation. Of these, arguably the most remarkable is a small orthodox
Protestant party, the *Staatkundig Gereformeerde Partij* (SGP). The SGP,
founded in 1918, adheres to the ideal of a theocracy, rejects 'the ideology
of equality as unchristian', wishes to ban (public) manifestations of non-
Christian religious convictions, and holds that 'the man is the head of the
woman'. This last position is the reason for denying women full-fledged
party membership.[18]

Despite its anti-democratic stance, and law suits by one of its female
members,[19] the SGP never prompted much critical discussion, presumably
due to its small membership (two to three members in Parliament), which
meant that it was hardly a real threat to democracy. This situation changed
when human rights and women's rights organisations challenged the legitimacy of the exclusion of women from SGP membership (discussed in more

---

[16]   For an example of a case see Centrale Raad van Beroep (Central Board of
Appeal; the highest Dutch court in labour disputes involving public officials), 21
February 2008, LJN: BC5658. The applicant wanted to be exempted from the legal
obligation to buy health insurance because of his anthroposophic convictions. In
this particular case, the request was turned down, because there was no consistency
in his rejection of insurance. He had insured his house and car, for example.

[17]   Wet van 21 December 2000 tot wijziging van Boek 1 van het Burgerlijk
Wetboek in verband met de openstelling van het huwelijk voor personen van
hetzelfde geslacht, *Staatsblad* 2001, 9.

[18]   See the party's political programme *Toelichting op het program van beginse-
len van de Staatkundig Gereformeerde Partij*, (2nd edn, 2003) available in Dutch at:
http://wwww.sgp.nl/Media/download/5257/Toelichting%20Pr.v.B.pdf.

[19]   In the 1980s a few progressive SGP local sections decided to accept women
as members. One of these was Ms Riet Grabijn-van Putten. She sued the party
several times in order to gain access to the national party congress. After some
15 years she gave up her struggle. Human and women's rights organisations then
took over. See for instance Martin van Amerongen, 'Riet Grabijn-van Putten',
De Groene Amsterdammer (10 July 1996) at http://www.groene.nl/1996/28/riet-
grabijn-van-putten; Robert Chesal, 'Vrouwenrechten: Dag des Oordeels nadert
voor de SGP', *Radio Nederland Wereldomroep* (8 April 2010) at http://www.rnw.
nl/nederlands/article/vrouwenrechten-dag-des-oordeels-nadert-voor-de-sgp.

detail in 6.2). Here the point to emphasise is the fact that even parties that adhere to a political programme that is fundamentally hostile to democracy – though admittedly the SGP also agree to strive for their aims through peaceful and democratic means only – are allowed to participate fully in the public sphere, and even receive funds on an equal footing with other political parties.

5.4   Accommodation of 'New' Religions and their Manifestations

Religion and religious organisations are generally considered to be important for the realisation of social cohesion and the wellbeing of their members or adherents. Although policies to integrate migrants focus primarily on ethnicity and country of origin, religion is acknowledged as being an influential aspect, and increasingly so. The government is 'neutral but not indifferent'.[20] So far policies regarding 'new' ethnic minorities in the Netherlands focus mainly on non-discrimination and equal opportunities, including as applied to religion. On that basis in the past the government has subsidised quite a few places of worship, including churches, mosques and *mandirs*, for different groups of newcomers. These groups, after all, had a disadvantage as compared to established religious communities in the Netherlands.[21]

Other examples of accommodation include legislative changes allowing ritual slaughter and the scattering of the ashes of the deceased. One problem that so far has not been tackled is the wish of many Muslims for non-terminable property rights over graves. Though burial is still quite common in the Netherlands, rights to graves are generally only granted for a fixed period, because of a shortage of space. Therefore, many Muslims choose to be buried in their country of origin, Turkey and Morocco in particular.[22]

Not all 'new' religions are introduced by immigrants. In the wake of the increasing invocation of freedom of religion by newcomers, especially Muslims, others also seem to frame their interests more and more in terms of (freedom of) religion. The extension of religious rights to, in particular, Muslims seems to have stimulated legal claims by other believers, adherents of both familiar faiths, such as Jews, and unfamiliar faiths.[23]

---

[20]   Ben Koolen, 'Integratie en religie. Godsdienst en levensovertuiging in het integratiebeleid etnische minderheden' (2010) 1 *Tijdschrift voor Religie, Recht en Beleid* 5, 9.

[21]   Ibid, 9–13.

[22]   Ibid, 10.

[23]   An example of the former is the Jewish woman who claimed to be the victim

Freedom of religion exists except to the extent that each person has responsibilities under the law. As described in section 2 of this chapter the Constitution only posits procedural limits. In practice legislation limiting the freedom of religion, either explicitly or in a more general context, often indicates grounds that may justify the imposition of limitations on freedom of religion. Still, because of the fundamental value of religious freedom, restrictions are not accepted easily. An example is the case of a Rechabite.[24] Rechabites do not build houses, but live in tents or caravans because of a nomadic ideal. The applicant felt hindered in the exercise of his religious freedom because the local authorities refused to grant him an exemption from a local camping regulation, which forbade camping except on designated campsites. However, the authorities had made an exception for an experiment to house homeless people and drug addicts in caravans. The court followed its regular line of reasoning: freedom of religion is not absolute and the city's refusal is based on legislation. Thus, the main requirements were fulfilled. However, according to the court 'the authorities could in fairness not have refused the exemption'. For the applicant it was important to be close to his daughter who lived in the city. The city must take care of public interests such as public health and the protection of the environment. However, in the eyes of the court these could hardly be said to have been jeopardised by making an exception for the applicant. Given the weight of the right to freedom of religion, the exception should therefore have been granted.

In special circumstances a faith-based claim may even overcome criminal law prohibitions. For example, a member of the Santo Daime church was caught smuggling *ayahuasca* tea into the Netherlands. Drinking this tea is part of ceremonial worship. However, the tea is regarded as a drug in the Netherlands and is therefore prohibited. The lower court of Haarlem asked an expert to investigate whether the public health hazards were serious enough to justify interference with the right of the accused and the other members of his church to manifest their religion.[25] On the basis of this expert report, and taking into account precautions that had been taken by the church, the court concluded that the interference was not justified. With

---

of discrimination on grounds of religion because the entrance exam for dentistry training was held on a Saturday. The ETC agreed with her. The university should have offered her an alternative date: ETC decision 2008-4. An example of the latter is the case of the Rechabite, discussed below.

[24] Rechtbank Leeuwarden, 3 December 2009, LJN: BK4873. On Rechabites see Frank S Frick, 'The Rechabites reconsidered' (1971) 90(3) *Journal of Biblical Literature* 279.

[25] Rechtbank Haarlem, 26 March 2009, LJN: BH9844.

this verdict the court diverged from a Supreme Court decision just two years earlier, that did allow criminal sanctions because of the possession of the tea.[26]

5.5 Accommodation of Religion in Horizontal Relationships

Protection of freedom of religion is not restricted to the relationship between the state and its citizens. The General Equal Treatment Act extends the protection against discrimination on the grounds of religion that is enjoyed in relation to the state, to relations between private parties acting in the public sphere. The Act is applicable to some of the most important areas of society, such as the labour market, education and consumer rights. The Act follows the construction of the European directives on sex equality – that is, direct discrimination is prohibited unless an exception has been included in the Act itself. Indirect discrimination is prohibited unless it is objectively justified. Although only a modest number of complaints received by the Equal Treatment Commission concern religion, these complaints attract the most media attention, by far (see 6.2 for some examples).[27]

For religious organisations some exceptions to the prohibition of discrimination have been made in the General Equal Treatment Act. An important exclusion from the scope of the Act is to be found in Article 3, which states that it does not apply to legal relations within religious organisations, while the second section contains an exemption for holders of religious offices, such as Catholic priests.[28] A second exception is laid down in Articles 5(2) (employment) and 7(2) (goods and services). The

---

[26] Hoge Raad, 9 January 2007, LJN: AZ2497.

[27] For an example of generous accommodation by a court see Rechtbank Den Haag, 20 August 2007, LJN BC3697. The court ordered social services to annul a reduction of the social welfare benefit paid to a Muslim woman whose refusal to dress in a less 'traditional' way had been regarded by the social services as an impediment to her finding a job for which she was responsible. However, the Amsterdam court ruled differently in a comparable case concerning a Muslim man who refused to trim his beard and shake hands with women: Rechtbank Amsterdam, 17 December 2009, LJN: BK7175.

[28] The generous exceptions for religious organisations have drawn the attention of the European Commission. See Met redenen omkleed advies van de Europese Commissie gericht tot Nederland wegens het niet correct omzetten van artikel 2, lid 1, artikel 2, lid 2, onder a, artikel 2, lid 2, onder b, en artikel 4, lid 2, van Richtlijn 2000/78/EG, Brussels, 31 January 2008, 2006/2444, Annex C(2008)0115, 6. At the time of writing the Dutch government was reconsidering the formulation and scope of these provisions.

exception laid down in Article 7(2), for instance, allows private schools, including denominational schools, to restrict access to their schools, provided that their demands are 'necessary for the realisation of their religious basis'. The restrictions may not be based on the 'single fact' of someone's political conviction, race, sex, nationality, sexual orientation or civil status. These exceptions were instigated to accommodate objections, in particular by Protestant parties, who feared that the Act would, for instance, force denominational schools to accept homosexual teachers.[29] In practice this situation has only twice led to discrimination complaints.

Sometimes parents ask the courts to order a denominational school to accept their child's application. A case that was decided on the basis of Article 7(2) of the General Equal Treatment Act, discussed above, concerned parents claiming access to an orthodox Protestant school for their son.[30] His application had been rejected on the grounds that his sister was known to wear trousers (at home), his parents owned a television set, and because his parents held divergent views on school policies. The Court rejected the school's argument that the refusal was necessary in the light of its religious foundation, because the school had failed to substantiate its claim of a consistent policy in this respect. Accordingly, the school was ordered to accept the boy's application.

A case with a different outcome concerned a father who had, himself, been a student at an orthodox Jewish school. Regardless, his son was denied access on the basis that he had not been born to a Jewish mother. The school regarded the latter to be an indispensable prerequisite to qualify as Jewish.[31] Private schools, including denominational schools, are funded by the state on an equal footing with public schools (Article 23(7) of the Constitution; see section 2 of this chapter). Nevertheless, the Supreme Court decided that funding did not entail obligations for the school regarding student access. Special circumstances aside, the (social) right to education has no horizontal effect, according to the Supreme Court. This case is generally regarded as representing the Dutch stance on freedom of religion in education. According to one commentator, the Dutch court's position regarding freedom of religion in education is 'timid' compared with the approach taken by international courts.[32]

---

[29]   ETC decisions 1999-38 and 2007-100.

[30]   Hof Amsterdam, 24 July 2007, LJN: BB0057.

[31]   Hoge Raad, 22 January 1988, LJN: AD0151 (*Maimonides Lyceum*) NJ 1988, 891, comment EAA.

[32]   See para 7 note EEA to *Maimonides* (ibid). See also the contrasting approach of the UK Supreme Court to this issue in *R (on the application of E) v Governing Body of JFS and the Admissions Appeal Panel of JFS* [2009]

Religious organisations, such as churches, enjoy significant autonomy. However, this autonomy is not without its limits. In a case concerning the dismissal of a minister, the higher court of Arnhem pointed out that, even though the state – including the courts – should not interfere in internal church affairs, that principle should not mean that individuals would lose their fundamental right of access to justice. Accordingly, the court decided that it was competent to decide the case. Because the minister had not first followed the church's own procedure for such conflicts, the court nevertheless declared the claim inadmissible, as that procedure fulfilled all of the (civil law) criteria for a fair trial.[33]

6. LIMITS TO THE ACCOMMODATION OF RELIGION

Despite the state's benevolent stance regarding religion and its various possible manifestations, accommodation is not unlimited. Opinions on the question of where to draw the line differ significantly and debates continue on such matters. In this section the two most important legal restrictions on demands for accommodation are presented, by exploring cases that have caused considerable public debate.

6.1 State Neutrality

Accommodation issues that (might) jeopardise state neutrality constitute a first category of case to give rise to considerable debate. We limit ourselves here to the issue whether public officials such as public school teachers, police officers on duty or judges sitting in court should be allowed to wear a headscarf or other religious symbols.[34]

So far public school teachers have been regarded as being free to wear a headscarf in the classroom. Public schools may rightly require their teachers to display a neutral attitude towards all religions and beliefs, and not to indoctrinate their pupils with specific world views, yet it cannot be presumed that such a neutral attitude is lacking because a teacher wears

---

UKSC 15; (2010) 2 WLR 153 discussed in Peter Edge's chapter in this volume (Chapter 3).

[33] Hof Arnhem, 19 January 2010, LJN: BL0003.

[34] On headscarf debates in the Netherlands see Sawitri Saharso and Doutje Lettinga, 'Contentious citizenship: policies and debates on the veil in the Netherlands' (2008) 15(4) *Social Politics: International Studies in Gender, State and Society* 455.

a headscarf or any other religious symbol. Whether s/he has the required openness must be assessed on an individual basis. This line of reasoning, as developed by the Dutch Equal Treatment Commission in its case law, has been the basis for the guidelines issued by the Ministry of Education, Culture and Science, and seems to be generally adhered to.[35]

However, as far as police officers and judges are concerned, the general mood is different. Judges are not allowed to wear religious symbols, or any other visible signs of a specific conviction or belief.[36] The emphasis in this case is not just on the need for judges to *act* in an unbiased and neutral way, but rather on their *appearing* impartial in the eyes of the public. Religious or other attire showing personal convictions or beliefs is deemed to jeopardise this appearance of neutrality towards the parties or suspects.[37] The ETC appears to endorse this approach as being compatible with the General Equal Treatment Act.[38]

In the case of police officers a similar line of reasoning has been used, not allowing headscarves to be worn with a police uniform, although this is a more contentious position. Though only a few years ago plans were under way to design matching headscarves, more recently the policy has changed into what has been called 'lifestyle neutrality'. In order to enhance the trust and confidence of the general public in the police authority, police officers should appear neutral and thus abstain from showing specific personal attributes such as piercings, tattoos or religious or political symbols. The ETC has been rather critical of this standard on the grounds that it may well lead to indirect discrimination on the basis of religion. The Commission warned the government it should be able to provide very convincing arguments for limiting religious freedom in this way. In this context it has pointed to the practice in countries such as Canada and the UK, where police officers are allowed to wear a headscarf or turban without

---

[35]   *Leidraad kleding op scholen* (Guideline dress codes in schools), available in Dutch only on the website of the central government, http://www.rijksoverheid. nl/documenten-en-publicaties/vragen-en-antwoorden/mag-een-school-bepaalde-kl eding-verbieden.html.

[36]   So far the prohibition has not been laid down in formal legislation, but is based on the prevailing dress codes.

[37]   See the letter of the Minister of Justice to the Parliament, 'Brief van de Minister van Justitie aan de Tweede Kamer van 30 augustus 2001', *Kamerstukken II* 2003/2004, Antwoord op kamervragen, aanhangsel 1073.

[38]   This is generally inferred *a contrario* from a decision in which the ETC held that it would not be compatible with the General Equal Treatment Act to preclude a law clerk from wearing a headscarf during a court session. The ETC emphasised that the law clerk is not part of the judiciary as such.

any apparent negative consequences.[39] Police unions have also criticised the lifestyle neutrality standard, but the majority in the Dutch Parliament seems to be in favour.[40]

6.2   Rights and Freedoms of Others

A second category of cases giving rise to considerable controversy concerns accommodation of religious practices that (might) engage the rights and freedoms of others; that is cases (potentially) involving conflicting rights.

A first issue to mention in this category concerns the position of the marriage official who refuses to marry same-sex couples because of religious convictions regarding homosexuality. When marriage was made accessible for same-sex couples in 2001, explicit statements were made in Parliament to the extent that officials with conscientious objections would not be forced to officiate at such marriages. In 2002, the ETC considered this position as not infringing the General Equal Treatment Act, as long as homosexual couples would not be barred from getting married because of a lack of officials willing to perform the service.[41] However, in the wake of extensive debate on this issue in subsequent years, the Commission changed its position in 2008. It referred to its former decision as a pragmatic solution rather than a principled balancing of the interests at stake. The Commission this time emphasised that, in acting as a state representative, a marriage official is not allowed to discriminate on the grounds of sexual orientation, even if this stems from religious convictions.[42] Until 2012 Dutch governments were not willing to implement this decision, which means that local governments are still free to employ marriage officials with conscientious objections to same-sex marriage. Recently a change in mood saw a bill put forward in Parliament that is expected to pass with a clear majority. It will prohibit the

---

[39]   ETC, 2007/08: 'Advies inzake uiterlijke verschijningsvormen politie "Pluriform uniform?" (Advice on the appearance of the police "Pluriform uniform") at http://www.cgb.nl/publicaties/publicatie/221129/2007_08_advies_inzake_uiterlijke_verschijningsvormen_politie_pluriform_uniform.

[40]   See the information on the site of the *Politiebond*, a Dutch police union: http://www.politiebond.nl/index.php?pagina=uitgave&uitgave_id=56&artikel_id=463&titel_id=1.

[41]   ETC decisions 2002-25 and 2002-26.

[42]   ETC decison 2008-40. The ETC explained its change of position more fully in an advice on the subject: ETC 2008/04: 'Advies inzake gewetensbezwaarde ambtenaren van de burgerlijke stand: "Trouwen? Geen bezwaar!" (Advice on conscientious objections of marriage officials: "Marriage? No objection!")'.

appointment of new marriage officials who object to performing same-sex marriages. In this way the discrimination will gradually cease to exist.[43]

A second accommodation issue involving the rights and freedoms of others that inspired some heated discussions in the public media concerns the wish of some Muslims to be allowed to refrain from shaking hands, though this is the generally accepted greeting ritual in the Netherlands in almost any social situation. This stems from their wish to avoid physical contact with persons of the opposite sex. Several cases have come up in which the persons involved were not employed or were dismissed for this reason.[44]

The ETC line has been protective of accommodating the wish not to shake hands, while the courts so far have decided differently. Two cases are illuminating in this respect. The first concerned a Muslim man who was denied a job as a customer manager at the Social Services Department of the city of Rotterdam because of his refusal to shake hands with women.[45] The municipality stated in its defence that it had to protect women against sex discrimination by a civil servant. The Commission accepted this argument, yet held that this, in itself, did not necessitate the requirement that the applicant should shake hands with both men and women. Other respectful ways of greeting, not involving physical contact, are feasible, as the applicant had offered to do. The District Court of Rotterdam, however, considered that a customer manager is an important contact person between the local authorities and the citizens. The Court ruled that the city of Rotterdam has the right to choose 'to observe the usual rules of etiquette and of greeting customs in the Netherlands' in its contact with citizens. As a result, the Court considered it justifiable to reject a candidate who is not willing to observe those rules of etiquette for this specific position.[46]

The second case concerned a female teacher in a public school, who decided not to shake hands with men anymore and was subsequently dismissed. The ETC considered this to constitute indirect discrimination on grounds of religion and did not accept the justifications put forward by the employer for reasons similar to those in the first case: the teacher was

---

[43] 'Voorstel van wet van de leden Dijkstra en Schouw tot wijziging van het Burgerlijk Wetboek en de Algemene wet gelijke behandeling met betrekking tot ambtenaren van de burgerlijke stand die onderscheid maken als bedoeld in de Algemene wet gelijke behandeling', *Kamerstukken II*, 2011–2012, no 33 344, nr 1–2.

[44] See for more details M Hertogh, 'What's in a handshake? Legal equality and legal consciousness in the Netherlands', (2009) 18 *Social and Legal Studies*, 221.

[45] ETC decision 2006-202.

[46] Rechtbank Rotterdam, 6 August 2008, LJN: BD9643.

prepared to greet everyone in the same (sex-neutral) way and in a polite manner, but without shaking hands.[47] In subsequent legal procedures however, the Central Board of Appeal did not agree with this line of reasoning. It held that the school had a legitimate aim in requiring teachers to shake hands irrespective of sex, as the school wanted to comply with prevailing customs in Dutch society. This was deemed particularly important, as the school had many pupils and teachers of multi-ethnic descent. Pupils have to be prepared for a society in which shaking hands is the prevailing custom for greeting and showing respect. The dismissal of the teacher was therefore judged to be lawful.[48]

To conclude this section we turn back to the case of the SGP, the political party that does not allow full membership to women (see 5.3).[49] For a long time the right of the SGP to express and act on their discriminatory position was relatively uncontested, but during the past decade legal proceedings have been brought by several human rights and women's rights groups to challenge the legitimacy of the exclusion of women, and to force the state to stop supporting the SGP and put an end to this discriminatory practice. Interestingly the SGP proceedings have resulted in two diametrically opposed judgments by the highest administrative court, the Afdeling Bestuursrechtspraak van de Raad van State (ABRvS) on one hand and the highest civil court, the Supreme Court, on the other.[50] Without going into the complicated details of how this could happen, the fact in itself is telling. If anything, it shows the deep division between the different positions that were pitted against each other in the public debates. The ABRvS emphasised the paramount importance of democratic pluralism and the freedom of religion and association for political parties. Democracy

---

[47]   ETC decision 2006-220.

[48]   Centrale Raad van Beroep, 7 May 2009, LJN: BI2440.

[49]   When the 2nd and 3rd (combined), 4th and 5th Dutch reports were presented, the UN Women's Rights Committee (CEDAW) expressed its concern that 'there is a political party represented in the Parliament that excludes women from membership, which is a violation of Article 7 of the Convention'. UN Docs A/56/38, 2001, para 219; UN Doc CEDAW/C/NLD/CO/4, 2 February 2007, para 25; UN Doc CEDAW/ C/NLD/CO/5, 5 February 2010, paras 10 and 13.

[50]   Afdeling bestuursrechtspraak Raad van State, 5 December 2007, LJN BB9493, AB 2008, 35, comment RJB Schutgens and JJJ Sillen; Hoge Raad 9 April 2010, LJN BK4549; NJ 2010, 388, comment EA Alkema. See also Barbara Oomen, Joost Guijt and Matthias Ploeg, 'CEDAW, the Bible and the State of the Netherlands: the struggle over orthodox women's political participation and their responses' (2010) 6 *Utrecht Law Review*, 158 available at www.utrechtlawreview. org, who discuss how this legal struggle was experienced within the religious community.

is fundamentally jeopardised if political parties are not free to express whatever views they may hold (of course, as long as they do not incite to violence). This freedom was to be given priority over the equal rights of women, as women would not, as such, be barred from standing for election and public office. Any female SGP members could join another party or establish one that would not bar women. On this basis, the state was not allowed to stop subsidising the SGP on an equal basis with other parties.

The Supreme Court, on the other hand, gave priority to the equal rights of women over the right to freedom of religion and association. It held that the SGP was free to hold its religiously inspired views of women and to express them, but was not allowed to *act* on the basis of those views in a discriminatory manner. On this basis the Supreme Court has ordered the state to take action against the SGP without terminating the subsidy (which was not allowed by the ABRvS) and with as little interference as possible with the fundamental rights of the SGP. Everyone is now wondering how the state is going to solve this riddle. In the meantime, the complaint against the Supreme Court decision lodged by the SGP with the European Court of Human Rights has been held inadmissible as being 'manifestly ill-founded'. In its decision, the European Court reiterates the importance of gender equality and points out that according to established case law a political party may not pursue political aims that are themselves incompatible with fundamental democratic principles. The judgment is very brief; the Court holds that the application of the European Convention leads to the same conclusions as reached by the Dutch Supreme Court on the basis of the UN Convention on the Elimination of all Forms of Discrimination against Women and the UN Covenant on Civil and Political Rights taken together.[51]

7. THE FUTURE OF FAITH IN THE NETHERLANDS

The Netherlands has developed in the last couple of centuries from a state that was basically founded on Protestantism into one that does not privilege any religion, but rather (as a general rule) holds all of them in esteem – out of respect not just for freedom of religion, but also because of the possibilities that religions offer to enhance social cohesion and inclusion. Not all remnants from the Protestant past have disappeared of course. The weekly calendar, to name an obvious example, is still organised around the

---

[51] European Court of Human Rights, 10 July 2012, *Staatkundig Gereformeerde Partij v The Netherlands*, Application no 58369/10.

Christian Sunday as a day of rest. Similarly, the dress code for the Dutch judiciary neatly fits its Christian traditions.

So far the claims of religious groups to be accommodated according to their religious wishes and needs have clearly fitted this historical practice. However, 'new' religious groups increasingly have a hard time in securing respect for their beliefs. The tensions stemming from 9/11, Islamic terrorism and the murder of the Dutch film maker Theo van Gogh by a young radical Muslim need not be explored here further to understand some of the dynamics at work in this regard.

Thus, the Netherlands seems to have arrived at a crossroads. Both characteristic elements of the Dutch position on the freedom of religion, inclusion and neutrality, are ever more frequently called into question. On the one hand, state neutrality towards religions itself is questioned, not only by orthodox religious parties such as the SGP, but also by others, such as the new Party for Freedom (*Partij voor de Vrijheid*). This stance has given rise to a significant number of proposals in relation to Islam in particular, such as banning Islamic face-covering dress from the public sphere and the – deliberately insulting – proposal for a 'head rag tax' (*kopvoddentax*).

Others do not question state neutrality as such, but instead plead for a less prominent role for religion in the public sphere generally. Inclusive neutrality should be exchanged for exclusive neutrality, somewhat similar to the French *laïcité*. No judges with headscarves, no face-covering dress in public, no political parties denying membership to women, no accommodation of marriage officials refusing to officiate at same-sex marriage, etc. Even the nearly sacrosanct funding of denominational schools on an equal footing with public schools (as enshrined in Article 23 of the Constitution) is criticised these days.

The judiciary has so far retained its rather balanced approach, but the SGP cases make it very clear that questions regarding freedom of religion and its limits present some hard nuts to crack in a society that is increasingly 'multi-faith'. Moreover, religious diversity is becoming even more apparent because adherents of traditional faiths seem to frame their needs increasingly in legal terms, such as the recognition of the Jewish Sabbath and the right to wear a visible cross.

Having arrived at this crossroads, the question is whether the Dutch approach of inclusive neutrality will survive the current torrents, or whether it will have to give way to a more exclusive neutrality, somewhat similar to the French model. Whatever happens, it is certainly to be hoped that neutrality and impartiality, as defining characteristics of the Dutch position, will not succumb.

3. Secularism and establishment in the United Kingdom

Peter W Edge

1. INTRODUCTION

During his State visit to the United Kingdom in 2010, Pope Benedict XVI chose to include in his address at Holyroodhouse a very explicit warning about the position of religion in the United Kingdom.[1] After praising the stand the UK took against 'Nazi Tyranny', he continued:

> As we reflect on the sobering lessons of the atheist extremism of the twentieth century, let us never forget how the exclusion of God, religion and virtue from public life leads ultimately to a truncated vision of man and of society and thus to 'a reductive vision of the person and his destiny'.

Later, he closed his address by returning to the theme:

> Today, the United Kingdom strives to be a modern and multicultural society. In this challenging enterprise, may it always maintain its respect for those traditional values and cultural expressions that more aggressive forms of secularism no longer value or even tolerate. Let it not obscure the Christian foundation that underpins its freedoms; and may that patrimony, which has always served the nation well, constantly inform the example your Government and people set before the two billion members of the Commonwealth and the great family of English-speaking nations throughout the world.

In this brief overview of the UK position, I will consider the constitutional protection of religious interests in the UK, and the nature of relationships between state and religious organisations. In particular, I will consider how far the law in a number of areas of particular tension reflects a con-

---

[1] Address of His Holiness Benedict XVI, Palace of Holyroodhouse, Edinburgh, 16 September 2010 available at http://www.vatican.va/holy_father/benedict_xvi/speeches/2010/september/documents/hf_ben-xvi_spe_2010091 6_incontro-autorita_en.html.

flict between particular religious values and cultural expressions and an assertive secular state, albeit a secular state with an established church.

2. THE CONSTITUTIONAL PROTECTION OF RELIGIOUS INTERESTS

The United Kingdom is distinctive, although not quite unique, in that it lacks a category of law that could be classed as 'the constitution', although it clearly possesses laws that deal with constitutional matters. In particular, protection of individual and indeed collective rights was effected by the normal legal and administrative mechanisms, while church–state relations, discussed in the section that follows, were similarly dealt with piecemeal.

This system of rights protection was subject to extensive criticism, and in 1998 Parliament legislated to provide mechanisms for enforcing the European Convention on Human Rights (ECHR) in the United Kingdom. Although falling short of a guarantee effective against all organs of the state, primarily because of the need to accommodate Parliamentary sovereignty, this new legislation constitutes the closest approximation to a positive guarantee of religious rights yet seen in the United Kingdom. The Human Rights Act 1998 (HRA) does not represent a fully-fledged British Bill of Rights, but rather seeks to bring the guarantees of the ECHR into English law. It is an oversimplification to say that the HRA 'incorporates' the ECHR into English law. Rather, it provides a number of distinct mechanisms by which English law may be brought into line with the ECHR.

The two most significant enforcement mechanisms under the HRA are the rule of statutory interpretation contained in section 3, and the new ground for challenging administrative action in section 6. Before the HRA, the courts would only look to the ECHR if legislation were ambiguous. The HRA shifts to a stronger position where 'so far as it is possible to do so, primary and subordinate legislation must be read and given effect in a way which is compatible with the Convention'.[2] This rule is not an absolute prohibition on the courts interpreting legislation as contrary to the Convention, however, as it '(b) does not affect the validity, continuing operation or enforcement of any incompatible primary legislation; and (c) does not affect the validity, continuing operation or enforcement of any incompatible subordinate legislation if (disregarding any possibility of revocation) primary legislation prevents removal of the incompatibility'.[3]

---

[2] Human Rights Act 1998 s 3(1).
[3] Human Rights Act 1998 s 3(2).

Where it is not possible to give a compatible interpretation to it, the legislation must be given full effect. Unlike, for instance, the system under the United States Constitution, the courts have no authority to ignore or strike out Acts of Parliament, or statutory instruments lawfully deriving authority from such Acts. If they are unable to make the legislation fit with the Convention, they must apply it as it stands, although section 3 has proved a powerful mechanism for shaping UK law into conformity with ECHR obligations. As Samuels concludes in his review of the section, 'interpretation of the language of the statute may be stretched, even stretched to the limit'.[4] In the instances when the courts are unable to resolve a conflict in favour of compatibility with the ECHR, however, they may, under section 4, make a declaration that it is incompatible with the Convention, which can be used to speed corrective legislation through Parliament. Additionally, section 6 provides for particular decisions by administrative bodies to be overturned when those bodies act in a way incompatible with Convention obligations. The section renders it unlawful for a public authority to act in a way that is incompatible with the Convention, unless it was bound to act as it did by primary legislation, or was acting to give effect to primary legislation that was itself incompatible with the Convention.[5]

The HRA has had a wide-ranging impact on UK law, but of most significance to this chapter is the effect it has given to Article 9 of the ECHR, which contains the principal guarantees of religious interests under the Convention. In a significant departure from the previous model of protecting religious interests in the UK, legal recourse may now be had to a general guarantee of religious rights. The UK courts have given considerable weight to the jurisprudence of the organs of the ECHR on the meaning of the Convention,[6] so the reach of this domestic guarantee is subject to those limitations that are found in Article 9. At the same time, other Convention rights have similarly become the subject of general guarantees. As we will see below, this has created the possibility of frank, juridified, clashes between religious and other interests.

---

4 A Samuels, 'Human Rights Act 1998 section 3: A new dimension to statutory interpretation?' [2008] *Statute Law Review* 130, 138.

5 See further A Williams, 'A fresh perspective on hybrid public authorities under the Human Rights Act 1998: Private contractors, rights-stripping and the "chameleonic" horizontal effect' [2011] *Public Law* 139; D O'Brien, 'Judicial review under the Human Rights Act 1998: Legislative or applied review?' [2007] *European Human Rights Law Review* 550.

6 R Masterman, 'Interpretations, declarations and dialogue: Rights protection the under the Human Rights Act and Victorian Charter of Human Rights and Responsibilities' [2009] *Public Law* 112.

The possibility of the HRA creating difficulties for religious individuals and organisations was anticipated during its passage through Parliament. As a result, a section was introduced to the HRA during its Parliamentary stage specifically to allay the concerns of religious organisations.[7] At a late stage during the passage of the Human Rights Bill through Parliament, concern arose that its provisions would extend to the Church of England, and possibly to other religious bodies that have charitable status.[8] A number of bodies lobbied for an exclusion from the Bill for religious organisations exercising public functions, although some religious organisations (such as Christians for Human Rights) strongly objected to such exclusion. The fundamental concern was that '[t]he Bill, instead of regarding Churches as autonomous bodies, as the European Court does, defines them as public bodies. They would therefore in unacceptable ways become subject to the authority of the civil courts for certain purposes.'[9] Particular manifestations of this concern arose in relation to possible requirements on religious organisations to conduct same-sex weddings, employ in religious schools teachers not professing the school's religion, or appoint women bishops.[10] These concerns resulted in a variety of amendments being proposed in Parliament, the most radical of which would have resulted in the exclusion of religious organisations from the remit of the legislation, even when exercising a public function.

In response, the government sponsored an amendment to the Bill, removing this special treatment but adding reassurance in the form of section 13 of the Act. This provides, in subsection 1:

> If a court's determination of any question arising under this Act might affect the exercise by a religious organisation (itself or its members collectively) of the Convention right to freedom of thought, conscience and religion, it must have particular regard to the importance of that right.

---

[7] See P Cumper, 'The protection of religious rights under section 13 of the Human Rights Act 1998' [2000] *Public Law* 254; P Cumper, 'Religious organizations and the Human Rights Act 1998' in PW Edge and G Harvey (eds), *Law and Religion in Contemporary Society: Communities, Individualism and the State* (Ashgate, 2001).

[8] A Thorp, 'The Human Rights Bill: Churches and religious organisations', (1998) House of Commons Research Paper 98/26.

[9] See http://www.fpchurch.org.uk/Magazines/fpm/1998/July/article9.php.

[10] See more broadly H Charlesworth, 'The challenges of human rights law for religious traditions' in MW Janis and C Evans (eds), *Religion and International Law* (Martinus Nijhoff, 1999).

The impact of this obligation 'to have particular regard' was anticipated to be slight, and when deployed in argument before the courts, does not appear to have been given additional weight.[11]

3.   THE NATURE OF CHURCH–STATE RELATIONS

The Establishment of the Church of England has had a significant impact on the global structuring of church–state relations, most notably through the legacy of British colonialism. In North America, the British colonies were influenced by the experience of Establishment in England in seeking their own, diverse, forms of the relationship.[12] The most significant clause of the original constitution in relation to religion prohibits religious tests before entry to any federal office.[13] As Madison argued, '[a] religious sect may degenerate into a political faction in a part of the Confederacy; but the variety of sects dispersed over the entire face of it must secure the national councils against any danger from that source'.[14] The US constitutional provisions dealing with religion were initially read as limiting the power of the federal government. By the 1930s, however, the Supreme Court accepted that the Fourteenth Amendment requires all state and local governments to adhere to the fundamental principles of liberty and justice that lay at the base of the civil and political institutions of the country, and that could be found stated authoritatively in the Bill of Rights, even those that on their terms bound only the national government.[15]

The US experience provides a sharp contrast to the experience of church–state relationships in the United Kingdom. Here, the story of church–state relations from the Reformation to the early twentieth century can largely be framed in terms of increased tolerance of religious communities (and their members) falling outside the dominant churches of England and Scotland; occurring alongside a retention of the paramount position of those dominant churches, particularly the Church of England in England, in public

---

11 See for instance *Suryananda v The Welsh Ministers* [2007] EWCA Civ 893.

12 Contrast Fundamentals of West Jersey (West Jersey), 1681, Art X, with Connecticut Code of Laws, 1650 (Connecticut), both in DS Lutz (ed), *Colonial Origins of the American Constitution: A Documentary History* (Liberty Fund, 1998).

13 US Constitution, Art I, s 7(2).

14 James Madison, 'Federalist Paper no 10: The utility of the Union as a safeguard against domestic faction and insurrection', 1787 in A Hamilton, J Madison and J Jay, *The Federalist Papers* (Wilder, 2008) 39.

15 *Palko v Connecticut* 302 US 319 (1937); see also *Hamilton v Regents of the University of California* 293 US 245 (1934).

life and the involvement of the state in those churches. In the twentieth and early twenty-first centuries, however, this increase in toleration has been combined with an increased separation of the Church of England from the United Kingdom state. The Church of England retains, however, a number of constitutional privileges in the United Kingdom, most notably in its representation in state bodies.

The Christian church in England predates England itself:

> When England gained a unifying monarchy and became a single state in the ninth and tenth centuries, the archbishopric of Canterbury and the church had already been functioning as a unifying factor for two centuries.[16]

The Reformation of the sixteenth century initially aimed at a separation of a national, Catholic, church under the King from 'Roman' Catholicism under the Pope. Although subsequently coming to incorporate Protestant elements into its theology and practice, the Anglican Church retained elements of Catholicism, and today is a broad national church, so that particular adherents may stress either the Protestant or the Catholic elements in its composition.[17] The establishment of a non-Roman Catholic identity for this national church was intimately tied to the needs of the English state, and a number of key legal elements retain this linkage, although other forms of religious belief, and religious organisations, are now accepted as legitimate.[18]

The Church of England no longer retains an effective monopoly over public life and positions in the state.[19] Nonetheless, the position of the Church of England in the life of the state remains exceptional. The sovereign is the Supreme Governor of the Church of England,[20] although not *ipso facto* a minister of that church.[21] The sovereign also possesses very

---

[16]   A Hastings, *Church and State: The English Experience* (University of Exeter Press, 1991) 10.

[17]   See T Thomas (ed), *The British: Their Religious Beliefs and Practices 1800–1986* (Routledge, 1988).

[18]   See K Hylam-Smith, *The churches in England from Elizabeth I to Elizabeth II: Volume II 1833–1998* (SCM Press, 1988) 211–33; E R Norman, *Church and Society in England 1770–1970* (Clarendon Press, 1976) 416–75; G Davie, *Religion in Britain since 1945: Believing without Belonging* (Blackwell, 1994) 139–61.

[19]   For a discussion of the key moves away from this monopolistic position, see St JA Robilliard, *Religion and the Law* (Manchester University Press, 1984) 199–203.

[20]   See Act of Supremacy 1558, s 9.

[21]   The Thirty-Nine Articles of Religion 1563, Art 37.

wide powers of appointment to offices within the Church of England.[22] Although the sovereign is responsible for a range of functions within the life of the Church of England, there is no provision for delegation of these functions in the event that the sovereign should be of a different denomination or religion. Rather, there are absolute limits on the religion of the sovereign.

In 1688 the Protestant Parliament offered the Crown to the Protestant William and Mary, Prince and Princess of Orange. As part of the Bill of Rights 1688, which confirmed this constitutional change, Parliament excluded from the throne anyone in communion with the Roman Catholic Church or professing 'the Popish religion' and/or anyone marrying a 'Papist'.[23] The Bill of Rights also contains, by implication, a positive requirement that the person becoming sovereign should be a Protestant at that time.[24] These provisions were supplemented by a requirement that the sovereign take an oath, normally at coronation, renouncing certain aspects of Roman Catholic doctrine,[25] a negative obligation replaced in 1688 by a positive one to protect the Protestant religion,[26] and in 1910 by a shorter form containing the positive declaration that the sovereign was 'a faithful Protestant'.[27] In 1700, the succession to the Crown was laid down by statute, and limited to Protestants.[28] The same Act reaffirmed the relevant provisions of the Bill of Rights,[29] and provided that 'whosoever shall hereafter come to the possession of this Crown shall join in communion with the Church of England as by law established'.[30]

The position of the Church of England in relation to the sovereign, accordingly, remains uniquely powerful. Important though the position of the head of state is, however, both in practical and rhetorical terms, in the UK the head of government is the Prime Minister. In contrast with other members of the executive, there is an important limitation on this post, based on religious affiliation. The Roman Catholic Relief Act 1829 was primarily intended to remove restrictions upon the role of Roman Catholics in public life. A number of sections, however, were intended to

---

[22] See Halsbury's *Laws of England* (4th edn) (Butterworths, 2004) vol 14, para 358.
[23] Bill of Rights 1688 (the spelling has been modernised).
[24] Ibid.
[25] Ibid.
[26] Coronation Oath Act 1688.
[27] Accession Declaration Act 1910, Schedule.
[28] Act of Settlement 1700 s 1.
[29] Ibid, s 2.
[30] Ibid, s 3.

ensure that particular functions were not discharged by Roman Catholic officials. Under the Act, '[i]t shall not be lawful for any person professing the Roman Catholic religion directly or indirectly to advise His Majesty . . . touching or concerning the appointment to or disposal of any office or preferment in the . . . Church of England . . . or in the Church of Scotland; and if such person shall offend in the premises he shall, being thereof convicted by the due course of law, be deemed guilty of a high misdemeanour, and disabled for ever from holding any office, civil or military, under the Crown.'[31] This provision was repeated, in relation to that religion, in the Jews Relief Act 1858.[32] A problem arises when these limits make it a high misdemeanour for an individual to fulfil some of the duties of their office, even though it is lawful for them to hold the office. Statutory provision has been made for such functions to be transferred from a Roman Catholic (but not Jewish) Lord Chancellor to another Minister of the Crown.[33] Yet no such provision has been made concerning the functions of Prime Minister. Along with their other legal and political powers, the Prime Minister is responsible for advising the sovereign on a range of key appointments within the Church of England, including the appointment of bishops. Although it should be remembered that the Prime Minister acts on the advice of others (notably the Crown Nominations Commission, which consists almost entirely of Church of England officials and representatives) the sovereign is bound to accept this advice. The effect of this is that, although there is no bar on a Roman Catholic or Jew occupying the post of Prime Minister and discharging most functions, properly carrying out some of the duties is not only unlawful, but would also expose the Prime Minister to criminal sanctions, including being barred from any office under the Crown – which would include ministerial and Prime Ministerial office. In practice, however, the post of Prime Minister

---

[31] Roman Catholic Relief Act 1829, s 18, as amended by the Statute Law Revision (no 2) Act 1888; Statute Law Revision (Northern Ireland) Act 1976. See *R v Kennedy* (1902) 86 LT 753.

[32] Jews Relief Act 1858, s 4; Statute Law Revision (Northern Ireland) Act 1980, s 1, Schedule, Pt XIV.

[33] Lord Chancellor (Tenure of Office and Discharge of Ecclesiastical Functions) Act 1974, ss 1, 2; the situation is complicated by the Jews Relief Act 1858, s 3, which expressly barred Jews from the office of Lord Chancellor, but was repealed by the Promissory Oaths Act 1871, which was itself repealed. Currently 'it is unclear whether a person professing the Jewish religion would be appointed Lord Chancellor without clarifying legislation' (Halsbury's *Laws of England* (4th edn) (Butterworths, 2002) vol 8, para 477, fn 7), although Sir Rufus Issacs occupied the post during the existence of the 1871 Act.

is mainly a creature of convention, and so can be changed informally.[34] It would not be impractical for any duties of a Prime Minister that would expose a Roman Catholic holder of that office to prosecution to be exercised by another Minister of the Crown, without even the need for legislation to formalise such an arrangement. The practical consequence of this is that Roman Catholic or Jewish Prime Ministers would exercise a slightly smaller range of power than their predecessors.

As well as the connection between the Church of England and the state in relation to the head of state and head of government, the Church enjoys a unique position in the national legislature. The bicameral Houses of Parliament are dominated by the directly elected House of Commons which, having lost its last remaining religious limit on membership,[35] is composed of individuals from a range of religious backgrounds. The second chamber of Parliament, the House of Lords, however, retains an element of privilege for the Church of England. In 2011,[36] of the 830 members of the House of Lords, 90 were hereditary peers who had inherited their position in the legislature;[37] 692 were life peers, who had been elevated to the peerage in recognition of distinction in public life, often service within the political system;[38] 23 were law lords, senior British judges formerly appointed to the Lords primarily to perform its then judicial tasks, but with a role in legislation; and 25 were Lords Spiritual.[39] The Lords Spiritual are all members of the Anglican hierarchy.[40] Originally, all bishops of the Church of England sat in the Lords, but the increase in the number of bishoprics was not fol-

---

[34]   See JF McEldowney, *Public Law* (Sweet and Maxwell, 1994) 78–81, 265.
[35]   House of Commons (Clergy Disqualification) Act 1801, repealed by House of Commons (Removal of Clergy Disqualification) Act 2001.
[36]   See   http://www.parliament.uk/mps-lords-and-offices/lords/lords-by-type-and-party/.
[37]   This is a useful simplification. In 1999, 665 of the 1321 members of the House of Lords were hereditary peers. As the first stage of the reform of the House, the House of Lords Act 1999 reduced this number to 92, elected by the existing hereditary peers.
[38]   For instance, former Prime Ministers James Callaghan (Lord Callaghan of Cardiff) and Margaret Thatcher (Baroness Thatcher). The statement in the text is an obvious simplification of the forces that lead to the appointment of a life peer to the House of Lords.
[39]   See *Modernising Parliament: Reforming the House of Lords* (Cmd 4183, 1998) paras 3.2–3.5.
[40]   The Human Rights Act may have impacted on the appointment of these officials; see J Rivers, 'From toleration to pluralism: Religious liberty and religious establishment under the United Kingdom's Human Rights Act' in RJ Ahdar (ed), *Law and Religion* (Ashgate, 2000).

lowed by an increase in the number of seats.[41] Today the Archbishops of Canterbury and York, the Bishops of London, Westminster and Durham, and the 21 most senior of the remaining bishops, sit in the House of Lords.[42] They retain their position so long as they hold their bishopric, in practice retiring from both roles before the age of 70.[43]

It is possible for other religious organisations to gain a voice in the national legislature, through the granting of life peerages to those in positions of leadership or responsibility within the different faith groups.[44] One such obvious example is the appointment of the current Chief Rabbi (Lord Sacks) as a life peer. There are, however, significant differences between a life peer and a Lord Spiritual. Life peers ordinarily retain their position for life, in contrast to Lords Spiritual who, on ceasing to hold their position in the Church of England hierarchy, lose their place in the Lords' Chamber. The appointment of a Lord Spiritual is effectively automatic, and as of right to the most senior Bishops, while appointments such as that of the Chief Rabbi are ad hoc and at the discretion of the political figures recommending the creation of life peers. Weller sees these appointments as having:

> been solely on the basis of a recognition of the individual concerned, rather than as part of an explicit attempt to reflect the wider range of religious traditions and communities now present in our increasingly pluralizing society.[45]

It follows that the question of which religious figure to appoint to represent a religious organisation or community can be contentious. In discussing the Chief Rabbinate, Newman notes:

---

[41] See Halsbury's *Laws of England* (4th edn) (Butterworths, 2002) vol 14, para 528.

[42] See Bishoprics Act 1878. This excludes the Bishop of Sodor and Man, who has a seat in the legislature of the Isle of Man; and the Bishop of Gibraltar in Europe. See P Goodrich, 'A Bishop in the House of Lords' [1997] *Law and Justice* 63.

[43] Ecclesiastical Offices (Age Limit) Measure 1975; Bishops (Retirement) Measure 1986.

[44] 'Other ecclesiastical groupings may be represented through the nomination of Life Peers. The Roman Catholic Archbishop of Westminster is not included, and only recently the Chief Rabbi, head of the Jewish faith, has been made a Life Peer' – McEldowney, *Public Law* 55. Additionally, members of the House may themselves follow a particular faith – see for instance Ahmed Versi, 'House of Lords loses a Muslim', *Muslim News* (London, 26 November 1999).

[45] P Weller, *Submission to the Royal Commission on the Reform of the House of Lords* (unpublished, 29 April 1999) para 6.5.

the extent to which the 'host society' has welcomed the intervention of successive chief rabbis in politics – even to the extent of awarding one of them a seat
in the House of Lords – might well in itself have weakened the status of the chief
rabbinate within the Jewish community itself. And the extent to which the State
has turned to the chief rabbinate and regarded it as the official spokesman of
the community has further alienated those groups within the community who
are unhappy about many of its aspects.[46]

The composition of the House of Lords was radically changed in 1999, with
the removal of the majority of the hereditary peers from the House, causing
it to be numerically dominated by life peers. This measure was seen by its
supporters as the first stage of a further-reaching reform, however, that
could include consideration of the position of the Lords Spiritual. The Royal
Commission, which reported in 2000, recommended a reduction in the size
of the Church of England's representation, the inclusion of other Christian
faith representatives, and the allocation of places for other religious communities. The White Paper that followed endorsed a reduced, but remaining,
Church of England presence, and the appointment of other religious representatives. As Parliament and the executive moved implementation of the
White Paper forward, they became increasingly less committed to the extension of religious representation, and the difficulties of reform generally led
to the dropping of the legislative plans in 2004. It is striking that, in relation
to the position of the Lords Spiritual, an equality narrative initially pushing
towards extension of places in the legislature to other religious groups, when
faced with the practical difficulties of doing this, began to transform into an
argument for abolition of the special treatment of the Church of England.
A second White Paper, in 2007, put forward a number of possibilities for the
future shape of the House of Lords, all with a reduced Church of England
representation. In May 2011 the coalition government published a Draft Bill
proposing a reformed House of Lords with a reduced membership of 300,
80 per cent of whom would be elected, with the remainder appointed. It was
proposed that Church of England bishops would retain seats in the House
of Lords, although these would be reduced in number to 12.[47] At the time of
writing the plans for Lords reform have been dropped.[48]

---

[46]   See A Newman, 'The office of Chief Rabbi: A very English institution' in
N Aston (ed), *Religious change in Europe, 1650–1914* (Clarendon Press, 1997);
R Gledhill, 'Chief Rabbi post for progressives', *The Times* (London, 17 February
1999) 4.
[47]   House of Lords Reform Draft Bill, Cm 8007 (May 2011) paras 91–103,
available at http://www.official-documents.gov.uk/document/cm80/8077/8077.
pdf.
[48]   See eg the Joint Committee on the Draft House of Lords Reform Bill

This review of the formal involvement of the Church of England in the key organs of the United Kingdom suggests that the Church enjoys considerable privileges in relation to control of state power. This risks being misleading. The role of the sovereign should not be overstated; the difficulties of a Prime Minister faced with the limits on Roman Catholic and Jewish advisers to the Crown are surmountable; and as we have seen the small minority of the House of Lords who sit as representatives of the Church of England are by no means certain to continue to hold their place.

During the twentieth century, state involvement in the doctrine of the Church of England through law has declined markedly. Although Parliament has the authority to legislate over the internal affairs of any religious community, in practice legislation tends to be limited to the Church of England. Following the Reformation, the bulk of ecclesiastical legislation was passed by Parliament. The doctrinal inheritance of the Church of England therefore includes state laws, both legislation and decisions of state courts. As a result, the national courts still have a role in resolving doctrine, for instance the question whether a structure referred to as an 'altar' rather than a 'table' was permissible.[49] By the early twentieth century the extent of the legislative programme made this inconvenient for Parliament, which in any case was no longer composed exclusively of members of the Church of England. In 1919 an Act of Parliament created the National Assembly of the Church of England,[50] later renamed the General Synod.[51] Although Parliament retains the authority to legislate over the Church the General Synod is now the principal legislature for the Church of England.[52] The General Synod has the authority to legislate by Measures on fundamental issues concerning the constitution, doctrine, conventions, customs and practices of the Church.[53] A Measure may even amend or repeal an Act of Parliament, and for most purposes has the same effect as an Act of Parliament.[54]

– First Report (26 March 2012) at http://www.publications.parliament.uk/pa/jt201012/jtselect/jtdraftref/284/28402.htm.

[49] *Re St Stephen's* (1987) 2 All ER 578.

[50] Church of England Assembly (Powers) Act 1919.

[51] Synodical Government Measure 1969. See also Church of England (Worship and Doctrine) Measure 1974.

[52] See *ex parte Haynes-Smith* [1928] 1 KB 411. The General Synod has a range of legislative powers, of which only the Measure is discussed in the text. For other forms of legislation see L Leeder, *Ecclesiastical Law Handbook* (Sweet and Maxwell, 1997) paras 2.29, 2.23–4.

[53] *R v The Ecclesiastical Committee of the Houses of Parliament, ex parte the Church Society, The Times*, 4 November 1993 (Div Ct).

[54] See Church of England Assembly (Powers) Act 1919, ss 3, 4; *ex parte*

Outside the Church of England, the general position of the UK state in relation to religious doctrine is fairly categorically stated. A recent statement by Eady J may serve to illustrate the general position:

> the courts will not attempt to rule upon doctrinal issues or intervene in the regulation or governance of religious groups. [This is] partly a matter of a self-denying ordinance, applied as a matter of public policy, and partly a question of simply recognising the natural and inevitable limitations upon the judicial function.[55]

There are well-established instances in which this is not possible, for example where the doctrinal issue is tied to property rights, the terms of a trust or the like; or where the doctrinal issues have been stated in an Act of Parliament. As mentioned earlier, some non-Anglican religious organisations have made use of Acts of Parliament to provide a foundation for their legal organisation. As an example of this, the Methodist Church Act 1976 provides that 'the constitution of the Methodist Church and the doctrinal standards shall be as declared and defined in the Deed of Union',[56] and that 'Conference shall be the final authority within the Methodist Church with regard to all questions concerning the interpretation of its doctrines'.[57] A more disturbing development, however, concerns state involvement in Islamic doctrine.[58]

Following the terrorist attacks in London on 7 July 2005, the 7/7 bombings, a significant thread of UK counter-terrorism strategy has been the use of soft power, primarily state financial power and reputation, to support Islamic groups compatible with that strategy, even to the extent of seeking to influence doctrinal arguments within Islam to promote a form of Islam compatible with state goals. In the aftermath of 7/7, Islamic working groups taking part in the government review *Preventing Terrorism Together* recommended a new national advisory body of mosques and imams; creation of continuous professional development programmes for imams and mosque officials; and 'particular emphasis on developing skills around inter-faith dialogue, youth work, counselling, management, communication,

---

Haynes-Smith; *ex parte Williamson*, *The Times*, 9 March 1994 (CA). It will be recalled that, for the purposes of the HRA, these measures are to be treated as primary legislation.

55 In *Singh Ji Maharaj v Eastern Media Group* [2010] EWHC 1294 (QB).
56 Methodist Church Act 1976, s 3(1).
57 Ibid at s 3(2).
58 For a fuller discussion of the issues in this section, see PW Edge, 'Hard law and soft power: Counter-terrorism, the power of sacred places, and the establishment of an Anglican Islam', (2010) 12(2) *Rutgers Journal of Law and Religion* 382.

citizenship and English'.[59] As a result of these recommendations there followed the launch of the Mosques and Imams National Advisory Board (MINAB), as 'an independent community led initiative' in 2006.[60] Despite this emphasis on its independence, however, it has been identified as an integral part of the UK counter-terrorism strategy (CONTEST), and been extensively criticised for receiving a substantial amount of state funding.[61] On the second point, continuous professional development has been supported by initiatives such as the Preventing Violent Extremism Community Leadership Fund, which provides ongoing support for capacity building and training of imams, including providing a course to equip newly qualified imams 'to engage with British culture and humanitarian values, and *to find parallel values within the Qur'an*'.[62] Although CONTEST is currently being reviewed by the UK government, a recent speech by Baroness Neville-Jones, the Security Minister, states as an ongoing aim 'empowering communities with the theological and technological expertise necessary to challenge terrorist ideology'.[63]

4. SECULAR VALUES AND THE ACCOMMODATION OF MINORITY FAITH PRACTICES

One way of avoiding explicit flashpoints involving overarching claims as to religious interests, and in particular the accommodation of minority faith practices, is to avoid having a legal framework for such claims. Even since the HRA, however, it is still possible for decision makers and courts to cast resolution of disputes in such a way as to avoid framing the dispute as a clash between religious and other, competing, interests. A good example

---

[59] '"Preventing Extremism Together" Working Groups August–October 2005' at 69; available at http://www.communities.gov.uk/documents/communities/pdf/152164.pdf.

[60] See http://www.minab.org.uk/.

[61] See I Bunglawala, 'Minab: Community initiative, or quango?' *The Guardian* (London, 15 May 2009) available at http://www.guardian.co.uk/commentisfree/belief/2009/may/15/minab-mosques-imams-islam.

[62] Hansard HC Deb 12 Jan 2009, vol 468, col 236W (Sadiq Khan, Parliamentary Under-Secretary (Community Cohesion and Fire and Rescue Service)).

[63] P Neville-Jones, 'The government's expectations: What should CONTEST deliver?', speech at Cityforum, 28 February 2011, available at http://www.home office.gov.uk/media-centre/speeches/counter-terrorism-speech.

is *Ghai*,[64] a case concerning a claim to the right to open-air cremation in accordance with the claimant's religious beliefs. Ghai's local council had decided that it was not able to set aside land for open-air funeral pyres because of the law on cremation. At first instance, Cranston J dealt with the case as a clash between the existing body of law, and a *prima facie* religious rights claim under ECHR Article 9. In the Court of Appeal, however, the case turned entirely on a technical point – the correct interpretation of 'building' under the Cremation Act 1902, section 2. The implications of Ghai's interests falling under Article 9 were not considered, as it was possible to resolve the case in his interest purely on this technical basis.

It does seem, however, that the twenty-first century has begun with a number of legal flashpoints – areas where the practices of faith communities, whether or not held by a small minority in the UK, are subject to state restriction or regulation, and this regulation is resisted in part through legal argument. I will discuss three.

Discrimination Law

Discrimination law is of relevance here, both in the workplace and in relation to the provision of goods and services. During the twenty-first century the potential for conflict between religious interests, and non-discrimination norms, has become more acute. Partly, this is due to an extension of the grounds regarded as violating non-discrimination norms. In addition to the relatively established grounds of race, gender and marital status, the UK has seen the extension of discrimination law to age, disability, religion and sexual orientation. As the grounds have increased, the potential for conflict not only between religious interest claims, but between religious claims and other grounds, has also increased. We can also see the potential for conflict increased by the extension of non-discrimination norms from the workplace to other areas, such as the provision of services. Two brief, high-profile, examples will illustrate this point.

Catholic Care was a charity set up to provide the services of an adoption agency, funded partly by payments from the local authorities and partly from charitable giving by the Roman Catholic Church. Catholic Care carried out its activities in accordance with the tenets of the Catholic Church, in particular not providing adoption services to unmarried couples, including same-sex cohabiting couples or civil partners. The regulations made under the Equality Act 2006 made it unlawful to discriminate

---

[64]   *R (on the application of Ghai) v Newcastle City Council and Ors* [2010] EWCA Civ 59.

on the grounds of sexual orientation in the provision of goods, facilities or services to the public or a section of the public.[65] During the preparation of the regulations the Catholic Church (amongst others) lobbied for an exception for religious adoption agencies to allow them to continue not providing their services to same-sex couples. The government declined. When the regulations were coming into effect, a number of agencies found a way to accommodate them with their relationship with a church, others severed their ties with religious organisations in order to provide services for same-sex couples, while some subcontracted their adoption agency work, and others closed.[66] Catholic Care, and others, sought to take advantage of an exception in the regulations that allowed a person to provide benefits only to persons of a particular sexual orientation if 'he acts in pursuance of a charitable instrument, and the restriction of benefits to persons of that sexual orientation is imposed by reason of or on grounds of the provisions of the charitable instrument'.[67] Catholic Care's charitable instrument did not contain such a limit, but the charity sought to amend its instruments to include one. The proposed amendment required the consent of the Charity Commission, which was refused. The High Court outlined the reach of the exemption under the regulations, and referred the case back to the Charity Commission to resolve. The Charity Commission ruled that the prohibition of discrimination on the grounds of sexual orientation was a fundamental principle of human rights law, and exceptions might only be permitted where there were particularly convincing and weighty reasons, which were not present in this case.[68] The religious element of the case was dealt with briefly. The Commission held that it 'was not satisfied that the attitudes and views of those providing part of the funding for a service provided by the charity would justify discrimination on the grounds of sexual orientation by the charity itself',[69] and that '[t]o the extent that the attitudes of the donors to the charity (ie Catholic Care) [we]re based on religious conviction, they [we]re insufficient to justify the discrimination by the charity because of the public nature of the charity's activities'.[70]

---

[65] Equality Act (Sexual Orientation) Regulations 2007. See now The Equality Act 2010.

[66] *Catholic Care (Diocese of Leeds) v Charity Commission for England and Wales* [2010] EWHC 520 (Ch) [8].

[67] Equality Act (Sexual Orientation) Regulations 2007, reg 18.

[68] Charity Commission for England and Wales, Catholic Care (Diocese of Leeds). Decision made on 21 July 2010, at http://www.charitycommission.gov.uk/Library/about_us/catholic_care.pdf.

[69] Ibid, para 106.

[70] Ibid, para 107.

Another high-profile dispute, albeit one not dependent on a recent change in the law, concerned the admissions policy of a Jewish faith school that received state support – a dispute that eventually reached the UK Supreme Court. In *JFS*,[71] the school gave preference to children whose Jewishness was recognised by the Office of the Chief Rabbi – that is, children whose mothers were Jewish by descent, or whose mothers were converts by the standards of Orthodox Judaism. The mother of the claimant, who had been refused a place, had converted to Judaism before his birth, but under the auspices of a non-Orthodox synagogue, and not in accordance with the requirements of Orthodox Jews. The UK Supreme Court found that her son had been racially discriminated against – the school applied racial criteria to admissions, albeit motivated by a religious belief that these criteria were required by Jewish religious law. As Lord Phillips held, '[a] person who discriminates on the ground of race, as defined by the Act, cannot pray in aid the fact that the ground of discrimination is mandated by his religion'.[72]

The British courts have also demonstrated a preparedness to extend the reach of discrimination law into religious organisations. In *Percy*,[73] the Judicial Committee of the House of Lords found that the relationship of ministers of the Church of Scotland with their Church could be the subject of legal regulation. In the process, the Law Lords rejected suggestions in some earlier cases that relations between ministers and their religious organisation should be presumed not to have a legal dimension. As Lord Nicholls observed: 'it is time to recognise that employment arrangements between a church and its ministers should not lightly be taken as intended to have no legal effect'.[74] Baroness Hale put it even more bluntly:

> But insofar as those authorities may be explained by a presumed lack of intent to create legal relations between the clergy and their Church, I cannot accept that there is any general presumption to that effect. The nature of many professionals' duties these days is such that they must serve higher principles and values than those determined by their employers. But usually there is no conflict between them, because their employers have engaged them in order that they should serve those very principles and values. I find it difficult to discern any difference in principle between the duties of the clergy appointed to minister to

---

[71]   *R (on the application of E) v Governing Body of JFS and the Admissions Appeal Panel of JFS* [2009] UKSC 15; [2010] 2 WLR 153.

[72]   Ibid, [35].

[73]   *Percy v Church of Scotland Board of National Mission* [2005] UKHL 73; [2006] 2 WLR 353.

[74]   Ibid, [26].

our spiritual needs, of the doctors appointed to minister to our bodily needs, and of the judges appointed to administer the law, in this respect.[75]

There is some evidence, however, that the courts may take a different approach where a religious organisation sees the state intrusion consequent on legal relations between the organisation and its ministers as contrary to their 'foundation and structure . . . the essential beliefs of the church'.[76] This needs to be proven by the facts in a particular case, however, rather than being presumed simply because of the nature of ministry.

Religious Rights Claims

As might be expected following the HRA, and the addition of religious discrimination to the prohibited forms of discrimination, we have seen a number of significant cases based explicitly on religious rights before the courts.[77] One implication of this is that such cases highlight the existence of specifically religious rights, rather than the general human rights of individuals who happen to be motivated by religion. These cases also raise wider questions about the relationship of religion to law. This can create the possibility for explicit conflict between the religious and the secular. An interesting recent example is the view of Laws LJ in *McFarlane*,[78] a case concerning dismissal of a relationship counsellor who asked to be exempted from counselling same-sex couples where issues of psychosexual therapy were involved. During the case, which turned primarily on discrimination law, a former Archbishop of Canterbury (George Carey) suggested, in a very wide-ranging witness statement, that the courts had 'a lack of sensitivity to religious belief'.[79] Laws LJ drew a distinction between the right to hold and express a belief, which he found unproblematic, and protecting the content of beliefs on the ground only that they are based on religious precepts.[80] The latter could not be justified:

> It is irrational, as preferring the subjective over the objective. But it is also divisive, capricious and arbitrary. We do not live in a society where all the

---

[75] Ibid, [152].

[76] *McDonald v Free Presbyterian Church of Scotland* [2010] UKEAT 0034_09_1001; see also *New Testament Church of God v Stewart* [2008] ICR 282.

[77] For an open-access collection of commentaries on such cases, see 'R3D: The Religious Rights and Religious Discrimination Commentary', hosted at https://wiki.brookes.ac.uk/display/r3d/Home.

[78] *McFarlane v Relate Avon Limited* [2010] EWCA Civ B1; [2010] IRLR 872.

[79] Ibid, [20].

[80] Ibid, [22].

people share uniform religious beliefs. The precepts of any one religion – any belief system – cannot, by force of their religious origins, sound any louder in the general law than the precepts of any other. If they did, those out in the cold would be less than citizens; and our constitution would be on the way to a theocracy, which is of necessity autocratic. The law of a theocracy is dictated without option to the people, not made by their judges and governments. The individual conscience is free to accept such dictated law; but the State, if its people are to be free, has the burdensome duty of thinking for itself.[81]

If the relationship between religion and law, particularly as articulated through religious rights, comes to be seen more broadly in this way, the implications for secularism in the English jurisdiction are clear.

Love Rights and Personal Law

The regulation of marriage and civil partnership is an important example of an area of law that currently serves to protect a secular space by excluding religion from being under active challenge on the basis of non-discrimination values.[82] In the UK, there are, for example, a well-established number of routes by which a valid marriage may be made, some religious, others secular. The secular routes were not only permitted to be exempt from religious activity, but were required to be so – that is to say, religious elements were legally prohibited. The difficulties with this exclusion, in terms both of its policing and of the impact on some individuals who were poorly placed to take advantage of the religious routes but wished their marriage to be religious, were exacerbated by the introduction of civil partnerships – limited to persons of the same sex – in 2004. Unlike marriage between persons of different sexes, civil partnerships did not have a religious route, and the legislation was careful to prohibit even the use of registered places of worship in these ceremonies. This was not accidental. Lord Falconer of Thoroton, speaking while Lord Chancellor, saw two major differences between marriage and civil partnership. First, civil partnership was open to same-sex couples only, while marriage was open to opposite-sex couples only. Second, 'opposite-sex couples can opt for a religious or civil marriage ceremony as they choose, whereas civil partnership is an exclusively civil procedure'.
     He added that:

---

[81]   Ibid, [24].
[82]   See at length PW Edge and D Corrywright, 'Including religion: reflections on legal, religious, and social implications of the developing ceremonial law of marriage and civil partnership' (2011) 26(1) *Journal of Contemporary Religion* 19.

> The government has been very clear throughout the process that it has no plans to bring in same-sex marriage. Marriage is an institution for opposite-sex couples with its own historical traditions. Civil partnership provides a separate and distinct relationship, which is secular in nature and only open to same-sex couples.[83]

The comprehensive exclusion of religion from civil partnerships is unsurprising, given the concerns noted above during the passage of the HRA, and the clear stance of some religious organisations against same-sex relationships. It is clear, however, that not all religious organisations share this view, and that some religious organisations see no distinction between marriage and civil partnership, and would wish to be involved in the ceremony of making both. Attempts have been made in Parliament to allow this, and the UK government, at the time of writing, is holding consultations on this point.[84]

5.   CONCLUSION

The legal structures of the UK have not been supportive of formal, over-arching, visions of the place of religion and religious organisations within the legal order. The late twentieth and early twenty-first centuries, however, have created a number of instances in which the place of such organisations has become contested both at the policy level, and the level of individuals seeking to rely upon their legal rights. There seems to be emerging a confident assertion of state values that do not include religious values, over religious values as such. The absence of an existing structure regulating the position of religious organisations in relation to the state – whether one similar to the US First Amendment, or to the bodies of 'ecclesiastical law' not uncommon elsewhere in the European Union such as Spain – may facilitate this. The constitutional emphasis in England (in particular on the Church of England) may thus contribute to a position where the constitutional order of the state seems anything but secular, while the body of law developing within that constitutional order is just that.

---

[83]   Lord Falconer of Thoroton, 'Church, state and civil partners' (2007) 9(1) *Ecclesiastical Law Journal* 5–9.

[84]   See   http://www.homeoffice.gov.uk/publications/about-us/consultations/equal-civil-marriage/.

4. Law, religion and belief in Germany

Gerhard Robbers

1. THE CONSTITUTIONAL PROTECTION AFFORDED TO RELIGION

The German Federal Constitution starts with the words: 'Conscious of their responsibility before God and man, inspired by the determination to promote world peace as an equal partner in a united Europe, the German people, in the exercise of their constituent power, have adopted this Basic Law.'

This *invocatio dei* in the preamble of the Constitution makes reference to the idea of God; it is not an *advocatio dei*, which would directly place the Constitution under the will of God, as is the case with many other countries' constitutions such as those of Ireland and Greece. The preamble does not restrict its reference to the Christian idea of God. It would have been inconceivable that in 1949, after the murder of the Jews by the Germans and in the attempt to reconnect Germany with its pre-Nazi and anti-Nazi good traditions, the new German constitution should have excluded the Jewish idea of God. It is generally understood that the preamble of the Basic Law does not refer to any particular religious vision of God (be it the Christian, Jewish or Muslim one), or any other specific concept of God.

The reference to God is, instead, one that relates to religion per se. The preamble of the German Federal Constitution, by making reference to God, acknowledges the existence of transcendence, and the idea that there is more than the visible world. By this reference to responsibility before God the preamble of the German Constitution accepts that there is something more and other than the state and its constitution, something that goes beyond what is made by humankind. It is thus acknowledging that the state, as created and structured by the constitution, is not all-encompassing, and in this sense the reference to God in the German Constitution is anti-totalitarian (that is, an acknowledgement that the state is 'not total').

The Constitution of the Federal Republic of Germany, known as the

'Basic Law' or *Grundgesetz* (GG), guarantees freedom of religion. Article 4 of the Federal Constitution reads:[1]

Article 4 [Freedom of faith, conscience, and creed]
(1) Freedom of faith and of conscience, and freedom to profess a religious or philosophical creed, shall be inviolable.
(2) The undisturbed practice of religion shall be guaranteed.
(3) No person shall be compelled against his conscience to render military service involving the use of arms. Details shall be regulated by a Federal law.

The relationship between the state and religious communities is further specified in Article 140 of the Basic Law. This provision consolidates Articles 136–39 and 141 Constitution of the Weimar Republic (WRV), promulgated on 11 August 1919, into the present Basic Law. These provisions of the Weimar Constitution form an integral part of the Basic Law, and they create a general structure of guarantees, which in German legal terminology is called an 'institutional guarantee'.[2]

---

[1] The German Federal Constitution is called the Basic Law (*Grundgesetz* or GG).

[2] See the Constitution of the Weimar Republic (*Weimarer Reichsverfassung* or WRV), officially known as the Constitution of the German *Reich* (*Verfassung des Deutschen Reichs*). Article 140 Basic Law and Articles 136, 139 and 141 of the WRV read as follows:

Article 140 Basic Law [Provisions respecting religious societies]
The provisions of Articles 136, 137, 138, 139, and 141 of the German Constitution of August 11, 1919 shall be an integral part of this Basic Law.

Article 136 (Weimar Constitution)

(1) Civil and political rights and duties shall be neither dependent upon nor restricted by the exercise of religious freedom.
(2) Enjoyment of civil and political rights and eligibility for public office shall be independent of religious affiliation.
(3) No person shall be required to disclose his religious convictions. The authorities shall have the right to inquire into a person's membership in a religious society only to the extent that rights or duties depend upon it or that a statistical survey mandated by a law so requires.
(4) No person may be compelled to perform any religious act or ceremony, to participate in religious exercises, or to take a religious form of oath.

Article 137 (Weimar Constitution)

(1) There shall be no state church.
(2) The freedom to form religious societies shall be guaranteed. The union of religious societies within the territory of the *Reich* shall be subject to no restrictions.

In relation to matters relating to religion and belief the Basic Law specifically provides for religious education in public schools,[3] and it also

---

(3) Religious societies shall regulate and administer their affairs independently within the limits of the law that applies to all. They shall confer their offices without the participation of the state or the civil community.

(4) Religious societies shall acquire legal capacity according to the general provisions of civil law.

(5) Religious societies shall remain corporations under public law insofar as they have enjoyed that status in the past. Other religious societies shall be granted the same rights upon application, if their constitution and the number of their members give assurance of their permanency. If two or more religious societies established under public law unite into a single organisation, it too shall be a corporation under public law.

(6) Religious societies that are corporations under public law shall be entitled to levy taxes on the basis of the civil taxation lists in accordance with *Land* law.

(7) Associations whose purpose is to foster a philosophical creed shall have the same status as religious societies.

(8) Such further regulation as may be required for the implementation of these provisions shall be a matter for *Land* legislation.

Article 138 (Weimar Constitution)

(1) Rights of religious societies to public subsidies on the basis of a law, contract, or special grant shall be redeemed by legislation of the *Länder*. The principles governing such redemption shall be established by the *Reich*.

(2) Property rights and other rights of religious societies or associations in their institutions, foundations, and other assets intended for purposes of worship, education, or charity shall be guaranteed.

Article 139 (Weimar Constitution)

Sunday and holidays recognised by the state shall remain protected by law as days of rest from work and of spiritual improvement.

Article 141 (Weimar Constitution)

To the extent that a need exists for religious services and pastoral work in the army, in hospitals, in prisons, or in other public institutions, religious societies shall be permitted to provide them, but without compulsion of any kind.

[3] The relevant provision, Art 7 ss 2 and 3 GG reads:

(2) Parents and guardians shall have the right to decide whether children shall receive religious instruction.

(3) Religious instruction shall form part of the regular curriculum in state schools, with the exception of non-denominational schools. Without prejudice to the state's right of supervision, religious instruction shall be given in accordance with the tenets of the religious community concerned. Teachers may not be obliged against their will to give religious instruction.

provides explicit rules on equal treatment in regard to religious opinion or affiliation.[4] Finally, the constitutional provisions of the German Federal states, called *Länder*, protect religion in a way often similar to the Federal Constitution, but if conflicts arise between the two the Federal Constitution's provisions prevail over those of the *Länder*.

2.   THE NATURE OF CHURCH–STATE RELATIONS

The basic principles of the law governing religion are found in Article 4 GG.[5] It requires a positive stance towards religion, and the free exercise of faith is protected in order to guarantee every individual the right to believe what they wish. Freedom of religion in a negative aspect (for example, the right not to have a creed and/or the right to not belong to a particular religious organisation) is also included. In addition, religious freedom guarantees the right to act according to one's beliefs, so that 'conscientious' beliefs can present a problem in certain criminal cases. For example, in one such case, a woman was critically ill, but refused medical treatment on the basis of her religious convictions. Her husband, of the same faith, respected her

---

Concerning religious education Article 141 GG provides special rules for historically based special cases that apply especially in Berlin and Bremen. Article 141 GG reads:

The first clause of section 3 of Article 7 shall not apply in any *Land* in which *Land* law otherwise provided on 1 January 1949.

[4]   Art 3 s 3 GG reads:

(3) No person shall be favoured or disfavoured because of sex, parentage, race, language, homeland and origin, faith, or religious or political opinions. No person shall be disfavoured because of disability.

Art 33 s 3 GG reads:

(3) Neither the enjoyment of civil and political rights, nor eligibility for public office, nor rights acquired in the public service shall be dependent upon religious affiliation. No one may be disadvantaged by reason of adherence or non-adherence to a particular religious denomination or philosophical creed.

Furthermore, as mentioned above, Art 136 WRV provides:

(1) Civil and political rights and duties shall be neither dependent upon nor restricted by the exercise of religious freedom.
(2) Enjoyment of civil and political rights and eligibility for public office shall be independent of religious affiliation.

[5]   For the following, see also Gerhard Robbers, *Religion and Law in Germany* (Kluwer, 2010) 86ff.

wishes and, as a result, the woman died. The Federal Constitutional Court quashed his conviction for neglect of a duty to help, because the husband could not be held responsible. Thus, in certain circumstances, truly acting in accordance with one's faith and conscience can avoid criminal liability for those who might otherwise break the law.[6]

Freedom of religion/belief also allows for the state to offer the opportunity for inter-denominational school prayer in public schools, as long as participation is completely voluntary. The state must make sure that it provides an atmosphere of tolerance. Thus, if someone wishes to not participate, s/he must not face social exclusion but, rather, teachers and the school must actively create an atmosphere of understanding and respect.[7] In situations creating a degree of control over an individual's surroundings, the state is required to provide for the religious needs of such a person – for example, in a penal institution or during compulsory schooling.[8]

Compared to the various church–state models currently found in Europe, Germany takes what may be called a 'middle of the road' approach. The Basic Law lays down a system under which religious communities are separate from the state while, at the same time, a constitutionally secured form of cooperation exists between the two spheres. Cooperation presupposes a separation between the state on one hand and religious, as well as ideological, communities on the other. Indeed, separation of the state from religious/ideological communities in Germany is strict and specific in the sense that the state and the communities respect the self-definition and independence of the other. This enables cooperation on the basis of equal standing of and respect for the other's field of exclusive competence.

Freedom of religion or belief underpins the system of cooperation between secular and religious institutions in Germany. The legal basis for the German church–state relationship is structured by several basic principles of which neutrality, tolerance, parity and pluralism are the most important, while openness to religion is also a dominant feature of the system. 'Neutrality' means that the state is required to not identify with a specific church. Thus, there is to be no Established Church (Article 137, section one WRV in conjunction with Article 140 GG). The state is not permitted to show favour to a particular religious community, nor to judge such an organisation's particular merits or ideologies to be true. Thus, institutions that have a secular or humanistic world view must be placed on an equal footing with religious groups, and vice versa. This means that anti-religious

---

[6] See BVerfG 19 October 1971, BVerfGE 32, 98.
[7] See BVerfG 16 October 1979, BVerfGE 52, 223.
[8] Ibid.

state policies would be incompatible with this principle of neutrality, which prohibits the making of decisions in favour of state atheism. Neutrality also entails non-intervention in the affairs of religious communities, as made clear in Article 137, section three WRV in conjunction with Article 140 GG: 'Every religious community regulates and administers its own affairs independently within the framework of the general law that applies to all.' The right of religious self-determination must accordingly be respected, regardless of the legal status of the religious congregation.

Neutrality has dual meanings. In a negative sense, it means that the state must not identify with a specific religious or philosophical concept, teaching or institution, while, in a positive sense, it requires the state actively to support religion and to make provision for the space that religion needs within which to flourish, such as, for example, the needs of religious communities in planning law and the construction of places of worship. This concept of positive neutrality is recognised and implemented by the courts and state authorities but, of late, some scholars have argued that the state should adopt a more distant stance towards religion, favouring a much stricter separation between the state and its religious communities.[9]

The principle of 'tolerance' obliges all state authorities to respect the many different religious and non-religious creeds that exist today. While neutrality is applied mainly to organisations in the field of religion and belief, tolerance tends to focus more on the individual. In this regard tolerance refers to a *positive* tolerance, not merely of enduring different views, but rather the active duty to create an atmosphere of tolerance in society. This was underscored by the Federal Constitutional Court in its early decisions on prayer in the state school system. Thus, while it is legal for state schools to offer prayers and religious services for their pupils, attendance must be completely optional, so that those who want to opt out must be free to do so. If a pupil is treated less favourably because of opting out (or participating), the school must seek to rectify the situation, and is required to create a general atmosphere of tolerance within and outside the classroom.[10]

In Germany 'parity' means the obligation to treat all religious communities equally. Equal treatment of religions is a key feature of the law on religion. This does not mandate identical treatment, but rather requires the equal treatment of that which is equal, and distinctions in treatment

---

[9] Gerhard Czermak, *Religions- und Weltanschauungsrecht. Eine Einführung* (Springer, 2008) 85ff.
[10] BVerfG 16 October 1979, BVerfGE 52, 223ff; HessStGH 27 October 1965, KirchE 7, 275ff; BVerwG 30 November 1973, BVerwGE 44, 196.

of areas that are not equal, according to the extent of the differences. Similarly, 'pluralism' is another basic feature of the German system of the law on religion, and it means that everyone has full freedom of religion or belief, with no preference being shown by the state to any particular religion.

German law also provides that religious institutions may rely on freedom of faith, which exists as a *corporative* right (that is, a right of the religious body, as a corporation). It is important to note that the German law on religion presupposes that, in general, religions are synonymous with communities, and that believers traditionally form groups or associations. Regardless of their specific legal structure these groups/associations can acquire legal-entity status. Thus, the Catholic Church, the Protestant churches, the Jewish faith communities, Jehovah's Witnesses, etc form religious communities that enjoy legal personality in their own right. This system of organisation has its traditional roots in both Roman law and the Christian tradition, and is an approach based on the assumption and expectation that the state will find representatives of religious groups with which it can deal and cooperate. In Germany, the fact that faiths such as Islam tend not to form such entities automatically has created problems, although Muslims in Germany have formed associations that take care of the religious needs of their members. In time, these associations may come to be recognised as religious communities by the state administrative authorities and the courts, and in this connection several cases are currently pending before the courts.

A basic feature of the German system is its openness to religion. Religion is regarded as something positive and a phenomenon that also forms part of the public sphere. Accordingly, in contrast (say) to France, German law does not refer to laicism or secularism, for these are not concepts recognised in German law. Thus, terms such as 'laicism' and '*laicité*' tend to be used only rarely and, if so, just by those who advocate a fundamental change of the system to adopt a basically hostile state stance towards religion and religious communities.[11]

A constant and intense debate is thus going on concerning the relationship between the state and religion, religion and culture, and the basic foundations of the German legal and political system in Christianity and its links with Judaism and other religions.[12]

---

[11] See Stefan Mückl, 'Trennung und Kooperation – das gegenwärtige Staat-Kirche-Verhältnis in der Bundesrepublik Deutschland' in Burkhard Kämper and Hans-Werner Thönnes (eds), *Thema Staat und Kirche*, vol 40 (Aschendorff, 2007).

[12] Ernst-Wolfgang Böckenförde, 'Die Entstehung des Staates als Vorgang der

3. THE HISTORICAL, POLITICAL AND SOCIAL CONTEXT OF SECULARISM

History

It would probably not be fair to describe German society as being, on the whole, secular. Religion continues to remain a powerful factor in both public and private life. Indeed, in recent years, there has been a resurgence of some forms of religion and belief. However, in order to properly understand contemporary German society, some reference to the nation's history is necessary.

The sixteenth-century Reformation and the associated religious wars resulted in a general equilibrium and balance of power between the Protestant and Catholic churches, which provided the basis not just for religious pluralism in Germany, but also for state supremacy over the churches. This supremacy was gradually loosened during the course of the nineteenth century, which witnessed the rise of atheism as a strong force in society.

The 1918 revolution at the end of World War I put an end to the remaining state supremacy over the churches. For example, Article 135 of the 1919 WRV guaranteed full freedom of religion or belief, and declared that the general laws of the state would remain applicable. The institutional guarantees of Articles 136–41 WRV provided religious freedom and freedom of manifestation of religion or belief for all individuals, as well as for every religious and non-confessional, philosophical community. This high degree of religious self-determination was only limited by the principle of 'laws valid for all', which was taken to refer to those laws that are indispensable for the nation's very existence and wellbeing.[13] The 1919 Weimar Constitution thus resulted in a separation of church and state, albeit one that recognised and allowed for cooperation in matters such as the provision of religious instruction in the public school system, as well as other matters such as the imposition of church tax and the existence of a military chaplaincy.

The complete moral and legal breakdown under National Socialism

---

Säkularisation' in Ernst-Wolfgang Böckenförde (ed), *Staat, Gesellschaft, Freiheit. Studien zur Staatstheorie und zum Verfassungsrecht* (Suhrkamp,1976).

[13] Johannes Heckel, 'Das staatskirchenrechtliche Schrifttum der Jahre 1930 und 1931' (1932) 37 *Verwaltungsarchiv* 280ff; for an overview of the discussion see Konrad Hesse, 'Das Selbstbestimmungsrecht der Kirchen und Religionsgemeinschaften' in Joseph Listl (ed), *Handbuch des Staatskirchenrechts I* (2nd edn) (Duncker & Humblot, 1994); Stefan Korioth in Roman Herzog, Rupert Scholz, Matthias Herdegen and H Klein (eds), *Maunz-Dürig, Grundgesetz. Kommentar*, 56th update 2009 (CH Beck, 2003).

in Germany brought an end to freedom and to the physical existence of millions of Jews and other people. The Nazi rulers tried to take over the churches. The struggle that arose from this is known as the '*Kirchenkampf*' ('church struggle'). Within the Protestant Church of Germany a Nazi bishop was appointed. In this context a small yet important minority of *Bekennende Kirchen* (confessing churches) maintained resistance against Nazi rule over the Protestant Church. In 1934 the Barmen Declaration of the *Bekennende Kirche* reaffirmed that the German church was not an 'organ of the state' for the purpose of strengthening the Nazi agenda, but was only subject to Christ and his mission. In addition, many parts of the Roman Catholic Church opposed the Nazi regime, while Jewish resistance against the Nazis was important, as shown by the revolt in the Warsaw ghetto in 1943. Resistance was also important among other religious groups such as the Jehovah's Witnesses and the Seventh Day Adventists, while the resistance group *Weiße Rose* (White Rose) had a Christian basis.

With the liberation of Germany in 1945 at the end of World War II, religious freedom took a foremost place in the new constitutional order. It can be argued that the suffering of the Jewish people (regardless of their individual beliefs), the relatively strong moral positions of the Catholic Church and of parts of the Protestant churches, and the fundamentally anti-religious policy of the National Socialist regime were reasons for the far-reaching guarantee of freedom of religion and belief in the new constitution. Germany's acceptance of responsibility for the murder of millions of European Jews by the Nazis was the catalyst for Germany giving its Jewish religious communities, although still small in number, the space for a highly visible role in society.[14]

Whilst the 1949 and 1968–74 constitutions of the German Democratic Republic (East Germany) promised freedom of religion,[15] the state was explicitly atheist, discriminated against religion and often persecuted individual believers. Nonetheless, the Communist state accepted the existence of religious communities and, as a result, opposition to the regime could be mobilised under the umbrella of the churches. Thus, the Protestant and Roman Catholic churches were key political actors during the German reunification at the end of the 1980s. Throughout the existence of the German Democratic Republic, from 1949 to 1990, the churches remained a counterpart to the ruling system. They maintained their independence in spite of manifold, and often successful, attempts by the regime to place its own people in church offices as unofficial collaborators of the Secret Service.

14　See Robbers (note 5 above) 213ff.
15　1949 Constitution: Arts 41–8; 1968–74 Constitution, Art 39.

The regime accepted the churches and other religious communities as somewhat autonomous institutions, so that, for example, their property was not expropriated by the state. Moreover, contacts between church institutions in East and West Germany remained largely intact, and these contacts were often used for the secret transfer of money and to pay to help people emigrate from the East into the West who had been arrested for attempting to escape from the Republic. During that time the Protestant Church came largely to see itself as being a 'church in socialism', in contrast to a 'church for socialism' or a 'church against socialism'. The Protestant Church, historically far stronger in the country than the Roman Catholic Church, also protected people who opposed the Communist regime in the late 1980s. In substance, this development was closely linked to the events in Poland that were supported by the Roman Catholic Church. The famous Monday Demonstrations that contributed to the final breakdown of the Communist regime started from the Protestant church of Saint Nikolai in Leipzig in 1989 following 'prayers for peace' that began in 1982. During the demonstrations, hundreds of thousands of citizens of the German Democratic Republic gathered to protest against the regime and to demand full freedom of travel. Many of the demonstrators were not church members, and they were often non-believers, but found a place to meet, discuss and demonstrate in a space that had been created by religious communities.[16]

Religious Affiliation

The religious affiliation of the German population differs across the various *Länder*. The north of Germany is predominantly Protestant, and the southern part is predominantly Roman Catholic while, in some parts of Germany, there are equal numbers of these two Christian traditions and in others a majority of people do not have any religious affiliation. This especially is the case for the eastern part of Germany which, from 1949 to 1990, was the Communist-ruled German Democratic Republic. Indeed, taking into account the rule of National Socialism, these 'Eastern' parts of Germany experienced a total of 57 years of decidedly anti-religious government after 1933.

Within Germany and its population of about 82 million people, the Roman Catholic Church had about 24 909 000 members, while the Protestant Church had approximately 24 195 000 members (in 2009).[17] The Roman

---

[16] See Robbers (note 5 above) 42.
[17] Statistisches Bundesamt Deutschland (ed), 'Bevölkerung', available at https://www.destatis.de/DE/Publikationen/StatistischesJahrbuch/Bevoelkerung.pd.

Catholic Church is structured in twenty dioceses and seven archdioceses. Among the religious orders and congregations for monks there are 113 independent provinces, abbeys and priorates for 62 different communities, with about 5000 monks in more than 460 monasteries.[18] The orders for nuns have 331 generalates, provincialates, abbeys and independent individual monasteries with about 22000 nuns who live in more than 1700 convents.

The Protestant Church, usually either Lutheran or Reformed (that is, Calvinist) consists of numerous, separate, territorially based *Landeskirchen* (*Land* churches), with each church an independent unit. Together they form the Evangelical Church in Germany (EKD) with 24832000 members. A number of smaller Protestant churches known as the *Freikirchen* (free churches) have chosen to stay outside this federation, and they have approximately 323200 members.

Today in Germany there are also significant minority faith populations. For example, as a result of Jewish immigration from Eastern Europe, there are now 108 Jewish communities with over 105000 members.[19] In addition, there are between 3.8 and 4.3 million Muslims in Germany, of whom between 1.6 and 2 million have German nationality, but these figures are based on rough estimates, since there is no official register. The numbers are calculated primarily on the basis of immigration from Muslim countries such as Turkey (about 2.5 million), the former Yugoslavia (540000), Iran (70000), Morocco (164000), Afghanistan (89000), Iraq (98000), Lebanon (128000), Pakistan (68000), and Syria (35000).[20] Of Germany's Muslims about 74 per cent are Sunni, 12.7 per cent Alevis, 7 per cent Twelver Shi'is, and 1.7 per cent Ahmadis according to their own statements.[21] Whilst Muslims today live in all parts of Germany, they tend to be concentrated particularly in major cities such as Berlin, Cologne, Hamburg, Stuttgart and Munich. Finally, in Germany there are about 1.3 million Orthodox Christians, approximately 1.6 million people who are affiliated to other smaller religions and an estimated 21–28 million inhabitants who profess themselves to hold no religion.[22]

---

[18] Deutsche Ordensobernkonferenz (ed) 'Zahlen und Fakten von Ordensgemeinschaften', available at www.orden.de/index.php?rubrik=3&seite =t1s&e2id=51.

[19] Zentralrat der Juden in Deutschland (ed), 'Mitglieder', available at www. zentralratdjuden.de/de/topic/5.html, July 2010.

[20] Bundesamt für Migration und Flüchtlinge (ed), *Muslim Life in Germany* (2009), 76. Available at www.deutsche-islam-konferenz.de/cln_117/SharedDocs/ Anlagen/DE/DIK/Downloads/WissenschaftPublikationen/MLD-Vollversion-eng -dik,templateId=raw,property=publicationFile.pdf/MLD-Vollversion-eng-dik.pdf.

[21] Ibid, 92.

[22] Forschungsgruppe   Weltanschauungen   in   Deutschland   (ed),

In recent decades, many of the long-established Christian groups in Germany have witnessed falling numbers. In contrast, during this period many people have adopted secularism, atheism or agnosticism. However, there has been an increasing tendency for many to take a fresh interest in religious matters and ideas over the last couple of years, and this has led not only to a growth of new, smaller or esoteric religions, but also to a new turning to the traditional (and more recent) faiths in Germany.[23] For example, according to a 2007 study, 70 per cent of the German population declare themselves to be religious while 28 per cent classify themselves as definitely not religious.[24] There are considerable differences between the east and the west of Germany. In the west, 78 per cent of people describe themselves as religious, in contrast to only 36 per cent in the *Länder* that belonged to the former German Democratic Republic. Similarly, 63 per cent of the people in the east of Germany declare themselves as *not* religious, compared to 19 per cent in the west.

In Germany as a whole, 52 per cent of people describe themselves as 'averagely religious', and 18 per cent classify themselves as 'highly religious'. Even the latter is subject to regional difference, for in western areas, 21 per cent are highly religious, and in eastern the figure is just 8 per cent. Finally, the complexity of belief and membership of a large organisation is illustrated by the fact that within the nation's two largest churches between 79 and 82 per cent of members declare themselves as being religious.

Secularism

The German constitution does not say that the state is secular, for 'secular' is not a term used in German constitutional law. Instead, the Federal Constitutional Court interprets the Constitution so that the German state has to be 'neutral' in respect of religion and related world views, as explained above.

While neither the Constitution nor the Federal Constitutional Court speak of a secular state, the notion of a secular state has become strong

---

'Religionszugehörigkeit, Deutschland. Bevölkerung. 1950–2008', available at http://fowid.de/fileadmin/datenarchiv/Religionszugehoerigkeit_Bevoelkerung__1 950-2008.pdf; Bertelsmann Stiftung (ed), *Religionsmonitor 2008* (Gütersloher Verlagshaus, 2007) (short report of the results: Stefan Huber and Constantin Klein, 'Kurzbericht zu ersten Ergebnissen des Religionsmonitor der Bertelsmann-Stiftung (Befragung in Deutschland)', available at http://www.bertelsmann-stif tung.de/bst/de/media/xcms_bst_dms_23407_23408_2.pdf (2.9.2012).

[23] See Bertelsmann Stiftung, ibid.
[24] Ibid.

in German constitutional theory. Indeed, in this regard, it has almost become a principle of constitutional law. But even though the Federal Constitutional Court does not explicitly use the term, many scholars have turned to it, including constitutional court judges. A very prominent, former constitutional court judge, Professor Ernst-Wolfgang Böckenförde, has introduced the term in constitutional law thinking.[25] In this regard, in short, it means that the secular state leaves the sacred sphere to the people and to religion.

If one were to use the term *secular* for the purposes of German constitutional law doctrine, one could probably say the following, based on the current interpretation of the Federal Constitution: the state, as such, does not base its legitimacy on religious (or anti-religious) assumptions. The state is an entity as much for believers as it is for non-believers. The secular state should not work for further secularisation in the sense of 'fighting' religion. On the contrary: the secular state does not foster anti-religious ideas; nor does it discriminate against religion. The state does not assume competence in religious issues, for it cannot decide religious questions. The state must not intervene in religious organisations. By making decisions in religious questions the state would violate its own secular identity. It is the state that has to refrain from being religious, not society. This rebuts any assumption that religions would be excluded from public debate, a notion that also would violate the basic principle of democracy.

From a German perspective, to be secular means that the state and religious communities should remain separate, and that the one may not intervene in the autonomous sphere of the other. Their respective institutions are separated. This makes cooperation possible, for only distinct bodies can cooperate. Furthermore, separation does not exclude cooperation, for the state has to cooperate with many non-governmental institutions, and it would amount to clear discrimination if the state were to cooperate with the likes of economic enterprises, trade unions, sports associations and human rights organisations, but not with religious communities. What is more, there is no state church or state religion in Germany, so the state does not identify with any specific religion; nor may a citizen be compelled to have, or to profess, a specific religion or none.

From the very start, Article 137, section 1 WRV, in conjunction with Article 140 GG, has made non-identification and non-intervention mandatory, while the state must not discriminate against religion generally nor a specific religion in particular. In addition, not merely is the German state obliged not to intervene without justification in the sphere of freedom, but

---

25 See Böckenförde (note 12 above) 42.

it must actively support freedom. In other words, the state has a responsibility to make a religious life possible. Thus, just as the state supports leisure activities (for example sports and theatres), economic enterprises and political organisations, so too must it support religion. Otherwise the state would discriminate against religion. To make religious life possible is a task for the secular state for the sake of its secular nature. If the state were to discriminate against religion, it would take a *religious* decision. The secular state is a state of freedom of religion and belief, otherwise it would endanger its own very identity.

4. THE RELATIONSHIP BETWEEN SECULAR VALUES AND THE ACCOMMODATION OF MINORITY FAITH PRACTICES

The relationship between 'secular' and 'religious' values is not always clearly defined.

In Europe generally, and Germany in particular, 'secular' values usually are derived from religious values, while, on the other hand, religious values are sometimes sacralisations of secular values. The religious roots of human rights, democracy, and pluralism (that is, the religious roots of secular values) may be forgotten by some, but they should not be ignored, for it would be wrong to ignore or deny these roots that are still alive and that continue to nourish present statehood.

In Germany the largest non-Christian faith group is Islam. Today Islam is increasingly visible in the German public sphere, and presents the greatest challenge to the development of German law on religion.[26] For example, Muslim organisations are mostly structured as registered associations under general civil association law. No Muslim organisation has, as yet, been acknowledged as a religious community under public law, although a number of organisations have applied for this status, which carries with it certain rights, including the right of churches to levy taxes on their members.

The most important Muslim organisations, and individual Muslims who represent the variety of Muslim ways of life in Germany, participate actively in the German Islam Conference. This Conference, established by the German Federal Minister of the Interior, discusses issues of Muslim life in Germany, and tends to change in accordance with changes of Minister.

---

[26] See Gerhard Robbers, 'Germany' in Jörgen Nielsen (ed), *Yearbook of Muslims in Europe* (Koninklijke Brill NV, 2009), 141ff.

Muslim organisations actively participate in inter-religious dialogues, while several inter-religious initiatives have been subsidised by public funds.

The local mosque community is the smallest organisational unit. As mentioned above, these communities are usually structured as associations. To date most mosques have been formed by members from the same national background. The majority of these mosque associations are active on a national level, and there are more than a dozen such associations, with estimates suggesting that between 10 and 15 per cent of Muslims in Germany are affiliated to them. Estimates suggest that there are approximately 2600 Muslim mosques/prayer houses in Germany, of which 206 are *classical* mosques, with minarets and domes. In addition, about 120 more mosques are currently awaiting construction, while there are already more than 120 teaching houses, and in excess of 100 Alevite associations have their own Cem-houses, although there are no exact figures available for this branch of Islam.[27]

The *muezzin*'s call is regarded as being part of a Muslim's freedom of religion, so in Germany it is legal to have it broadcast by loudspeakers. In determining the volume of the call, the interests of the faithful have to be balanced against those of the general population. In relation to the construction of religious buildings more generally, urban planning law provides for the religious needs of the local population. The religious associations also have to be heard in order to establish the actual need for the construction of buildings of worship.

In Germany, there are some 700 000 Muslim pupils in public schools. Islam is usually covered in classes of culture and language, which are typically taught in Turkish and Farsi. Some of the *Länder* work together with the Turkish authorities to define the syllabus for this religious instruction, while others work together with local mosque associations in this regard. There are strong moves to integrate Muslim religious instruction in public schools in the same structure as is provided for the more traditional religions in Germany.[28]

Another area of controversy has been burial rites. It is estimated that about 90 per cent of Muslims who have died in Germany in recent times have been buried in their former home countries. However, this applies mainly to first-generation Muslims, and the nation's burial law has been substantially amended to meet the needs of Muslim burial practice.

---

[27] See http://de.statista.com/statistik/daten/studie/72323/umfrage/muslimische-moscheen-und-gebetsraeume-in-deutschland/.

[28] See http://www.deutsche-islam-konferenz.de/cln_110/SubSites/DIK/DE/Startseite/home-node.html?__nnn=true.

Several *Länder* have repealed the former duty to use a coffin, as well as the minimum time before burial. In many cemeteries, including some operated by Christian churches, areas for Muslims have been specifically developed in which it is possible, without too much of a problem, to orient the grave towards Mecca and bury amongst other Muslims.

Muslim religious festivals are not explicitly or specially protected, as are Christian and Jewish religious holidays. However, Muslims and members of other minority faiths have a right to time off from employment to attend holy days and religious services, if their absence is feasible taking into account the needs of their employers.[29] Some laws explicitly regulate the free time afforded to pupils and school teachers for attending the services of their religious communities, and the amount of protection that is offered tends to differ between the various *Länder*. In the absence of particular legal provisions, determinations of free time usually involve a balance being struck between the religious needs of the believer and the needs of his/her employer or school.

Halal food and religious dress are two other issues that have led to the accommodation of Muslim faith practices. Halal slaughter is permitted under conditions specified by law[30] and, while some state authorities have tried to make ritual slaughtering more difficult, no problems of access to halal food have been reported in public institutions such as prisons and in the armed forces, where it is available on request. In general, everybody is free to wear religious garments or symbols. The headscarf as a religious garment is not prohibited in the areas of education and employment. Thus, for example, the Federal Constitutional Court has held that an employer has to tolerate a Muslim woman employee who works as a sales person in a perfume shop wearing a Muslim headscarf.[31] However, complete coverage of the face has not been tolerated at school for pedagogical reasons. Following intense public debate, a number of *Länder* (Baden-Württemberg, Hessen, Bremen, Berlin, Lower Saxony, Bavaria, Saarland and North Rhine-Westfalia) have introduced specific laws to prohibit teachers or other public officials from wearing specific religious symbols. For example, the law of Baden-Württemberg reads:

> Teachers at public schools are not allowed to exercise political, religious, ideo-logical or similar manifestations that may endanger or disturb the neutrality of the country towards pupils or parents or the political, religious or ideological

---

[29]   See Robbers, *Religion and Law in Germany* (note 5 above) 331.
[30]   In Germany, animal protection law provides for exemptions from the requirement to stun the animal prior to slaughter.
[31]   BVerfG, decision of 30 July 2003 – 1 BvR 792/03.

peace of the school. Particularly illegitimate is behaviour that can appear to pupils and parents to be a teacher's demonstration against human dignity, non-discrimination, the rights of freedom or the free and democratic order of the constitution. The exercise of the task of education and the respective exhibition of Christian and occidental educational and cultural values or traditions does not contradict the duty of behaviour according to sentence 1.

The Federal Administrative Court has ruled that all laws prohibiting religious garments in public schools must be interpreted in a way that treats all religions equally while respecting the German cultural tradition. However, this issue continues to arouse great controversy, and remains a challenge in terms of determining the limits of religious freedom for Muslims in Germany.

Only civil marriage is given legal effect in Germany. Because most Muslims in Germany are of Turkish background, Shari'a family law does not play a major role in the country, but exceptions apply for marriage contracted abroad and amongst foreigners. Everyone remains free to enter into marriage before a religious institution, but such a marriage has no effect in state law. In the same way, the state only recognises divorces that have been granted in accordance with the law of the land, while issues such as inheritance are exclusively governed by law passed by the state, as opposed to those created by a religious tradition.

5.   CONCLUSION

Muslim immigration, increased religious pluralism, and the current rise of religion in society have all created challenges for Germany in the field of law and religion. Today the law in Germany is deeply rooted in Christian values and those of an Enlightenment based on the Christian tradition, as well as being influenced by a variety of other ideas and cultures. In order to meet the needs of intensified pluralism, German law must adjust further and find new, appropriate ways to accommodate religion or belief. The path to follow is that of inclusion rather than that of exclusion. While increased pluralism requires openness to law and society, religions and beliefs also need to adapt to a society of pluralism.

The German law on religion is capable of meeting these challenges. It is based on the human right of freedom of religion or belief for everyone. Over centuries this law has developed to accommodate various religions and denominations, predominantly to secure peace and equality between Protestantism and Roman Catholicism as two competing, albeit basically equally strong, forces. There has been much experience of religious pluralism in German law and society over many centuries, and German legal and social thinking has been deeply affected by the complete legal and moral breakdown under National Socialism. The challenges of immigration, cultural diversity and religious plurality in contemporary Germany are discussed openly, albeit sometimes in a very controversial atmosphere. It seems that the law often takes the lead, while some parts of society and the media still need greater flexibility and openness.

5. Religion in the constitutional order of the Republic of Ireland

Eoin Daly

1. INTRODUCTION

The relationship between law and religion in the Republic of Ireland is unusual and interesting. It is set within an apparent paradox: that of a notoriously close church–state relationship in the political and institutional practice of the independent state, juxtaposed against a broadly liberal constitutional framework that accords ostensibly strong priority to religious freedom and equality on religious grounds. The historically close relationship between the Irish state and the Roman Catholic Church was constructed on a largely informal basis, which finds no clear footing in the constitutional and legislative framework pertaining to religion. The quasi-establishment of the dominant church throughout the earlier part of the state's history was facilitated, rather than being actively stipulated or formalised, by the constitutional text. Indeed, as will be seen, this elusive constitutional compromise allowed for a mediation of the two distinct traditions of Irish nationalism: the secular republican tradition represented by the Jacobin-influenced, anti-sectarian revolutionaries of the eighteenth century;[1] and the romantic Gaelic nationalism that associated Irish identity with Christianity and, to some extent, more specifically with Roman Catholicism. Thus, a recurrent theme in this chapter is the tension, in the constitutional framework, between a liberal and republican heritage that emphasises equality before the law and therefore leans against religious 'establishments', and a parallel tendency to promote recognition of the determinate religious needs and traditions of the people.

The constitutional framework for the state–religion relationship must be set in context as one facet of the broader state–religion relationship in

---

[1] The anti-sectarian and republican conception of national identity in Ireland was expressed by Theobold Wolfe Tone (a key figure in the revolutionary group the United Irishmen) in the pamphlet *An Argument on behalf of the Catholics of Ireland* (1791).

its institutional, practical, affective and even aesthetic dimensions. This chapter describes the main themes in the constitutional adjudication and regulation of church–state issues within the framework of the 1937 Constitution, which at one level appears to echo and doubly enforce the traditionally close state–religion relationship in practice and, on another, has provided something of a check on it, safeguarding individual freedoms, and not just freedom of religion, against the instrumentalisation of state power by dominant religious forces. Nonetheless, many of the constitutional guarantees in the state–religion sphere have lain dormant through the state's history, having never been effectively used to challenge those alliances of civil and religious power that infringe basic liberties.

Any analysis of law and religion in a given polity extends beyond the narrow analysis of how law checks the impact of the state on religious life, and of religious influence on the polity. As will be seen, the very authority of the Constitution is predicated simultaneously on the religious, the plebiscitary and the popular: it offers a peculiarly prescient vindication of Witte and Alexander's observation that 'law and religion are distinct spheres and sciences of human life, but they exist in dialectical interaction, constantly crossing over and cross-fertilising each other ... religion gives law its spirit and inspires its adherence to ritual and justice'.[2] Indeed, as will be explored, a broad swathe of constitutional affirmations is explicitly linked to the transcendental, the metaphysical and the divine. Just as Christianity partly underpinned the common law,[3] Christian and sometimes Catholic values provided the background set of moral values against which constitutional adjudication was conducted, as the ultimate legitimation in view of which constitutional rights were expounded and applied. The dissipation of the denominational ordering of the public sphere more generally has reverberated in the sphere of constitutional adjudication, and the use of religious references in constitutional interpretation has dissipated in line with broader trends of secularisation.

2.   RELIGIOUS INFLUENCES ON THE CONSTITUTIONAL ORDER

Since there is little statutory law dealing directly with religion, the most significant legal basis for the state–religion relationship is found in the

---

[2]   John Witte and Frank Alexander, *Christianity and Law: an Introduction* (Cambridge University Press, 2008) 1.
[3]   See, for example, *Donoghue v Stevenson* [1932] AC 562.

1937 Constitution. While this contains comparatively detailed provisions dealing specifically with religion, it is necessary first to look at the broader religious influences on its overall scheme and ethos – both in terms of the historical religious forces that helped shape its provisions, and the enduring religious references that continue to supply, at least in part, its deeper normative and philosophical identity.

The main political purpose of the 1937 Constitution was to assert independence from Britain at further, both institutional and symbolic, levels – the 1922 Constitution, the first of the independent polity, having been associated with the divisive Anglo-Irish Treaty and the dominion status it accorded to the Irish Free State. The new Constitution was purged of any symbolic association with the British Crown, being replete, in both preamble and main text, with institutional and symbolic affirmations of national identity – where the 'Irish nation [affirmed] its inalienable, indefeasible and sovereign right to choose its own form of Government' (Article 1), the state being affirmed as 'sovereign, independent and democratic' (Article 5) and 'all powers of government, legislative, executive and judicial, deriv[ing], under God, from the people' (Article 6).

Moreover, the Constitution's assertion of national sovereignty and its formulation of a national identity embraced an explicitly religious dimension, with the preamble both invoking 'the most Holy Trinity' and 'humbly acknowledging all our obligations to our Divine Lord, Jesus Christ, who sustained our fathers through centuries of trial . . . gratefully remembering their heroic and unremitting struggle to regain the rightful independence of the Nation'. Indeed, Article 44, which treats specifically of 'Religion', juxtaposes liberal-rights guarantees against exhortatory, even bellicose affirmations of the privileged position accorded to religion in the new constitutional order, even asserting 'the Homage of Public worship is due to Almighty God'. McCrea even suggests the Constitution 'defines its ultimate notion of the good in explicitly religious terms'.[4] Religion, in a broadly non-sectarian sense, was recognised as a public good that the state is bound, by Article 44.1 of the Constitution, to 'honour and respect'. Originally, the Constitution also recognised 'the special position of the Holy Catholic Apostolic and Roman Church as the guardian of the Faith professed by the great majority of the citizens'.[5] However, also recognised were the Protestant churches, Jewish congregations and other religious

---

[4]   Ronan McCrea, 'The recognition of religion within the constitutional and political order of the European Union', *LSE 'Europe in Question' Discussion Paper Series*, Paper no 10, September 2009, 6.

[5]   Article 44.1.2.

groups existing in Ireland at the time.[6] However, the 'special position' provision, while never having had any justiciable legal effect, was abolished by referendum in 1972 – along with reference to the minority denominations.[7]

The contemporaneous influence of the Catholic Church on Irish politics is well documented,[8] and this certainly had a determinative effect on the new Constitution. However, this influence may have been overstated; the Vatican, to which the draft Constitution was submitted for approval, neither expressly approved nor disapproved, while the Protestant and Jewish congregations were also consulted – and were reportedly quite satisfied with the text. Thus, in view of the overwhelming Catholic majority at the time, the contemporary text reflects the constitutional framers' successful resistance to pressures to establish the Catholic Church formally, with the provisions having been characterised as a 'skilful endorsement of religious pluralism'.[9] Hogan and Whyte even characterise the Article 44 provisions, guaranteeing freedom of conscience and religion, as reflecting a philosophy of 'nineteenth century liberalism'[10] while Hogan argues that the Catholic influence on the Constitution has been overstated, with its competing narrative, secular-republican values, having been overlooked.[11] Interestingly, it has been noted that 'the adoption of a document in 1937 that made no effort to conceal the sectarian sources of its deepest commitments did not appreciably alter the identity of a polity that had previously been governed by a constitution notably lacking in any explicit religious identification'.[12]

In any event, the effect of Catholic social teaching was marked in comparison with the more liberal tenor of the 1922 Constitution, particularly in relation to the definition and scope of fundamental rights. This is particularly salient in the areas of family and marriage, with 'the State recognis[ing]

---

[6]   Article 44.1.3 recognised the 'Church of Ireland, the Presbyterian Church in Ireland, the Methodist Church in Ireland, the Religious Society of Friends in Ireland, as well as the Jewish congregations and the other religious denominations existing in Ireland at the date of the coming into operation of this Constitution'.

[7]   Fifth Amendment of the Constitution (1972).

[8]   See generally Dermot Keogh, 'The Irish constitutional revolution: an analysis of the making of the Constitution' in Frank Litton (ed), *The Constitution of Ireland 1937–1987* (Institute of Public Administration, 1988) 74.

[9]   Gerard Hogan and Gerry Whyte, *JM Kelly: The Irish Constitution* (Butterworth, 2003) para 7.6.248.

[10]   Ibid.

[11]   Gerard Hogan, 'De Valera, the Constitution and the historians', (2005) 40 *Irish Jurist* 293.

[12]   Gary Jacobsohn, 'Constitutional identity', (2006) 68 *Review of Politics* 361, 385–6.

the family as the natural and fundamental unit group of Society, and as a moral institution possessing inalienable and imprescriptible rights, antecedent and superior to all positive law' (Article 41). Until 1995, the Constitution prohibited laws allowing for divorce, while it still pledges the state to 'guard with special care the institution of Marriage . . . and to protect it against attack'.[13]

In a broader field of view, the influence of religion is also felt in the deeper, natural-law philosophy that impregnated the new constitutional order and that was to gain significance in certain landmark judgments on constitutional rights. The positivist and Diceyan inheritances of the previous British constitutional order were resoundingly discarded. This philosophy was evident in the formulation of (family) rights 'antecedent and superior to all positive law' and, for example, of the right to private property as a 'natural right, antecedent to positive law',[14] with children being described as possessing (unspecified) 'natural and imprescriptible rights', and parents, 'inalienable' rights over their children's education.[15]

This quasi-religious, moral and political legitimation of the Constitution itself, and the quasi-metaphysical or 'natural' qualities attributed to constitutional rights, markedly influenced subsequent jurisprudence. Religion and natural law represented the underlying, interpretative values, as the philosophical legitimation of the Constitution, in the light of which sometimes rather vague and open-ended constitutional provisions were expounded in case law. An activist period of Supreme Court jurisprudence was heralded in the 1960s with the articulation of a doctrine of unenumerated constitutional rights linked to natural law. Walsh J affirmed:

> The Constitution acknowledges God as the ultimate source of all authority . . . In view of the acknowledgment of Christianity in the preamble and the reference to God in Article 6, it must be accepted that the Constitution intended the natural human rights I have mentioned as being in the latter category ['the law of God promulgated by reason and is the ultimate governor of all the laws of men'] rather than simply an acknowledgment of the ethical content of law in its ideal of justice.[16]

Thus, religion and natural law together were to represent the primary sources for the identification of the unenumerated rights that were linked to the Christian values of 'prudence, justice and charity' set out in the

---

13   Article 41.3.1.
14   Article 43.1.
15   Article 42.1.
16   *McGee v Attorney General* [1974] IR 284, 317.

preamble along with the 'dignity and freedom of the individual'. In Walsh J's terms, again, 'justice is not subordinate to the law', but the positive law was to adjudicate, crystallise and appropriate morally controversial notions of 'justice' influenced by Christian and sometimes explicitly Catholic values. The real significance of this lay not perhaps in any formulation of a novel relationship between law and justice, but rather in the far-reaching empowerment of the judiciary as the 'least dangerous' branch, charging itself with extensive constitutional power rooted in political, moral, and even theological, interpretative endeavours. In *Ryan v Attorney General*,[17] Kenny J cited the papal encylical *Pacem in Terris* in declaring an unenumerated constitutional right to bodily integrity, in the context of a constitutional challenge to the fluoridation of public water supplies. The 'Christian and democratic nature of the State' was asserted as a further interpretative basis for ascertaining unenumerated constitutional rights. Yet barely a decade later, in *McGee v Attorney General*,[18] the Supreme Court reached a conclusion directly opposed to another papal encyclical, *Humanae Vitae*, in striking down the statutory prohibition on the sale and supply of contraceptives as contrary to the unenumerated right of marital privacy. Although 'justice' was above 'law' and presumably unalterable, Walsh J affirmed that the values of 'prudence, justice and charity', which expressed the natural law ethos of the Constitution, were capable of being 'conditioned by the passage of time'. Thus, the understanding of the Constitution at the time of its enactment, as allowing for such socially conservative legislation as per its 'original' or historical meaning, was not in itself dispositive. Somewhat paradoxically, therefore, constitutional rights were formulated against the moral background both of religious natural law and of the more contingent determinative force of evolving social mores. Henchy J articulated an alternative interpretative basis for unenumerated rights – 'the essential characteristics of the individual personality of the citizen in his or her capacity as a vital human component in a social, political and moral order posited by the Constitution'.[19] This has a more secular ring, but also inevitably invites morally controversial adjudication on questions of human dignity. The capacity of religiously inspired natural law to circumscribe as well as to conceive fundamental constitutional rights was evident in *Norris v Attorney General*.[20] The Supreme Court reasoned that, if the people enacted a Constitution that they understood as being

---

[17]   [1965] IR 294.
[18]   [1974] IR 284.
[19]   *Norris v Attorney General* [1984] IR 36.
[20]   Ibid.

consistent with Christian teachings on homosexuality, they could not have
intended it as invalidating the longstanding statutory prohibition on male
homosexual conduct, which the plaintiff had claimed violated the unenumerated right to privacy.

Constitutional jurisprudence has not been immune from broader social
trends towards secularisation in Ireland, even without constitutional revi-
sions such as the Fifth and Fifteenth Amendments, which removed the
'special position' of the Roman Catholic Church and the prohibition on
divorce, respectively. Even in the 1970s, in *McGee v Attorney General*,[21]
it was held that, in ascertaining unenumerated constitutional rights with
reference to 'natural law', the courts could not 'be asked to choose . . .
between the different views of religious denominations'.[22] In the *Abortion
Information* case,[23] the Supreme Court rejected the rather outlandish
contention that a constitutional amendment duly passed by referendum
– in this case, one allowing for the provision of information on abortion
services[24] – could be invalid on the basis of its repugnancy to 'natural law'.
The Court affirmed the supremacy of the constitutional text over natural
law as any independent, free-standing entity, and emphasised the primacy
of popular sovereignty as a constitutional value.[25] Thus, the influence of
religion as a source for the interpretation of constitutional law has dissipated somewhat in recent decades, with Walsh J's ideal of Christian values
supplying the background moral values for constitutional interpretation
being all but forsaken. Moreover, in a recent case,[26] in which the plaintiff
unsuccessfully claimed that frozen embryos enjoyed the constitutional right
to life accorded to the 'unborn', many Supreme Court judges have explicitly
disavowed any role in uncovering the theological or metaphysical basis of
the ideals and principles – such as the sanctity of 'unborn' life – expressed
in the Constitution. In a stark contrast to the interpretative methodology
of some of her predecessors, Denham J stated:

> This case is not about the wonder and mystery of human life. This is a court of
> law which has been requested to make a legal decision on the construction of

---

21   [1974] IR 284.

22   Ibid, 317–18.

23   *Re Article 26 and the Regulation of Information (Services outside the State
for Termination of Pregnancies) Bill 1995* [1995] 1 IR 1.

24   Fourteenth Amendment of the Constitution Act (1992). Under Art 46 of
the Irish constitution of 1937, constitutional amendments may be enacted only by
way of referendum, after an Act to amend the Constitution has first been enacted
by the *Oireachtas*.

25   [1995] 1 IR 1.

26   *Roche v Roche* [2009] IESC 82.

an article of the Constitution. The question raised is whether the term 'unborn' in the Constitution includes the frozen embryos in issue in this case. This is not an arena for attempting to define 'life', 'the beginning of life', 'the timing of ensoulment', 'potential life', 'the unique human life', when life begins, or other imponderables relating to the concept of life. This is not a forum for deciding principles of science, theology or ethics.[27]

Thus, the religious basis for constitutional adjudication, as the set of background moral values against which constitutional rights are interpreted, has all but disappeared – and indeed, is left without adequate substitute.[28]

3. CONSTITUTIONAL STRICTURES ON THE CHURCH–STATE RELATIONSHIP

As already noted, Hogan in particular suggests that the influence of Catholicism on constitutional order may have been exaggerated.[29] This is reflected in the fact that it accords no particular institutional privilege to any church or to organised religion generally, and affords religions an essentially private status.[30] In this sense, despite its symbolic and exhortatory affirmations of religious identity, the Constitution follows a broadly liberal model in its regulation of the state–religion relationship. Thus, the notoriously close relationship between the state and the Catholic Church was constructed on an informal basis; while the legislative agenda typically reflected Catholic concerns, this had no particular constitutional footing.[31] Indeed, legislation itself has almost never used explicitly religious criteria. With the exception of a rather incongruous recent provision limiting the legal sale of 'Mass cards' to those approved by certain Catholic authorities,[32] neither has the state ever formally delegated any civil or legislative authority to the dominant church.

Thus, contrary to frequent perceptions of the Constitution as privileging

---

27 Ibid.
28 On this theme generally, see S Mullally, 'Searching for foundations in Irish constitutional law', (1998) 33 *Irish Jurist* 333.
29 Hogan (note 11 above).
30 Denominations are guaranteed the right to 'manage their own affairs' in Article 44.2.5, which would seem to rule out any form of publicly administered religious activity.
31 See generally Gerard Hogan, 'Church–state relations in Ireland from independence to the present day', (1987) 35 *American Journal of Comparative Law* 47, and John Whyte, *Church and State in Modern Ireland* (Gill and Macmillan, 1980).
32 Charities Act 2009, s 99. See generally Eoin Daly, 'Regulating religious function: the strange case of Mass cards', (2010) 9 *Hibernian Law Journal* 55.

or establishing Catholicism, all direct references to specific religions have
been expunged since the Fifth Amendment, while Article 44, alongside
its protections of religious freedom, sets out a principle of church–state
separation of sorts, providing: 'the State guarantees not to endow any
religion'.[33] This is much more limited than the equivalent provision in
the United States Constitution prohibiting laws respecting any 'establishment' of religion, because its scope is limited to financial support for
religion, rather than prescribing a broader neutrality of the state towards
and between religions. However, the meagre jurisprudence on the endowment clause illustrates how the scope of an already limited constitutional
secularism has been further circumscribed, in its interpretation, by virtue
of the more socially and politically conservative context in which it was
enacted, when compared to its United States equivalent. In the only case
that relied directly on the non-endowment clause, *Campaign to Separate
Church and State v Minister for Education*,[34] the plaintiffs challenged the
state's funding of chaplains' salaries in comprehensive and community
(secondary) schools, both Catholic and Protestant, as an unconstitutional
'endowment' of religion. The court held that the Constitution envisages the
extensive system of state support for denominational education – subject
to the values of parental choice exalted in Article 42 – and that the provision of chaplains' salaries has to be viewed in this light. It was interpreted
less as a form of support for religion per se, than as support for the type of
education that parents wanted their children to receive. The constitutional
framers could not have envisaged the state's funding of denominational
schools as constituting an 'endowment' of religion; therefore, neither
could provision for chaplains' salaries be construed as such. Thus, the religious aspect of state-funded chaplaincies and instruction was attributed
to private choice rather than state largesse – the state was merely funding
education, the religious dimension of which was depicted, uncritically, as
the product of family and community choice. Through a broader lens, the
apparent potential of Article 44.2.2 to recast the church–state relationship
along liberal, separationist lines has been stymied by a narrow, conservative
interpretation that emphasises the value accorded to religion in the broader
constitutional order, irrespective of the literal meaning of 'endowment'.
In his concurring *Campaign* judgment, Keane J interpreted Article 44 as
recognising that 'religion plays an important part in Irish life . . . [given] the
importance of the part played by religion in the lives of so many people'.[35]

---

[33] Article 44.2.2.
[34] [1998] 3 IR 321.
[35] Ibid, 358–9.

An interesting obiter dictum in the *Campaign* ruling, nonetheless, was the affirmation that, although the 1937 Constitution did not explicitly adopt the prohibition on religious 'establishment' contained in the Anglo-Irish Treaty of 1921, it nonetheless *implicitly* prohibits religious establishment. Barrington J observed that it would be effectively impossible to 'establish' a church without violating the prohibition on religious discrimination in Article 44.2.3.[36] However, this referred to a much narrower sense of 'establishment' than that developed in United States jurisprudence, being limited to the historical European 'establishments' of official churches.[37]

4.   RELIGION AND EDUCATION IN THE CONSTITUTIONAL ORDER

Unlike the establishment clause in the United States context, the weak constitutional restraint on the church–state relationship represented by the non-endowment clause did not prevent the development of a sometimes rather notoriously close relationship between church and state in practice, particularly in the provision of health and education services. Due to the 'fundamentally different' development of primary education in Ireland under British rule, the state never provided a system of public education owned and administered by local authorities. This was partly owing to nationalist resistance to what was perceived as the imposition of British state education.[38] Thus, the diluted form of constitutional church–state separation contained in the Article 44 provisions did not prevent the Catholic Church from 'carv[ing] out for itself a more extensive control over education . . . than in any other country in the world'.[39] In 2010, over 97 per cent of recognised primary schools were operated by a religious denomination, and 91 per cent by the Roman Catholic Church,[40] with no parallel

---

[36]   Ibid, 358.

[37]   In contrast, Justice Douglas noted in *Abington School District v Schempp* that 'establishment of a religion can be achieved in several ways. The church and state can be one; the church may control the state or the state may control the church; or the relationship may take one of several possible forms of a working arrangement between the two bodies.' 374 US 203, 229 (1963).

[38]   Aine Hyland, 'The multi-denominational experience in the national school system in Ireland', (1989) 8 *Irish Educational Studies* 89.

[39]   Whyte (note 31 above), 31.

[40]   See *Information on Areas for Possible Divesting of Patronage of Primary Schools* (Department of Education and Skills, 2010), 1. See also, generally, Alison Mawhinney, *Freedom of Religion and Schools: the Case of Ireland* (VDM, 2009)

system of non-denominational, state-run schools. The end-result of this is that families in many parts of Ireland may enjoy little choice other than to avail themselves of public education through institutions committed to imparting beliefs other than their own. Indeed, the Constitution foresees a heavily denominational public education system,[41] with the consequences of this historic model, for religious freedom and parental choice, having become a subject of intense controversy in recent years.[42] In this regard, the Constitution does not *prescribe* the provision of religious schooling – in fact it does not accord any privileged status to religions as educators per se – but it is rather *permissive* as to the model and infrastructure through which the state discharges its educational responsibilities. Reflecting a logic of subsidiarity, Article 42 establishes that the state must 'provide *for* free primary education'. This was intended to reconcile the state's responsibility to ensure the provision of free primary education with a preference for delegating this function to the churches. Curricular responsibilities and running costs were to be borne by the state, but the 'ethos' and ownership of schools to be entrusted to denominations. As a result Article 44 itself, addressing religion, only explicitly mentions denominational schools in prohibiting discrimination in their funding by the state,[43] while Article 42 explicitly makes parents, not churches, sovereign over the religious and moral values in which children are educated.[44] Thus, it is parental authority, rather than any intrinsic constitutional value or privilege attributed to religion per se, that legitimates the framework of state support for denominational schools; indeed, the *Campaign* judgment described the provision of denominational education as a 'right' of parents.[45] Moreover, in *O'Shiel v Minister for Education*,[46] the High Court held that the state cannot constitutionally refuse recognition to a school whose ethos represents the preference of an 'appreciable' number of parents in a locality – it cannot

---

50; Conor O'Mahony, *Educational Rights in Irish Law* (Thomson Round Hall, 2006) 125.

    [41]   Article 44.2.4 states, '[l[egislation providing State aid for school shall not discriminate between schools under the management of different religious denominations, nor be such as to affect prejudicially the right of any child to attend a school receiving public money without attending religious instruction at that school'.

    [42]   See Alison Mawhinney, 'Freedom of religion in the Irish primary school system: a failure to protect human rights?', (2007) 27 *Legal Studies* 379.

    [43]   Article 44.2.4°.

    [44]   Article 42.1 sets out 'the inalienable right and duty of parents' to 'provide . . . for the religious and moral . . . education of their children'.

    [45]   [1998] 3 IR 321, 358.

    [46]   [1999] 2 IR 321.

provide a single model of free primary education on a 'take it or leave it' basis, without having regard for parental 'choice'. Yet it also held that this does not prevent the state from imposing 'rational criteria' in the process of school recognition – which inevitably means that some communities' claims will be excluded.[47] Thus, the limited concept of pluralism expressed in Articles 42 and 44 does not mean that the state is obliged to 'provide for' free primary education in schools appropriate to all beliefs existing in society, in all areas – a self-evident impossibility – which means that the formal pluralism of the denominational model, which the Constitution underpins, represents a rather limited tool for the protection of religious freedom in education. Exercising the good of school 'choice' – the new, secularised legitimation of the denominational model – is limited to those groups that possess sufficient numbers and resources to attract state recognition for schools specifically appropriate to their peculiar beliefs.[48] In the absence of this, non-Catholics who attend Catholic schools are entitled under Article 44.2.4 to withdraw from religious instruction classes, but the *Campaign* ruling confirmed that this does not entitle them to be shielded from the religious beliefs and exercises pervading the broader school environment. This validated the long-standing policy of the 'integrated curriculum', whereby the religious ethos of a school may be integrated within all parts of the curriculum – and therefore curtails the efficacy of the 'right of withdrawal'.[49]

Again, the paradox and tension that the role of religion represents in the constitutional order in this field means that, through much of the history of independent Ireland, the prevailing justification for the denominational character of public education centred on the Catholic ethos of the independent state, while the broadly liberal orientation of the constitutional text emphasised the primacy of parental choice, independently of any intrinsic public good attributed to religion per se. In practice, the dominant role of the churches always belied the absence of any formal recognition accorded to them as privileged agents, as such, in the educational sphere, and that, today, leads to a certain constitutional ambiguity in this dominant position. The *Campaign* ruling justified the denominational character of recognised schools in terms not of any rights of school patrons or religious communities as such, but only of the rights of individual parents, holding whatever persuasion. However, this shift towards ends-neutral values

---

47 Ibid.
48 Eoin Daly, 'Religious freedom as a function of power relations: dubious claims on pluralism in the denominational schools debate', (2009) 28 *Irish Educational Studies* 235.
49 See generally Mawhinney (note 42 above).

of 'choice' contrasts somewhat with earlier jurisprudence. For example, Gavan Duffy J stated in *Re Tilson* that 'religion holds in the Constitution the place of honour which the community has always accorded to it',[50] while Walsh J affirmed in *Quinn's Supermarket v Attorney General* that 'we are a religious people'.[51]

Today, the legitimation of denominational education interpreted in the Constitution centres more explicitly on the secular goods of 'diversity' and 'choice' – on the claim of parents and communities to enjoy access to schools reflecting their specific beliefs – but this good of school 'choice' is inevitably distributed unequally, as a function of the demographic and social disparities between different groups. Within a formally pluralist system predicated on the recognition of schools representing a diversity of beliefs and world views, recognition of a specifically appropriate school depends (at least) on the existence of a 'critical mass' or viable number of persons of the relevant affiliation, that might warrant this recognition in a particular area.[52] The denominational model is underpinned and legitimated by the state's formal, constitutional neutrality between religions. However, formal equality between groups in the process of school recognition does not translate, inevitably, into equal religious liberty for individuals situated differently in terms of the resources and bargaining power they can draw upon, collectively with others, in negotiating the processes of school recognition.[53] Therefore, this formal constitutional pluralism operates, in reality, as a function of the power relations between, and within, different religious groups. The contemporary focus on 'diversity' in educational provision, as a recrafted legitimation of the 'patronage' model, is bounded by various demographic, political and resource-based limitations; the 'rights' into which it is translated are not fully adequate for persons differently situated in society, particularly the marginal minorities that are poorly positioned to instrumentalise the processes of school recognition. Thus, despite the trend towards a 'choice'-oriented discourse, religious freedom in education remains precarious and unequal in its distribution.

Echoing the previously explored theme of the relationship between reli-

---

[50]   [1951] IR 1, 14.
[51]   [1972] IR 1, 21.
[52]   In terms of the statutory provisions relating to school recognition, s 10(2) (a) of the Education Act 1998 provides that the Minister for Education must be satisfied that 'the number of students who are attending or are likely to attend the school is such or is likely to be such as to make the school viable'.
[53]   Daly (note 48 above).

gion and national identity in the constitutional order, Kenny J expounded the rationale for the denominational model in *Crowley v Ireland*:[54]

> The State is under no obligation to educate. The history of Ireland in the 19th century shows how tenaciously the people resisted the idea of [British] State schools . . . That historical experience was one of the State providing financial assistance [to denominational schools].[55]

Similarly, O'Higgins J stated:

> [Article 42 of the Constitution] *was intended to avoid imposing a mandatory obligation on the State directly to provide free primary education.* Such, if imposed, might have led to the provision of free primary education in exclusively State schools. Rather was it intended that the State should ensure by the arrangements it made that free primary education would be provided. When one remembers the long and turbulent history of the church schools in Ireland, and the sustained struggle for the right to maintain such schools by the religious authorities of all denominations in all parts of Ireland, one can well understand the care with which the words used must have been selected.[56]

On one hand, the denominational model in Irish education was depicted as a bulwark against the intrusion of the state in religious and familial life. On the other, this embraces a post-colonial and nationalist dimension: just as the rejection of British state education represented resistance to assimilation into a British identity, the state's commitment to the de facto Roman Catholic character of public education reflected the importance of religion as a cement of nationalist identity in the nascent state.[57]

In either case, whatever evolving narrative legitimates it, a rather optimistic conjectural assumption underpins the constitutional framework for religion and education – that basic rights can be satisfied by devolving public education to groups (not necessarily religious) which can give positive expression to the different beliefs prevailing in society – in preference to a model of uniform secular education. But this has proved inapt for the

---

54   [1980] IR 102.

55   Ibid, 126. However, Article 42.4 does not prevent the state from providing primary education directly, and the state has recently piloted an alternative model of 'community' primary schools administered by public bodies. The Dublin Vocational Educational Committee opened the first state-run primary school in Diswellstown, Co Dublin in 2008. See Patsy McGarry, 'A big first as two new state-run community schools open', *The Irish Times* (Dublin, 2 September 2008).

56   Ibid, 122, emphasis added.

57   See Kevin Williams, 'Education and religious identity in the Republic of Ireland', (1999) 47 *British Journal of Educational Studies* 317.

complex diversity of modern society, and has protected religious freedom in education in a highly unequal way.

5. RELIGIOUS FREEDOM AND THE CONSTITUTION – AN INCHOATE IMPERATIVE OF EXEMPTION

Given the exalted position of religion in the constitutional order, albeit in a broadly non-sectarian sense,[58] it is unsurprising that its provisions have been interpreted as according a broad primacy to freedom of religion in relation to competing social interests and claims. Along with the symbolic and exhortatory references to religion, there is ample textual basis for this view. For example, Article 44.2.1 guarantees 'freedom of conscience' along with the 'free practice and profession of religion', and Article 44.2.3 prevents the state from imposing any 'disability [or] discrimination on the ground of religious profession, belief or status'. Moreover, Article 44.2.5 protects the principle of denominational autonomy, in providing that '[e]very religious denomination shall have the right to manage its own affairs . . .'.[59]

While it is clear that the legislature may not interfere with religion *as such*, or target religion specifically in its enactments, the state (as noted below) is not only permitted, but also obliged, to exempt religions from the scope of generally applicable secular enactments that impinge inadvertently upon religious beliefs and practices. There has been no suggestion, along the lines of the controversial US Supreme Court judgment in *Employment Division v Smith*,[60] that religious freedom simply requires the object, aim and form of legislation to be religiously neutral and 'generally applicable', or that the courts cannot ascertain the effect of 'neutral' legislation upon specific religious practices. This insistence that the Constitution requires legislative and judicial cognisance of the determinate religious traditions in society was illustrated in *Quinn's Supermarket v Attorney General*.[61] In this case the plaintiff supermarket challenged Ministerial regulations on trading hours

---

[58]   Notwithstanding references to 'Almighty God' in Article 44 and the Trinity in the preamble, it has been determined that the Constitution protects non-Abrahamic religious beliefs, as well as non-religious and atheist belief systems: *Corway v Independent Newspapers* [1999] 4 IR 484.

[59]   '. . . own, acquire and administer property, movable and immovable, and maintain institutions for religious or charitable purposes.'

[60]   494 US 872 (1990).

[61]   [1972] IR 1.

under which it had been prosecuted,[62] because they exempted kosher shops from their ambit in order to facilitate Sabbath observance. It claimed that this represented unconstitutional discrimination on the grounds of religious 'belief, profession or status' under Article 44.2.3. The court accepted that Article 44.2.3 precludes, *prima facie*, all 'distinctions' based upon 'religious belief, profession or status',[63] and that 'discrimination' could not be constructed solely as 'discrimination *against*'.[64]

This was held to be unconstitutional *prima facie* as a legislative 'distinction' on religious grounds. Thus, it appeared that the Constitution, on its literal terms, embraced an unusually strict and formalist conception of religious equality, precluding the legislature from taking account of the effect of generally applicable secular enactments on discrete religious communities. However, reading this provision in the context of the Constitution as a whole, the Supreme Court held that strict non-discrimination had to be qualified where its application would undermine religious freedom, given that the 'overall purpose' of Article 44 was to protect religious freedom.[65] This form of differential legislative treatment, then, was not only constitutionally permissible, but also, potentially, constitutionally required:

> Any law which by virtue of the generality of its application would by its effect restrict or prevent the free profession and practice of religion . . . would be invalid having regard to the provisions of the Constitution, unless it . . . saved from such restriction or prevention the practice of religion of the person or persons who would otherwise be so restricted or prevented.[66]

However, on the facts of the case, the Court struck down the impugned law because it granted a wider exemption to kosher shops than was necessary to compensate Jewish shopkeepers for loss of trade on the Sabbath, going beyond what was *necessary* to maintain religious freedom.[67] The

---

[62] Victuallers' Shops (Hours of Trading on Weekdays) (Dublin, Dun Laoghaire and Bray) Order, 1948 (SI No 175 of 1948), pursuant to s 25 of the Shops (Hours of Trading) Act, 1938.

[63] This was based partly on the interpretation of the Irish text of the provision – *aon idirdhealú do dhéanamh* – as approximating to 'distinction' rather than 'discrimination'. [1972] IR 1, 16.

[64] Ibid.

[65] Ibid, 11. Walsh J stated: 'The preamble to the Constitution acknowledges that we are a Christian people and Article 44, s 1, sub-s 1, acknowledges that the homage of public worship is due to Almighty God but it does so in terms which do not confine the benefit of that acknowledgment to members of the Christian faith' ibid, 23.

[66] Ibid.

[67] Ibid, 26.

advantage of this reading is, primarily, that it preserved the primacy of religious freedom, but also upheld the strict scope of non-discrimination in situations where it was not necessary to qualify non-discrimination for the sake of religious freedom.

However, the *Quinn's Supermarket* doctrine left many salient questions unresolved, a problem compounded by the fact that there have subsequently been few cases involving religious freedom claims. In particular, it left unresolved the question of any difference between the constitutionally *permissible* and constitutionally *required* accommodation of religion, through exemption from generally applicable laws. Theoretically, it would appear that because exemption is unconstitutional 'discrimination' *except* where *necessary* to protect religious freedom, and religious freedom *requires* exemption where necessary, the only accommodation that is constitutionally permissible is one which is constitutionally required. If this is the case, then there is no zone of constitutionally permissible religious accommodation that is not constitutionally required. This contrasts with the doctrines developed to reconcile the 'establishment' and 'free exercise' clauses in United States constitutional law.[68] Moreover, the judgment did not elaborate any test that might determine the situations in which the public order interest underpinning a statute might preclude any such exemptions.[69] It also failed to set out whether generally applicable statutes were to be disapplied only for discrete religious communities on the basis of their recognised doctrines, or also for individual objectors whose beliefs deviated from the norms of those discrete religious communities recognised by the courts. Nor, finally, did the judgment ponder any broader implications of the courts' role in interpreting those religious beliefs and doctrines warranting the exemption of religious communities from generally applicable statutes.[70] The *Quinn's Supermarket* court simply took evidence from the Chief Rabbi concerning Sabbath requirements – whereas incongruously, the Supreme Court, in a later case concerning blasphemy, declared 'the State is not placed in the position of an arbiter of religious truth'.[71] This meagre case law inadvertently alludes to the familiar jurisprudential dilemma of how to protect religious belief while excluding any role for the state as an authority on religious doctrines.[72] Partly because of the rarity

---

[68] See generally *Estate of Thornton* v *Calder* 472 US 703 (1985).

[69] Article 44.2.1 limits the 'free practice and profession of religion' with reference to 'public order and morality'.

[70] On this difficulty generally, see Christopher Eisgruber and Laurence Sager, 'Does it matter what religion is?', [2009] *Notre Dame Law Review* 807.

[71] *Corway v Independent Newspapers* [1999] 4 IR 484.

[72] C Eisbruber and L Sager, *Religious Freedom and the Constitution* (Harvard

of litigation involving religion, Irish constitutional jurisprudence has yet to develop a coherent stance on this problem, although the meagre authority available suggests a much greater receptiveness to a jurisprudence of *recognition* – in other words a willingness to inquire into and ascertain the content of religious belief – in comparison to the more neutrality-oriented establishment clause jurisprudence in the United States.[73]

Irish legislation typically uses a rather general formula for accommodating religious practices, usually exempting religious practice or belief as a broad category, rather than enumerating particular denominations. Indeed, although there is no judicial authority on this point, this formula, accommodating religion as a broad category rather than recognising specific denominational needs, may be well suited to reconciling the requirement of non-discrimination between denominations seeking accommodation, with the *Quinn's Supermarket* concern for prioritising religious freedom over formal non-discrimination.[74] Thus, for example, 'Ministers of religion', presumably a broad category, are exempted from jury service by the Juries Act 1976.[75] In similarly general terms, the Prison Rules 2007 provide that 'each prisoner shall, in so far as is practicable and subject to the maintenance of good order and safe and secure custody, be permitted to practice and comply with the rules, observances and norms of behaviour of the religious denomination of which he or she is a follower or member'.[76] However, the Slaughter of Animals Act 1935 makes denominationally specific provision for Jewish and 'Mohammadan' slaughter methods, while the more recent Charities Act 2009 establishes a specific scheme for regulating the sale of Mass cards on the basis of the approval granted to retailers by specific Catholic authorities[77] – again, revealing the lack of

---

University Press, 2007).

[73] This was confirmed by the High Court's upholding of a recent statute enacted to regulate the sale of 'Mass cards' on the basis of the approval granted to retailers by specific Catholic authorities. See Eoin Daly, 'Competing concepts of religious freedom through the lens of religious product authentication laws', (2011) 13 *Ecclesiastical Law Journal* 298.

[74] Particularly since the Fifth Amendment, 1972, the deletion of references to any specific denomination makes it seem likely that the Constitution accords broad protection to 'religion' as a category, rather than to any exhaustive list of recognised denominations. In *Quinn's Supermarket* [1972] IR 1, Walsh J confirmed that the protections of Article 44 are not confined to the Christian and Jewish religions.

[75] First Schedule, Pt II.

[76] Section 34(1).

[77] The retailer must demonstrate the existence of an 'arrangement' either with a Catholic bishop, or the provincial of an order of priests. Charities Act 2009, s 99.

any clear jurisprudential stance on the constitutionality or otherwise of denominationally specific enactments. Thus, Irish law is incongruously poised between models of denominational neutrality and denominational recognition.

Curiously, while *Quinn's Supermarket* might suggest an expansive framework for religious freedom, there has been practically no litigation on the sorts of religious practice that have been the subject of controversial rulings elsewhere. For example, in 2008 the commissioner of the national police force ruled against permitting a Sikh member of the force to wear a turban, with no subsequent constitutional challenge, and little serious public discussion of what level of accommodation of such practices, if any, the Constitution requires.[78] It was argued by the commissioner that 'the prohibition was necessary to safeguard the impartiality of the police force in a context where religion has often threatened the peaceful coexistence of religious communities'.[79] Controversy also erupted surrounding the refusal of a school principal in Gorey, Co Wexford, to permit a pupil to wear the *hijab*,[80] but there is no legislation governing the specific requirements of freedom of religious manifestation and dress in Ireland's educational institutions, this being left to school management. Such claims have been adjudicated on an ad hoc basis with little sense, if any, of how the constitutional framework might order these. There has been a paucity of *analytic* or doctrinal consideration as to whether, and in what circumstances, religious freedom warrants the exemption of religiously motivated conduct from generally applicable secular laws and requirements, such as uniforms in schools and public services. There is little consistency: medical professionals are exempted from any requirement to dispense contraception or abortion information,[81] yet with the enactment of Ireland's Civil Partnership Act for same-sex couples in 2010, the claim of some Catholic civil registrars

---

[78]   Garda Síochána Press Office, 'Garda Uniform', Statement of 23 August 2007. Accessible at http://www.garda.ie/Controller.aspx?Page=3155&Lang=1.

[79]   Siobhan Mullally and Darren O'Donovan, 'Religion and Ireland's "public squares": education, the family and expanding equality claims', [2011] *Public Law* 284, 289.

[80]   Tom Hickey, 'Freedom as non-domination and the Islamic *hijab* in Irish schools', (2009) 31 *Dublin University Law Journal* 128.

[81]   The Health (Family Planning) Act 1979, s 11 states 'nothing in this Act shall be construed as obliging any person to take part in the provision of a family planning service, the giving of prescriptions or authorisations for the purposes of this Act, or the sale, importation into the State, manufacture, advertising or display of contraceptives'. Similarly, s 13 of the Regulation of Information (Services outside the State for Termination of Pregnancies) Act 1995 provides that no person may be obliged to provide information on abortion services available outside of the State.

to exemption from same-sex ceremonies was roundly rejected and even ridiculed across the political spectrum (this event in itself dramatically illustrating the diminishing hold of religion on public life).[82] Yet despite a threadbare jurisprudence, Mullally and O'Donovan note: 'as the implicit contract between Church and State unravels, the cleavages between faith communities, and between religious citizens and secularists, are likely only to increase.'[83]

Interestingly, in an era of immigration, there has been no equivalent in Ireland of the discourse in states such as France and Germany surrounding the state's role in supervising or overseeing the internal affairs of minority religions in order to promote social cohesion or 'national values'. Even in secularist France, the state played an instrumental role in establishing a public representative body for Muslims, the *Conseil Français du Culte Musulman*, and there was much discussion of the possibility of amending the law so as to allow the state to subsidise 'moderate' mosques.[84] There is no equivalent of these initiatives in Ireland, illustrating how the legal relationship between state and religion is born of a markedly more *laissez faire* ethos[85] – following a judicial model of religious privatisation notwithstanding the historically close *political* relationship of church and state.

In a somewhat incongruous case that confounds the general sense of a

---

[82]   Senator Paschal Donohoe noted on his website: 'the law is the law. We cannot choose what parts of the law we want to implement based on our own views or beliefs. We've seen to our cost as a country what happens when the universal application of law to all, regardless of their status and wealth, is either subverted or nor implemented.' Press release, 'Freedom of conscience and the Civil Partnership Bill', 2 December 2009, available at http://www.paschaldonohoe. ie/?p=2752 (accessed 4 July 2011). The then Minister for Justice, Dermot Ahern, said that it would be 'against public policy to permit State officials to choose not to perform certain of their official functions on the grounds that to do so would be contrary to their religious beliefs'. See Marie O'Halloran, 'No exemption from bill on grounds of belief – Ahern', *Irish Times* (Dublin, 28 January 2010).

[83]   Mullally and O'Donovan (note 79 above).

[84]   See Malika Zeghal, 'La constitution du Conseil Français du Culte Musulman: reconnaissance politique d'un Islam Français?', (2005) 129 *Archives de sciences sociales des religions* 1.

[85]   It might be noted, nonetheless, that the state has taken steps to implement Article 16C of the Treaty of Lisbon, committing member states to 'open, regular and transparent' dialogue with religious associations and non-confessional bodies, and committing the Union to respecting the status under national law of churches and religious associations. See the speech of Bertie Ahern, ex-Taoiseach, on this theme, on 4 February 2008, http://www.taoiseach.gov.ie/eng/Government_ Press_Office/Taoiseach's_Speeches_2008/Speech_by_the_Taoiseach,_Mr_Bertie_ Ahern,_T_D_,_at_a_Reception_in_honour_of_Sean_Cardinal_Brady_in_Dublin_ Castle,_on_Monday_4_February,_2008_at_7_00_p_m_.html.

primacy accorded to religious freedom, the statutory restriction of freedom of religious expression in broadcasting was upheld as constitutionally valid by the Supreme Court. The broadcasting legislation impugned in *Murphy v IRTC*[86] prohibited TV and radio advertisements having religious ends.[87] According a surprisingly broad scope to the 'public order and morality' proviso that constitutes the only constitutional basis for restricting freedom of religious 'profession', the Supreme Court held that the restriction was warranted in the light of the potentially divisive nature of religious broadcasting, and the concern that the rich would have access to the airwaves to the detriment of poorer rivals.[88] Thus, Ireland's history of religious strife was used to justify curtailment of an apparently innocuous form of broadcast solely on the basis of its religious character – suggesting a rather broad deference to the legislature in the regulation of religious practice.[89]

6.   THE RELIGIOUS FREEDOM–RELIGIOUS EQUALITY DICHOTOMY IN CONSTITUTIONAL JURISPRUDENCE

The dichotomy articulated in *Quinn's Supermarket* between religious freedom and religious equality has subsequently been interpreted in surprising and often incoherent ways, suggesting an over-extensive qualification of non-discrimination for the sake of sometimes spurious claims of religious 'freedom'. Recall that religious freedom was to trump non-discrimination on religious grounds where these values conflicted. This may be located in a broader ideological dichotomy between freedom and equality; however, there has been little consideration of or reflection on the very coherence of a blanket juxtaposition of these values.

In particular, this conceptual dichotomy has been used to accord constitutional validity to legislation exempting state-funded denominational

---

[86]   [1999] 1 IR 26.

[87]   Radio and Television Act 1988, s 10(3).

[88]   [1999] 1 IR 26. This conclusion was upheld by the European Court of Human Rights in *Murphy v Ireland*, Application No 44179/98, 10 July 2003.

[89]   The regulation of speech touching on religious matters arose again with the enactment of a statutory prohibition on blasphemy within the Defamation Act 2009, as is specifically mandated in Article 40.6 of the Constitution. Section 36(2)(a) defined blasphemy as the publication or utterance of matter that is 'grossly abusive or insulting in relation to matters held sacred by any religion, thereby causing outrage among a substantial number of the adherents of that religion'. However, it exempts material having 'genuine literary, artistic, political, scientific, or academic value', and there have been no prosecutions of the offence.

schools, in particular, from statutory prohibitions on religious discrimination, both in employment and pupil enrolment. Something of a 'right
to discriminate' has been extrapolated from the *Quinn's Supermarket*
doctrine. It has been generally assumed that a strict application of the
non-discrimination guarantee would undermine the religious freedom of
schools that would otherwise be forced to recruit teachers and enrol pupils
not professing the institution's religion.

For example, in *McGrath and Ó Ruairc v Trustees of Maynooth College*,[90]
the plaintiff lecturers, also priests, were dismissed from the defendant
Catholic college, which was in receipt of state funding, as a result of their
leaving the priesthood and publicised disagreement with Church teachings.
The Supreme Court dismissed the challenge, partly on the basis that the
constitutional guarantee against discrimination on grounds of religious
'status' did not apply to private bodies, even when in receipt of public
funding.[91] However, it also relied on the *Quinn's Supermarket* doctrine,
and its dichotomy of religious freedom and strict non-discrimination, in
holding that the 'primary aim' of the constitutional prohibition on religious discrimination was 'to give vitality, independence and freedom to
religion'.[92] To construe the non-discrimination provision as unqualifiable,
Henchy J stated, would 'lead to a sapping and debilitation of the freedom
and independence given by the Constitution to the doctrinal and organisational requirements and proscriptions which are inherent in all organised
religion'.[93]

Thus, the state has to 'recognise *and buttress*' the 'internal discriminations
... which flow from the tenets of a particular religion'.[94] This expanded
the 'liberty–equality dichotomy' identified in *Quinn's Supermarket* in a
significant way. It qualified the non-discrimination principle not just as it
applies to the general applicability of laws, but also as it relates to the *practice* of religious discrimination against human persons, in the sense of unfa-
vourable treatment on religious grounds. This implies that the Constitution
warrants not only religious 'discrimination' in the technical sense of
exemption from generally applicable laws, but also a 'right to discriminate'
for religious denominations themselves, even where they are engaged in
essentially public functions. This was subsequently carried further by the
Supreme Court in *Re Article 26 and the Employment Equality Bill 1996*.[95]

---

90   [1979] ILRM 166.
91   Ibid, 214.
92   Ibid, 187.
93   Ibid.
94   Ibid.
95   [1995] 1 IR 1.

The bill was referred to the Supreme Court by the President to assess its constitutionality. This case affirmed the constitutionality of exempting from the statutory prohibition on religious discrimination in employment any 'religious, educational or medical institution which is under the direction or control of a body established for religious purposes or whose objectives include the provision of services in an environment which promotes certain religious values'.[96] Such institutions were exempted from employment equality on religious grounds where necessary 'to uphold the religious ethos of the institution'.[97] This applies, for example, to the recruitment of teachers for denominational schools.[98] Citing *Quinn's Supermarket*, the Supreme Court again held that religious discrimination is permissible where it is necessary to give 'life and reality' to the constitutional guarantee of religious freedom.[99]

Similarly, the Equal Status Act 2000 provides that a denominational school does not impermissibly discriminate in enrolment if 'it admits persons of a particular religious denomination in preference to others or it refuses to admit as a student a person who is not of that denomination and, in the case of a refusal, it is proved that the refusal is essential to maintain the ethos of the school'.[100] The constitutionality of this particular provision has not yet been challenged. However, just as the religious freedom of denominational schools is thought to preclude the application of non-discrimination rules to employment, it would likely be argued that it also precludes legislation requiring schools to admit pupils not professing the sponsored religion to an extent likely to undermine the 'ethos' of those schools. This would likely be inferred from what the High Court, in a different case, termed the right of parents 'to have their children educated in denominational schools'.[101]

However, this depiction of religious freedom and non-discrimination as broadly conflicting values has been stretched beyond reasonable use since its inception in *Quinn's Supermarket*.[102] It overlooks ways in which religious freedom and religious equality might be considered not as antagonistic and

---

[96] Employment Equality Bill 1996, s 37(1).
[97] Ibid.
[98] [1997] 3 IR 321, 351. This was termed 'positive discrimination' by counsel for the Attorney General.
[99] Ibid, 360.
[100] Section 7(3)(c).
[101] *Greally v Minister for Education* [1999] IR 1, 9.
[102] For a critique of this position, see Eoin Daly and Tom Hickey, 'Religious freedom and the "right to discriminate" in the school admissions context: a neo-republican critique', [2011] *Legal Studies* 615.

opposed, but rather as being complementary and even interdependent. There is a certain absurdity in the use of a 'primacy of religious freedom' doctrine to justify, for example, the practice by which publicly funded denominational schools may require baptismal certificates from applicant pupils, which is reportedly widespread.[103] Little consideration has been given to the ways in which legislative permission for religious discrimination in enrolment, and other contexts, may in fact enable and facilitate interference in the religious freedom of those discriminated against. Simply, the requirement to produce evidence of religious affiliation in order to access what may be the only publicly funded schools in a particular area may impose a penalty on non-adherents on the basis of their religious choice. It may set, as the price of access to publicly funded education, or at least to the normal range of school choice, the feigning of belief or the non-disclosure of alternative beliefs, or non-belief.[104]

The Supreme Court insisted in *Employment Equality Bill* that the non-discrimination principle could be qualified *'only insofar* as this may be *necessary to give life and reality* to the guarantee of the free profession and practice of religion'.[105] Non-discrimination should yield only where *necessary* to protect religious freedom. However, it appears that this criterion of necessity has been stretched beyond all plausibility in legislation allowing for religious discrimination. The religious freedom claim protected in the context of school enrolment – the interests of parents and religions in maintaining a relatively exclusive confessional environment, albeit while receiving public funding as 'recognised' schools – seems to embrace an inchoate range of religious claims as potentially within the scope of religious 'freedom'. Hogan and Whyte speculate that an imperative much broader than what might reasonably be regarded as religious *freedom* – 'the promotion of social conditions conducive to the fostering of religious beliefs'[106] – is accepted as broadly qualifying the non-discrimination guarantee. It is curious that, while the interests of certain citizens in attending publicly funded schools committed to a relatively unfettered confessional

---

103   In particular, it was reported in 2007 that a number of children of Nigerian origin in an area of north Co Dublin could not gain access to any local schools because they did not hold Catholic baptismal certificates. An 'emergency' non-denominational school, catering almost exclusively for children of African nationalities, was subsequently established in Balbriggan. See H McDonald, 'Ireland forced to open immigrant school', *The Guardian* (London, 25 September 2007) and R Boland, 'Faith before fairness', *The Irish Times* (Dublin, September 2007).

104   See Mawhinney (note 40 above).

105   [1997] 3 IR 321, 358 (emphasis added).

106   Hogan & Whyte (note 9 above), 2054.

ethos is deemed to be constitutionally protected, there is no constitutional guarantee that all citizens will have access to schools suitable to their beliefs. Moreover, without these alternatives, they may be subject to discrimination in access to other schools as not professing the required religion – surely a qualitatively greater interference in their freedom to practise their faith or not practise the dominant faith. Again, the salient theme is one of inequality in the distribution of religious freedom in a formally neutral constitutional framework.

7. CONCLUSION

The underlying ethos and philosophy of the constitutional provisions dealing with religion synthesise familiar liberal and republican values with what might be described as a romantic nationalist viewpoint. This resists any liberal abstraction of religious freedom from the religious traditions and identities of the people, and instead emphasises shared religious identity as one of the anchoring points of national identity.[107] The religious ethos of the Constitution, at least in its aesthetic and symbolic (if not institutional) dimensions, recalls Dworkin's description of liberalism's apprehension of 'ghostly entities like collective will or national spirit',[108] of any romantic nationalism that might attribute an essentially religious character to the people. This echoes John Rawls's conception of citizens as 'claim[ing] the right to view their persons as independent from and not identified with any particular conception of the good'.[109] However, this religious ethos of the broader constitutional order, as its philosophical and moral basis, has dissipated somewhat along with the weakening hold of religion, generally, on the public sphere. Broadly speaking, constitutional adjudication has mirrored the unravelling of the 'implicit contract' between church and state.[110] The constitutional provisions addressing religion specifically are poised between a liberal requirement of state neutrality in religious matters, and a recognition of the centrality of religion to national identity. Mullally and O'Donovan suggest that, 'for the moment, the shift

---

[107] See Eoin Daly, 'Precarious religious liberties in education: the salience of demographic and social contingencies under a formally pluralist public philosophy' in Zvi Bekerman and Thomas Geisen (eds), *International Handbook of Migration, Minorities and Education* (Springer, 2012).

[108] Ronald Dworkin, *Taking Rights Seriously* (Duckworth, 1978), xi.

[109] John Rawls, *Justice as Fairness: a Restatement* (Harvard University Press, 2001), 21.

[110] Mullally and O'Donovan (note 79 above).

from "ethnos" to "demos" is not yet complete, and inherited religious traditions continue to constrain the pursuit of greater pluralism and equal citizenship'.[111] However, given the surprising paucity of litigation on religion in Irish courts – despite the controversial and fraught history of church–state relations – the doctrinal aspect of church–state jurisprudence remains underdeveloped. What is more, a coherent doctrinal theory of constitutional religious freedom has yet to emerge. The distinctiveness of the role of religion in Ireland's constitutional order thus lies primarily in the oscillation between the competing narratives of secular republicanism, and of a nationalism that firmly links religion to national identity.

---

[111]   Ibid, 306–7.

6. Religion and secular values in Spain: a long path to a real religious pluralism

Eugenia Relaño Pastor

1. INTRODUCTION

The demise of Franco's dictatorship heralded a new period in Spanish history, one that paved the way for a transition to democracy. The old systems were overturned, including the powerful role the Roman Catholic Church had played for more than 30 years in Spanish politics. Spain, quite suddenly and profoundly, had ceased to be a Catholic state.

Yet in the period leading up to the establishment of the new Spanish Constitution in 1978, calls by secularist groups for a strict separation between Church and State were not successful. The new Constitution enshrined the principle of State neutrality and incorporated the principle of religious freedom according to international human rights norms. But it also explicitly declared that the State did not have an official religion, and stated that public authorities 'should take into account the religious beliefs of Spanish society and shall maintain appropriate cooperative relations with the Catholic Church and other confessions'.

The constitutional right to religious freedom was further developed in the Organic Law of Religious Freedom (*Ley Orgánica de Libertad Religiosa*: LOLR), passed in 1980, which outlined the individual aspects of religious freedom as well as the nature of relations between the State and religious communities. Though more than 30 years have now passed since the LOLR was enacted, it still has not been fully implemented, revealing perhaps its inherent inability to protect the collective dimension of the right of religious freedom. Whilst such protections may have been adequate for Spanish society a generation ago, today in twenty-first century Spain there is an urgent need to adapt the legal framework to a multi-cultural and multi-religious society.

In spite of the fact that no official government census has ever been conducted in Spain on issues of faith, for the Spanish Constitution states that no individual is required to answer questions regarding religion or equivalent beliefs, an independent government agency (the Centre for Sociological Investigation) periodically collects data on religious trends. In April 2010 one of its surveys reported that 73.2 per cent of respondents considered themselves as being Catholic, although 53.1 per cent of these almost never attended Mass.[1]

All other Christian groups, constituting less than 10 per cent of the Spanish population, include Protestant and evangelical denominations, Christian Scientists, Jehovah's Witnesses, Seventh-Day Adventists, Eastern Orthodox and Mormons (members of The Church of Jesus Christ of Latter-Day Saints).[2] An additional portion of Spanish society, again less than 10 per cent, are followers of Islam, Judaism, Buddhism, Hinduism and Baha'ism.[3]

Increased global immigration has changed the traditional face of Spanish society, bringing with it a serious need to cope with religious diversity. Current laws and practices dealing with religious minorities are frequently challenged and attacked. This chapter will explore the problem by providing an overview of church and state relations (Parts 2, 3 and 4) before outlining the unequal legal status of religious denominations (Part 5). It will then conclude with an analysis of the central shortcomings of the current system as well as a possible direction for moving forward (Parts 6, 7 and 8).

2.   HISTORICAL BACKGROUND TO CHURCH–STATE RELATIONS IN SPAIN

Precedents

In the latter part of the fifteenth century, following King Ferdinand and Queen Isabella's reunification of the country under Catholicism, Spain

---

[1]   Centre for Sociological Investigation (CIS), at http://www.cis.es/cis/opencms/-Archivos/Marginales/2840_2859/2847/e284700.html.

[2]   The Federation of Evangelical Religious Entities (FEREDE) estimates there are 1.2 million evangelical Christians and other Protestants, 800,000 of whom are immigrants. FEREDE at http://www.redevangelica.es/.

[3]   According to Islamic Commission of Spain and Ministry of Justice (MOJ) reports in 2009 there were approximately 1.4 million Muslims in Spain. Approximately 72 per cent are immigrants without Spanish nationality. See http://www.euro-islam.info/2010/03/08/islam-in-spain/. The Federation of Jewish Communities (FCJE) estimates that there are 48,000 Jews: see http://www.fcje.org/index.php/quienes-somos/historia.

framed political unity in terms of religious unity.[4] To be a Spaniard and to be a Catholic were understood as being equivalent, two sides of a single national identity. Such a liaison gave Catholicism a fundamental role in the Spanish national consciousness for the next five centuries where, previously, religious pluralism had existed. During the Middle Ages members of the three monotheistic religions – Christianity, Judaism and Islam – had lived side by side in relative harmony. Each religion was able to keep its customs and its own laws, though this tolerance did not translate into equality. Under both the Christian and the Islamic kingdoms, non-believers were subjected to restrictions (payment of special taxes, exclusion from public office, imposition of special clothing, etc) not imposed upon members belonging to the ruling religious community.[5]

With the Spanish kingdom unified under Catholicism, Jews and Muslims who refused to convert were expelled from the country. Catholics who abandoned their faith, espousing instead the Protestant doctrines of Luther or Calvin, were persecuted and publicly condemned by the Spanish Inquisition. This is why, until the end of the twentieth century, Protestantism was virtually non-existent in Spain, and only a few scattered Jewish and Muslim communities remained.[6]

Later, in the Constitution of 1812, Catholicism was established as Spain's state religion. This was reaffirmed in the Constitutions of 1845 and 1876, as well as indirect mentions in the Constitutions of 1837 and of 1869. During the nineteenth century, religions other than Catholicism were tolerated to a degree, and citizens were free to engage in religious practices such as establishing schools, publishing newspapers and printing and circulating the Bible.

A significant part of twentieth-century Spanish politics revolved around church–state relations, which oscillated between two extremes: on one hand, a confessional state and, on the other, an anti-religious, and more precisely anti-Catholic, hostility. We can find a clear and relevant example of the latter approach in the Spanish Second Republic.

---

[4]   Frances Lannon, *Privilege, Persecution and Prophecy: The Catholic Church in Spain, 1875–1975* (Oxford University Press, 1987) 670.

[5]   Agustin Motilla, 'Religious pluralism in Spain: striking the balance between religious freedom and constitutional rights', [2004] *Brigham Young University Law Review* 575, 577.

[6]   Javier Martínez-Torrón, 'Religious freedom and democratic change in Spain', [2006] *Brigham Young University Law Review* 777, 780.

Spanish Second Republic (1931–6)

The 1931 Republican Constitution, as well as subsequent legislation on religious issues, adopted an unquestionably anti-Catholic attitude. Republican legislatures and governments, especially at the beginning and the end of the Republic, were determined to reduce the social influence of the Catholic Church, which they considered excessive and incompatible with a democratic and secular state. They failed to accept the incontrovertible fact that the church held enormous sway within Spain's social structure. Consequently, Republican governments refused to enact moderate legislation that could reconcile ecclesiastical influence with a democratic system.[7] As some scholars have pointed out, there was something anomalous in the decidedly anti-religious policy of the Second Republic. The religious policies were intended to reduce religion to a purely individual and private matter in a country in which almost all of the population declared themselves to be Catholic.[8]

The Second Republic's reign was short. The actions of ecclesiastical leaders on one side, and political officials and members of the media who supported the Republic on the other, created a potent atmosphere of tension and hostility. This environment intensified further following the burning of churches and convents by anti-clerical groups.[9] Meanwhile, Republican policy on religion, as manifested in the Constitution of 1931, was based on three fundamental aspects: the separation of Church and state; the recognition of religious freedom (although religious groups presenting a danger to State security were to be dissolved, and all groups had to be entered in a special registry within the Ministry of Justice); and the subjection of religious faiths to special laws.

Reducing religion to a purely individual and private matter, the Republic would no longer give financial aid to any religious group. Article 26 of the Constitution of 1931 provoked the most hostile opposition: any state favour, aid or support to churches, religious associations or institutions was prohibited and the Jesuits, as a religious order, were dissolved. These measures presupposed a fundamental change in the status of the Catholic Church and, at the same time, presented an opening for non-Catholic denominations. The Catholic Church rejected and condemned the new

---

[7]   Juan Ferreiro Galguera, *Relaciones Iglesia–Estado en la Segunda República Española* (Atelier, 2005).

[8]   Gabriel Jackson, *The Spanish Republic and the Civil War 1931–1939* (Princeton University Press, 1985).

[9]   José María Sánchez, *The Spanish Civil War as a Religious Tragedy* (University of Notre Dame Press, 1987).

constitutional provision, following the doctrine of Pope Leo XIII.[10] The Spanish Catholic hierarchy adhered to this doctrine and reproved the Republic for its support of an atheistic state.

The Franco Dictatorship

The story of clerical support for General Franco during the Spanish Civil War (1936–9) is well known. Behind the rhetoric of the 'great spiritual crusade', the Spanish Catholic Church seized an opportunity to re-christianise the nation that had been impossible just a few short years before.[11] And with the advent of Franco's new regime,[12] clericalism returned. Franco restored the State's old privileges in religious matters and those of the church in the political arena. The religious beliefs of non-Catholics were still permitted, but restricted to the private sphere.

Franco issued the *Fuero de los Españoles*, the Fundamental Law of the regime, in 1945. In its most important section, Article 6, the profession and practice of the Catholic religion, which was that of the Spanish state, enjoyed official protection. The statement 'Spain is a Catholic nation' received impressive confirmation in August 1953 with the conclusion of the Concordat between the Holy See and Spain. The 38 articles of the Concordat spelled out the obligations of the State to the church and those of the church towards the State. Regarding the former, the Concordat pronounced that the Roman Catholic and Apostolic Faith would continue to be the only religion of Spain, and would enjoy all the rights and prerogatives (education, religious marriage, subsidies and jurisdiction exemptions) in accordance with divine law and canon law. In return, the State gained little from this Concordat, only the right to name the bishops.[13] Consequently, during the first half of the Franco era (1936–58), the Spanish legal system became subject to Catholic doctrine and morals.[14]

In contrast, during the second half of the period (1958–75), the Catholic Church initiated what would become a slow process of disentangling itself

---

[10]   Fernando de Meer, *La cuestión religiosa en las Cortes Constituyentes de la II República* (EUNSA, 1975) 80.

[11]   William J Callahan, 'The evangelization of Franco's New Spain', (1987) 4 *Church History* 491, 496.

[12]   Julián Casanova, *La Iglesia de Franco* (Temas de Hoy, 2001) 215.

[13]   Alberto de la Hera, 'Las relaciones entre la iglesia y el estado en España (1953–1974)', (1977) CCXI *Revista de Estudios Políticos* 5,18.

[14]   The Principles of the National Movement (1958) states '[t]he Spanish nation considers it an honour to faithfully comply with the laws of God according to the doctrines of the Holy Roman Catholic Church, the only true Church, the faith inseparable from our national conscience, which faith inspires our legislation'.

from the State.[15] The Church–State model had quickly exhibited short-comings. The Concordat of 1953 showed its fragility as illegal groups and unions began using Catholic institutions for their own purposes,[16] while the Second Vatican Council produced an intense shock for both the Church and State systems. As a result of the Council's doctrinal pronouncements, Spain had to modify fundamental laws, replacing the existing system based on mere toleration of 'non-Catholics', who were required to prove that they were 'non-Catholics' in order to practice their religion with official recognition of religious freedom to their faith. The enactment of the Religious Freedom Act 1967, granting religious freedom to non-Catholic faiths, ensured this change.[17] Notwithstanding this official recognition of religious freedom, the Catholic character of the State was not undermined.

In 1974 national Catholicism reached its end, as did the political regime that had sponsored it. The momentum for democratisation appeared unstoppable. Paradoxically, when Franco died in November 1975, Spain was both the most confessional European State and the State with the worst relationship with the Holy See.[18] In July 1976, just days before Adolfo Suarez was named President of Spain, the state and the Catholic Church signed an Agreement by which the State waived its privilege to name bishops and the church waived its privilege to legal exemption. This new Agreement contained a preamble that integrated the doctrines of the Second Vatican Council, thereby opening negotiations that concluded with the signature of four specific agreements on 3 January 1979 one week after the Constitution was promulgated.

3. FREEDOM OF RELIGION IN THE CONSTITUTION OF 1978

The Constitution of 1978 goes beyond Catholic confessionalism, and the radical secularism of the Second Republic, by proclaiming that Spain has no official religion and by recognising religious liberty. This Constitution, as a result of a new social and political context characterised by consensus,

---

[15] Eugenia Relaño Pastor, 'Spanish Catholic Church in Franco regime: a marriage of convenience', (2007) 20(2) *International Journal for Theology and History* 275, 283.

[16] Jose Antonio Souto Paz, 'Perspectives on religious freedom in Spain', (2001) *Brigham Young University Law Review* 669, 687.

[17] María Blanco, *La primera ley española de libertad religiosa: génesis de la ley de 1967* (EUNSA, 1999).

[18] Relaño Pastor, 'A marriage of convenience' (note 15 above), 286.

provided a positive framework for the development of religious freedom and Church–State relations in Spain. It included the protection of individual and collective religious freedoms while fostering positive, cooperative relationships between the State and various religious groups. Rather than restricting, preventing or controlling religious groups, as had been done during the Second Republic, the Constitution of 1978 obliges public authorities to cooperate actively with religious entities.

The Constitution protects the exercise of freedom of religion and conscience by every individual and group. Article 16, section 1 guarantees the individual and collective right to 'freedom of ideology, religion and worship', with the manifestation of such freedoms subject to those restrictions necessary to 'maintain public order as protected by law'. Section 2 protects individual freedom of expression by recognising that no one can be forced to declare his or her religious beliefs, while section 3 prohibits the establishment of a state religion and requires the state to 'maintain appropriate cooperation with the Catholic Church and the other [religious] denominations'.[19]

Article 14 states that 'Spaniards are equal before the law and may not in any way be discriminated against on account of birth, race, sex, *religion*, opinion or any other condition or personal or social circumstance' (emphasis added). Additional constitutional provisions directly or indirectly relating to freedom of religion and belief include Article 30 (conscientious objection to military service), Article 27 (right to education and freedom of teaching), Article 20 (freedom of expression) and Article 22 (freedom of association).[20]

The Spanish Constitution establishes a framework for religious pluralism and tolerance, and the fundamental text is based on important principles to be taken into consideration for effective protection of any human rights, particularly religious freedom:

---

[19] Article 16 states:

1. Freedom of ideology, religion and worship of individuals and communities is guaranteed, with no other restriction on their expression than may be necessary to maintain public order as protected by law;
2. No one may be compelled to make statements regarding his or her ideology, religion or beliefs;
3. No religion shall have a state character. The public authorities shall take into account the religious beliefs of Spanish society and shall consequently maintain appropriate cooperation with the Catholic Church and other confessions.

[20] Alberto de la Hera and Rosa María Martínez de Codes (eds), *Spanish Legislation on Religious Affairs* (Ministerio de Justicia, 1998) 25, 39.

1. *Respect and protection of fundamental rights inherent in human dignity* (Article 10.1).[21] This principle implies that any and every individual holds those fundamental rights that are inherent in human dignity. Religious groups, such as churches or religious communities, also hold these rights, insofar as fundamental rights are exercised by persons collectively.
2. *Pluralism* (Article 1.1).[22] In order for citizens to exercise their basic human rights, a government must recognise and ensure the value of pluralism. Because there can be no liberty without freedom of choice, each individual must be able to choose among a variety of options, beliefs, ideas, ideological convictions, perspectives, and philosophical or religious world views.
3. *Participation* (Article 9.2).[23] The constitutional principle of participation in political, economic, cultural and social life includes not just individuals but also religious and philosophical groups taking part in decision-making processes in any issue that may directly affect them.

In addition to these general constitutional principles, four guiding principles are cited in the Spanish Constitution that inspire Church and State relations, the judicial system and actions of the government:[24]

1. The first principle is *religious freedom* (Article 16.1). In governing public authorities, this principle requires that public powers have no authority in religious matters. Religious freedom should not only be

---

[21] Article 10 states:

1. The dignity of the person, the inviolable rights which are inherent, the free development of the personality, the respect for the law and for the rights of others are the foundation of political order and social peace.
2. Provisions relating to the fundamental rights and liberties recognised by the Constitution shall be construed in conformity with the Universal Declaration of Human Rights and international treaties and agreements thereon ratified by Spain.

[22] Article 1.1 states: 'Spain is hereby established as a social and democratic State, subject to the rule of law, which advocates freedom, justice, equality and political pluralism as highest values of its legal system.'

[23] Article 9.2: 'It is the responsibility of the public authorities to promote conditions ensuring that freedom and equality of individuals and of the groups to which they belong are real and effective, to remove the obstacles preventing or hindering their full enjoyment, and to facilitate the participation of all citizens in political, economic, cultural and social life.'

[24] Joaquín Calvo Álvarez, *Los principios constitucionales del Derecho Eclesiástico español en las sentencias del Tribunal Constitucional* (EUNSA, 1999).

recognised and protected, but also promoted according to the axiom 'maximum freedom possible, minimum restriction necessary'.

2. The second principle is *equality with respect to religion/s*. Article 14 recognises equality both 'in the law' (preventing laws from creating unequal or discriminatory situations among citizens) and 'of the law' (legal consequences resulting from laws must be equal). Article 14 prohibits discrimination on ideological or religious grounds. Therefore, differences among legal statutes of several religious communities are legitimate only if they are not the result of discrimination. The equality principle also implies a substantive equality, requiring the state to take action to protect and enforce equality – that is, public powers should intervene to promote the necessary conditions for real and effective equality between individuals and groups, removing any obstacles that prevent or hinder full equality.

3. The third principle is *state neutrality*. Article 16.3 establishes that 'no denomination shall have the character of a state religion'.

4. And lastly, the *principle of cooperation* with religious groups (Article 16.3) is not intended to positively validate religious interests or religion itself. Rather, it exists only as an instrument to ensure that citizens obtain the full enjoyment and exercise of the right to freedom of conscience. State cooperation with churches, which is required by the Constitution, implies that religion is considered a positive reality in Spain as far as it is the result of the exercise of the freedom of religion.

4.   SPANISH STATUTORY TREATMENT OF RELIGION

The constitutional right to religious freedom was developed by a statute, the LOLR, enacted in 1980. The LOLR deals both with the individual aspects of religious freedom, and with the main issues regarding the relationships between the state and religious denominations.[25] Because state relations with the Catholic Church had already been largely defined by agreements negotiated in 1979 shortly after the adoption of the Constitution of 1978, LOLR focused on non-Catholic denominations.

LOLR enumerates the individual and group rights included in the

---

[25] Ley Orgánica 7/1980, de Libertad Religiosa, 5 July 1980. María José Ciaurriz, *La libertad religiosa en el derecho español. La ley Orgánica de Libertad Religiosa* (Tecnos, 1984).

constitutional guarantees of religious freedom. Article 2.1 guarantees individuals the following religious rights:

1. The free exercise of any or no religious belief, the right to change religious beliefs and the right to express religious beliefs openly;
2. Freedom of religious worship, celebration of religious holidays, marriage rites and funeral rites, and religious assistance in schools, the armed forces, prisons, hospitals and welfare institutions;
3. Freedom to instruct or be instructed in religious teachings, the right to choose religious education according to personal convictions and the right to religious information; and
4. Freedom to meet, join and develop religious activities.

With regard to collective rights, churches and religious communities possess the right to establish places of worship, to educate and appoint their religious leaders, to proselytise, and to maintain relations with other religious organisations, whether in Spain or outside.

Spanish legislation lacks a single label for religious groups. Many terms are used in legal texts, for example 'religious association', 'religious denomination', 'religious community', 'church', 'confession' and 'entity'. The most common label is 'religious denomination'.[26] The LOLR does not define what a religious denomination is but it recognises as religious entities those denominations that can prove a specific religious purpose. But what is a religious purpose? Article 3.2 LOLR outlines those activities, purposes and entities that are deemed *not* to be religious, that is those related to psychic or para-psychic phenomena, or those that spread 'humanistic or spiritualist' values. The major issue, therefore, is how state law distinguishes religious values from 'spiritualistic' values: for the former get legal protection under the religious freedom guarantees while the latter do not.

If entities or denominations have religious purposes, the LOLR provides them with the possibility of special protection by granting them legal recognition. In order to receive legal recognition as a religious entity, the law requires that the organisation submit to a process of inscription in the Register of Religious Entities.[27] Once registered, the denomination enjoys autonomy and freedom of internal organisation, is able to create

---

[26] Agustín Motilla, 'Aproximación a la categoría de confesión religiosa en el derecho español', (1988) 4 *Anuario Derecho Eclesiástico del Estado* 107, 119.

[27] Art 5 LOLR.

associations for achieving its ends and gains special protection of its beliefs and rites.[28]

Enactment of the LOLR can be considered a crucial step in the advancement of religious pluralism within Spain, since this was the first time that a broad spectrum of individual and group religious rights (albeit with certain limitations) was officially recognised, with limits prescribed similar to those established by international human rights law.[29] These limitations include 'violation of others' fundamental rights and liberties' (Article 3.1) and 'public health, security and morality as constituent elements of public order' (Article 3.2).

The LOLR was passed in order to develop Article 16 of the Constitution further, and to fulfil the state's duty to cooperate with religious denominations through specific instruments. Article 7 LOLR allows the state to make agreements with minority religions similar to those already entered into with the Catholic Church. These agreements are treated as ordinary positive law emanating from Parliament. In order to enjoy active participation with the State through a formal cooperation agreement, a religious denomination has to be recognised as having well-known roots in Spain. To date, objective criteria for determining this status have not been established.

In 1992 the State signed agreements with the Federation of Evangelical Religious Entities of Spain (FEREDE), the Federation of Israelite Communities of Spain (FCI) and the Islamic Commission of Spain (CIE).[30] The signing of these agreements was a watershed in Spanish history as minority religions, which had been persecuted for centuries, acquired special status under the law.[31]

---

[28]   If a group is not allowed to register as a religious entity, it can obtain legal personality in Spain through registration in the general Registry of Associations. In any event, legal personality, acquired in either of these ways, is not a condition for the exercise of religious freedom in Spain, which is guaranteed by Article 16 of the Constitution 'with no other restriction on their expression than may be necessary to maintain public order as protected by law'.

[29]   Article 18(3) of the International Covenant of Civil and Political Rights 1966 and Article 9(2) of the European Convention of Human Rights 1950.

[30]   Law 26/1992, of November 10, Approving the Agreement of Cooperation Between the State and the Islamic Committee of Spain (BOE 1992, 272); Law 25/1992, of November 10, Approving the Agreement of Cooperation Between the Spanish State and the Federation of Jewish Communities of Spain (BOE 1992, 272) and Law 24/1992, of November 10, Approving the Agreement of Cooperation Between the Spanish State and the Federation of Evangelical Religious Entities of Spain (BOE 1992, 272).

[31]   Motilla, 'Religious pluralism in Spain' (note 5 above), 583. See Ana Fernández-Coronado González, *Estado y confesiones religiosas: un nuevo modelo de relación: (los pactos con las confesiones, leyes 24, 25 y 26 de 1992)* (Civitas, 1995).

5. THE SPANISH MULTI-TIER SYSTEM OF CHURCH–STATE RELATIONS

Legal Status of the Catholic Church

Article 16.3 requires the State to cooperate with the Catholic Church. Such cooperation has a long history, dating back at least to the eighteenth century (Concordats of 1753, 1851 and 1953). Following Spain's transition to democracy, the four agreements signed in 1979 between the Spanish state and the Holy See (collectively comprising a new Concordat) replaced the Concordat of 1953. As a Concordat, the four agreements were incorporated as an international treaty in Spanish law, meant to make the traditional privileges of the Catholic Church compatible with democratic constitutional principles.

The agreements contain certain peculiarities that could be considered as constituting discriminatory legal treatment of religious minorities, as compared to the Catholic Church. The Agreement concerning Legal Affairs recognises, among other things, Sundays and Catholic holidays as state holidays, while it grants civil effect to canonical marriage and ecclesiastical courts' decisions about the nullity of a marriage, as well as the pontifical dissolution of unconsummated marriages. The Agreement concerning Education and Cultural Affairs provides for the teaching of the Catholic religion as a main subject in any school (though students are not required to attend such classes) and it grants civil effect to ecclesiastical academic degrees. And in the Agreement concerning Religious Assistance, the State and the Holy See agreed on permanent Catholic chaplaincies. Finally, in the Agreement concerning Economic Affairs, the Spanish state and Catholic Church designed a three-phase system to help the Church achieve financial self-sufficiency. The current system of state financing of the Catholic Church combines aspects of the general budget and tax assignment systems. Taxpayers have the option to assign a percentage of their income tax to the economic maintenance of the Catholic Church. In addition, the State provides the Church with income tax exemptions, exemption from taxes on goods and properties used for worship and fiscal benefits similar to those afforded to non-profit organisations.[32]

---

[32] Gloria Moran, 'The Spanish system of church and state', [1995] *Brigham Young University Law Review* 535, 543.

Cooperation Agreements with Religious Minorities

According to Article 7.1 LOLR, some religious denominations (that is, those that have been granted 'well-known roots' special status), are able to establish covenants or agreements with the state. To date, Protestants, Mormons, Jehovah's Witnesses, Jews, Muslims and Buddhists enjoy this special status. However, so far, the State has only signed agreements with FEREDE, FCI and the CIE. These three agreements are treated as ordinary positive law emanating from Parliament. The terms of the agreements are very similar and, amongst other things, provide rights that places of worship and burial are inviolable, the Sabbath is a day of rest and may be celebrated on a day other than Sunday if there is agreement between employer and employees, and that all Islamic and Jewish traditional religious festivals may be observed on days other than national Catholic holidays if employer and employees agree. Special accommodation is made for the dietary requirements and fasting times of the Muslim and Jewish communities; religious leaders qualify for legal status within the Social Security Service; members of the armed forces may receive religious assistance, including participation in religious activities, and they may attend places of worship outside armed service facilities in order to fulfil religious duties, when these activities are compatible with the needs of the armed services; Evangelical, Jewish and Muslim education is guaranteed in public schools, and also in private schools so long as it does not contradict the religious ideological framework of the private school; and communities may enjoy other tax exemptions similar to those provided for the Catholic Church.

Minority Religions Lacking Agreement with the State

This category includes those religious denominations recognised as 'religions' by the state and listed as such in the Religious Entities Registry. They may involve all of the rights listed in Articles 2 and 6 of the LOLR, including autonomy and freedom, in establishing organisational rules that may enable them to achieve their purposes as religious entities.

Religious Groups Lacking Legal Status

Groups that have not been officially recognised as religions do not receive specific religious protection. The only legal organisational alternatives are to obtain legal personality through entry in the Registry of Associations (Article 22, Spanish Constitution) or to exercise their constitutional rights of assembly, free speech and freedom of religion.

6. SHORTCOMINGS OF THE INSTITUTIONAL PROTECTION OF RELIGIOUS FREEDOM

To Be Registered as 'a Religion'

One of the main struggles faced by any religious minority within Spain is for recognition of legal status. In order to be entered in the Religious Entities Registry, a religious group must prove that it is a religious organisation, and it must submit religious objectives at the time of listing in the Religious Entities Registry.[33] Until recently the paradigm of what constituted a religion rested on the traditional archetype of the Catholic Church. The General Authority for Religious Affairs (the administrative body in charge of entries in the Registry) required data regarding the number of followers, the period of establishment in Spain and the organisation's purpose.[34] The religious denomination's application was often rejected if it did not meet certain standards, either in terms of the numbers of members, the length of time established in Spain or the legality of the aims of the organisation.

However, in 2001, a very significant Constitutional Court ruling changed this trend.[35] The Court annulled the General Authority for Religious Affairs' denial of inscription for the Church of Unification. This ruling stated that inscription could be denied only when a religious group's activities might endanger individual rights and freedoms.[36] Clearly, the Court found that the right to inscription is part of the constitutional principle of religious freedom, as it facilitated the collective exercise of this right. Accordingly, the Court ruled that denial of inscription would undermine the fundamental right of religious freedom as recognised in the Spanish Constitution.

Recognition as a Religion Having 'Well-known Roots'

The fact that a religion must be recognised as having 'well-known roots' to enjoy active participation within the state creates the first major administrative obstacle. No objective criteria exist for determining whether a denomination has recognised roots in Spain. For example, the General

---

[33] Rosa María Martínez de Codes, 'The contemporary form of registering religious entities in Spain', [1998] *Brigham Young University Law Review* 369, 379.

[34] Agustín Motilla, *El Concepto de Confesión Religiosa en el Derecho Español Práctica Administrativa y Doctrina Jurisprudencial* (Centro de Estudios Políticos y Constitucionales, 1999) 106.

[35] Constitutional Court's decision 46/2001 (15 February 2001).

[36] Ibid, 8.

Authority for Religious Affairs decided that Protestantism, Judaism and Islam were historically rooted in Spain without looking at any data regarding the number of members or houses of worship they possessed in the country. Even today, the State continues to exercise a great deal of discretion in the conferral or denial of such status.[37] The Ministry of Justice's Advisory Commission on Religious Freedom recognised the 'well-known roots' of the Church of Jesus Christ of Latter-Day Saints on 23 April 2003. In spite of a large number of members and after a long time waiting for recognition, the Ministry of Justice granted 'well-known roots' status to Jehovah's Witnesses in 2006.[38] One year later, and more than seven years after its initial application, the Federation of Buddhist Communities also gained 'well-known roots' status.

Protection According to Religious Identity

In 1992, when the State concluded cooperation agreements with the three most important religious minorities in Spain – Protestants, Jews and Muslims – institutional pressure existed to create fewer agreements with broader federations of denominations rather than a larger number of agreements with individual denominations. But the focus on federations has numerous drawbacks.[39] First, an agreement with a federation minimises possibilities for agreements that satisfy the particular interests of individual beliefs. For example, the Evangelical Federation is a highly diverse group that includes Lutherans, Anglicans, Baptists, Methodists, Seventh-Day Adventists and members of the Greek Orthodox Church. Second, the interests of individual denominations within federations

---

[37]   The Advisory Commission on Religious Freedom has outlined the following elements of *notorio arraigo*: sufficient members of the petitioning faith; an adequate legal organisation that links all entities within the faith; a presence in Spain (whether legal or clandestine) for long enough to show that the faith has historical roots; the existence of social, cultural, service and similar activities to a relevant degree; sufficient reach, as determined by the faith's territorial spread, number of places of worship, etc; and finally, institutionalisation of religious ministers. The *notorio arraigo* should be interpreted on a case-by-case basis rather than as a demand that faiths satisfy certain concrete elements. Spain needs an approach that is broad and inclusive. That is, faiths qualify for this classification if they can demonstrate that they have a culture that is shared, permanent and has the possibility of a future. This shared culture should produce evidence – conspicuous evidence – of a geographic, socio-economic and cultural presence.

[38]   Jehovah's Witnesses have more than 100 000 members in Spain and are the second largest Christian denomination in the country.

[39]   Motilla, 'Religious pluralism in Spain' (note 5 above), 584.

are not always united. Indeed, misunderstandings and tensions between denominations develop frequently.[40]

However, the most striking feature of the three agreements is the similarity of their content. Though different religious beliefs face different problems requiring different solutions, the reiterative content of these agreements suggests that the government granted a 'bill of rights' for all religious denominations to adhere to, subverting the inherent nature of bilateral agreements. The texts of the agreements of 1992 contain uniform standards for FEREDE, FCI and the CIE (with religious exceptions on the issues of dietary foods, festivals and holidays, and the safeguarding of artistic heritage provided only for FCI and the CIE).[41]

The Equality Principle

As a multi-tier system of church–state relations is based upon the recognition of diverse legal status – social roots, membership size and tradition within the country – a situation often results in which principles of equality and neutrality can be undermined. As the state only cooperates formally with those religions recognised as having 'well-known roots' in Spanish society, this position ultimately infringes upon both constitutional provisions regarding the duty of public authorities to 'take into account' the religious beliefs of Spanish society and consequently maintain appropriate cooperation (Article 16.3, Spanish Constitution), and the constitutional principle of religious and philosophical groups having the freedom to participate in any issue that may directly affect them (Article 9.2, Spanish Constitution).

The religious minorities that signed the 1992 agreements complain about what they deem to be unjustified and discriminatory legal treatment in comparison with the Catholic Church. The main complaints focus on matters of religious education in public schools, religious assistance in military establishments, hospitals or penitentiaries, and the civil effects of religious marriage and state economic cooperation. While decisions made

---

[40] The Islamic Commission of Spain is made up of two federations of Muslim communities, each having 50 per cent representation. Because the Islamic Commission is the organ that interacts with the State, lack of understanding between the two federations has resulted in significant obstacles to the creation and implementation of their agreements. Iván Jiménez Aybar, *El Islam en España: aspectos institucionales de su estatuto jurídico* (Navarra Gráfica, 2004).

[41] Isidoro Martín Sánchez, 'El modelo actual de relación entre el Estado y el factor religioso en España', (2009) 19 *Revista General de Derecho Canónico y Derecho Eclesiástico del Estado* at http://www.iustel.com.

by the Catholic Church's ecclesiastical jurisdiction on the nullity or dissolution of marriages are given civil effect, the marital decisions of Jewish and Islamic religious courts are not granted any civil effect. And while the four agreements signed with the Catholic Church in 1979 preserved the State's obligation to provide religious instruction in all primary and secondary schools 'under the same conditions as for other basic disciplines',[42] the 1992 agreements only guarantee access to religious instruction for members of the parties where more than ten students have expressed interest in receiving such instruction in public schools.[43]

With regard to religious assistance in public centres such as military establishments, hospitals, penitentiaries, retirement homes or asylums, it is worth noting that, whereas permanent Catholic chaplaincies offering religious assistance are paid for with State funds, under the agreements religious minorities only enjoy a system of 'free access and free exit'. This system consists in allowing a religious minister, rabbi or imam to enter any public centre when their assistance is required, and in authorising individual members of a religious denomination to leave public centres for the purpose of religious worship.

As for economic cooperation between the State and religious denominations, the only beneficiary of direct economic aid from the State is the Catholic Church. Therefore tax assignment remains an exclusive privilege of that church. Minorities with agreements may deduct donations, and receive tax exemptions, only.[44] In 2005 the Foundation of Pluralism and Coexistence was launched to provide public financial support to Protestant, Jewish and Islamic federations. It is a state-backed foundation established with the agreement of the Council of Ministers in October 2004. The Foundation's aim is to 'contribute to the implementation of programmes and projects of a cultural, educational, and social integrational nature'.[45] The Foundation does not finance worship services, but rather

---

[42]   Souto Paz, 'Perspectives on religious freedom in Spain' (note 16 above), 704 and Javier Martínez-Torrón, 'Freedom of religion in the case law of Spanish Constitutional Court' [2001] *Brigham Young University Law Review* 711, 733.

[43]   The 1996 Convention on the Economic System for Evangelical and Muslim teachings states that the educational administration should pay the salary of the religious education teachers chosen by FEDERE and the CIE.

[44]   Article 11 of the Agreements establishes that the strictly religious activities these denominations carry out 'will have the right to the other fiscal benefits that the Spanish State's tax code provides at all times for non-profit entities and, in any case, to those benefits granted to private charitable organisations'. Additionally, those faiths that sign bilateral agreements with the state improve their tax and fiscal situations by becoming non-profit entities.

[45]   Bylaws of the Foundation for Pluralism and Coexistence, Art 7 (2005).

seeks to benefit religious groups in carrying out activities relating to education, cultural development and community service.[46]

However, the absence of equality between the Catholic Church and religious minorities with agreements appears insignificant when compared to the situation faced by religious denominations merely listed in the Religious Entities Registry. The religious denominations registered argue that they do not benefit from the principle of state cooperation at all. And it is true that registration as a religious denomination does not grant any specific guarantees over and above any other association registered under civil law.

Implementation of Minority Agreements

As previously pointed out, the Agreements of 1992 grant similar rights without taking into consideration the specifics of each religion. For those communities subject to the Cooperation Agreements, such rights were supposed to be extended or specified by public authorities. However, implementation of the rights guaranteed in the agreements has been flawed.

For example, two key issues for Islamic communities in Spain are the protection of places of worship and the right to education. Under the Agreement of 1992 between the state and the CIE, mosques and other recognised religious spaces are inviolable and profit from a favourable fiscal arrangement. The only requirements for Islamic communities wishing to open and build *oratorios* (places of worship) are consent from the CIE and a commitment to dedicate the place of worship only to prayer and religious education. Local governments are obligated to provide land for the building of such places of worship, but in practice this law is often ignored by municipalities. The building of places of worship is arguably the most important religious minority demand, and easily the most controversial, as protests by neighbours and resistance from local government fuels social conflict. At least 55 Spanish cities have witnessed conflicts over the construction of houses of worship since 1998, particularly in Catalonia, where many demonstrations against the construction of mosques have occurred.[47]

With regard to Islamic education, the agreement between the state and the CIE guarantees Muslim students the right to Islamic education in both public and private schools in cases where more than ten students

---

[46]   José María Contreras, 'The direct financing of religious minorities in Spain', [2007] *Brigham Young University Law Review* 575, 596.

[47]   Ricard Zapata-Barrero 'Dynamics of diversity in Spain: old questions, new challenges', in S Vertovec and S Wessendorf (eds), *The Multiculturalism Backlash: European Discourses, Policies and Practices* (Routledge, 2009) 208.

require such instruction. Teachers are to be proposed by the CIE and then appointed by education authorities. In practice, many schools do not provide this opportunity and local governments rarely give priority to Islamic education.

In 1996, the State approved a curriculum for compulsory Islamic religious instruction in primary and secondary schools but close to 15 years passed before the curriculum began to be implemented.[48] Though it has now been introduced into primary schools, only 35 teachers have been selected by the CIE and appointed by the state. In the opinion of Muslim communities, the teaching of Islam in public schools is rare.[49] And recent statistics seem to bear this out: in 2007, while 120 000 students applied for classes in Islam, only 12 000 received them.[50] Most Muslim associations attribute the delay in implementation to governmental lack of interest, while the government attributes the delay to disagreements between the two main Muslim federations over the submission of a teacher shortlist.[51]

7. SECULAR VALUES AND MINORITIES

Spain is a secular state, neutral in religious terms, yet not secularist.[52] Whilst public authorities may adopt a neutral stance with regard to religion, keeping themselves independent from ecclesiastical structures, at the same time they recognise religious freedom and provide all appropriate measures to ensure that religious freedom is fully achieved.

According to Spanish constitutional principles on religious freedom, public authorities must ensure that beliefs can be expressed freely and publicly, as part of the core freedom of religion. The only permissible restrictions on the exercise of this right are 'public order' and the 'protection of

---

[48]   María José Ciáurriz and others (eds), *La enseñanza islámica en la Comunidad de Madrid* (Facultad de Derecho Servicio de Publicaciones Universidad Complutense, 2004) 85.

[49]   Iván Jiménez-Aybar, 'Marco jurídico del Islam en España' at http://afri canomadar.org/wp-content/uploads/2009/03/institucion-del-islam-en-espna.pdf.

[50]   2008 Report on International Religious Freedom (Spain) at http://www. state.gov/g/drl/rls/irf/2008/108473.htm.

[51]   Jiménez-Aybar (note 49 above).

[52]   In a secular state, public authorities adopt a neutral stance with regard to religion and they seek to remove all obstacles to promote the necessary conditions so that citizens may exercise their religious freedom fully and freely. It would be hard for a secular state to maintain that the best form of neutrality would be to remove religious convictions from the public sphere. Such an attitude would be typical of a secularist state and not that of a secular state.

the rights and freedom of others'. Any question concerning limitations on religious freedom should take into consideration the principle of pro-portionality – that is, taking account of the circumstances of the specific situation and the principle that minimal restrictions should be imposed on fundamental freedoms.

One area in which the secular nature of the state has been particularly challenged by minorities is that of religious symbols in the public sphere. Several legal conflicts have arisen in recent years, both in the workplace and within educational institutions. The best-known case concerning accom-modation of religious symbols in the workplace was heard by the Superior Court of Justice of Baleares.[53] A driver for the Municipal Company of Public Transportation of Palma de Mallorca wore a *kippa* (Jewish head covering for men) at work. Even though Article 26 of the Worker's Collective Agreement did not allow such attire to be worn, the driver defended his right to wear it. The Court ruled that, although the employer held the right to determine the work uniform of employees, any such deci-sion should respect an employee's fundamental rights. Moreover, it stated that such a case should not be decided on general principles but rather upon a specific and detailed analysis, using the proportionality test. Taking into consideration the specific circumstances, the Court stated that the driver should be allowed to wear the *kippa*.[54]

With regard to religious symbols worn in schools, several cases regard-ing the wearing of headscarves have been resolved while others are still pending in court.[55] Each school has the authority to decide whether or not to allow headscarves to be worn, with some schools banning their students from doing so. When female students have dropped out of school for this reason, the central government or regional authorities have demanded their readmission because the constitutional right to education must prevail over the internal rules of the school.[56] Until now the right to wear a headscarf

---

[53] Sentence of the Superior Court of Justice of Baleares (9 September 2002) AR/2003/3.

[54] However the Sentence of the Superior Court of Justice of Madrid (October 27 1987) took the opposite position about accommodating the religious needs of a Muslim woman who refused to wear a summer uniform consisting of a blue skirt above the knees, blouse and long-sleeved jacket.

[55] In 2010 Najwa Malha, a Spanish female Muslim student, was dismissed from a secondary school in Pozuelo (Madrid) for ignoring the school's rule that forbade the wearing of headscarves. She was transferred to another school where she was permitted to wear the *hijab*. The Education Directorate of the Autonomous Community of Madrid upheld the first school's decision. Currently a judicial appeal against the administrative decision is pending in court.

[56] In 2002, in the city of San Lorenzo de El Escorial, a female student had

has not been an important legal concern in Spain. Both litigation and legislative initiatives on the issue have been minimal. However, due to increased attention by the mass media to the wearing of headscarves, and the banning of headscarves in several municipalities,[57] it is likely that more of such cases will be brought before the courts. The challenge of future cases will be to make the free exercise of religion compatible with protection of the legal elements that make up what is known as 'public order'. Protection of the rights and freedoms of others (one element of the public order protection) is not a sufficient reason to restrict the exercise of religious freedom.

In addition, two further cases illustrate the clash between secular and religious minority values, in the context of parental and group interests in directing a child's upbringing colliding with the general public interest. The first case focuses on religious symbolism inside school classrooms. Most schools do not have religious symbols in classrooms, though some classrooms may have a crucifix on the wall. In 2002, parents of Muslim students in Barcelona requested that school authorities should remove crosses from classrooms. The Secretary of Education of the Catalonian government instead ordered that the students be transferred to a public school at which no religious symbols were displayed in the classrooms. Thus the issue of whether state neutrality requires religious symbols, including the crucifix, to be taken away from classrooms was not addressed.

This question was similarly avoided by the Supreme Court of Madrid in a decision in October 2002.[58] In this case, atheist parents requested that crosses be removed from schools. The Court determined that the Ministry of Education is the public authority responsible for the final decision. More recently, in December 2009, the Superior Court of Castilla y León ruled that in a particular school the crucifix should be removed only from

---

attended no classes at a private school financed by public funds because the director forbade her to wear her Islamic headscarf. The school was reported to the Secretary of Education of the Autonomous Community of Madrid, which ordered that the student be admitted to another school without any condition concerning her headscarf. The first school was permitted to prevent her attending classes if she wore a headscarf, but (since it had no specific rules about students' attire) the second school was compelled to admit her.

[57] In 2010 a few municipalities (most of them in Catalonia) prohibited women from wearing headscarves and the PP (right-wing political party) presented a Draft Bill in the Senate to urge the government to prohibit women from access to public spaces if wearing a *burqa* or *niqab*. The proposition was adopted by 131 votes to 129. However on 20 July 2010 Congress struck down a PP-sponsored Draft Bill banning wearing of the *burqa* in public.

[58] Sentence of the Superior Court of Justice of Madrid (15 October 2002) n 1105/2002.

classrooms from which parents have requested the removal of religious symbols.[59] In such cases, a minority, whether religious or atheist, challenged a religious symbol representing mainstream values. While the cross is a Christian symbol belonging to the Spanish majority's religion, it may also have cultural and historical meaning linked to the identity of the country and, hence, could be accepted as a cultural symbol and not as a religious one.[60]

The second controversial issue in schools arose when protests were lodged by Catholic parents over a public school's decision to make a class entitled 'Education for Citizenship' compulsory for all students.[61] The parents were not opposed to the class in principle, but rather objected to what specifically was being taught in it. For example, besides lessons in democracy and human rights, students were being presented with teachings on moral conduct.[62] Such teaching conflicts with the rights of parents, guaranteed under Spanish law, to oversee the moral education of their children. When the Supreme Court ruled on these cases in 2009, its decision denied the existence of a right to object to the course subject, but left room for possible objections to textbooks or other teaching material not conforming with the state's obligation to ensure a pluralist, objective and neutral education.[63]

Over the years, other issues related to the accommodation of religious minorities have developed. For example, in 1985, a Seventh-Day Adventist Church member was dismissed from her job when she refused to continue working on Saturdays. The Constitutional Court ruled in favour of the employer and reaffirmed the principle that Sundays are the standard day of rest in secular, western society.[64] Today such a conflict could be resolved

---

[59]   Sentence of Superior Court of Castilla y León (14 December 2009) n 3285/2009.

[60]   That is one of the dilemmas addressed by the European Court of Human Rights in *Lautsi v Italy* (App no 30814/06) (ECtHR, 18 March 2011) (GC).

[61]   Dionisio Llamazares, *Educación para la ciudadanía democrática y objeción de conciencia* (Dykinson, 2008).

[62]   Sentences of the Supreme Court (11 February 2009) n 905/08, n 949/08 and n 1013/08.

[63]   The reasoning of the Court is very similar to that in *Folgerø v Norway* (App no 15472/02) (ECtHR, 29 June 2007)(GC) and *Zengin v Turkey* (App no 1448/04) (ECtHR, 9 October 2007) .

[64]   Constitutional Court's decision 19/1985 (13 February 1985). Adoración Castro Jover, 'Libertad religiosa y descanso semanal', (1990) VI *Anuario Derecho Eclesiástico del Estado* 307 and Alex Seglers, 'La "acomodación" de las festividades religiosas y la nueva protección por discriminación indirecta en el orden laboral', (2004) XLIV, n 88 *Ius Canonicum* 649.

differently, utilising Law 62/2003 (on fiscal and administrative measures and social order), which protects citizens from indirect discrimination. If the case of the Seventh-Day Adventist employee described above were to be reviewed now, the employer's refusal to accommodate an employee's religious beliefs might well be considered a violation of religious freedom (so long as the employer had not provided a reasonable justification for his decision).

8.   CONCLUSION

From this fairly brief overview of the shortcomings of the legal framework that exists in Spanish Church–State relations, we may conclude that the system needs fine-tuning. Changes are clearly needed to fulfil the equality principle as prescribed in the Spanish Constitution. By recognising a different legal status for religious denominations according to discretionary criteria (such as the concept of religion, or the meaning of 'well-known roots') many religious communities have been denied the constitutionally mandated state cooperation with religions and, consequently, have been effectively discriminated against.

In April 2009, President Zapatero announced that reform of the Organic Law on Religious Freedom would be sent to Parliament for debate. Since then extensive debate has raged both in academia and the media about which aspects of the law require reform. On one hand, secularist groups are calling for a ban on religious symbols in public spaces, as well as a general prohibition on the wearing of a *burqa* (full body covering for women). On the other hand, religious minorities are demanding that reforms focus on protection for places of worship and burial, as well as enhanced cooperation with autonomous regions and municipalities on religious issues. The debate on religion and secular values in Spain continues.

Ongoing controversies related to the wearing of a headscarf or *burqa*, the building of mosques or the demand for Muslim religious education have uncovered two main streams in Spanish society intent upon curtailing religious freedom and equality in Spain. At one end of the spectrum are the secularists, standing for the removal of any religious values from the public sphere, wilfully ignoring religious dimensions meaningful to some parts of society. At the other end is mainstream Catholicism, relying on its historical and collective legitimacy to protect the status quo of the Spanish Catholic Church.

However, there is a 'third way', one that takes a multi-cultural and multi-religious society as a starting point, and the effective protection of religious freedoms as the goal. In order to align fully with existing constitutional principles on religious freedom, it is anticipated that the new Religious Freedom Law could well take such a 'third way', one sensitive to the public promotion of the greatest level of diversity compatible with harmonious coexistence.

7. The rise and contradictions of Italy as a secular state

Marco Ventura

1. INTRODUCTION

Conflicts in the civil and religious history of Italy have been reflected in the struggle for the definition of the religious and ideological identity of the Italian state. Since unification in 1861, Italy has been formally a Catholic state – but liberalism until 1922 and Fascism from 1922 to 1943 preferred to design secular policies for an increasingly secularised country. In considering such matters this chapter will offer an extremely simplified overview of the evolution of Italy as a secular state after it became a republic in 1946 and adopted a new Constitution in 1948. Two different periods and patterns will be examined: pluralistic secular Italy (between 1948 and 1992) and Christian secular Italy (from 1994 onwards).

The thesis of this chapter is that, over the 150 years since the unification of Italy in 1861, while the country underwent a process of spontaneous social secularisation largely similar to the rest of western Europe,[1] Italians split over how to cope with a society in which the influence of religion was shrinking. Was social secularisation to be resisted and the traditional role of the Catholic Church in Italian society and politics to be preserved? Or was social secularisation to be accepted and even encouraged in view of a more modern, free and developed Italy?

The latter was the response that the leaders of unification gave between 1861 and 1922. This period coincided with what Italians referred to as the

---

[1] See generally Réne Rémond, *Religion and Society in Modern Europe* (Blackwell, 1999). For the history of the concept of secularisation see Hermann Lübbe, *Säkularisierung. Geschichte eines ideenpolitischen Begriffs* (Karl Albert, 1965). As far as theories of secularisation are concerned, this chapter is mainly influenced by Charles Taylor, *The Secular Age* (The Belknap Press, 2007). I discussed my understanding of the interaction between secularisation, law and religion in Europe in Marco Ventura, 'The changing civil religion of secular Europe', (2010) *George Washington International Law Review* 947.

età liberale, the liberal age, when liberalism in the economy and in politics was the dominant ideology. Many of those who endorsed liberalism (that is, liberals for the purpose of this chapter) were Catholics who confronted their church's views for the sake of a modern, developed Italy.[2] Together with Socialists and Republicans, liberals supported the policy of Italy's emancipation from the Catholic Church, and led the struggle for unification against the *Papa Re* (the 'Pope King'), who refused to accept the end of the Pontifical states, opposed the unity of Italy, and urged Catholics to boycott Italian politics. This group also dominated the political scene until of the end of World War I, and contributed to the construction of a liberal secular state, in the sense of a secular state inspired by liberalism. After the rise and fall of Fascism, many Catholics joined the liberal camp to promote the Republican Constitution of 1948, in which the preference for Catholicism was reduced if not cancelled – and the Concordat of 1984, in which Italy and the Holy See agreed that Italy was no longer a Catholic state. This group saluted as a major achievement the decision handed down in 1989 by the Italian Constitutional Court, which recognised *laicità* as a supreme principle of the state,[3] and the Court's successive decisions that defined Italy as a *stato laico*, a secular state in the sense of a pluralistic and neutral state, not indifferent to religion, but respectful of equality and non-discrimination on religious grounds.[4] In this view the recognition of Italy as a *stato laico* was the accomplishment of the struggle for a non-Catholic, pluralistic and religiously neutral state.[5]

In contrast to this approach, conservative Catholics defended the temporal and spiritual mission of the Catholic Church, and opposed the unification of Italy and the introduction of a liberal (that is, liberal-oriented) government. When they realised Italy was here to stay, and the Pontifical states could not be resurrected in their previous shape, the conservatives fought for a strict interpretation of the principle that Italy was a Catholic state, according to the proclamation of the Statuto Albertino, the 1848 Constitution of the Kingdom of Sardinia-Piedmont that had become the

---

[2] See Guido Verucci, *L'Italia Laica Prima e Dopo l'Unità* (Laterza, 1981). The link between Catholic liberalism and the development of *laicità* in Italy is underlined in Luciano Caimi, 'Laicità', in Enrico Berti and Giorgio Campanini (eds), *Dizionario delle Idee Politiche* (AVE, 1993) 420.

[3] C cost 11 April 1989, n 203, in (1990) *Quaderni di Diritto e Politica Ecclesiastica* 1, 193.

[4] Such definition results from the several decisions on *laicità* handed down by the Constitutional Court since 1989. See Giovanni Barberini, *Lezioni di Diritto Ecclesiastico* (Giappichelli, 2001) 285–8.

[5] See Anna Ravà, 'Corte Costituzionale e religione di stato', in *Studi in Onore di Pietro Rescigno* (Giuffrè, 1998).

Constitution of Italy in 1861. After the advent of Fascism in 1922, supporters of Italy as a Catholic state were rewarded by the Lateran Pacts of 1929, that sealed the 'conciliation' between Italy and the Holy See and consecrated the Statuto Albertino's proclamation of Italy as a Catholic state. After World War II, they managed to secure the recognition of the Lateran Pacts in the 1948 Republican Constitution. When the Concordat of 1984 acknowledged the end of Italy as a Catholic state, and when the Constitutional Court in 1989 recognised *laicità* as a supreme principle of the state, the conservatives promoted a pro-Catholic version of *laicità*, based on the argument that Italy as a *stato laico* was still bound by a political and legal preference for the Catholic Church. They argued that this was the obvious implication of the church membership of most Italians, and of the Catholic roots and identity of Italy. This second camp accepted Italy as a *stato laico* but, unlike the first camp, they qualified *laicità* as being 'positive', 'inclusive' or 'sensible', and struggled to understand *laicità* as the new form of the Catholic identity of the Italian state.

Throughout the history of the Italian state and its various legal developments, these two camps and visions have changed in their social, political and ideological natures. Indeed, today, in socially secularised, multi-cultural and multi-religious Italy, the contrast is still obvious between devotees of a pluralistic secular Italy, nostalgic for the liberal, Republican and socialist ideal of separation between the state and the church, and those subscribing to the vision of a Christian secular Italy, nostalgic for Italy as a Catholic state.

2.   PLURALISTIC SECULAR ITALY (1948–92)

After the collapse of Fascism, the civil war between 1943 and 1945, and the liberation in 1945, Italians voted in 1946 to end the monarchy and to become a republic.[6] The first Republican Constitution was voted for in 1947, and enacted in 1948. The next 40 years marked a deep transformation of Italian society and law, under the guidance of the new Constitution. Eventually, in the 1980s a fresh page was turned. In 1984, in a new Concordat between Italy and the Holy See, the state was recognised as no longer being a Catholic state. Five years later, in 1989, for the first time the

---

   [6]   A referendum to choose between monarchy and republicanism was held on 2–3 June 1946. Republicans prevailed by 2 million votes. Church and state dynamics in the referendum have been investigated in Luciano Musselli, 'Il referendum monarchia–repubblica e l'atteggiamento della chiesa', in *Studi in Onore di Lorenzo Spinelli* (vol 3) (Mucchi, 1989).

Constitutional Court defined *laicità* as a supreme Constitutional principle.[7] Contradictions and complexities remained, but undoubtedly Italy was no longer a Catholic state, but rather a secular state in the specific sense of the Italian *stato laico*.

The Republican Constitution – neither Catholic nor Secular

The Constitution of 1948 opened a new era based on democracy, equality and fundamental rights. The Constitution marked a significant change of direction, but could not avoid some contradictions. The state that emerged from the alliance between the left (Socialists and Communists), the Christian Democrats and the *laici* (representatives of those political parties that were neither on the left nor Christian democratic), was not a Catholic one. The proposal to mention the Holy Trinity or to include some other form of invocation of God was rejected. The constituent assembly did not even consider retaining Article 1 of the Statuto Albertino, which had granted Catholicism the status of state religion. Article 3 of the Constitution prescribed equality on the grounds of religion.[8] Article 8 provided that all religious denominations had to be granted the same measure of freedom, opening the way to a number of *intese* (that is, agreements between the state and non-Catholic denominations).[9] Article 19 proclaimed religious freedom in the broadest terms, with *ordre public* not considered as a legitimate reason for imposing restrictions.[10]

However, ultimately the change was not radical. After all, the main issue that remained was how to deal with the Lateran Pacts of 1929 that were still in force after the transition to democracy and Republicanism.[11] The Lateran Pacts comprised a Concordat regulating 'the conditions of

---

[7] See note 3, above.

[8] Art 3, para 1 of the Constitution (cost): 'All citizens have equal social dignity and are equal before the law, without distinction of sex, race, language, religion, political opinion, personal and social conditions.' For all articles of the 1948 Constitution, see the English version established by the Presidency of the Republic of Italy at http://www.quirinale.it.

[9] Art 8, para 1 cost: 'All religious denominations are equally free before the law.'

[10] Art 19 cost: 'Anyone is entitled to freely profess their religious belief in any form, individually or with others, and to promote them and celebrate rites in public or in private, provided they are not offensive to public morality.'

[11] For the proceedings of the debate at the Constituent Assembly on the legal status of the Catholic Church and the Lateran Pacts see Aldo Capitini and Piero Lacaita (eds), *Gli Atti dell'Assemblea Costituente sull'Art 7* (Lacaita, 1959).

religion and the church in Italy',[12] a Treaty settling the *questione romana* (that is, the original conflict between Italy and the Holy See over the unification of Italy) and giving birth to the Vatican City and a financial agreement. As a whole the Pacts were dominated by the pattern of Italy as a Roman Catholic state. Some political forces, in particular liberals and socialists, vocally demanded the removal if not of the Treaty, at least of the Concordat. The Christian Democrats, however, under pressure from the Holy See, found it unacceptable to denounce the Lateran Pacts and were unwilling to reopen the *questione romana*. A solution was found when the party announced that it would support a future reform of the Concordat, leading to the Communists offering their support to this proposal for the sake of 'religious peace' in the country.[13] Article 7 of the Constitution was forged accordingly as an instrument that was meant first to protect both the state and the Catholic Church, as two 'independent and sovereign' entities, and, second, to secure the Lateran Pacts and to pave the way for their reform at a more convenient time.[14]

Whilst the Catholic Church retained its special legal status, reflecting its renewed political prestige and influence – and even though the Constitution recognised the Lateran Pacts in Article 7,[15] thus enabling Catholic conservatives to argue that nothing had changed and that Catholicism was still the state religion of Italy (based on Article 1 of the Lateran Treaty) – this Constitution was not the Constitution of a Catholic state.[16] This could not be the Catholic state of the *ancien regime* tradition, nor of the age of liberalism; nor (of course) could it be a Catholic state in the Fascist sense.

---

[12]   The Lateran Pacts were signed on 11 February 1929 and ratified by the Italian Parliament on 27 May 1929 (l, 27 May 1929, n 810).

[13]   Aldo Moro for the Christian Democrats made this point in his speech of 18 December 1946. See Capitini and Lacaita (note 11 above) 142. The future Prime Minister was speaking not only for his party, but also on behalf of the Catholic Church. Again, Moro stated that the Catholic Church would be open to 'revise some concordatarian norms in order to adjust the Concordat to the new historical circumstances'. Speech of 23 January 1947, in Capitini and Lacaita (ibid) 156 (the translation from Italian is the author's). The Christian Democrat Prime Minister, De Gasperi, made the same point in his speech on 25 March 1947. See Capitini and Lacaita (ibid) 463.

[14]   Art 7, para 1 and 2 cost: '(1) The State and the Catholic Church are independent and sovereign, each within its own sphere. (2) Their relations are regulated by the Lateran Pacts. Amendments to such Pacts which are accepted by both parties shall not require the procedure of Constitutional amendments.'

[15]   Ibid.

[16]   A canon lawyer at the Catholic University of Milan, Orio Giacchi, addressed the issue and used the expression *stato laico* in a book written during the Constitutional debate. See Orio Giacchi, *Lo Stato Laico* (Vita e Pensiero, 1947).

Catholic Italy was still there, socially and politically, and to some extent legally, but Italy was now framed within a Constitution based on pluralism, freedom and equality. Many welcomed the Constitution as the death knell of the Catholic state and, indeed, as the beginning of a true Italian secular state. But it would take a long journey, with slow and sometimes contradictory developments, before Italy would officially be recognised as a *stato laico*.

Legalised Social Secularisation

In the Cold War context, with Italy playing a strategic geopolitical part, the Christian Democrats (the majority party from 1948 to 1994) opposed initiatives to change the Constitution so as to withdraw the privileges of the Catholic Church and afford greater rights for religious minorities. The Holy See also proved resistant to any attempt at reforming the Concordat of 1929.[17] The social and political secularisation of the 1960s and the 1970s, with Italian Catholics more inclined to support liberal reforms after the Second Vatican Council, changed the picture, however. Divorce and abortion were legalised, first by Parliament and then, when Catholic conservatives supported by the Catholic Church asked Italians to strike down the laws in referendums, the changes were approved by Italians themselves.[18] There was now a secular Italy, in politics, in society and increasingly in the law itself. As the country massively embraced consumerism and social liberation, the law changed accordingly, with the legalisation of divorce

---

[17]   As for the definition of Italy as a Catholic or a secular state in the 1950s, in 1954 Arturo Carlo Jemolo observed that neither the expression 'confessional state' (that is, Catholic state) nor the expression *stato laico* are used in the Italian Constitution. Arturo Carlo Jemolo, *Lezioni di Diritto Ecclesiastico* (Giuffrè, 1954) 51. Also see Arnaldo Bertola, 'Appunti sulla nozione giuridica di laicità dello stato', in *Scritti di Sociologia e Politica in Onore di Don Luigi Sturzo* (Zanichelli, 1953).

[18]   Divorce for civil marriages was introduced in 1970. See l, 1 December 1970, n 898. Law 898 of 1970 was applicable to concordat-based marriages as well, that is for those marriages under Catholic canon law that enjoyed civil effect under the Concordat of 1929. The Act was challenged in 1974 through a referendum called by anti-divorce Catholics, but almost 60 per cent turned out, supporting the law of 1970. See Giambattista Sciré, *Il Divorzio in Italia. Partiti, Chiesa, Società Civile dalla Legge al Referendum (1965–1974)* (Bruno Mondadori, 2007). Abortion was legalised in 1978, subject to specific restrictions. See l, 22 May 1978, n 194. A referendum aiming at abrogating the act, thus going back to a full ban on abortion, was defeated in 1981, with 68 per cent of voters supporting the law. The referendum had been promoted by Catholic associations. See Giambattista Sciré, *L'Aborto in Italia. Storia di una Legge* (Bruno Mondadori, 2008).

and abortion, the enactment of new family laws giving better protection to women and the passage of more liberal criminal and labour legislation. 'Bottom-up' social dynamics and 'top-down' legal developments both led to the creation of a more socially and legally secular country.

While norms regulating church and state relations inherited from the Fascist era looked increasingly outdated, the legal doctrine of *laicità* gradually developed. The example of France, which had proclaimed *laïcité* in the Constitution of 1946 and again in that of 1958, was powerful.[19] In a French publication of 1960 Arturo Carlo Jemolo defined *laicità* as the equality of rights for all, regardless of religious affiliation.[20] In 1961 Professor Sergio Lariccia provided a new reading of church and state relationships, in which *laicità* had a prominent place.[21] In 1963 the legal philosopher Nello Morra published an encyclopaedia entry on *laicismo*, which provided some clarification on the different possible uses of the term.[22] In 1967 Professor Giuseppe Caputo published a revolutionary essay on the religious definition of the state, in which he suggested the issue had to be historicised and understood through new concepts.[23] The most common treatises of the time were still reluctant to use the expression *laicità*.[24] However, by the late 1970s, a new generation of judges and legal experts could study church and state law in texts, in which it was suggested that *laicità* was the natural implication of Constitutional principles.[25] For some, the new social

---

[19]   On the circulation of models of the secular state in Mediterranean Europe see Marco Ventura, 'Parcours de la laïcité dans une Méditerranée marginale', in A Dierkens and Jean-Philippe Schreiber (eds), *Laïcité et Sécularisation dans l'Union Européenne* (Editions de l'Université de Bruxelles, 2006). On *laïcité* in France see Francis Messner, Pierre-Henri Prélot and Jean-Marie Woehrling (eds), *Traité de Droit Français des Religions* (Litec – Editions du Juris-Classeur, 2003) 393, and Chapter 8 by Sylvie Bacquet in this volume.

[20]   Arturo Carlo Jemolo, 'Le problème de la laïcité en Italie', in *La Laïcité* (Paris, 1960). On Jemolo's approach to the issue of *laicità* see Arturo Carlo Jemolo, *Coscienza Laica* (Carlo Fantappiè (ed), Morcelliana, 2008).

[21]   Sergio Lariccia, 'Stato e chiesa (rapporti tra)', in *Enciclopedia del Diritto XLIII* (1961).

[22]   Nello Morra, 'Laicismo', in *Novissimo Digesto Italiano* (1963).

[23]   Giuseppe Caputo, *Il Problema della Qualificazione Giuridica dello Stato in Materia Religiosa* (Giuffrè, 1967). In the book the author made no significant use of the term *laicità*.

[24]   See in particular Pietro Antonio D'Avack, *Trattato di Diritto Ecclesiastico Italiano* (Giuffrè, 1943) and following editions.

[25]   See Sergio Lariccia, *Diritti Civili e Fattore Religioso* (il Mulino, 1978). For an authoritative point of view on the state of the art on the same subject amongst political scientists see Valerio Zanone, 'Laicismo', in Norberto Bobbio and Nicola Matteucci (eds), *Dizionario di Politica* (UTET, 1976).

and legal dispensation meant that the time was ripe for getting rid of the Concordat and for the introduction of a true separation.[26] In contrast, others believed that Italy could be considered a *stato laico* without giving up the Concordat; but of course this path would require that the Lateran Concordat be reformed in order to adjust to the spirit of the time and the letter of the Constitution.[27]

The End of Italy as a Catholic State and the Proclamation of *Laicità*

In 1971 the Constitutional Court acknowledged that the 'supreme principles' of the Constitution prevailed over the Concordat, and claimed the power to strike down specific concordatarian norms if deemed unconstitutional.[28] In 1982, for the first time, the Court struck down an article of the Lateran Concordat, providing for automatic civil recognition of ecclesiastical rulings on marriage nullity.[29] The way was open for a modification of the Concordat, without the agreement of the Holy See, by way of the Constitutional Court's decisions.[30] An increasingly secular public, a more liberal Christian Democratic party, and the governments led by Giovanni Spadolini (1981–2) and Bettino Craxi (1983–7), the first non-Catholic Prime Ministers in the Republic's history, pushed the Italian bishops and the Holy See to accept that a change was inevitable. Prominent Catholics had prepared the field by studying how *laicità* could be reconciled with Catholic teachings.[31] Before the Constitutional Court could destroy the

---

[26]   See Marco Ventura, 'Diritto e religione come questione di coerenza', in Gianni Long (ed), *Libertà Religiosa e Minoranze* (Claudiana, 2007).

[27]   For an overview of the debate between separation and reform of the Concordat see Anna Ravà (ed), *Individuo, Gruppi, Confessioni Religiose nello Stato Democratico* (Giuffrè, 1973). Also see Carlo Cardia, *La Riforma del Concordato. Dal Confessionismo alla Laicità dello Stato* (Einaudi, 1980).

[28]   C cost 24 February 1971, 30 (1971) *Giurisprudenza Costituzionale* 150, 153 [3].

[29]   C cost 22 January 1982, 18 (1982) *Giurisprudenza Costituzionale* 138.

[30]   For the key role of the Constitutional Court in church and state developments see Sara Domianello, *Giurisprudenza Costituzionale e Fattore Religioso. Le Pronunzie della Corte Costituzionale in Materia Ecclesiastica (1957–1986)* (Giuffrè, 1987) and *Giurisprudenza Costituzionale e Fattore Religioso: le Pronunzie della Corte Costituzionale in Materia Ecclesiastica (1987–1998)* (Giuffrè, 1999).

[31]   Giuseppe Lazzati, rector of the Università Cattolica del Sacro Cuore from 1968 to 1983, represented an example of those Italian lay Catholics who believed that, while Catholic lay people were asked to play a prominent role in Italian politics, the Catholic Church had nothing to lose by accepting Italy as a secular state. Thus *laicità* was praised both within the church (by way of praising the role of the lay faithful) and in the public sphere (by way of praising the secular

Concordat, a new one was signed in 1984 by the Vatican Secretary of State Agostino Casaroli and the then Socialist Prime Minister Bettino Craxi.[32] At point 1 of the additional protocol, the parties agreed that 'the principle of the Catholic religion as the sole religion of the Italian State, originally referred to by the Lateran Pacts, shall be considered to be no longer in force'.[33]

The term *laicità* was not mentioned in the new Concordat of 1984. But in his speech to the Senate of 3 August 1984, asking for ratification of the Concordat, Bettino Craxi stated that reform stemmed from the option for a 'full' '*laicità dello stato*'.[34] The task of defining *laicità* further rested on experts and, possibly, on judges or on future parliaments.

The formal and bilateral recognition that Italy was no longer a Catholic state was applied in legislation as well as in the courts. All remnants of the former Catholic state were progressively dismantled, with examples being the abolition of both the requirement to swear an oath before giving evidence in court, and the law of blasphemy. In both cases the Constitutional Court declared unconstitutional the relevant provisions inspired by state Catholicism.[35] The status of non-Catholic denominations was also improved, with *intese* signed between the government and Protestant and Jewish denominations between 1984 and 1993.[36]

---

state). See Giuseppe Lazzati, *Laicità e Impegno Cristiano nelle Realtà Temporali* (AVE, 1985).

[32] The new Concordat, formally an agreement modifying the 1929 Lateran Concordat, was signed on 18 February 1984 and ratified by the Italian Parliament on 25 March 1985 (l, 25 March 1985, n 121). English version at http://www. religlaw.org/document.php?DocumentID=578.

[33] Ibid.

[34] Bettino Craxi, 'Discorso a conclusione del dibattito per la ratifica degli Accordi di Villa Madama', Senate, 3 August 1984, in Gennaro Acquaviva (ed), *La Grande Riforma del Concordato* (Marsilio, 2006) 166.

[35] As for blasphemy the Constitutional Court ruled unconstitutional several norms of the criminal code of 1930 based on the preference for Catholicism as the state's religion. See C cost 18 October 1995, 440, in (1995) *Quaderni di Diritto e Politica Ecclesiastica* 1047; C cost 10 November 1997, 329, in (1997) *Quaderni di Diritto e Politica Ecclesiastica* 981; C cost 13 November 2000, 508, in (2000) *Quaderni di Diritto e Politica Ecclesiastica* 1041; C cost 9 July 2002, 327, in (2002) *Quaderni di Diritto e Politica Ecclesiastica* 1051; and C cost 18 April 2005, 168, in (2005) *Quaderni di Diritto e Politica Ecclesiastica* 1065. As for the oath in the civil procedure, see C cost 30 September 1996, 334, in (1996) *Quaderni di Diritto e Politica Ecclesiastica* 870.

[36] The following *intese*, or agreements, were signed by the Italian government and the representatives of particular denominations, and then approved by Parliament: with the Waldensian Church (21 February 1984), the Union of Italian Seventh-Day Adventist Churches (29 December 1986), the Assemblies of God

Based on the Second Vatican Council's reference to 'sounder coop-eration' between the Catholic Church and the 'political community',[37] 'mutual collaboration' between the state and the Catholic Church was established as a key principle at Article 1 of the Concordat of 1984.[38] The principle was extended to all denominations: cooperation between the state and faith communities, together with the Constitutional preference for bilateral relationships between the state and religious denominations (through the Concordat for the Catholic Church and the *intese* with the other denominations), became a central aspect of *laicità* and religious freedom in Italy.

In 1988 the Constitutional Court recognised that even though the majority of Italians were Catholics, this would have no legal consequences. According to the Court, 'any discrimination based on the fact that a major-ity or minority of people belong to a given denomination is unacceptable'.[39]

A year later, in 1989, for the first time Italy was formally acknowledged by the Constitutional Court as a secular state. In a seminal decision, Italian *laicità* was construed by the Court as a supreme principle deduced from the Constitution, in particular from the principles of equality, non-discrimination on grounds of religion and independence of the state from the Catholic Church. According to the Court, the 'supreme principle' of *laicità* had to be considered as 'one of the aspects of the form of State outlined by the Constitution'.[40] Such a principle was 'not synonymous with indifference towards the experience of religion',[41] but represented 'the

---

in Italy (29 December 1986), the Union of the Jewish Communities in Italy (27 February 1987), the Union of Evangelical Christian and Baptist Churches in Italy (29 March 1993) and the Evangelical Lutheran Church in Italy (20 April 1993). Texts published in Giovanni Barberini (ed), *Raccolta di Fonti Normative di Diritto Ecclesiastico* (8th edn) (Giappichelli, 2007) 70.

[37]   Second Vatican Council, *Constitution Gaudium et spes*, n 76.

[38]   See Act 121 of 1985 (note 32 above).

[39]   C cost 8 July 1988, 925, in (1989) 1 *Quaderni di Diritto e Politica Ecclesiastica* 637, 640 [10]. (The translation from Italian is the author's). Two months earlier, the supreme administrative court, the Consiglio di Stato, had dismissed for the first time a claim that to display a crucifix in state schools' classrooms was incompat-ible with a state that was no longer a Catholic state. In its ruling, the Consiglio di Stato stated that the crucifix belonged to the Italian historical heritage (*patrimonio storico*). See Cons St 27 April 1988, 63 (1989) 1 *Quaderni di diritto e politica eccle-siastica* 197, 198.

[40]   C cost 11 April 1989 (note 3 above), 200, 4. Translation from Italian by Carlo Panara, 'In the Name of God: state and religion in contemporary Italy', (2011) 6 *Religion and Human Rights* 75, 80.

[41]   C cost 11 April 1989 (note 3 above). (The translation is the author's.)

state's guarantee that religious freedom will be safeguarded, in a framework of denominational and cultural pluralism'.[42]

If the Constitution of 1948 moved cautiously towards the definition of Italy as a *stato laico*, the Concordat of 1984 made a fundamental contribution, by declaring that Italy was no longer a Catholic state. Against this background, in 1989 the Constitutional Court made explicit that the Constitution had shaped Italy as a *stato laico* (in this specific sense of a secular state), devoted to a positive understanding of religion conducive to religious freedom, as well as denominational and cultural pluralism. Forty years of Republican and Constitutional experience had thus led to a pluralistic secular Italy.

3. CHRISTIAN SECULAR ITALY (1994–)

The crumbling of the Berlin Wall impacted heavily on Italy. At the beginning of the 1980s Italian judges had tried unsuccessfully to investigate the collusion of the Istituto per le opere di religione, the Vatican bank, with the network of criminals and prominent Italian personalities in politics, finance, media and the army who planned a soft, anti-democratic revolution under cover of a Masonic lodge: the Holy See used the Lateran Treaty and the sovereignty of Vatican City to shut the door on the investigation.[43] Ten years later the judiciary again featured as the main actor in the pursuit of corrupt politicians, including Christian Democrats. Tension was high at the crossroads of politics, justice and the church. The social atmosphere had changed. Faced with the scandal of widespread political corruption, public opinion largely supported the *mani pulite* ('clean hands') judicial investigation and the ensuing trials leading to the collapse of the Christian Democratic and Socialist parties, with Bettino Craxi, the former Socialist Prime Minister who had signed the Concordat of 1984, fleeing to Tunisia in 1994 to avoid prison.[44] The ruling political class of the past decades was swept away.

---

[42]   Ibid. (The translation is the author's.) A different translation is provided in Panara (note 40 above): *laicità* (which Panara translates as 'secularism') 'does not imply indifference to religions by the State[. O]n the contrary it is a guarantee of protection of religious freedom in a system based on confessional and cultural pluralism.'

[43]   See Anna Ravà, 'La Banca Vaticana nell'Europa delle banche', in Franco Belli and Vittorio Santoro (eds), *La Banca Centrale Europea* (Giuffrè, 2003).

[44]   Bettino Craxi never returned to Italy and died in exile, in Tunisia, on 19 January 2000.

Paradoxically, in the post-1989 era, the Catholic Church was confronted again with the Communist threat. As a matter of fact, Communists were at the same time both losers and winners. They were expected to win the elections of 1994, but they also needed to change if they wanted to overcome the global collapse of Communism. Accordingly, the Italian Communist Party was transformed in 1991 into the Democratic Party of the Left. Electoral reforms and the new political landscape, featuring the secessionist Lega Nord and Forza Italia, the new party founded by media tycoon Silvio Berlusconi, reshaped Parliament following a bipolar scheme. With Christian Democrats and Socialists disbanded, in 1994 Berlusconi's Forza Italia prevailed over the Democratic Party of the Left by 0.7 per cent of votes. Italy was entering a phase in which the political landscape would be sharply divided between the two rival poles of the centre-right (dominated by the charismatic Berlusconi), and the centre-left. The social and political divide of this bipolar era influenced Italy's approach to the global economic crisis and in geopolitical matters – while accompanying the Italian transition to a multi-cultural and multi-religious society. Ultimately, the relationship between religion, politics and the law was reshaped. On one hand, the pluralistic secular Italy consecrated between 1984 and 1989 was strengthened, mainly in case law and jurisprudence.[45] On the other hand, the centre-right governments and the Catholic bishops backed by the Holy See emphasised that the identity of Italy was Christian (that is, Catholic), and that Italian *laicità* had to be interpreted in the sense of giving Catholicism a special place in law, as well as in the country. While social secularisation deepened, Italy found itself divided between the two models/narratives of pluralistic secular Italy, and Christian (that is, Catholic) secular Italy.

Unfolding *'Laicità'*

Under the lead of Cardinal Ruini, President of the Italian Catholic bishops since 1991, a new doctrine was established affecting how the Catholic Church would interact with Italy now that the Christian Democrats were no longer present to mediate between the Bishops, society and the world of politics. The bishops would play a much more active and direct role in Italian public life. They would fight *laicismo*, the alleged political project aimed at marginalising the Catholic Church and bringing Italy into line with the

---

[45] See Francesco Rimoli, 'Laicità (dir cost)', in *Enciclopedia Giuridica Treccani* (1995). Mario Tedeschi (ed), *Il Principio di Laicità nello Stato Democratico* (Rubbettino, 1996).

rest of secularised Europe.[46] With non-Italian Popes now interacting with domestic Italian politics, the international role of Italy was emphasised as the champion of Christianity and bulwark against the spreading in Europe of social secularisation and political and legal secularism.[47]

A strategy was outlined by which the bishops would try to influence both sides of the new bipolar political spectrum in order to gain the best possible advantages for the Catholic Church in terms of legislative measures inspired by the Church's views, but also in terms of the funding of Catholic activities. The Bishops' Conference would claim a prominent position for the church in the name of the Christian identity and roots of Italy. Italian Catholic politicians would be required to stand for 'non-negotiable values', namely the defence of the embryo, of marriage, of the traditional family and of Catholic schools. The Holy See deemed that compromises in these areas, which had been accepted by Catholic bishops in other western countries, were impossible for Italy.[48]

The new strategy of the Catholic episcopate was partially countered by the centre-left coalition in power from 1996 to 2001 under the lead of Romano Prodi, a self-proclaimed 'adult Catholic', and a strong believer in a Catholic laity capable of standing against the political tactics of the ecclesiastical hierarchy. During this period, in 1997, the Constitutional Court handed down another key decision, pushing the principle of *laicità* further in the direction of a pluralistic secular Italy. The Court established that '*laicità* or non-confessionality' meant more than that religious freedom had to be protected by a state that could not be indifferent towards religion; it also proclaimed that *laicità* implied 'the equidistance from and the impartiality of the law towards all religious denominations'.[49] Consequently, according to the Court, no positive or negative bias towards any faith or denomination could be consistent with the Constitution.

In 2000 the Constitutional Court summarised its case law on *laicità* and gave the following encompassing definition:

---

[46] On the use of the term *laicismo* in the 1990s see Edoardo Tortarolo, *Il Laicismo* (Laterza, 1998).

[47] In his speech to the General Assembly of the Italian Catholic Church on 19 October 2006, Benedict XVI called upon the Italian church to transform Italy into the example in Europe of the resistance against de-Christianisation and 'insidious secularism'. See Benedetto XVI, 'L'Italia: bisognosa e favorevole', (2006) *Il Regno Documenti* 671, 673 (the translation is the author's).

[48] See Marco Ventura, 'Le transizioni del Cattolicesimo Italiano', (2006) 6 *il Mulino* 1066.

[49] C cost 10 November 1997 329, in (1997) *Quaderni di Diritto e Politica Ecclesiastica* 981, 983 [2] (the translation is the author's).

Under the fundamental principles of equality of all citizens before the law regardless of their religion (Art 3 cost) and equal freedom of all religious denominations before the law (Art 8 cost), the state's approach to different religious denominations must be equidistant and impartial, with no regard for the quantitative more or less widespread membership of this or that religious denomination (Constitutional Court decisions 925 of 1988, 440 of 1995 and 329 of 1997) nor for the bigger or smaller social reaction to the violation of the rights of one denomination or the other (again Constitutional Court decision 329 of 1997) . . . Such a position of equidistance and impartiality reflects the principle of *laicità* that the Constitutional Court has deduced from the system of the Constitutional norms, a principle which enjoys the status of 'supreme principle' (Constitutional Court decisions 203 of 1989, 259 of 1990, 195 of 1993 and 329 of 1997) and which characterises as pluralist the form of our State within which different faiths, cultures and traditions have to coexist in equality of freedom.[50]

In 2000 the Cassation Court applied the principle of *laicità* to the controversial display of the crucifix in polling stations. A polling staff member had claimed that the presence of the crucifix in the polling station violated his freedom of conscience and refused to perform his duties. He was convicted for refusing to perform his duties as a public officer and then acquitted by the Appeal Court of Turin. Asked to rule on the appeal against the acquittal, the Cassation Court confirmed the acquittal on the grounds that the crucifix was the symbol of the Italian Catholic state, and therefore its compulsory display was inconsistent with *laicità*, the secular character of the Italian state.[51]

In the same year (2000) the centre-left government, led by former Communist Massimo D'Alema, further applied *laicità*, when on 20 March it signed *intese* with Buddhists and Jehovah's Witnesses,[52] after the Council

---

[50]   C cost 20 November 2000 508, in (2000) *Quaderni di Diritto e Politica Ecclesiastica* 1041, 1041–2 [3] (the translation is the author's). For a less literal and more fluid translation see Panara (note 40 above) 80. Panara translates *laicità* as 'secularism'.

[51]   Cass 1 March 2000, n 439, in (2000) *Quaderni di Diritto e Politica Ecclesiastica* 846. For a study of the case see Antonello De Oto, 'Presenza del crocefisso o di altre immagini religiose nei seggi elettorali : la difficile affermazione di una laicità effettiva', (2000) *Quaderni di diritto e politica ecclesiastica* 837. For an account of the personal struggle of the protagonist of the case (Marcello Montagnana) against state's Catholicism as embodied in the display of the crucifix, see Sergio Luzzatto, *Il Crocifisso di Stato* (Einaudi, 2011) 10.

[52]   For a preliminary version of the agreement with the Jehovah's Witnesses see (1999) *Quaderni di Diritto e Politica Ecclesiastica* 459. For amendments to the final version see (2000) *Quaderni di Diritto e Politica Ecclesiastica* 492. For the final version of the agreement with the Union of Italian Buddhists see (2000) *Quaderni di Diritto e Politica Ecclesiastica* 606.

of State had dismissed the claim that Buddhism could not be considered a true religion.[53] The march of pluralist secular Italy towards a fully inclusive treatment of non-Christian faiths seemed unstoppable.

Christian Secular Italy is Shaped

Since the 1990s, Italy, historically a country of net emigration, has experienced rapid and massive immigration. This has resulted in a major reshaping of the religious landscape with, in particular, a growing Muslim multi-national community. The centre-left, and the many Catholics supportive of a pluralistic secular Italy, believed that *laicità* was the best principle to guide a sensible policy in the light of such new religious and social issues. The same group argued that new *intese* were needed, and that a new general Act on religious freedom, replacing the old Act of 1929, was necessary. Most centre-left voters, including many Catholics, believed that the Catholic Church should contribute socially, but should avoid 'playing politics' in order to preserve or increase the advantages still granted by the law. At the same time the centre-left put forward new liberal policies in ethically sensitive areas, such as those relating to the family, education, health care and life sciences, in promoting the rights of the disadvantaged, including minorities, women and homosexuals.

However, the events of 9/11 and the second electoral victory of Prime Minister Berlusconi in 2001 changed the picture. The official doctrine of church and state professed by experts remained apparently the same. Courts dealt with religious issues according to the established pattern of religious freedom.[54] The Constitutional Court and the Cassation Court did not change their understanding of Italian *laicità*. But the centre-right government and the administrative organs applied the law according to the former status of Italy as a religiously non-neutral state. Of course, it was impossible to regress to the Fascist discourse of Italy as a Catholic state. Rather, the 1950s argument – that most Italians were Catholics – was used. And soon, coinciding with the European discussion on whether the

---

[53]   Cons St 29 November 1989, n 2158, in (1991–2) 1 *Quaderni di diritto e politica ecclesiastica* 531.

[54]   See Marco Ventura, 'The permissible scope of legal limitations on the freedom of religion or belief in Italy', (2005) 19(2) *Emory International Law Review* 913. In particular on the issue of new religious movements, see Marco Ventura, 'Les nouveaux mouvements religieux: une catégorie invisible dans la soi-disant Italie chrétienne', in Nathalie Luca (ed), *Quelles Régulations pour les Nouveaux Mouvements Religieux et les Dérives Sectaires dans l'Union Européenne?* (Presses Universitaires Aix Marseille, 2011).

European Constitution should refer to the continent's 'Christian roots', centre-right politicians and Catholic bishops claimed that Italy should be mindful of its Christian heritage and identity. In the monopolistic Catholic history of the country, the terms Christian and Catholic bore the same meaning for most Italians. Thus, claiming that Italy had to be faithful to its Christian legacy and identity was tantamount to an invocation of the state's support for the Catholic Church.

Equality between the Catholic Church and other denominations, especially Islam, was actively opposed, with the new Parliament refusing to enact (earlier discussed) agreements in 2000 with Buddhists and the Jehovah's Witnesses. Racism and xenophobia were on the increase, and the Lega Nord, a crucial ally of Berlusconi, actively campaigned against Muslims, citing worrying examples from 'multiculturalist' European countries, or from France with its system of *laïcité*.[55] With the links within the European Union growing closer, the legal impact of the Union on Italian church and state relations was also perceived as threatening. For example, in the *Pellegrini* case in 2001, the European Court of Human Rights condemned Italy for violation of defence rights in a procedure under the Concordat for civil recognition of the ruling of an ecclesiastical court.[56] 'The Italian courts', the European Court ruled, 'breached their duty of satisfying themselves, before authorising enforcement of the Roman Rota's judgment, that the applicant had had a fair trial in the ecclesiastical proceedings.'[57] Further condemnation in Strasbourg of the Italian Concordat system came in 2009 in the *Lombardi Vallauri* case. The Court examined the dismissal by the Law Faculty Council of the Catholic University of Milan of an application for a teaching job by legal philosopher Luigi Lombardi Vallauri, an invited professor at the Faculty since 1976. The dismissal was based on negative advice from the Vatican Congregation for Catholic Education. Under the terms of the Italian Concordat, the applicant had no right of access to the motivation of the Vatican advice, and no right to appeal. The Court found that the Faculty's

---

[55] The Catholic sociologist Luca Diotallevi suggested that because of its close connection with French *laïcité*, *laicità* was inappropriate for Italy and ought to be dropped in favour of the American model of religious freedom. See Luca Diotallevi, *Un'Alternativa alla Laicità* (Rubbettino, 2010).

[56] *Pellegrini v Italy* (2002) 35 EHRR 2. See Marco Ventura, 'The application of the freedom of religion principles of the European Convention on Human Rights in Italy', in Norman Doe and Russell Sandberg (eds), *Religious Freedom in the European Union* (Peeters, 2011) 223–30.

[57] *Pellegrini* (ibid) [47].

deliberation had breached the right of the applicant to a fair trial as well as his freedom of expression.[58]

Eager to please the Catholic Church, Prime Minister Berlusconi championed the traditional values of the Italian family. In 2004, under his majority, the Italian Parliament passed an Act banning assisted donor reproduction for couples not civilly or canonically married.[59] The law was challenged in a referendum, which failed to achieve a quorum, following a campaign by Italian bishops pressuring voters to abstain. With more than 70 per cent of Italians avoiding the poll, this was a major victory for Cardinal Ruini's strategy,[60] which was duplicated two years later, when the Bill that had been intended to legalise civil heterosexual partnerships (introduced by the centre-left second Prodi government) was actively opposed by the Catholic bishops and eventually dropped.[61]

Statutes and case law avoided any formal reference to the 'Christian' character of the state. But in the political discourse of the centre-right coalition and of the Catholic bishops there was a heavy resort to the rhetoric of Christian (that is, Catholic) Italy. Also, the centre-right allied with the Catholic Church in order to avoid more equality legislation on religious minorities, to prevent the church from losing legislative advantages (for example in the public funding of Catholic schools), and to keep Italian legislation far from the standard of the rest of western Europe, in particular on reproductive rights, family law and end of life care.

Christian Secular Italy Legalised

From 2001 to 2006, and even more after the fresh electoral victory of Prime Minister Berlusconi in 2008, the pattern of Christian (that is, Catholic) Italy has become the dominant discourse and a label that coincides with a dramatic lack of vision and policy for the new multi-cultural and multi-religious Italy. The Berlusconi government and the Catholic bishops stigmatised multi-culturalism, but could not offer non-Catholic Italians any alterna-

---

[58] Italy was condemned for violation of the defence rights of a legal philosopher teaching at the Catholic University of Milan whose contract had not been renewed on the grounds of his departure from Catholic teaching: *Lombardi Vallauri v Italy*, App no 39128/05 (ECtHR, 20 October 2009).

[59] L 19 February 2004, n 40.

[60] The referendum took place on 12–13 June 2005. Cardinal Ruini's call for abstention was issued in March 2005. See Luigi Accattoli, 'Ruini: referendum, non si deve votare', *Corriere della Sera* (Milan, 8 March 2005) 15. See generally Panara (note 40 above) 87–91. Another example was the debate on euthanasia and advance health care directives; see Panara (ibid) 81–7.

[61] See Panara (note 40 above) 93–4.

tive other than to be assimilated in an all-Christian (that is, all-Catholic) Italy. New agreements were signed by the centre-left Prodi government on 4 April 2007 with Buddhists, Jehovah's Witnesses, Mormons, Hindus, the Ecumenical Patriarchate of Constantinople and the Apostolic Church.[62] As happened with the agreements signed in 2000, the centre-right victory in the 2008 elections instituted a government (with a parliamentary majority) hostile to the agreements. Only in August 2012, after the fall of Berlusconi in 2011 and the establishment of the Monti government, did Parliament enact the agreements with Mormons, the Ecumenical Patriarchate of Constantinople and the Apostolic Church. Still the most sensitive agreements, those with Buddhists, the Jehovah's Witnesses and Hindus have not been approved. Once again, important religious communities have been excluded from symbolic recognition and benefits that had been enacted by Parliament, such as state funding through the *otto per mille* – a proportion of income tax that taxpayers are free to assign to a denomination of their choice amongst those that have signed an agreement with the government.

By the same token, after discussion in Parliament in 2007 a religious freedom bill replacing the outdated Act of 1929 on 'admitted cults' was not carried.[63] The centre-right was afraid of promoting alien religious groups, and of recognising Muslim communities. When debated in Parliament, Catholic bishops stated that they accepted the law, but disapproved of the reference to *laicità* in the bill, and urged Parliament not to alter the imbalance between the privileged Catholic Church and other denominations.[64]

In 2007, the Ministry of the Interior issued a 'Charter of values of citizenship and integration', aimed at introducing immigrants to Italian constitutional principles. The Charter declared that Italy was a secular state, based on the 'Jewish-Christian tradition' of Italy. Once again, Christian secular Italy was the dominant narrative and theory.[65]

---

[62] Texts of the *intese* in (2007) *Quaderni di Diritto e Politica Ecclesiastica* 539.

[63] See Marco Ventura, hearing before the House of Deputies, 11 January 2007, in *Resoconto stenografico Indagine conoscitiva* 5, Seduta di giovedì 11 gennaio 2007, 8–11, 65. See generally Valerio Tozzi and others (eds), *Proposta di Riflessione per l'Emanazione di una Legge Generale sulle Libertà Religiose* (Giappichelli, 2010).

[64] See the hearing before the House of Deputies of Mons Giuseppe Betori, Secretary-General to the Catholic Bishop's Conference, 16 July 2007, in *Resoconto stenografico Indagine conoscitiva* 7, Seduta di lunedì 16 luglio 2007, 4–5.

[65] See the Ministry of Interior, 'Charter of Values of Citizenship and Integration', 23 April 2007 available at http://www.interno.it/mininterno/site/it/sezioni/sala_stampa/speciali/carta_dei_valori/index.html. Italy is defined as 'a secular country based on complete religious freedom, both individual and collective'. The Charter also states that 'the Italian secular State recognises the positive contribution of the different religions to the collectivity and has the intention to

The strategy and discourse aimed at qualifying the principle of *laicità* through reference to Christian Italy proved particularly intense with regard to Islam. Life was generally made hard for Muslim communities, whose right to a decent place of worship was constantly denied in practice, thanks to a lack of clear procedures and a hostile bureaucracy.[66] Since 2005, the Italian Ministry of the Interior, both under the centre-left and the centre-right governments, has promoted talks with Muslim representatives within the 'Consulta per l'Islam italiano' (formally a committee of experts).[67] Talks between Italian officials, experts and Muslim representatives on the main issues at stake (for example the status of imams, the dignity of Muslim women, the operation of mosques, anti-Semitism and the wearing of headscarves) did not produce any substantial agreement and were halted in 2009. However in 2010 a new body, the 'Comitato per l'Islam italiano', was created and began providing the Ministry of Interior with policy papers on the status of imams, and the application of Muslim family law in Italy. The Monti cabinet, established in November 2011, has tacitly terminated the Comitato.

Since the Cassation Court's 2000 decision banning display of the crucifix in polling stations, and the decisions by the administrative courts against Soile Lautsi's claim that the same principle had to apply to the display of the crucifix in state classrooms (see below), the crucifix has come to symbolise the clash between the defenders of pluralistic secular Italy and the proponents of Christian secular Italy.[68]

The issue of the crucifix represented the best opportunity for the Holy See and the Italian Bishops' Conference to test the alliance with the centre-right coalition, to strengthen the new discourse on Christian Italy and to achieve some formal recognition of this new principle. After the 2009 decision of the European Court of Human Rights in *Lautsi*,[69] in which

---

enhance the moral and spiritual legacy of each one of them'. At the same, the 'Jewish-Christian tradition' of Italy is acknowledged, and it is stated that 'Italy has developed in the perspective of Christianity that has permeated its history and, together with Judaism, has paved the way to modernity and to the acquiring of the principles of freedom and justice'.

[66] See Stefano Allievi, *La guerra delle moschee. L'Europa e la sfida del pluralismo religioso* (Marsilio, 2010).

[67] The Consulta was instituted on 10 September 2005. See decreto del Ministero dell'Interno at http://www1.interno.gov.it/mininterno/ site/sezioni/ servizi/legislazione/religioni/legislazione_691.html.

[68] For the debate on the crucifix between 2000 and 2004 amongst legal experts see Roberto Bin and others (eds), *La laicità crocifissa?* (Giappichelli, 2004).

[69] *Lautsi v Italy* (App no 30814/06) (ECtHR 3 November 2009); (2010) 50 EHRR 42. There was found to have been a breach of Art 2 of Protocol 1 (the

Italy was found to have violated the rights of parents and pupils by the compulsory display of the crucifix in state classrooms, the Italian government appealed against the decision to the Grand Chamber of the Court and joined the administrative courts in the interpretation of *laicità* as a principle belonging to the Christian roots and identity of Italy.[70] The crucifix was thus proclaimed as being the symbol of *laicità*,[71] in the sense that it symbolised a secular state with a Christian (that is, Catholic) preference, to be defended accordingly. This interpretation was inconsistent with the Constitutional Court's jurisprudence and with Italian legal doctrine.[72] But such a defence of the crucifix offered Prime Minister Berlusconi a great opportunity to present himself as the sole barrier against the further secularisation of Italy, and as the most efficient adversary of those who would like Italy to follow the 'secularist' path of western Europe.

With the blessing of the Holy See, the *Lautsi* case allowed the Italian government to seal a diplomatic alliance with Russia against allegedly 'secularist' western Europe.[73] In its appeal the government presented a manipulated version of church and state relations in Italy, on the basis of which, in 2011, the Grand Chamber of the European Court reversed the 2009 ruling.[74] Eager to make the point that national systems of church and state relations are safe from European interference, the Court accepted the manifestly untrue account put forward by the Italian government

---

right to education in conformity with parents' religious and philosophical convictions) taken together with Art 9 (the right to freedom of thought, conscience and religion).

[70] The clearest intellectual expression of this change was a book published with a supporting foreword by Foreign Minister Frattini of the centre-right government and by the Secretary to the Council of Ministers Letta. See Carlo Cardia, *Identità Religiosa e Culturale Europea. La Questione del Crocifisso* (Allemandi, 2010). On the transition from secular Italy to Christian Italy in church and state studies see Marco Ventura, 'Grillo parlante o Pinocchio? Come sta nascendo il diritto ecclesiastico dell'Italia multiculturale', in Antonio Fuccillo (ed), *Multireligiosità e Reazione Giuridica* (Giappichelli, 2008).

[71] The Council of State, the supreme administrative court, affirmed in 2006 that the crucifix is a 'symbol able to express the high foundation of the values shaping the secular character of the present State's legal system' (the translation is the author's). Cons St 13 February 2006, 556 (2006) *Quaderni di diritto e politica ecclesiastica* 776, 782.

[72] For the legal doctrine at the time, see Salvatore Prisco, 'Laicità', in Sabino Cassese (ed), *Dizionario di Diritto Pubblico* (Giuffrè, 2006) vol 4. Also see Paolo Stefanì, *La Laicità nell'Esperienza Giuridica dello Stato* (Cacucci, 2007).

[73] See Marco Ventura, 'La tradizione come diritto', *Corriere della Sera* (Milan, 19 March 2011) 23.

[74] *Lautsi v Italy* (App no 30814/06) (ECtHR, 18 March 2011) (GC).

on religious pluralism in Italian state schools,[75] and decided not to take into account Italian Constitutional *laicità*,[76] and the contradictions of Italian legislation and case law.[77] The Grand Chamber accepted two basic assumptions that reflected the new rhetoric of Christian secular Italy. First, religion embodies culture and traditions: though it is first of all a religious symbol, the crucifix bears a cultural meaning that identifies the civil community and prevails over personal considerations and choices. If you're Italian, you must be a Catholic as well, because Catholicism is the historical legacy of the country. Second, Christianity (ambiguously used to mean Catholicism) is the religion of the majority of Italians and as such it must prevail, especially if one agrees with the European Court that 'a crucifix on a wall is an essentially passive symbol'.[78] Aside from non-Catholic Christians, and believers in other faiths or convictions, many Italian Catholics felt outraged at such a blasphemous exploitation of their faith.[79] But the government, political parties from all sides, the Presidency of the Republic, Catholic bishops and the Holy See were unanimous in welcoming this ruling.[80]

In its 2011 ruling, the Grand Chamber of the Strasbourg Court granted Christian secular Italy a legal recognition that had proved impossible to obtain from the Italian Constitutional Court and from the Italian Parliament. The lesson was that *laicità* in the sense of pluralistic secular Italy and *laicità* in the sense of Christian (that is, Catholic) secular Italy represents two models that are condemned to both coexist and compete. Against the background of a heavily secularised and increasingly multi-religious Italian society, Italy is indisputably a *stato laico*. But *laicità* remains a deeply contradictory principle.

---

[75] 'According to the indications provided by the Government, Italy opens up the school environment in parallel to other religions', *Lautsi* (GC) (ibid) [74].

[76] '[It is not] for the Court to rule on the compatibility of the presence of crucifixes in State-school classrooms with the principle of secularism as enshrined in Italian law.' Ibid [57].

[77] 'As regards the Government's opinion on the meaning of the crucifix, the Court notes that the Consiglio di Stato and the Court of Cassation have diverging views in that regard and that the Constitutional Court has not given a ruling (see paragraphs 16 and 23 above). It is not for the Court to take a position regarding a domestic debate among domestic courts.' Ibid [68].

[78] Ibid [72].

[79] See the press communiqué of the association Noi siamo Chiesa at http://www.noisiamochiesa.org/?p=559.

[80] See Marco Ventura, 'La "guerra santa" per il crocifisso', *Corriere della Sera* (Milan, 6 May 2011) 53.

8. Religious freedom in a secular society: an analysis of the French approach to manifestation of beliefs in the public sphere

Sylvie Bacquet*

1. INTRODUCTION

France, with its quasi-obsessive tradition of secularism (*laïcité*), is often singled out from its European neighbours for its strict approach to regulating religious symbols in the public sphere.[1] By adopting Law n° 2004–228 banning the wearing of religious symbols at school,[2] France has unequivocally resisted a relaxation of the prohibition of manifestation of religious beliefs in the public sphere. This legislation is the culmination of France's long tradition of *laïcité*, which goes back to the nineteenth century and originated in the conflict between the Catholic Church and the French Republic. As such, the law is deemed to mark an important feature of the separation of powers and the independence of the state from religious pressure. More recently and following the same stance, the French Parliament went even further by approving a Bill banning the wearing of the full veil in public.[3] The law that the French Senate adopted with an overwhelming

*   I would like to thank my colleague and friend Dr Lisa Webley for her ongoing support throughout the work of producing this chapter. The many inspiring conversations we have had over the months have given me invaluable guidance and provided me with a solid foundation for it. I am also thankful to my friend Lindsay Martin for her help in formatting the final document.

[1]   France is the only European country to provide explicitly for secularism in its Constitution. Although not officially a member of the European Union, Turkey (which declares itself secular) does likewise.

[2]   Loi n° 2004–228 du 15 mars 2004 encadrant, en application du principe de laïcité, le port de signes ou de tenues manifestant une appartenance religieuse dans les écoles, collèges et lycées publics. For the full text see: http://legifrance.gouv.fr/affichTexte.do?cidTexte=JORFTEXT000000417977.

[3]   Projet de loi interdisant la dissimulation du visage dans l'espace public, n°

majority (246 to 1) came into force on 11 April 2011 and provides that in the public sphere no one can wear a garment intended to fully cover the face.[4] While the wording of the law does not single out religious attire, it is clear that it was intended to target the small minority of Muslim women who wear the *niqab* or *burqa* in France.[5] Proponents of the law allege that full face coverings, the *burqa* and *niqab* in particular, infringe republican values (especially *laïcité*, equality between men and women, citizenship and freedom of worship).[6]

While France is a secular country *par excellence*, protection of human rights (including freedom of thought, conscience and religion) has been a constant preoccupation of the state since the revolution of 1789. Article 10 of the 1789 Declaration of the Rights of Man and Citizen provides that '[n]o one may be disturbed on account of his opinions, even religious ones, as long as the manifestation of such opinions does not interfere with the established Law and Order'.[7] Freedom of religion is also afforded constitutional protection. Article 1 of the Constitution of 4 October 1958 states, 'France shall be an indivisible, secular, democratic and social Republic. It shall ensure the equality of all citizens before the law, without distinction of origin, race or religion. It shall respect all beliefs.'[8] It appears therefore that freedom of thought is positively protected, in compliance with Article 9(1) of the European Convention on Human Rights (ECHR).[9] Freedom to display religious symbols in public, however, is restricted by *laïcité*, which is

---

2520, déposé le 19 mai 2010. For the full text see http://www.assemblee-nationale.fr/13/pdf/projets/pl2520.pdf.

[4]   Article 1 – 'nul ne peut, dans l'espace public, porter une tenue destinée à dissimuler son visage'.

[5]   Strictly speaking, the *niqab* is a veil covering the whole face apart from the eyes, whilst the *burqa* is a garment that covers the full body including the face, with a small opening for the eyes. Often the terms are used interchangeably and in France the term *burqa* often that takes precedence although it is assumed that opposing the *burqa* means also opposing the *niqab* as the difference between the two face coverings is minimal.

[6]   Liberté de culte.

[7]   The French Declaration of the Rights of Man and Citizen 1789. For the full text see http://www.assemblee-nationale.fr/histoire/dudh/1789.asp.

[8]   The 1958 Constitution is available at http://www.legifrance.gouv.fr/affichTexte.do?cidTexte=LEGITEXT000006071194.

[9]   Art 9(1) of the ECHR states, '[e]veryone has the right to freedom of thought, conscience and religion; this right includes freedom to change his religion or belief and freedom, either alone or in community with others and in public or private, to manifest his religion or belief, in worship, teaching, practice and observance'.

enforced through the legislation[10] permissible under Article 9(2) ECHR.[11] Nonetheless, the French ban on religious symbols in the public domain, at schools or otherwise, has often been accused of breaching human rights,[12] exacerbating religious and ethnic differences or resulting in indirect discrimination.[13] Indeed, one might legitimately question the extent to which freedom of religion may be successfully protected in a country that prides itself on republicanism and *laïcité*. Can one legitimately assume that the minority of Muslim women who choose to wear the *burqa* or the *niqab* are free to practise their religion while they are excluded from public life unless they are prepared to give up their religious attire?

This chapter seeks to examine how, if at all, France has tackled the challenge of reconciling freedom of religion with secularism, two values that may seem incompatible. It looks at the protection afforded to freedom of religion in the French constitution as well as the country's core values of republicanism and secularism. It also considers the socio-political context leading to the adoption of both the 2004 law banning religious symbols at school and the most recent law that bans full face coverings in the public sphere. This chapter attempts to provide an understanding of how both laws came to be seen as a necessity for the enforcement of the notion of *laïcité*, a cornerstone of French republicanism, and provides a starting point for the debate on whether those laws and secularism more generally are compatible with freedom of religion.

2.   HISTORICAL AND THEORETICAL BACKGROUND TO THE LAW OF 1905

Religion vs the State

Since 1905 and the enactment of the law separating church and state, France has been a secular society. The enactment of this law, a key

---

[10]   Mainly and in particular, the law of 1905, the law of 2004 and the recent law on the full face covering. This will be discussed, in part 4 of this chapter.

[11]   Art 9(2) states, '[f]reedom to manifest one's religion or beliefs shall be subject only to such limitations as are prescribed by law and are necessary in a democratic society in the interests of public safety, for the protection of public order, health or morals, or the protection of the rights and freedoms of others'.

[12]   See Human Rights Watch, 'France: headscarf ban violates religious freedom' (26 February 2004) at http://www.hrw.org/english/docs/2004/02/26/france7666. htm.

[13]   See for instance Joan Wallach Scott, *The Politics of the Veil* (Princeton University Press, 2007).

feature of republicanism, marked the end of a long battle between the state and the church in the struggle for power. Many of the ideas that shaped France's republican policy, including *laïcité*, originated in the century of the Enlightenment (eighteenth century) with philosophers such as Montesquieu, Rousseau, Voltaire and Diderot promoting the use of reason and logic over the blind following of the king and the church. The Enlightenment century culminated in the French Revolution of 1789 that signified the end of the power of the church and of the monarchy.[14] It is in this context that the relationship between the state and religion as we know it today has evolved in France. At the outset, therefore, there existed a negative view of the state towards religion. Religion, embodied within the church, was the enemy of the state in the struggle for power. With the enactment of the law of 1905, religion was relegated to the private sphere and France officially became a secular state.

The law of 1905 is based on two key principles: freedom of conscience and the separation of church and state, and these provide the foundations for *laïcité*. Freedom of conscience is guaranteed under Article 1 and includes freedom of worship provided that this does not interfere with public order.[15] Critics of this article argue that it is the result of a war against Catholicism and that freedom of worship alone does not guarantee freedom to practise one's religion.[16] Yet the article was adopted by a large majority in both chambers of the French Parliament.[17] Separation of church and state is governed by Article 2,[18] which provides that the state does not recognise, remunerate or fund any religion. As such, it becomes religiously neutral. As rightly pointed out by Jacques Robert, though, the law of 1905 is quite outdated since it does not take into account those religious groups that were absent from France at the time of drafting. In particular, Muslims are not taken into account.[19] Moreover, despite the French

---

[14]   On the history of *laïcité* see generally Jean Beaubérot, *Histoire de la laïcité en France* (PUF, 2000).

[15]   'La République assure la liberté de conscience. Elle garantit le libre exercice des cultes sous les seules restrictions édictées ci-après dans l'intérêt de l'ordre public.'

[16]   Conseil d'Etat, 'Rapport public: jurisprudence et avis de 2003 – un siècle de laïcité', (2004) 259, http://lesrapports.ladocumentationfrancaise.fr/BRP/044000121/0000.pdf.

[17]   Ibid.

[18]   'La République ne reconnaît, ne salarie ni ne subventionne aucun culte'; full text available at http://www.legifrance.gouv.fr/affichTexte.do?cidTexte=LEGITEXT000006070169&dateTexte=20101027.

[19]   See Jacques Robert, 'Religious liberty and French secularism', [2003] *Brigham Young University Law Review* 637, 656.

claim to *laïcité*, the calendar of the Republic is essentially Christian. Except for the national holidays such as Bastille Day, all holidays are Christian (Ascension, Easter, Christmas).[20] Thus it can be said that, although the state aspires to be neutral, Catholics are put in a more favourable position in that they can practise their religion more freely than Muslims or Jews since it is facilitated by the calendar. For instance, going to Church on Sunday is possible whereas attending Friday prayers or respecting the Sabbath may not be possible if one is employed.

The neutrality of the state is essentially what became known as *laïcité* and, in order to understand how it became a key feature of the French Fifth Republic, one must look at the theories that have shaped the doctrine over the centuries.

Republicanism

France is a constitutional republic, currently governed by the Constitution of the Fifth Republic, which dates from 1958.[21] The Constitution is grounded on republican theories that emerged during the Enlightenment and crystallised with the French Revolution of 1789. Republicanism is traditionally defined as universalist in nature in that it purports to establish a French identity and requires that the individual transcends any cultural, social or religious belonging in order to achieve individual autonomy, as opposed to multi-culturalism, which traditionally seeks public recognition of cultural diversity.[22] As such, republicanism presupposes that the state is free of any influence from the church in particular and from religion in general. In return the state will not interfere with religion: by refusing to recognise one religion it agrees not to deny any.[23]

The constitution is based on three pillars – *Liberté* (freedom), *Egalité* (equality), *Fraternité* (citizenship)[24] – that are rooted in republican theories. The French philosophers of the Enlightenment considered individual autonomy as key to realising the right to *liberty* since, according to them, real freedom could not be achieved without freedom from religion and tradition. They saw school education as vital in contributing to the learning

---

[20] Ibid 659.

[21] The 1958 Constitution (note 8 above).

[22] See generally Cécile Laborde, 'The culture(s) of the Republic, nationalism and multiculturalism in French republican thought', (2001) 29(5) *Political Theory* 716.

[23] 'Si l'état ne reconnaît aucune religion il doit n'en méconnaître aucune.'

[24] Slogan of the First Republic – see Art 2 of the Constitution.

of individual autonomy,[25] and it is interesting to note that the term *laïcité* was first used in the context of schools in the preamble to the Constitution of 1946.[26] With this in mind, state schools have the role of developing children's autonomy so that they may exercise their right to liberty through distancing themselves from their original affiliation.[27] It follows therefore that *equality* is achieved by putting cultural differences aside rather than via the recognition and reinforcement of cultural differences as in multi-culturalism. *Fraternity* comes from a common inclination of citizens to participate actively in the free political community.[28] As Laborde puts it, '[t]he bond of citizenship would be eroded if society were fragmented into a collection of identity groups seeking recognition rather than work[ing] towards the public interest'.[29] Thus fraternity requires autonomy, in order to flourish.

While it may indeed be important to distance oneself from cultural, social and religious affiliation in order to achieve a certain level of autonomy and ultimately exercise one's right to liberty (including the freedom to choose one's religion, or choose none), the goal of creating a universal community of citizens that share a single culture sits uneasily with the diverse social reality in France. As Jennings points out, the French Republic is ambivalent in nature. It is a culturally and ethnically diverse society (in part due to the large population of immigrants of North African origin) but yet is not one that describes itself as a pluralist society. Instead, the Republican tradition still holds strong within French society and in particular within the field of education.[30] French social policy has tended to focus on integration rather than on the recognition of collective rights that is essential to multi-culturalism. In fact, republicanism focuses on the recognition of the individual, rather than the group and its ability to exist outside its historical, social, cultural and religious affiliation. Secularism therefore is a prerequisite for republicanism since autonomy can only be achieved if religion is kept separate from the state.

---

[25]   Laborde (note 22 above) 718.

[26]   Art 13 '. . . L'organisation de l'enseignement public gratuit et laïque a tous les degrés est un devoir de l'Etat' (. . .the organisation of public and free education at all levels is a duty of the State).

[27]   Catherine Kintzler, *La république en questions* (Minerve, 1996).

[28]   Ibid.

[29]   Laborde (note 22 above) 720.

[30]   Jeremy Jennings, 'Citizenship, republicanism and multiculturalism in contemporary France', (2000) 30 (4) *British Journal of Political Science* 575, 576.

3.   THE FRENCH *LAÏCITÉ* AS A CORE PRINCIPLE OF THE REPUBLIC

While the law of 1905 established the separation between church and state that is key to *laïcité*, it did not make any explicit reference to the word *laïcité*. This term came to be recognised later, in both the 1946 and 1958 Constitutions (Article 1). The French *laïcité* derives from freedom of conscience as well as the principle of equality of citizens and in France the term presupposes the separation of church and state so that no religion has a privileged status within the Republic and individuals are entitled to freedom of opinion and faith. Three main principles govern the concept of *laïcité*: neutrality of the state, freedom of conscience and pluralism.[31]

Neutrality of the state is the main prerequisite for *laïcité*. Article 1 of the French Constitution guarantees equality before the law to all citizens, regardless of origin, race or religion.[32] This entails a duty on the state to appear religiously neutral in the provision of public services. Thus, the principle of neutrality of public servants (*neutralité des agents du service public*)[33] stipulates that manifestation of beliefs or the wearing of religious symbols are forbidden for those working on behalf on the state including the police, school teachers, government ministers, local council workers, public medical personnel, etc. This injunction against the display of religious symbols preserves the public sphere as a secular space, while allowing the private sphere to be imbued with religious identity, free from interference by the state.

This principle implies a clear division between a citizen's private life on one hand and the public sphere on the other. It becomes difficult for citizens to practise their religion outside the private sphere. At a time when the dominant religion was Christianity, the distinction between belief and practice might not have been viewed as an infringement of one's freedom of religion, for Christianity is mainly a belief-based religion that does not generally require a public display of faith. In today's diverse French society, however, it is necessary to distinguish between those religions that are belief-based such as Christianity and others that are more practice-based and, as such, require that their members publicly display their faith, such as

---

[31]   Conseil d'Etat (note 16 above) 272–8.

[32]   'Elle assure l'égalité devant la loi de tous les citoyens sans distinction d'origine, de race ou de religion.'

[33]   Conseil d'Etat 3 mai 1950 Demoiselle Jamet in Bernard Stasi, 'Commission de réflexion sur l'application du principe de laïcité dans la République: rapport au Président de la République' (December 2003) para 2.2, available at http://www.ladocumentationfrancaise.fr/var/storage/rapports-publics/034000725/0000.pdf.

Sikhism, Islam and Judaism (in its most Orthodox form). The turban (for instance) is an essential element of the Sikh faith; members of the Sikh religion are required to wear it by the Sikh Code of Conduct as promulgated by the various gurus.[34]

With the principle of neutrality of the agents of the state, a Sikh man or a practising Muslim woman are faced with the choice of either manifesting their religion or working for the French government. If they choose the latter, they must give up their religious practice, at least while they are on duty. This inevitably leads to religious discrimination as it excludes some religious groups from certain professions unless they are prepared to renounce their religious practice while in service.[35] Those who support the principle of the neutrality of the state argue that public administration must remain neutral and that those working for the public sector are free to manifest their beliefs, just not while they are at work.

The lay state guarantees *freedom of conscience*: individuals are free to choose a religious or spiritual position, or to choose none, to change it, or even cease to adhere to it. The state aims to ensure that no single group or community is allowed to impose on anyone their particular faith. It seeks to protect individuals from any physical or moral pressure on religious or spiritual grounds.[36] This is particularly important at school where the state has a duty to protect schoolchildren from any social pressure but at the same time allow them to form their own opinion on the various religions. In the secular state, therefore, religious freedom is guaranteed by protecting the individual from religious pressure particularly during childhood when the individual is most vulnerable.[37] This provides the rationale for the 2004 legislation on manifestation of belief at school, and will be discussed in further detail in part 4 of this chapter.

Pluralism, the third pillar of *laïcité*, is enshrined in Article 2 of the law of 1905. By renouncing the idea of a state religion, the Republic places all religions on the same level. No single religion will have a special status and as such the old distinction between official and non-official religions

---

[34]   See further Neha Singh Gohil and Dawinder S Sidhu, 'The Sikh turban: post-9/11 challenges to this article of faith', (Spring 2008) 9 *Rutgers Journal of Law & Religion* 1; Ranvir Nayar, 'French Sikhs defend the turban', BBC News (Paris, 17 January 2004) available at http://news.bbc.co.uk/1/hi/world/europe/3403775.stm.

[35]   This is argued by Desmond M Clarke, 'Freedom of thought in schools: a comparative study', [1986] *International & Comparative Law Quarterly* 283.

[36]   Stasi (note 33 above) para 1.2.2.

[37]   Henrik Palmer Olsen and Stuart Toddington, *Architectures of Justice* (Ashgate, 2007) 165.

is abolished.[38] The state therefore has a duty to protect those minority religions against any form of discrimination.

Over a century after the law of 1905, the French *laïcité* keeps being debated and has been a source of controversy especially since the law of 2004 that took *laïcité* even further by banning religious symbols at school. In the next section we look at the more recent legislation on *laïcité* and how religious minorities have been accommodated.

4. *LAÏCITÉ* IN CONTEXT: ACCOMMODATION OF MINORITIES

Socio-political Background

Following decolonisation of North Africa, France found itself with a large population of North African immigrants who are now well established in France and whose children are often French citizens.[39] It is estimated that there are currently between 5 and 6 million Muslims living in France, which makes it the largest Muslim community in Europe.[40] This influx of immigrants and their establishment in France has resulted in an increasingly diverse and multi-cultural French society that perhaps conflicts to a certain extent with the underlying principle of universalism that has dominated French ideology during the various republican regimes.[41]

French Muslims have indeed remained largely part of a poorer minority, mostly uneducated and marginalised, generally living at the outskirts of big cities in what have become known as *banlieues*. Strictly '*banlieue*' means suburb but over the years it has come to be used pejoratively to denote those poorer suburbs, mainly populated by immigrants who mostly live in council estates (called '*cités*') and receive state benefit often linked to unemployment. Allegedly as a result of poverty and unemployment, the poorer suburbs have become a breeding ground for street crime

---

[38]   Before the law of 1905 only Catholicism, Protestantism and Judaism were recognised religions and therefore in receipt of state funds. Robert (note 19 above) 640.

[39]   See generally Jane Freedman, 'Secularism as a barrier to integration? The French dilemna', (2004) 42(3) *International Migration* 5, 7–9.

[40]   AFP, '5 à 6m de musulmans en France' (*Le Figaro*, 28 June 2010) at http://www.lefigaro.fr/flash-actu/2010/06/28/97001-20100628FILWWW00407-5-a-6m-de-musulmans-en-france.php. Note that due to the absence of census data on ethnic minorities in France, it is impossible to quote exact figures.

[41]   For an account of the history of immigration and its resonance on *laïcité* see Wallach Scott (note 13 above) 21–41.

making them even less attractive to small businesses and private housing schemes. Also, local public schools have tended to achieve very poor success rates which adds to the stigma associated with the *banlieues*.[42] It is no surprise, then, that in the late 1990s some suburban schools became the theatre of a series of incidents involving Muslim headscarves.[43] These later became known as *l'affaire des foulards* (the headscarves affair) and eventually led to the adoption, in 2004, of the law banning religious symbols at school.

L'affaire des foulards started in October 1989 when three Muslim girls were expelled from a school in one of the poor, marginalised Parisian suburbs. The girls had refused to remove their headscarves, which the school principal alleged were in contravention of the principle of *laïcité*. In November 1989 the Conseil d'Etat (French constitutional court) ruled that the wearing of religious symbols was not incompatible with the principle of *laïcité* as long as the said symbol was not worn in a polemical or ostentatious manner.[44] The decision whether a particular symbol would be considered ostentatious was left to schools.[45] These events attracted a lot of media coverage at a time when international attention was already turned towards Islam,[46] with the start of the first Palestinian *intifada* as well as the Iranian *fatwa* against Salman Rushdie.[47] As a result, what began as a small school incident grew into a wider national debate on the place of Muslims in France. The headscarf became a symbol of Muslim identity in the secular Republic. More and more young Muslims took to wearing the headscarf and protests claiming the freedom to wear a headscarf in the classroom were organised in the schools of various French cities.[48]

In September 1994 following more school incidents Francois Bayrou,

---

[42]   See generally statistics published by the French Ministry of Education available at http://www.education.gouv.fr/cid3014/indicateurs-de-resultats-des-lycees. html. For instance in Lycée Henri Wallon in Aubervilliers, north of Paris, largely populated by immigrants, the pass rate at the Baccalaureate in 2008 was 71 per cent; Lycée Jacques Brel La Courneuve, another *banlieue*, achieved only 63 per cent while the Lycée Blaise Pascale in Orsay, south of Paris and therefore a relatively rich suburb, achieved a pass rate of 98 per cent and Lycée Victor Hugo in Paris achieved 93 per cent.

[43]   See generally Freedman (note 39 above) 7–10.

[44]   Avis n° 346.893 relatif au port de signes d'appartenance religieuse, CE 27 Novembre 1989.

[45]   Décision n° 130394, CE 2 Novembre 1992.

[46]   See generally Pierre Tévanian, 'Le voile médiatique. Un faux débat: "l'affaire du foulard islamique"', (2006) 25(1) *Communication* 362.

[47]   Wallach Scott (note 13 above) 71–2.

[48]   See for example Judith Rueff, 'Le défilé des intouchables', *Le Monde*, Archives (Paris, 24 October 1989).

then Minister of Education, issued a decree prohibiting ostentatious signs of religious affiliation at school, although discreet ones were permitted.[49] The decree suggested that schools revise their rules and regulations to take this into account but, following the decree, more protests ensued and there were a number of exclusions from schools that gave rise to various court decisions.[50] In deciding whether to overturn an exclusion the courts had to look at whether the wearing of the religious symbol in question amounted to an act of proselytism or propaganda. If so then exclusion could be upheld. A number of exclusions were overturned, for instance when pupils had been excluded solely on the ground of their wearing a headscarf that the school had deemed incompatible with *laïcité*. Moreover, in a decision of 26 July 1996 the Conseil d'Etat overturned the decision of a university to deny access to female students wearing headscarves on the ground that the university had received an anonymous security threat.[51] The court held that the security threat could have been addressed without the need to deny access to those students. On the other hand, in a decision of 27 November 1996,[52] the Conseil d'Etat confirmed 17 exclusions of students who had organised protests against a change in their school's rules and regulations following the decree. The Conseil considered that the students had gone beyond their right to manifest their religion by disrupting the normal functioning of the school.

Over the years, there were more and more cases of exclusion and more and more litigation as schools were left with the responsibility of deciding whether the wearing of a particular religious symbol could be seen as proselytism.[53] This led to much confusion and inconsistency, and in 2003, in order to clarify the situation, the then President Jacques Chirac decided to introduce a law that would ban all religious symbols at school. He commissioned the Stasi report on *laïcité* in the Republic,[54] which eventually led to the adoption of the law of 2004.

---

[49]   Circulaire n° 1649 du 20 Septembre 1994, available at http://www.assem blee-nationale.fr/12/dossiers/documents-laicite/document-3.pdf.

[50]   See for example, Philippe Depalle, 'Deux élèves portant le foulard islamique sont exclues d'un lycée de Nevers', *Le Monde*, Archives (Paris, 24 October 1995).

[51]   Requête n° 170106 du 26 Juillet 1996.

[52]   Requêtes n° 170207 et 170208 du 27 Novembre 1996.

[53]   See for example Caroline Monnot and Xavier Ternisen, 'L'exclusion de deux lycéennes voilées divise l'extrême gauche', *Le Monde*, Archives (Paris, 9 October 2003).

[54]   Stasi (note 33 above).

Legal Framework

The law of 15 March 2004: religious symbols at school

The Stasi report was submitted to President Chirac on 11 December 2003 by the Stasi Commission,[55] named after the ombudsman charged with the enquiry. The Commission comprised mainly scholars and intellectuals and the inquiry was based on interviews with stakeholders including politicians, religious leaders, trade union representatives, human rights NGOs, local representatives, school headmasters and teachers, and students.[56] The Stasi report led to the adoption of the law of 2004 banning the wearing of conspicuous signs of religious affiliation in public schools.

The report reaffirmed the strong tradition of *laïcité* and recalled its importance within the Republic, especially for schools and public services. The Commission acknowledged that *laïcité* was confronted with a new religious and spiritual diversity and noted that reasonable adjustments had already been made, notably in relation to planning permission for new religious buildings, accommodation of religious holidays, dietary requirements linked to religious belief and incorporating some religious studies in the school curriculum.[57]

The report provides examples of infringements on *laïcité* that the Commission considered to be a threat to the neutrality of public services and of the state. In schools, for instance, the Commission noted that disruption was caused by repeated absences for prayer, or fasting, or young girls refusing to take part in PE lessons. Exams were also disrupted when female Muslim students refused to go through identity checks or to be examined by a male examiner. In public hospitals, similar problems had occurred with husbands or fathers refusing to have their daughter or wife treated by a male doctor. The same kinds of difficulty were also reported in prisons.[58]

The Commission considered that these infringements were responsible for what they called '*repli communautaire*' (communitarism). In France this term is used to describe a situation in which minorities live in self-sufficient communities rather than integrate with the majority.[59] The report highlighted that schools or sports no longer helped to improve the situation. The Commission noted for instance that community sports teams had

---

[55] Commission de réflexion sur l'application du principe de laïcité dans la République.

[56] The Commission conducted about 100 public interviews and about 40 private ones.

[57] Stasi (note 33 above), para 3.1.1.

[58] Ibid, para 3.2.1.

[59] See generally Wallach Scott (note 13 above).

developed that no longer took part in competitions at federation level; women also tended to be automatically excluded by faith communities from local swimming pools and stadiums.[60] The Commission pointed out that the concept of *mixité*, which in France advocates mixed access to public places such as sporting facilities, was being compromised by those practices, which in turn resulted in a reduction of equality between the sexes.[61]

Moreover, the Commission noted that women's rights in those communities were in decline – 'la situation des filles dans les cités relève d'un veritable drame' (the situation of young women on estates is a real concern).[62] The report notes that young women were victims of sexism and were on the receiving end of verbal, psychological and/or physical pressure and violence. Some were forced to wear modest clothing and the report noted that, while some women willingly choose to wear the headscarf, others are put under pressure to wear it. Pressure usually comes both from within the family (for example from a brother or father) and from the wider community, for the perception is that, were they not to wear a veil, young women would be regarded as indecent or unfaithful.[63]

Finally, the Commission noted the rise of racism and xenophobia especially targeted at Muslims, as well as the rise of anti-Semitism,[64] and made a number of recommendations in addition to outlawing conspicuous signs of religious affiliation at school. These included the drawing-up of a Charter on *laïcité*,[65] the establishment of a national school for Islamic studies,[66] the creation of Muslim chaplaincies in the army, alternatives to pork and fish on Friday in public service cafeterias,[67] and the recognition of some Muslim and Jewish holidays.[68]

In a speech on 17 December 2003, President Chirac announced that a law banning conspicuous religious signs at school would be put before Parliament, but the proposal to add additional public holidays to the school calendar to accommodate important religious festivals was rejected at the outset by the President. However, Chirac recommended that exams should not be set on those days. In relation to hospitals, he noted that nothing

---

[60]   Stasi (note 33 above), para 3.3.1.
[61]   Ibid, para 4.1.2.2.
[62]   In the words of the head of an association; ibid, para 3.3.2.1.
[63]   Ibid.
[64]   Ibid, para 3.3.2.2. On anti-Semitism in France see Sylvie Bacquet, 'An analysis of the resurgence of anti-Semitism in France', (2004) 1(4) *Journal of Diplomatic Language*.
[65]   Stasi (note 33 above), para 4.1.1.1.
[66]   Ibid, para 4.3.2.
[67]   Ibid, para 4.3.3ff.
[68]   Ibid, para 4.4.

could justify a patient refusing to be treated by a doctor of the opposite sex and advocated a law to this effect. The proposal to create a Charter on *laïcité* was retained and the President also insisted on the need to protect women's rights and the principle of *mixité*.[69] The Charter on *laïcité* was eventually adopted in 2007 and disseminated to public service establishments such as hospitals and universities.[70]

The law banning the wearing of conspicuous signs of religious affiliations in public was voted through on 10 February 2004 in the National Assembly by a large majority (494 to 36). It introduced Article L141–5–1 of the Education Code, which states that '[d]ans les écoles, les collèges et les lycées publics, le port de signes ou tenues par lesquels les élèves manifestent ostensiblement une appartenance religieuse est interdit' ('in primary and secondary public education, the wearing of conspicuous signs of religious affiliation is forbidden').

The law is particularly short but there is an accompanying application decree that specifies that the signs or dress that are forbidden are those that affiliated with a particular religion such as the Islamic veil (in all its forms), the Jewish *yarmulke* or a large cross. Presumably, the Sikh turban would also fall under this category. Discreet religious signs are allowed and the law does not forbid any attire or symbol worn by pupils having no religious significance.[71] In cases of breach, the application decree recommends that a dialogue is opened between the student and all those involved. Exclusion must be a last resort.[72]

The law came into force in September 2004 in time for the start of the new school year. The atmosphere was tense as two French journalists and their driver had been taken hostage by a group calling itself the Islamic Army in Iraq a month earlier, and the hostage takers had demanded that the law be cancelled.[73] But despite ongoing fears and tension, the first day of school was relatively smooth and only 240 religious symbols were reported, mainly Islamic headscarves. This figure gradually rose during

---

[69] Jacques Chirac, 'Discours relatif au respect du principe de laïcité dans la république', Fil-info-France (Paris 17 December 2003) at http://www.fil-info-france.com/actualites-monde/discours-chirac-loi-laicite.htm.

[70] Charte de la Laïcité dans les services publics, Avril 2007, available at http://www.sante.gouv.fr/IMG/pdf/charte_laicite-2.pdf.

[71] Circulaire n° 2004–084 du 18 mai 2004 JO du 22 Mai 2004, available at http://www.legifrance.gouv.fr/affichTexte.do?cidTexte=JORFTEXT00000025246 5&dateTexte=.

[72] Ibid.

[73] Lemonde.fr, 'Attente dans l'espoir de la libération des journalistes français en Irak', *Le Monde* Archives (Paris 31 August 2004). The two journalists were subsequently freed.

the first week of that term but remained reasonable.[74] Some have put this down to the hostage situation but it has also been argued that it was as a result of a better understanding of *laïcité* following the success of the national and academic programmes designed to assist the enforcement of the new law.[75]

Those in favour of the law argue that the headscarf is a symbol of oppression of women and that in order to guarantee their freedom of religion (including freedom from religion), women need to be able to take it off if they so choose. French schools cannot endorse what might constitute a symbol of repression against women.[76] As such, the law is seen as promoting equality and protecting the secular state and pupils from any social and religious pressure.

The opponents of the law have argued that it was enacted to target the French Muslim minority[77] as part of a fear of the rising Islamic fundamentalism.[78] They have also argued that the law will reinforce France's already strong policy of assimilation and integration.[79] Saxena argues that minority groups are required to surrender their identity in the name of assimilation.[80] It is true that, with *laïcité*, it becomes difficult for minorities to manifest their identity outside the private sphere, especially those that follow a practice-based religion.

The law has also frequently been accused of breaching human rights, in particular, Articles 9 and 14 of the ECHR as well as Article 2 of Protocol 1 (right to education). The European Court of Human Rights has never so far declared the French law incompatible with the ECHR, however, since the prohibition is 'prescribed by law' and therefore falls within the state's margin of appreciation. The right of belief is considered to be absolute, but the right to manifest that belief is considered to be qualified and thus

---

[74] Hanifa Chérifi, 'Application de la loi du 15 mars 2004: Rapport a monsieur le ministre de l'éducation nationale de l'enseignement supérieur et de la recherche' (juillet 2005), available at ftp://trf.education.gouv.fr/pub/edutel/rapport/rapport_cherifi.pdf.

[75] Ibid, 36. These have included information days for those who would be responsible for implementing the law, the publication of various guides around the issue of *laïcité* and the setting-up of supporting commissions for schools: see further Ch I(2) of the same report.

[76] Olsen and Toddington (note 37 above) 163.

[77] Wallach Scott (note 13 above) 1.

[78] Jessica Fourneret, 'France: banning legal pluralism by passing a law', (2006) 29 *Hastings International & Comparative Law Review* 223.

[79] See Freedman (note 39 above).

[80] Mukul Saxena, 'The French headscarf law and the right to manifest religious belief', [2007] *Detroit Mercy Legal Review* 765, 767.

capable of restriction as long as that restriction is prescribed by law, in defence of a legitimate aim and proportionate. In July 2009, the European Court upheld a number of exclusions for failure to comply with the law. The Court recognised that the law of 2004 places a restriction on the manifestation of religion but since the law carries the legitimate aim of protecting the rights and freedom of others as well as public order, it is a justified interference and the expulsions were not disproportionate. The claims based on Article 14 were also rejected because the law applies to all religious symbols and the claim that the exclusions were an infringement to the right to education was also rejected since distance learning was available.[81] In addition, one could argue that the presence of a number of private schools, including religious ones that are subsidised by the French government, provides an accessible alternative to secular state schools and thus the right to education is not compromised by the law of 2004.[82]

Despite the fact that the law has been found not to breach Convention rights, it remains the case that for the minority of Muslim girls, Sikhs and Jewish boys who consider that wearing a veil, turban or *kippa* is an obligation of their religion, the law forces them to choose between their religion on one hand and *laïcité* on the other. It appears therefore that openly practising their religion is not compatible with *laïcité*. If they wish to continue to display their faith, they can continue to do so only in private or in limited public spaces. As a result, many religious students have moved to religious schools or opted for distance learning that will isolate them even more, thus making the process of integration even more difficult.

This position clearly poses problems in that some Muslims argue that wearing the headscarf is a requirement of the Qur'an not a question of choice;[83] similarly, for a Sikh, wearing a turban is a requirement of the religion.[84] While the law focused on all conspicuous religious symbols, it is true that its impact will mostly be felt by those who belong to a practice-based religion such as Islam, Sikhism and Judaism. The Catholic majority in France is unlikely to be affected: Catholics seldom wear large crosses and

---

[81] For instance see the cases of *Aktas v France* App no 43563/08 (ECtHR, 30 June 2009), *Bayrak v France* App no 14308/08 (ECtHR, 30 June 2009), *Gamaleddyn v France* App no 18527/08 (ECtHR, 30 June 2009), *Ghazal v France* App no 29134/08 (ECtHR, 30 June 2009), *J Singh v France* App no 25463/08 (ECtHR, 30 June 2009) and *R Singh v France* App no 27561/08 (ECtHR, 30 June 2009).

[82] La documentation francaise, 'L'école républicaine', available at http://www.ladocumentationfrancaise.fr/dossiers/france-50-ans-transformations/ecole-republicaine.shtml>

[83] Fourneret (note 78 above) 234.

[84] Saxena (note 80 above) 780.

there is no such requirement in Catholicism – the wearing of a religious symbol is not considered an article of faith but rather an expression of faith. In that sense, the allegation that the legislation is discriminatory can be seen as well-founded. Indeed, the reference to large Catholic crosses in the decree has been accused of being a 'symbolic gesture' to avoid the charge of discrimination.[85]

More recently, it is the Muslim full-face covering (that is, the *burqa* or *niqab*) that has become the subject of controversy in France. While at the beginning of the new century such garments were almost non-existent in France, the practice gradually rose to reach 1900 at the beginning of the year 2009.[86] In October 2010, after over a year of being at the forefront of the public debate, the face veil was finally outlawed in public spaces. This legislation is discussed in the next sub-section.

The law of 11 October 2010: prohibition of full face coverings in public spaces

In June 2009 the (then) French President Nicolas Sarkozy launched the debate on the full face covering in a speech at the Palace of Versailles, when he declared that the *burqa* was not welcome in France and described it as a 'sign of subservience' and contrary to the Republic's principle of women's dignity.[87] Following Sarkozy's comments, the French National Assembly commissioned a special inquiry into the wearing of the full face covering in France and whether it undermines secularism. The report of the inquiry, which contains more than 600 pages, was published after a very thorough examination of the practice, and concluded that wearing a full face covering was an infringement to liberty and to the dignity of women. The report indicated that the inquiry had concluded that the practice of wearing a full face covering is not prescribed by religion but instead constitutes a cultural custom, amounts to excluding women from social life and is therefore against republican values. It recommended that the practice be outlawed in public places.[88]

---

[85]   Ibid, 767 and Wallach Scott (note 13 above) 3 and 4.

[86]   This number compares to 10000 to 30000 in the UK or 5 per cent of the Muslim population; see Jean-Pierre Langellier, 'Multiculturalisme britannique', *Le Monde*, Archives (Paris, 30 October 2006).

[87]   'Sarkozy speaks out against *burka*', BBC News (22 June 2009) at http://news.bbc.co.uk/1/hi/8112821.stm.

[88]   Assemblée Nationale, 'Rapport d'information au nom de la Mission d'information sur la pratique du port du voile intégral sur le territoire national' (26 janvier 2010) at http://www.assemblee-nationale.fr/13/rap-info/i2262.asp#P24_348.

Consulted on the issue, the rector of the Grand Mosque of Paris condemned the wearing of the *burqa* in France, saying that French Islam must be open and liberal, and that there is no need for French Muslims to hide behind a *burqa*.[89] The Head of the French Council of Muslim Faith indicated that, while he supported taking action to discourage women from wearing a full face covering, a legal ban would stigmatise a vulnerable group.[90] The general Muslim public is also divided on the issue, although it would appear that a majority are against the *burqa*.[91]

In June 2010, the Garraud Report noted that the face is synonymous with identity and thus the uniqueness of an individual, and that dialogue can only come from the face.[92] To hide one's face is to exclude oneself from the social contract that allows citizens to live together (*'le vivre ensemble'*).[93] Acknowledging that outlawing the practice carries some risks, the report discusses the possibility that a law might result in the stigmatising in particular of Muslim women dressing in this fashion, and of Islam more generally. Moreover, it might mean that women who refuse to give up the practice would be forced to remain at home, which will lead to them being even more isolated. Despite those reservations, the report recommended that a law be adopted, and on 14 September 2010 the French Parliament voted through a law prohibiting the full head covering. Article 1 provides that 'nul ne peut, dans l'espace public, porter une tenue destinée à dissimuler son visage' ('in public spaces, no one may wear a garment intended to fully cover their face').[94] The new law includes all forms of head coverings, not just the *burqa*, but it is clear from the way it came to be enacted that it was a reaction to the proliferation of full face coverings (*burqa* or *niqab*), even though in France the practice remains confined to a small minority of women.

Public space for the purpose of the law is defined at Article 2 and

---

[89]   Lemonde.fr, 'Des députés réclament une commission d'enquête sur le port de la *burka*', *Le Monde*, Archives (Paris, 18 June 2009).

[90]   'French MPs vote to ban Islamic full veil in public', BBC News (13 July 2010) available at http://www.bbc.co.uk/news/10611398.

[91]   Abdennour Bidar, 'La *burqa*, une pathologie de la culture musulmane', *Libération* (29 June 2009) available at http://www.liberation.fr/societe /0101576805-la-burqa-une-pathologie-de-la-culture-musulmane.

[92]   This is the equivalent of the Stasi report but for the 2010 law proposal.

[93]   Jean-Paul Garraud, 'Rapport n° 2648 sur le projet de loi inderdisant la dissimulation du visage dans l'espace public' (23 June 2010) at http://www.assemblee-nationale.fr/13/rapports/r2648.asp#P418_115159.

[94]   Loi n° 2010–1192 du 11 octobre 2010 interdisant la dissimulation du visage dans l'espace public, at http://legifrance.gouv.fr/affichTexte.do?cidTexte=JORFT EXT000022911670&categorieLien=id.

includes all public places including places open to the public or where a public service is delivered. These include the streets and thus the definition is wider in scope than previous bans on religious symbols in public service or public schools.[95] Exceptions to the ban include instances when a face covering is prescribed by law for reasons of health, sports or when worn during traditional or artistic manifestations.[96] In addition, the Conseil Constitutionnel, asked to review the law by Parliament in accordance with Article 61 of the French Constitution, has held that it conforms to the Constitution but added a reservation to the effect that the law could not apply in places of worship open to the public.[97] Presumably this would mean that women have to cover their face immediately before entering the place of worship, as travelling from their home in a full face covering would constitute an infringement of the law.

The law provides that breaches will result in fines of €150 for those caught wearing a full face covering, once a six-month grace period, to allow time to educate Muslim women about the ban, has elapsed. Anyone who forces a person to cover their face risks penalties of up to €30 000 euros and a one-year jail term.[98]

Those who oppose the law argue that it is an overreaction to a minor problem since the practice only concerns a small number of Muslim women and that it is part of a crusade against Islam which, in France, does not fit with *laïcité*. Those who support it, on the other hand, argue that the law was not enacted to address a religious problem since the *burqa* and the *niqab* are not a religious requirement of Islam.[99] It is, they maintain, a sectarian practice that is encouraged by a minority of Muslims, called the Salafi movement, who interpret the Qur'an to the letter. It is argued that the law aims to address national security issues and respect for women. In an age where CCTV has become the norm, there is a gap between the practice of covering one's face and issues of security. For instance, how can a teacher safely allow a child to leave school when picked up by someone with a full face covering – it may be difficult to be sure of the identity of the person coming to collect the child.[100]

---

[95]   Actions that are already forbidden in the streets of France include walking around naked and protesting with a hood.

[96]   Art 2(ii).

[97]   Décision n° 2010–613 DC du 7 octobre 2010.

[98]   Art 4.

[99]   Meeus, 'Copé: pourquoi il faut une loi anti-*burqa!*' (8 January 2010) available at http://www.lefigaro.fr/politique/2010/01/09/01002-20100109ART-FIG00050--pourq-u-oi-il-faut-une-loi-anti-burqa-.php.

[100]   Ibid.

The French law came after a number of other countries initiated bans on full face coverings including Belgium and Italy. Belgium was the first European country to pass legislation banning the full face covering despite the practice being confined to a very small minority of women.[101] In Italy, the practice has also been banned albeit not via primary legislation but through bylaws at local level.[102] In the Middle East, Syria has banned both the *niqab* and the *burqa* in universities,[103] while in Turkey religious clothing is banned from public places following the country's strict secular laws.[104]

It is too early to comment on the impact that the law will have on the French Muslim community. While the initiative to outlaw the practice in order to protect those women who are forced to hide behind a full veil is one that should be welcomed, one might also wonder what will become of those women once they have been removed from public life. The initiative of imposing a fine on those who impose the practice is well founded but it is likely that enforcement will be problematic. Will those women be forced to remain at home or will they be moved by their families to countries in which the practice is allowed? Have the French authorities hidden the problem away from society rather than addressing any underlying issues that might be better dealt with at local level case by case? Moreover, the ban appears to be predicated on the assumption that all women who wear the veil have been forced to do so, or indoctrinated into doing so, rather than choosing to exercise their autonomy in determining that this is how they wish to live. The state may be making paternalistic assumptions about women, and denying their autonomy, which appears to run contrary to the spirit of republicanism. Indeed, while the report recognises that, amongst those women who were interviewed, some claimed to be wearing the full face covering out of choice, the report describes this phenomenon as '*servitude volontaire*' (voluntary enslavement).[105] This, according to the Assemblée Nationale report, can be attributed to the desire of those women to adhere more strictly to the principles of Islam and to look like the wives of the Prophet, or to a willingness to distance themselves from a society that they

---

[101]   Baptiste Schweitzer, 'La Belgique interdit la *burqa*', *France Info* (29 April 2010) at http://www.france-info.com/monde-europe-2010-04-29-la-belgique-inter-dit-la-burqa-435918-14-15.html.

[102]   Cyriel Martin, 'Eclairage – comment l'Italie interdit la *burqa* sans faire de loi', *Le Point* (4 May 2010) at http://www.lepoint.fr/monde/eclairage-comment-l-italie-interdit-la-burqa-sans-faire-de-loi-04-05-2010-451037_24.php.

[103]   Constance Jamet, 'La Syrie interdit le *niqab* à l'université', *Le Figaro* (20 July 2010) at http://www.lefigaro.fr/international/2010/07/20/01003-20100720ART-FIG00388-la-syrie-interdit-le-niqab-a-l-universite.php.

[104]   See further *Leyla Sahin v Turkey* (Application 44774/98) [2006] ELR 73.

[105]   Rapport d'information (note 88 above) 42.

see as corrupted. This is not surprising if one considers that most of those who wear the full face covering are young French women under 30 years old who, for the most part, have converted to Islam.[106] In that sense it could be seen as the manifestation of a strong desire to show one's belonging to a particular culture and to be fully integrated into that culture, rather than as a form of extremism as is often claimed.

5. CONCLUSION: FREEDOM OF RELIGION VS *LAÏCITÉ*

This chapter has provided an overview of secularism in France – its historical, socio-political and legal basis – in an attempt to assess whether France has been successful in balancing freedom of religion with secular values. Freedom of religion as protected by Article 9 ECHR comprises both belief and manifestation of belief. It is the latter in France that is subject to controversy. The manifestation of belief through religious symbols is widely limited in France within the public sphere and especially at school, since it contradicts the principles of *laïcité*. While the limitations placed on manifestations of belief are prescribed by law as provided by Article 9(2) ECHR, those limitations have been the subject of much criticism, and one can indeed question the extent to which those limitations are proportionate to the aim sought, especially in view of the wide margin of appreciation afforded by the European Court on such matters.

There is no uniform policy in French schools. Instead, the uniform is the 'secular uniform'. Non-religious symbols are not outlawed – students can, for instance, attend school dressed as a Goth but they cannot wear a headscarf. This seems to give religion a special status, and thus has created a stigma against religion and more particularly Islam.

The underlying issue is that many of the principles underlying the notion of *laïcité* emerged as a reaction to the church and at a time when France was overwhelmingly Catholic. Following the independence of its colonies, however, France became a pluralist society and *laïcité* needed to be revised to accommodate the new demographic status. *Laïcité* does not as such pose problems to belief-based religions but to practice-based ones such as Islam, Judaism and Sikhism. Some French Muslim women undeniably have to choose between practising their religion, which for some might include wearing a form of face covering that they may consider to be prescribed by the Qur'an, and taking an active part in French public life, as the two

---

[106]   Ibid.

are not compatible. Private religious schooling has also been encouraged, which further reduces communitarism (as described above).

As a result, minorities find themselves more stigmatised and this leads to more exclusions thus undermining the initial aim of legislation, which was 'integration'. *Laïcité* is taken to such an extreme that it can be seen as the religion of the republic. The idea that, in order to be a French citizen, one must detach oneself from any religious and cultural background is one that may lead to ignorance and segregation rather than integration. It might also allow religious practice, relegated to the private sphere, to go unchallenged once it is hidden from view and from public debate. While it is important to support freedom from religion and the state has to protect its citizens from factional pressure, religion and culture are often intertwined and for certain minorities giving up their culture amounts to a surrendering of their identity.

9. Secularism, law and religion within the Cypriot legal order

Achilles C Emilianides

1. INTRODUCTION

The Republic of Cyprus was established as an independent and sovereign republic on 16 August 1960, when its Constitution came into force and the British sovereignty over Cyprus, as a crown colony, ceased. On 20 July 1974 the Republic of Turkey, one of the powers guaranteeing the independence, sovereignty and territorial integrity of Cyprus, invaded the country and occupied the northern part the island. As a result of the occupation, the Greeks and the other Christians of the region became displaced persons, having fled to the southern part of the island. Likewise, the Muslim Turks of the southern part of the island were induced to relocate to the north. The area occupied by Turkey amounts to 36.4 per cent of the territory of the Republic of Cyprus.

The Turkish occupation in Cyprus continues to the present day and therefore the Republic of Cyprus is prevented from exercising its powers over the occupied territory. Cyprus became a full member of the European Union on 1 May 2004. However, the application of the *acquis communautaire* in the occupied areas has been suspended, until a solution to the Cyprus problem is found. The analysis presented in this chapter refers exclusively to the government-controlled areas, and not to the areas occupied by Turkey since the 1974 invasion. In the areas not controlled by the government the vast majority of the population are Turkish Muslims.

The next part of this chapter examines the constitutional position of the five major religions of the island, namely the Christian Orthodox, the Islamic, the Roman Catholic, the Armenian and the Maronite faiths; the last three are considered collectively, since the main parameters of their legal status as 'religious groups' are identical. The subsequent part of the chapter analyses the typology of the Cypriot legal system as it touches religion. It is argued that the Constitution has introduced a pluralistic system of coordination between the Republic of Cyprus and the major religions and Christian creeds that is based upon the autonomy of religious organisations; the church and state model embraces the public dimension to religion, while attempting cooperation with religious communities. An assessment of the principles governing religious freedom in Cyprus on the basis of Article 18 of the Constitution is carried out in the fourth part of the chapter; the relevant constitutional provisions and leading case law are analysed with respect to individual, collective and organisational religious freedom. Finally, the Conclusion discusses certain of the challenges that the Cypriot model has to address in order to truly justify its pronounced pluralistic character.[1]

2. THE CONSTITUTIONAL POSITION OF MAJOR RELIGIONS

The Constitutional Position of the Orthodox Church

According to Article 110(1) of the Constitution, the Autocephalous Greek Orthodox Church of Cyprus shall continue to have the exclusive right of regulating and administering its own internal affairs and property in accordance with the Holy Canons and its Charter in force for the time being. It is further provided that the Greek Communal Chamber shall not act inconsistently with this right of the Orthodox Church.[2] Following the bi-communal violence that broke out in Cyprus in December 1963, the Greek Communal Chamber dissolved itself in 1965 and its competences were transferred under Law 12/1965 to the House of Representatives, the Council of Ministers, or the Ministry of Education and Culture. It should be accepted that none of the state organs to which the competences of the Greek Communal Chamber were transferred under Law 12/1965 may act inconsistently with the exclusive right of the Orthodox Church to regulate and administer its internal affairs and property. Article 110 therefore confirms that the state may not interfere in the internal affairs of the Orthodox Church.[3]

Moreover, Article 111 of the Constitution provides certain privileges

---

[1]   This chapter draws and expands upon research work previously published by the author in the form of journal articles and his recent book *Religion and Law in Cyprus* (Kluwer, 2011).

[2]   The Constitution provided for two Communal Chambers: a Greek and a Turkish Communal Chamber, which have legislative power in educational, cultural, religious and other matters of a purely communal nature.

[3]   See A Emilianides, 'The constitutional position of the Charter of the Church of Cyprus', [2005] 2 *Nomokanonika* 41 (in Greek).

for the Orthodox Church, with respect to the adjudication of issues relating to marriage and divorce of members of the Greek Orthodox Church. Prior to the First Amendment of the Constitution in 1989, Article 111 provided that family law matters should continue to be governed by the law of the Orthodox Church and be cognisable by the ecclesiastical courts of that church.[4] Following the First Amendment, however, all family law matters for members of the Orthodox Church came under the jurisdiction of the Family Courts and the (family) ecclesiastical courts were abolished; further, only issues relating to betrothal or ecclesiastical marriage, or nullity of ecclesiastical marriage, have continued to be governed by the canon law of the Orthodox Church since 1989.[5]

Article 110(1) establishes the right of the Orthodox Church to regulate and administer its own internal affairs and property, and stipulates that this right shall be exercised 'in accordance with the Holy Canons and its Charter in force for the time being'. For this purpose, the Holy Canons are not primarily those that relate to Church doctrine; doctrinal rules of all religions are safeguarded by Article 18 of the Constitution, which provides for the free exercise of religion, and therefore no special provision was needed. The aim of Article 110 is rather to safeguard the application of those canons that refer to the administration of the Church's internal affairs and property. In addition to the Holy Canons, the Constitution also refers to the Charter of the Church of Cyprus. The relevant provisions of the Charter in force are only safeguarded to the extent that they are not inconsistent with the Holy Canons, which are, thus, superior to the Orthodox Church's Charter.[6]

In the case of *The Holy Monastery of Mahairas*, the Supreme Court held, obiter, that the Charter does not have 'the status of a Law and is not superior to the laws of the State, in such a manner as to neutralise the effect of the Succession and Inheritance Law, Cap 195'.[7] It is suggested that the correct interpretation of this passage is simply that the Charter does not

---

[4] See G Serghides, *Internal and External Conflict of Laws in Regard to Family Relations in Cyprus* (Nicosia, 1988).

[5] See A Emilianides, *The Cypriot Law of Marriage and Divorce* (Sakkoulas, 2006) (in Greek). Following a lengthy period of resistance, the Orthodox Church eventually accepted the Constitutional amendment with the ratification of its new Charter on 13 September 2010.

[6] This was confirmed by the Major Synod convened in 1973 by then Archbishop, and President of the Republic, Makarios, with the participation of Patriarchs and Archbishops of other Orthodox churches. See C Tornaritis, *The Ecclesiastical Courts, Especially in Cyprus* (Nicosia, 1976) 30–31.

[7] *The Holy Monastery of Mahairas v Maria Papasavva* [2007] 1 CLR [Cyprus Law Reports] 436 (in Greek).

prevail over a law that does not concern the internal affairs or property of
the Church, such as the Succession Law, Cap 195 in the Laws of Cyprus,
1959 Edition; however, the Charter of the Orthodox Church should be
considered as prevailing over any legislation of the Republic of Cyprus, in
so far as it refers to matters that concern the internal affairs or the property
of the Church. A state law that regulates matters that fall within the ambit
of internal affairs (for example matters pertaining to the internal status of
the Holy Synod, the election of bishops, the ordination of clergymen or
the tonsure of monks), or property of the Orthodox Church, and that is
inconsistent with the provisions of the Charter of the Church in force at the
time, is therefore contrary to Article 110 of the Constitution.[8]

It should be further clarified that Articles 110 and 111 of the Constitution
refer to the Autocephalous Orthodox Church of Cyprus, which is in
communion with the Ecumenical Patriarchate and the other Orthodox
churches. The Cypriot Church of the Orthodox Christians who follow
the Old Calendar may not be considered as part of the Autocephalous
Orthodox Church of Cyprus,[9] to which the great majority of the population adheres, since it has its own separate administrative organisation,
with its own metropolises, bishops and priests, as well as its own charter,
which differs from the Charter of the Orthodox Church of Cyprus. Thus,
Orthodox Christians who follow the Old Calendar have opted to exercise
their constitutionally safeguarded rights and to separate themselves from
the Autocephalous Orthodox Church of Cyprus. In view of the above,
the church of those Orthodox Christians is not the church provided for in
Articles 110 and 111 of the Constitution and its position is not safeguarded
by express constitutional provisions.[10]

The Constitutional Position of Islam

Article 110(2) of the Constitution provides that all matters relating to or in
any way affecting the institution or foundation of *vakf* (a Muslim religious
or charitable foundation) or the *vakfs* or any *vakf* properties, including
properties belonging to mosques and any other Muslim religious institution, shall be governed solely by and under the laws and principles of *vakfs*

---

[8] Emilianides (note 3 above) 41.
[9] Namely Orthodox Christians who continue to adhere to the Old Julian
calendar, despite the fact that the Orthodox Church of Cyprus has adopted the
New Julian calendar, which mostly coincides with the Gregorian calendar. For
a detailed account see A Emilianides, *The Status of the Old-Calendar Church of
Cyprus* (Cyprus Institute of Church and State Relations, 2008) (in Greek).
[10] Ibid.

(*ahkamul evkaf*) and the laws and regulations enacted or made by the Turkish Communal Chamber. *Vakf* had a specific meaning at the time the Constitution came into operation. It denoted the entailing of a property itself (imposing an interdiction on its transfer) in such a manner that its benefit is given to men, on the condition that the property is to be regarded as the property of God. *Vakf* was thus the equivalent of 'dedication'. *Vakf* further denotes, however, the object of the dedication and not just the act. *Evkaf* is the plural of *vakf*, although *vakfs* may also be used.[11]

It is further provided that no legislative, executive or other act whatsoever shall contravene, override or interfere with the *ahkamul evkaf* and with related laws and regulations of the Turkish Communal Chamber. Article 110(2) of the Constitution thus safeguarded all matters relating to Muslim religious institutions, including *vakf* properties, or properties belonging to mosques, ensuring that they would be governed by the *ahkamul evkaf* and the laws and regulations enacted by the Turkish Communal Chamber. Thus, the autonomy of the Islamic religion with respect to its internal affairs and the administration of its property was provided for through provisions similar to those protecting the Orthodox Church and the three religious groups (see below).[12] The provision that not only the *ahkamul evkaf*, but also the laws and regulations enacted by the Turkish community would govern matters relating to *vakfs* or other Muslim religious institutions, was consistent with the recommendations of the Interim Committee of Turkish Affairs that had observed in its Report in 1949 that the system of administration of *vakfs* was in need of revision.[13] Thus, specific laws were enacted in order to revise the system.[14]

The state may not interfere with matters pertaining to the administration of *vakfs*, or *vakf* properties, or relating to other Muslim religious institutions. Thus, it is provided that neither the House of Representatives, nor the Council of Ministers, nor any other state organ, have competence

---

[11]   O Effendi, *The Laws of Evqaf* (2nd edn) (Nicosia, 1922); K Dizdar, 'The origin and administration of the Cyprus *evkaf*', in *Proceedings of the First International Cyprological Conference*, v II (Society for Cypriot Studies, 1973) 63.

[12]   A Emilianides, 'Islamic faith as one of the main religions: the case of Cyprus', in *Islam in Europe* (Slovak Institute for State–Church Relations, 2005) 220.

[13]   Cyprus Government Printing Office, *Interim Report of the Committee on Turkish Affairs: An Investigation into Matters Concerning and Affecting the Turkish Community in Cyprus* (Nicosia, 1949).

[14]   These are the Turkish Religious Head (Mufti) Law (Cap 340 of the Laws of Cyprus, 1959 edn), the *Vakfs* and *Evcaf* Law (Cap 337 of the Laws of Cyprus, 1959 edn, as amended by Law 60/1972) and the Establishment of a Department of *Vakfs* and Religious Matters Law of the Turkish Communal Chamber 57/1961.

in such matters. Any interference with *ahkamul evkaf,* and with related laws and regulations of the Turkish Communal Chamber, is invalid. The Constitution does not contain a provision similar to Article 111, granting Muslim religious institutions competence over the family relations of Muslims, in view of the radical amendments of the Turkish Cypriot institutions following the acceptance of the Kemalic reforms.[15]

The Constitutional Position of the Three 'Religious Groups'

A 'religious group' in the constitutional sense, according to Article 2(3) of the Constitution, is a group of persons, ordinarily resident in Cyprus, professing the same religion and either belonging to the same rite or subject to the same jurisdiction. The membership of such a group on the date the Constitution came into operation must have exceeded 1000, of whom at least 500 became citizens of the Republic on that date. This disparity between the required numbers of ordinary residents and citizens of the Republic stemmed from the fact that a great number of Roman Catholics and Armenians had retained British citizenship after the Constitution came into force.

The constitutionally recognised religious groups are the Armenians,[16] the Maronites and the Roman Catholics (Latins).[17] There is no future scope to constitutionally recognise new religious groups, even if such groups were to meet the numerical criteria provided for in Article 2(3) of the Constitution; nor is it possible to remove the constitutional status of a religious group from any of the three 'religious groups', even if the number of their members who reside in Cyprus, or are citizens of the Republic, falls below the numbers set out in Article 2(3).

According to that article, religious groups were required to opt to belong either to the Greek or to the Turkish community within three months of the Constitution coming into operation. All three religious groups opted collectively to belong to the Greek community and now reside in the unoccupied territories, with the exception of about 100 Maronites residing in Kormakitis. The Constitution further provides that any individual member of a religious group may choose not to abide by the option of

---

[15] A Emilianides, 'Private international law in Cyprus', in *Symposium on Cypriot Legal Issues* (Aristotle University, 1974) 91 (in Greek).

[16] See A Emilianides, *The Status of the Armenian Church of Cyprus* (Cyprus Institute of Church and State Relations, 2006) (in Greek).

[17] See A Emilianides, 'The legal status of the Latin community of Cyprus', in A Varnava, N Coureas and M Elia, *Minorities of Cyprus* (Cambridge Scholars Publishing, 2009) 229.

such group and, by a written and signed declaration, to opt to belong to a community other than that to which the main group is deemed to belong. However, all individual members of the three religious groups accepted the choice of their group.

The only criteria that *state* law may apply (ecclesiastical law is different), in order to specify whether a person should be considered as a member of a 'religious group', are whether such person is a citizen of the Republic and whether he/she resides ordinarily in Cyprus.[18] These criteria are contained in the definition of religious groups in Article 2(3). Accordingly, it was held in *Achcar v Saad* that a person may not belong to a 'religious group' if that person is not ordinarily resident in Cyprus.[19] Further, a person may not be considered to belong to the Greek community unless that person is a citizen of the Republic, since members of the Greek and the Turkish community are, by definition, citizens of the Republic of Cyprus.

According to Article 110(3) of the Constitution the three 'religious groups' shall continue to have every right with respect to religious matters that they had before the Constitution came into force. Furthermore, prior to the First Amendment in 1989, Article 111 of the Constitution had provided that family law matters would be governed by the law of the respective 'religious group' and would be cognisable by the ecclesiastical courts of that religious group. Following the First Amendment, family law matters of members of the 'religious groups' came under the jurisdiction of the Family Courts of Religious Groups; only issues relating to betrothal, or ecclesiastical marriage or nullity, continued to be governed by the canon law of the religious groups after 1989.[20] The family courts of the religious groups are composed of three judges in divorce proceedings and one judge in any other trial. Of particular interest is the establishment of the three-member family court in divorce proceedings; it is provided that the chair and one of the two members are appointed by the Supreme Court, while the other judge is a member of the religious group to which the parties belong to and is proposed by the representative of that religious group in the House of Representatives.[21]

It is obvious that the provisions of Articles 110(3) and 111 of the

---

18   Emilianides (note 5 above) 173ff.
19   *Achcar v Saad* [1979] 1 CLR 627 (in Greek).
20   Emilianides (note 5 above).
21   In practice the Maronite and Roman Catholic groups do not recognise the jurisdiction of their respective family courts and thus do not propose a judge. Conversely, the Armenian group recognises the jurisdiction of the Armenian Family Court and proposes an Armenian judge to represent their group on the bench of that family court.

Constitution as applied to 'religious groups' correspond to the relevant provisions of Articles 110(1) and 111 as applied to the Orthodox Church. While Article 110(1) of the Constitution is more detailed than Article 110(3), this is only because Orthodox Christianity is the religion of the great majority of the population, and so it was considered necessary that the extent of its competences be defined with greater clarity. However, this does not signify any difference in treatment between the Orthodox Church on one hand and the three 'religious groups' on the other.[22] Article 110(3) maintains the rights that the 'religious groups' had enjoyed prior to independence. These rights correspond to those of the Orthodox Church and relate to the religious groups' internal affairs and the administration of their property.

While, unlike Article 110(1), Article 110(3) does not prevent the Greek Communal Chamber from interfering in the rights of the 'religious groups', it is suggested that this is heavily implied.[23] Thus, when applying the competences transferred to it by the Greek Communal Chamber, the House of Representatives is not entitled to interfere in issues relating to the internal affairs of the religious groups, or the administration of their property.

Furthermore, under Article 109 of the Constitution each religious group had the right to elect member(s) to the chamber of the community into which such group has opted, as provided by a relevant communal law. This specific right of the three religious groups was additional to the right of electing and being elected to the House of Representatives. Following the self-dissolution of the Greek Communal Chamber, it was provided that, in addition to their individual right to stand and vote in parliamentary elections as citizens, the members of the three 'religious groups' elect one representative of each 'religious group' to represent their group in the House of Representatives. These representatives have the right to speak in the House of Representatives on all matters that concern their group, but do not have the right to vote; their remuneration and other benefits are equivalent to those of regular members of the House of Representatives.[24]

---

[22]   A Emilianides, 'The constitutional framework of the relations between church and state in the Republic of Cyprus', (2006) 1 *Nomokanonika* 46–7 (in Greek).

[23]   See also C Tornaritis, 'The legal position of the Armenian religious group', in C Tornaritis, *Constitutional and Legal Problems in the Republic of Cyprus* (2nd edn) (Nicosia, 1972) 90.

[24]   Emilianides (note 22 above) 70–71.

3.   NATURE OF CHURCH–STATE RELATIONS

It has been suggested that the constitutional protection of the Orthodox Church is wider than the respective protection of the three 'religious groups'; it has further been suggested that the relations between the Orthodox Church and the state in Cyprus are governed, as they are in Greece, by the 'State-law rule',[25] 'even if the control of the Church by the State is limited'.[26] These views are hardly convincing and have to be rejected. Despite the different terminology used, the aim of the Constitution is to treat the five major religions in an equal manner and not to distinguish between them. The Orthodox Church, the three religious groups and the Islamic religion all enjoy exclusive competence in their internal affairs, as well as over the administration of their property. Such autonomy derives from the legal regime that existed prior to independence, since the Constitution has not created a new internal legal regime for the various religions in Cyprus, but has maintained, essentially, the provisions of the Ottoman law.

Such similarity in treatment is also evident in the provisions of Article 23 of the Constitution that safeguards the right to property. Article 23(9) stipulates that no deprivation, restriction or limitation on the right to acquire, own, possess, enjoy or dispose of any movable or immovable property, belonging to any see, monastery, church or any other ecclesiastical corporation, nor any right over it or interest therein, shall be granted, except with the written consent of the appropriate ecclesiastical authority being in control of such property. The same right is accorded to all Muslim religious institutions. Under Article 23(10), no such deprivation, restriction or limitation may be imposed on the immovable or movable property of any *vakf*, except with the approval of the Turkish Communal Chamber and subject to *ahkamul evkaf*. Such property includes the objects and subjects of the *vakfs* and properties belonging to mosques or to any other Muslim religious institutions, or any right thereon or interest therein.

Certainly, the Orthodox Christian and the Islamic religions constitute one of the criteria for the bi-communal character of the Republic of Cyprus, since Article 2 of the Constitution provides that the Greek community comprises, *inter alia*, all citizens of the Republic who are members of the Greek Orthodox Church, while the Turkish community comprises,

---

[25]   Under which the Orthodox Church is a public body and the state legislates its Charter and internal organisation.

[26]   C Tornaritis, 'The constitutional position of the Autocephalous Greek Orthodox Church in the Republic of Cyprus' (1990) 4 *Cyprus Law Tribune* 485 (in Greek).

inter alia, all citizens of the Republic who are Muslims. This peculiarity does not, however, signify the recognition of a special status for either the Orthodox Church or Islam at the expense of the other religions;[27] such was simply a method of distinguishing between members of the Greek and the Turkish communities, with no further implications for the status of either religion.[28]

An analysis of the constitutional provisions shows that no single religion or creed is established as the official religion. As a result there is no prevailing, established or state religion in Cyprus. All religions and creeds in Cyprus deal with their own affairs exclusively, without in any way interfering in the affairs of the state. However, the five main religions of the Republic enjoy a special constitutional status. The state has recognised broad discretionary powers in their favour and does not have the right to intervene in their internal affairs, or in the administration of their property. Whenever matters of common interest arise, such as religious education, the state and the religious corporations debate in order to reach a common solution. If, however, this is not possible, the state may reach any decision, so long as it does not interfere in the internal affairs or the administration of the property of the constitutionally protected religions.[29]

It is further observed that the state is not confessional. Thus, when assuming their duties, state officials are not sworn in, but affirm their allegiance to, and respect for the Constitution and the laws made thereunder, and the preservation of the independence and territorial integrity of the Republic of Cyprus, pursuant to Articles 42(1), 59(4), 69 and 100 of the Constitution (with respect to the President of the Republic, the Ministers, the Representatives, and the members of the Communal Chambers, respectively). Accordingly, state officials do not have to profess any particular religion, nor even that a God exists, in order to be elected, or appointed. Their only required allegiance is towards the Constitution and the laws made thereunder.

In view of the above, it is suggested that the Constitution has introduced a system of coordination between the Republic of Cyprus and the major religions and Christian creeds.[30] Such a system differs substantially from the

---

[27]   As suggested by C Tornaritis, 'The relations between church and state according to Cypriot Law' (1967) 1 *Review of Public and Private Law* 15 (in Greek).

[28]   See C Papastathis, *On the Administrative Organisation of the Church of Cyprus* (Thessaloniki, 1981) 36–37.

[29]   See A Emilianides, 'State and church in Cyprus', in G Robbers (ed), *State and Church in the European Union* (Nomos Verlagsgesellschaft, 2005) 237; A Emilianides, 'Law and religion in Cyprus' (2008) 20 *Kanon* 7.

[30]   Emilianides (note 22 above) 37ff; Papastathis (note 28 above) 34.

'State-law rule' prevailing in Greece, since it is based upon the autonomy of religious organisations that are distinct from the state and deal exclusively with their own affairs. It further differs from the separation system, since the state has recognised broad discretionary powers with regard to the main religions' internal affairs, administration of their property, family matters, and in general matters of communal character. The model prevailing in Cyprus is essentially a pluralistic one, which recognises and embraces the public dimension to religion, while at the same time attempting cooperation with all religions. The significance of faith in people's lives is considered as worthy of protection by the state and, where its functions overlap with religious concerns, the state seeks to accommodate religious views in so far as they are not inconsistent with its interests.[31]

In consequence, pluralism is achieved through recognition that the state and the various religions occupy in principle different societal structures; religious neutrality is not, however, achieved simply because there is religious autonomy, but also through positive measures on behalf of the state, which aim at the protection of religions. Members of other religions and rites, such as Jews, Jehovah's Witnesses, Buddhists, Protestants or the Orthodox Christians who follow the Old Calendar, enjoy religious freedom under Article 18 of the Constitution, and are equal before the law, so that no legislative, executive or administrative act should discriminate against them. However, such religions are not considered as religious groups in the constitutional sense and, therefore, do not enjoy the special constitutional status of the five main religions of the island. Differences in treatment between the five constitutionally recognised religions and other religions of the island principally occur in the areas of religious education, direct financing and family law.

4.   SECULARISM AND HUMAN RIGHTS

The Right of Religious Freedom

Article 18 of the Constitution safeguards the right of religious freedom, including freedom of religious conscience and freedom of worship.[32] This Article corresponds in many ways to Article 9 of the European Convention

---

[31]   For pluralistic models in general see J Rivers, 'Irretrievable breakdown? Disestablishment and the Church of England', (1994) 3(4) *Cambridge Papers* 3.

[32]   C Tornaritis, *The State Law of the Republic of Cyprus* (Cyprus Research Centre, 1982) 145–8 (in Greek).

on Human Rights (ECHR), but it is more detailed, while its provisions cover sectors that are not recorded in Article 9. Article 18(1) provides that every person has the right to freedom of thought, conscience and religion. This right is far-reaching and profound. Freedom of thought, conscience and religion are safeguarded for any person, either a believer or an atheist, a citizen or a non-citizen of the Republic. Thus conscience and religion are not confined to belief in the relation of a human being to a Creator. Religion or conviction refers to theistic, non-theistic and atheistic convictions. It includes convictions such as agnosticism, free-thinking, pacifism, atheism and rationalism. It is, therefore, not limited in its application to traditional religions or to religions and beliefs with institutional characteristics or practices analogous to traditional religions.[33] Until a person attains the age of 16, the decision as to the religion to be professed is taken by his/her lawful guardian under Article 18(7) of the Constitution.

The Supreme Court has specified that Article 18 safeguards religious liberty, which is not to be confused with religious tolerance. It was held that:

> Tolerance as a legal concept is premised on the assumption that the State has ultimate control over religion and the churches, and whether and to what extent religious freedom will be granted and protected is a matter of state policy. The right of religious liberty is a fundamental right. The days that oppressive measures were adopted and cruelties and punishments inflicted by Governments in Europe and elsewhere for many ages, to compel parties to conform in their religious beliefs and modes of worship to the views of the most numerous sect, and the folly of attempting in that way to control the mental operations of persons and enforce an outward conformity to a prescribed standard, have gone. Mankind has advanced and the right to freedom of thought, conscience and religion is now a fundamental right.[34]

Article 18(4) guarantees the more particular manifestation of an individual's religious freedom, stipulating that every person is free and has the right to profess a faith and to manifest a religion or belief, in worship, teaching, practice or observance, either individually or collectively, in private or in public, and to change their religion or belief. While religious freedom is primarily a matter of individual conscience, it also implies the freedom to manifest one's religion, since such freedom is intrinsically linked with the very existence of religious convictions.[35] The term 'worship' embraces, but is not confined to, institutional forms of worship; it extends to ritual

---

[33] *Pitsillides v The Republic* [1983] 2 CLR 374 (in Greek).
[34] Ibid.
[35] *Kokkinakis v Greece* (App no 14307/88) (ECtHR, 25 May 1993); (1994) 17 EHRR 397.

and ceremonial acts giving direct expression to belief, as well as practices integral to such acts, including the building of places of worship, the use of ritual objects, the display of symbols and the observance of holidays and days of rest. The observance and practice of religion may include such customs as the observance of dietary regulations, the wearing of distinctive clothing or headcoverings, participation in rituals, and the use of particular language customarily spoken by a group.

Freedom to manifest one's religion entails the right to exercise religious activities in public, as well as trying to convince others, through teaching, to change their religion or belief. Further a person may establish and maintain communication with individuals and communities in matters of religion or belief at a national or international level. Any person may write, issue and disseminate texts or publications in order to manifest their religious beliefs and may teach such religious beliefs to others, and train, appoint, elect or designate by succession appropriate leaders called for by the requirements and standards of their religion, establish seminaries or religious schools.

The constitutional right to religious freedom further includes the negative aspects of that right, namely the right not to disclose one's religion. This was accepted by the Supreme Court in an obiter dictum in the case of *Elia*, where it was held that revealing in official documents the religion of a candidate for a position in the public service should be avoided in view of Article 18 of the Constitution. Thus, it was held that the fact that the official documents referred to the applicant as a Maronite was strictly prohibited by the Constitution.[36] While these comments of the Supreme Court were only obiter, it is considered that they accurately reflect the position under Article 18 of the Constitution; a person has therefore a constitutional right not to disclose their religion.

In a subsequent case before the Supreme Court, *Panayiotou*, it was held that while the simple fact that the candidate was referred to in an official document by the Public Service Commission as a Maronite did not constitute by itself discrimination on grounds of religion, such references in official documents ought in principle to be avoided, because they might cause suspicion of religious discrimination or inequality.[37] As a general rule, religion is not referred to in Cypriot official documents, such as passports or identity cards. Further, the application form for appointment or promotion in the civil service no longer requires information about the candidate's religion.[38]

---

[36]   *Elia v The Republic* [1985] 3 CLR 38 (in Greek).
[37]   *Panayiotou v The Republic* [1991] 3 CLR 1837 (in Greek).
[38]   Second Report Submitted by Cyprus pursuant to Article 25, paragraph 1 of

Clashes between Positive Law and Religious Practices

Interference with the right to religious freedom is in principle prohibited, irrespective of whether such interference is direct or indirect. No limitations whatsoever are permitted on the freedom of thought or conscience, or on the freedom to have or adopt a religion or belief of one's choice; such freedoms are protected unconditionally and are considered to be absolute. However, the freedom to manifest one's religion can be restricted, by virtue of Article 18(6), so long as such limitations are prescribed by law and are necessary in the interests of a) the security of the Republic, b) constitutional order, c) public safety, d) public order, e) public health, f) public morals or g) the protection of the rights and liberties guaranteed to every person by the Constitution. In view of the above, two general principles may be accepted: there has to be a legal basis for any interference with the fundamental right to religious freedom; and a restriction has to be prescribed by law, in accordance with the national law. Any such law must be adequately accessible and sufficiently precise, and must have been enacted by the appropriate organ. The interference has to be necessary for one of the constitutionally specified legitimate aims; a limitation that has been prescribed by law in order to facilitate interests other than those explicitly referred to in Article 18(6) of the Constitution shall not be considered legitimate.

In addition to the conditions mentioned above, any limitation on the freedom to manifest one's religion must be considered to be necessary in a democratic society, under the mandate of Article 9(2) ECHR, and this has been readily accepted by the Cypriot courts. Establishing that the measure is necessary in a democratic society involves showing that the action taken is in response to a pressing social need and that the interference with the rights protected is no greater than is necessary to address that need. Consequently, a test of proportionality should be applied. Any restrictions, furthermore, should not discriminate among religions. Thus, in certain cases the manifestation of religious freedom may be subject to limitations, in order to preserve social rights, as well as the rights of others.

Clashes between positive law and religious practices are not unusual. If the law is based upon a particular system of values, such as secularism, there could be circumstances under which the law requires to be done what the religion prohibits, and vice versa. Certain religions permit, or require, polygamy, religious divorces, marriage before the state legal age, some forms of animal slaughter or sacrifice, wearing a turban or a headscarf

---

the Framework Convention for the Protection of National Minorities, 27 October 2006, para 39.

or religious use of drugs, practices that might be contrary to the existing positive law in a specific European country. Other religions prohibit blood transfusion, military service, compulsory animal sacrifice, or compulsory wearing of crash helmets, contrary to what might be legally required. Certain religions argue that the observance of some Christian holy days amounts to religious discrimination; others argue that the obligation of children to attend schools violates their religious beliefs.

It could be argued that the general principle so far accepted in Cyprus, with respect to clashes between law and religion, is that religious freedom does not necessarily imply that religious practices that are contrary to what is prescribed by law shall be upheld. Furthermore, despite the fact that all religions are considered equal before the law, socially Cyprus constitutes a European and therefore a predominantly Christian civilisation. While there have been few cases concerning new religious movements, probably owing to the fact that the number of adherents to such religious movements in Cyprus is too low, it is far-fetched to expect that a court might recognise that there should be a religious exemption for drug use, or that members of a particular religion could be excluded from compulsory schooling on grounds of religious belief. State interests are normally expected to prevail over religious interests, unless reasons why religious interests ought to exclude the application of state legal provisions can be justified.

Organisational and Collective Religious Freedom

Article 18(2) of the Constitution provides that all religions whose doctrines or rites are not secret are free. For a religion to be constitutionally protected, it need not register with the authorities; the only requirement is that its doctrines or rites are not secret. There has been, so far, no court decision, or any other attempt to define religion in Cypriot law. In principle, however, not only mainstream religions, such as Christian denominations of many kinds, Jehovah's Witnesses, Judaism, Islam, Hinduism, Buddhism and Sikhism, but also less known religions, or new religious movements, ought to constitute religions for the purposes of Article 18(2), so long as their doctrines or rites are free. A sect, or a specific religious creed, may well be considered as a religion in the constitutional sense. The assessment of whether a particular creed forms a religion excludes any assessment by the state of the legitimacy of its beliefs or the ways in which such beliefs are expressed.[39]

---

[39] *Metropolitan Church of Bessarabia v Moldova* (App no 45710/99) (ECtHR, 13 December 2001); (2002) 35 EHRR 306.

What is more, Article 18(3) provides that all religions are equal before the law and no legislative, executive or administrative act of the Republic shall discriminate against any religious institution or religion. There should in principle be no discrimination between newly established religions, or religions that represent religious minorities. The leading case on discrimination between religions is *The Jehovah's Witnesses Congregation (Cyprus) Ltd.*[40] The Minister of the Interior had decided to omit members of the Jehovah's Witnesses from the annual list of officers authorised to conclude marriages, on the ground that officers of that congregation had ceased to be considered as such following the enactment of Civil Marriage Law 21/90. The Supreme Court held that, under Article 18 of the Constitution, freedom of religion should not be violated, either directly or indirectly, and that all religions whose rites are known are equal before the law. It further held that Law 21/90 should not have been interpreted in the manner adopted by the Minister of the Interior. Accordingly, it was held that members of the Jehovah's Witnesses should not have been omitted from the list of officers authorised to conclude marriages.

Were the organisational life of a religious community not protected by Article 18, 'all other aspects of the individual's freedom of religion would become vulnerable'.[41] A legal person that constitutes a religious organisation is capable of having or exercising the rights mentioned in Article 18. While a religious association is not capable of exercising the right of freedom of conscience, since this would be a metaphysical impossibility, such an association is capable of exercising the right to manifest its religion. The right of a religious community to religious freedom complements the individual right to religious freedom of the members of such community, so that non-discrimination against religious communities may be affected; equality of religions necessarily implies that a religious community enjoys certain rights as such, in addition to the rights of its members.

As already stated the administrative organisation of the five main religions of the island is explicitly safeguarded in Article 110 of the Constitution. This should not mean that other religions do not enjoy, to their full extent, all the freedoms safeguarded by Article 18. In the case of *Ktimatiki Eteria Neas Taxeos* the officers of the applicant company were Jehovah's Witnesses.[42] The applicants applied for a building permit

---

[40] *The Minister of the Interior v The Jehovah's Witnesses Congregation (Cyprus) Ltd* [1995] 3 CLR 78 (in Greek).

[41] *Hasan and Chaush v Bulgaria* (App no 30985/96) (ECtHR 26 October 2000), (2002) 34 EHRR 1339 (GC).

[42] *Ktimatiki Eteria Neas Taxeos v The Chairman and Members of the Municipal Committee of Limassol* [1989] 3 CLR 461 (in Greek).

to erect a two-storey building in part of Zakaki. The respondents refused the permit, without disclosing the real reasons for doing so. The applicants impugned the decision by which the permit was refused. During the proceedings it became apparent that the real reason for the refusal was public order or safety, because of the opposition of the Orthodox Church and the inhabitants of Zakaki to a building belonging to the Jehovah's Witnesses in their area. The Supreme Court annulled the lower court's decision and held that reasons for denying the right of a person or group to manifest their religion or belief can only be limited by law, according to Article 18 of the Constitution and Article 9 ECHR; an administrative organ cannot by itself refuse an application submitted to it on such grounds. Thus, the right to manifest one's religion applies not just to individuals, but also to churches and other religious communities; any restriction of that right should be in accordance with the law, should meet one of the specified legitimate aims and should be necessary in a democratic society; any interference will be unconstitutional if it is not proportionate to the pressing social need that it addresses.[43]

However, only activities of a religious organisation that refer to the exercise of their religious freedom are safeguarded by Article 18 of the Constitution; other activities are not. In the case of *Church of Nazarene International Ltd*, the petitioners argued that the state should not have refused to grant them a permit to buy offices in Cyprus, because that ran contrary to the principle of religious liberty enshrined in Article 18 of the Constitution and Article 9 ECHR.[44] The court acknowledged that the administration cannot hinder, directly or indirectly, the exercise of religious freedom, but held that in the circumstances of that particular case, there had been no violation of Article 18 of the Constitution. This was due to the fact that the petitioners had asked for a permit to buy offices in Cyprus for residence purposes, or vacation purposes, and not for any purpose directly or indirectly related to the exercise of religious freedom. Thus, Article 18 of the Constitution was deemed not to be applicable in the aforementioned case.

---

[43]   A Emilianides, 'The application of the freedom of religion principles of the European Convention on Human Rights in Cyprus', in A Emilianides (ed), *The Application of the Freedom of Religion Principles of the European Convention on Human Rights in the European Union* (Peeters, 2011).

[44]   *Church of the Nazarene International Ltd v Minister of Interior* [1996] 3 CLR 3091 (in Greek).

5. CONCLUSION: THE CHALLENGES OF A PLURALISTIC SYSTEM

A pluralistic system that intends to promote religions equally, while at the same time maintaining its secular character, is confronted with various legal challenges. Despite pronounced legal equality, the fact remains that 82 per cent of the population of Cyprus are Orthodox Christians and 13 per cent Muslims − most of whom currently reside in the occupied areas. Religion, and particularly the Orthodox Church, has a central role in civil society, and in the economy and culture of the island. The Archbishop's standing, as the leader of the Orthodox Church, is unlike that of any of his counterparts in other religious communities and rivals, in stature and importance, that of the President of the Republic. This social reality often challenges the lofty constitutional declarations about the intended equal standing of all religions before the law. Three challenges will be briefly referred to here and they relate to the areas of education, financing and the allocation of space.

In the field of education, religious lessons given in primary and secondary schools follow the doctrine of the Eastern Orthodox Church. Attendance is compulsory for Orthodox pupils; atheists or members of other religions, however, may be excused. In the 1996 Curriculum of the Ministry of Education and Culture, the subject of religious education appears under the title 'Christian Orthodox Education' and it is provided that the aim of the lesson is to enable students to realise that they are members of the Christian Orthodox Church, to learn the fundamental truths of Christianity and to experience a loving relationship with God.[45]

There is no possibility of religious education for members of other religions in public schools, with the exception of Maronites and Turkish Cypriots who have a sufficient number of pupils and combine both ethnic and religious characteristics. The fact that the state cannot offer religious education appropriate for every single individual religion or creed is not of course surprising; the great majority of pupils in non-Turkish public schools adhere to the Orthodox Christian religion and so it would be practically infeasible for the state to provide religious education that would meet the demands of all parents. This is why the state has opted to assist children belonging to religious groups to attend private schools of their choice, if

---

[45] Ministry of Education, *The National Curriculum of Cyprus* (Nicosia, 1996) 128 (in Greek). See also A Tapakis, *Religious Education in Primary and Pre-Primary Schools: A Guidebook for Primary and Pre-Primary School Teachers* (Holy Monastery of Kykkos, 2003) (in Greek).

they so desire, and, further, why pupils who are not Orthodox Christian may request to be exempted from religious education, including collective worship. However, in a predominantly Orthodox society, revealing one's religious beliefs for the purpose of exemption from religious education might also lead to discrimination. The exercise of the right to opt out of religious activities might entail significant discomfort or embarrassment for the students, or entrench religious differences at an early stage of the students' lives.

As far as funding is concerned, the Republic of Cyprus does not provide funding to religions per se. Significant assistance, however, is provided to religious communities through payment of salaries of the parish clergy in rural areas, the construction, or repair of their churches, monasteries and cemeteries, and for other religious purposes in the form of state aid. It should be observed that such state aid is provided by the central government and is in practice provided only to the five major religious communities and not to other religious organisations.[46] The question arises: should the state also fund other religions, or rites, such as the Jews, the Protestants or the Buddhists? Although such cases have not yet occurred since the number of adherents to such religions is small, it is quite possible that in the near future one of these religious communities might also apply to the government for financing. It is suggested that, although there is a distinction in the Constitution between the five main religious communities of the Republic, the government ought to assist other religious communities as well, to assist them to freely exercise their religious beliefs within the boundaries of the Republic.[47]

With respect to the allocation of space, the situation of two differing religious communities claiming use of the same sacred space has recently arisen with the established Sunni Muslims and the less established Shia Muslims claiming use of the Omeriye Mosque in Nicosia. As noted in the case of *Serif v Greece*, tension between competing religious groups is an unavoidable consequence of pluralism.[48] The role of Cypriot authorities in such a situation should not be to remove the cause of the tension, thereby eliminating pluralism, but instead to ensure tolerance and respect between the rival factions.[49]

---

[46]   See Report submitted by Cyprus pursuant to Article 25, paragraph 1 of the Framework Convention for the Protection of National Minorities, 1 March 1999, Part II, Article 5 D 11.

[47]   See A Emilianides, 'Il finanziamento delle cinque religioni: il caso Cipriota', (2006) 1 *Quaderni di Diritto e Politica Ecclesiastica* 123.

[48]   *Serif v Greece* (2001) 31 EHRR 561.

[49]   A Emilianides and others, 'Allocation of religious space in Cyprus', (2011)

Challenges such as those described above imply that achieving the right balance between secularism and promotion of religions, within a non-discriminatory pluralistic society, is not a theoretical exercise, but rather a highly practical one. It is only by putting the legal principles into actual practice and by taking into account the social realities in a never-ending quest for reform, that the Cypriot legal system might live up to its characterisation as 'pluralistic'.

---

23 *The Cyprus Review* 97.

10. The pendulum of church–state relations in Hungary

Renata Uitz*

1. INTRODUCTION

Freedom of religion or belief was not a particularly contentious issue in Hungary for the first two decades after the transition from Communism to democracy. Indeed, until the spring of 2011, it was a matter of less than moderate public concern. Unlike many countries in Western Europe, Hungary is not a primary target for immigration and asylum seekers, and it still does not have a very visible or sizeable Muslim community. In common with most other post-Communist EU member states, surveys found that Hungarians appeared not to regard religious discrimination as being a serious problem in Hungarian society.[1]

In the last population census of 2001, the majority of the population listed themselves as Roman Catholic (52 per cent), with the second largest segment being Calvinist Protestants (almost 16 per cent),[2] the third largest the Lutheran Protestants (or Evangelicals, as they are known in Hungary, with 3 per cent), with less than 1 per cent identifying as Jewish.[3] At the same

* Unless otherwise noted expressly, all translations from the Hungarian are mine.

[1] European Commission, 'Discrimination in the EU in 2009', Special Eurobarometer Survey 317, available at http://ec.europa.eu/public_opinion/archives/ebs/ebs_317_sum_en.pdf. In the same survey Hungarians perceived age and ethnicity-based discrimination as serious, and on these items the Hungarian discrimination perception index scored above the European average.

[2] In contemporary statutes Calvinists are referred to as 'Helvets', while Lutherans are mentioned as 'Augsburgians'. Contemporary Hungarian terminology mentions Calvinists as 'Reformed' Protestants, while Lutherans are 'Evangelicals'. My text keeps with 'Lutheran' and 'Calvinist' to the extent practicable, while 'Protestant' refers exclusively to 'old/traditional European' Reformation denominations.

[3] Census data from 2001 as available with the website of the Central Statistical Office (in English): http://www.nepszamlalas2001.hu/eng/volumes/18/tables/load2_38_1.html.

census, 15 per cent of the respondents declared that they did not belong
to a church, while 10 per cent refused to answer the question.[4] Religious
identification, admittedly, translates to less active religious participation in
Hungary than in other Central European democracies. In addition to the
two poles of practising religious believers and non-believers, in Hungarian
society there is also a significant layer of 'cultural Christians': those who
attend religious services less frequently and choose freely from religious
doctrine.[5] Lately a fourth group is emerging in the middle, for whom
emphasis is not on institutional religion but on belief in a personal God
and in the transmigration of souls.[6]

This chapter was written at a time of major constitutional and legislative change in Hungary. After winning a constitution-making majority
in the 2010 elections, the new conservative–Christian Democrat coalition
government adopted a new constitution in the spring of 2011, which was
quickly followed by a new legislative framework for church–state relations
in Hungary in the summer of 2011 (Act no 100 of 2011). For many this
fundamental change came as a major surprise, as religious liberty and
church–state relations had not been matters of dispute during the election campaign or in the preceding period. In early December 2011 it was
leaked in the press that the Constitutional Court was likely to invalidate
the statute for procedural improprieties in the legislative process. On 19
December 2011 the Constitutional Court did indeed find the new church
law unconstitutional for formal invalidity (164/2011 (XII 20) AB decision).
On the very same day, and before the decision of the Constitutional Court
was published in the *Official Journal*, Parliament withdrew the church law
in an amendment appended to the Act on National Minorities (Act no 179
of 2011, Article 241). Thus, the first Hungarian cardinal law never entered
into force.

A mere three days later, on 23 December 2011, Parliament held a debate
on a new church bill, and passed it into law, along with a corresponding amendment to the new constitution on 30 December 2011. This new
church law together with the freshly amended new constitution entered
into force on 1 January 2012. This law set conditions for the recognition of
religious communities as 'churches', and confirmed the legal status of 14

---

[4] For data protection reasons data of religious affiliation may only be collected with the consent (and upon the self-identification) of the respondent, in an
anonymous manner.

[5] Mónika Földvári, 'A vallásosság típusai a mai magyar társadalom gen-
erációiban' ('Modes of religiosity across generations in Hungarian society')
(2003/4) *Szociológiai Szemle* 20.

[6] Ibid, 29.

previously registered churches in its appendix. In late February 2012 this new church law was amended, as the church status of 18 more previously registered churches was confirmed by Parliament (Act no 7 of 2012). At the same time, Parliament refused to confirm the church status of 66 formerly registered churches in a resolution, without providing any reasons or explanation for the rejections (8/2012 (II 29) OGY resolution).

At the time of the adoption of the first church law of 2011, the individual right to freedom of religion and church–state relations were framed by the 'old' Constitution,[7] as well as the 1990 Act on freedom of conscience and religion.[8] In making registration open for all religious communities with 100 members or more (Article 9(1)(a)), the 1990 Hungarian law was among the most permissive of its kind, allowing for unprecedented religious diversity and opportunities for new faith-based initiatives. Over 300 churches had been registered in Hungary under this law during the first two decades of democracy.[9] Despite strong separationist language in the old Hungarian Constitution (Article 60(3)), and an easily accessible registration system, the Hungarian church–state regime of the first 20 years of transition to democracy is best described as cooperationist, with significant (mostly political and financial) advantages to the 'historic churches' over the 'small churches' – tags that are based on political distinctions beyond the neutral facade of the even-handed regulatory framework. At times this regime was also described as an example of 'active state neutrality'.[10]

On Easter Monday 2011, the President of the Republic signed into law a new Constitution for Hungary, which was adopted by a Parliament where a conservative–Christian coalition has held a more than 2/3 majority of the seats since the general elections of the spring of 2010. The new Hungarian Constitution (Fundamental Law) entered into force on 1 January 2012 and appears,[11] on its face, to bring little change to the existing church–state regime. The new Constitution continues to guarantee individual religious freedom (Article VII(1)), and also provides for the continued separation of church and state, proclaiming that the 'State and Churches shall be

---

[7] Act no 20 of 1949, available in an English translation on the website of the Hungarian Constitutional Court at http://mkab.hu/index.php?id=constitution.

[8] Act no 4 of 1990.

[9] US State Department, 'International Religious Freedom Report 2010 – Hungary', available at http://www.state.gov/g/drl/rls/irf/2010/148942.htm.

[10] Zsolt Enyedi, 'The contested politics of positive state neutrality in Hungary', (2003) 26(1) *West European Politics* 157.

[11] The English translation of the new Hungarian Constitution is available on the website of the Hungarian Parliament at http://www.kormany.hu/download/4/c3/30000/THE%20FUNDAMENTAL%20LAW%20OF%20HUNGARY.pdf.

separate. Churches shall be autonomous. The State shall cooperate with the Churches for community goals' (Article VII(2)). The express reference to 'cooperation for community goals' accounts for the status quo of the last 20 years.

There is a major change in tone, however. Unlike its predecessor, the new Constitution has several segments that read like an ode to Christianity. It proclaims in its introductory segment, entitled 'National Avowal', that '[w]e are proud that our king Saint Stephen built the Hungarian State on solid ground and made our country a part of Christian Europe one thousand years ago . . . [w]e recognise the role of Christianity in preserving nationhood. We value the various religious traditions of our country . . . [w]e promise to preserve the intellectual and spiritual unity of our nation torn apart in the storms of the last century' and '[w]e honour the achievements of our historical constitution and we honour the Holy Crown, which embodies the constitutional continuity of Hungary's statehood and the unity of the nation'. The extent to which such a strong attachment to Christianity will allow for the recognition of pluralism and tolerance in practice in a neutral fashion under the new Constitution remains unclear.

The amendment to the new Constitution that was added on 30 December 2011 authorises Parliament to determine 'recognised churches' (*elismert egyház*), and to specify conditions for the recognition of other churches, including the required length of operation, number of applicants and 'historical traditions and social support' (transitional provisions, Article 21(1)). The newest law, entitled 'on the right to freedom of conscience and religion, and the status of churches, religious congregations and religious communities' (Act no 206 of 2011), brought only minor changes compared to its immediate predecessor, the church law of July 2011 that never entered into force. Nonetheless, together with the amendment to the new Constitution, the latest church law creates a new regime for church–state relations or, to be more precise, re-creates a late-nineteenth-century state of affairs.

The new legal rules introduce a three-tier system of church registration. The top tier is acquired by 14 churches recognised *ex lege* in the appendix of the act, as 'recognised churches'. The list includes the Catholic Church, the Protestant Church (Calvinists), the Evangelical Church (Lutherans), three Jewish congregations, five Eastern Orthodox congregations, the Unitarians (Trinitarians), the Baptists and the Congregation of Faith. The middle range is acquired by churches to be registered by Parliament upon the request of at least 1000 persons [Article 14(3)], provided that the community has been present in Hungary for at least 20 years, or has been known internationally for at least 100 years (Article 14(2)(c)). The bottom tier is reserved for religious communities organised as associations.[12] With the exception of the 14 registered churches listed in the law, after a grace period all churches registered under the 1990 law are demoted to become associations (Article 34(1)). The associations, which meet statutory criteria, will need to seek re-registration with Parliament.

The new law emphasises the 'separate operation of state and church' (Article 8(1)) only to continue by emphasising that 'in order to achieve communal goals the state cooperates with the church' (Article 10(1)),[13] and adding that the state will take into account the 'actual social position' of churches in the future and in the course of their cooperation (Article 9(2)). This is a clear indication that equality in matters of religion is no more a cherished standard under Hungarian law: 'recognised churches' retain a constitutionally privileged status, while the language of the law saves state cooperation for churches, but not religious associations.

As past examples, as well as recent developments, indicate in Hungary, the status quo of peaceful church–state relations (and thus, indirectly, the scope of individual religious liberty)[14] depends not on the propensities of believers, but on political will. The need to adjust or improve any given regulatory framework does not seem to respond to a shortcoming in the law or a fundamental change in the religious scene,[15] but appears to follow – as if a pendulum – the gravity of the minute political aspirations of those in decision-making positions. Although historically Hungary probably does not differ from the rest of Europe in this respect, this is a disturbing continuum to observe in a constitutional democracy 20 years after transition.

This chapter will survey church–state relations in Hungary, reflecting on the dominant patterns of historical developments (part 2), the details of the most recent regulatory framework (part 3) and will, in closing,

---

[12] Associations are regulated by the Civil Code and act no 175 of 2011 on associations.

[13] Note that, unlike at other places, in this section the new law uses 'church' in the singular, and not 'churches' in the plural.

[14] On the intricate interconnections of individual freedom of religion and church–state relations in the transition context, and beyond, see W Cole Durham, 'Perspectives on religious liberty: a comparative framework', in Johann van der Vyver and John Witte (eds), *Religious Human Rights in Global Perspective: Legal Perspectives* (Kluwer, 1996).

[15] See for example Balázs Schanda, 'Stabilitás és bizonytalanság a magyar állami egyházjogban, Húsz évvel az 1990 évi IV törvény után' (Stability and uncertainty in Hungarian church regulation, Twenty years after Act no 4 of 1990), (2010) January *Jogtudományi Közlöny* 3, arguing that the current regime is not in need of a major overhaul.

discuss reservations concerning the new regulatory framework in the light of its evolution (part 4). The chapter argues that the new regime not only introduces a retrograde regulatory scheme, but also endangers the rights of unpopular and non-mainstream religious communities – an intended consequence that is at least doubtful in terms of prevailing human rights standards. Political nostalgia of the kind infused into legal regulation is most uncivilised in a community of nations built on principles of democracy, pluralism and tolerance, to borrow key terms from the relevant jurisprudence of the European Court of Human Rights.

2. HISTORICAL BACKGROUND: TOWARDS AND AWAY FROM TOLERATION

The pendulum of church–state relations is not unique to the post-Communist period in Hungary. It turns out to be a basic characteristic of church–state interaction ever since the Reformation, with the privileged position of the Catholic Church marking the pivot. This section does not intend to provide a comprehensive history of church–state relations in Hungary, but simply aims to highlight the formative forces behind a pattern of interaction that seems to be characteristic of the development of the relevant legal framework, and some underlying (if outdated) concepts.

Hungary has long-established ties with the Roman Catholic Church, going back to its foundation as an independent state and the coronation of its first monarch, István, who is also a saint for the Catholic Church alongside another early Hungarian king of the Árpád dynasty, László. According to (contested) tradition, the Holy Crown that was used to crown the pagan grand prince of the Carpathian basin, István (known by his former pagan name, as Vajk), as a Christian monarch was sent by Pope Sylvester II with the consent of the Holy Roman Emperor, Otto III. Following the solidification of the monarchy (and the rule of primogeniture) the rule of Catholic monarchs – who since 1526 belonged to the Habsburg family, which also provided the emperors of the Holy Roman Empire – was not seriously challenged until the Reformation. In cycles of struggle between Catholics and Protestants, periods of open violence were followed by periods of relative peace and toleration. In the midst of these struggles the Catholic Church preserved a privileged position for the longest period of time, as a key component in a well-embedded Habsburg state ideology.[16] Importantly, the principality of remote Transylvania and its grand dukes had a key

---

[16]   On this aspect see recently Marie-Elizabeth Ducreux, 'Emperors, kingdoms,

role in strengthening the position of Protestants in Hungary *vis-à-vis* the Habsburg court in Vienna.[17]

It is a little known fact that, following the peace of Augsburg of 1555, in 1568 – following a brief period of anti-Catholicism[18] – the Diet (Parliament) of Torda in Transylvania was the first in Europe to declare the equality of 'all four accepted denominations' (that is, Lutheran, Calvinist and Anti-Trinitarian (Unitarian)[19] in addition to Roman Catholic), under the rule of Grand Duke John Sigismund.[20] Toleration meant the equality of the four denominations and not the domination of the grand duke's personal religion: each community in a city and village could pick its religion, and dissidents were free to move away. The Declaration of Torda guaranteed both freedom from religious coercion for all, and the freedom for preachers to follow their own creed in their sermons.

Transylvania was not an unlikely place to proclaim toleration, as it is located at the boundary of Eastern and Western Christianity, and was also reached by all waves of the Reformation, and – primarily among its German inhabitants – had a strong Protestant aristocracy alongside its Catholic elite. In addition to the ethnic and religious diversity of Transylvania, one cannot ignore the fact that Grand Duke John Sigismund himself converted first to the Lutheran strain of Protestantism, then became a Calvinist and later joined the Anti-Trinitarians, while his wife, Isabella, remained a Roman Catholic.

The wave of religious toleration reached mainland Hungary after a local armed conflict (the Bocskai uprising of 1591/93–1606)[21] between the court in Vienna and the Hungarian Protestant aristocracy. During the war the ruling monarch, Rudolph I, required the Hungarian Diet to pass a

---

territories: multiple versions of the *Pietas Austriaca?*', (2011) 97(2) *The Catholic Historical Review* 276.

[17]   Currently Transylvania is part of neighboring Romania.

[18]   In 1556 Catholics were stripped of their rights in real property and were banished from Transylvania. A year later, in 1557, the Diet of Torda recognised the Lutheran faith and urged tolerance of Catholics.

[19]   On the arrival of Unitarians in Transylvania see A J Long, 'Unitarians', (2000) 112 *The Expository Times* 46.

[20]   For a rare English language discussion see István Keul, 'Early modern religious communities' in *East Central Europe: Ethnic Diversity, Denominational Plurality and Comparative Politics in the Principality Transylvania (1526–1691)* (Brill, 2009), 243–7. For a comprehensive discussion in Hungarian see Kálmán Benda, 'Az 1568. évi tordai országgyűlés és az erdélyi vallásszabadság' (The 1568 Parliament at Torda and freedom of religion), (1994) 56(3–4) *Erdélyi Múzeum* 1.

[21]   The uprising was named after its leader, István Bocskai. It remains disputed in the literature whether the Bocskai uprising was a religious conflict.

special statute prohibiting any discussion of religious affairs in Parliament, or in any public meeting.[22] The Bocskai uprising ended with the peace of Vienna in 1606, which also brought religious toleration for Calvinists and Lutherans (Protestants) while preserving the primacy of Roman Catholicism under Act no 1 of 1608 on religion. This statute was the result of a high-powered political deal in which the Hungarian estates agreed to elect the brother of the Emperor Rudolph I, to be crowned as Matthias II, in exchange for toleration.[23] The precepts of toleration applied not only to the high estates but also to the villages and peasants. Public and military offices in Hungarian affairs were opened for Hungarians, irrespective of their religious denomination.

The legal reinforcement of toleration for the accepted religions – with the primacy of Roman Catholicism intact – came in a detailed regulatory scheme adopted by Parliament in a series of statutes in 1647.[24] The acts were passed after the Grand Duke of Transylvania, George Rákóczi I, agreed to give up his struggle against the Habsburgs in a peace agreement in Linz, in 1645. The Toleration Act confirmed the rights established in the 1608 Act, and provided undisturbed access to church bells and cemeteries.[25] The prohibition of coercion in matters of conscience was reaffirmed in a separate article.[26] A separate act settled the return of seized Protestant church property in admirable detail.[27]

The end of the seventeenth century was a period of aggressive Counter-Reformation in Hungary. This period coincides with the grand dukes of Transylvania losing their control over high politics, and also the uncovering of an aristocratic conspiracy against the Habsburg court (the Wesselényi conspiracy of 1666–70). Although there were several prominent Roman Catholics among the surviving conspirators, the measures affecting Hungary not only included a show trial of the conspirators, but also another show trial of 33 Protestant preachers and schoolmasters in 1673 in Bratislava, which was followed by yet another show trial of 700 Protestant preachers and schoolmasters.[28] The ones who refused to

---

[22]   Act no 22 of 1604.
[23]   The same deal prohibited the Jesuit order from acquiring landed property in Hungary.
[24]   Acts no 5 to 15 of 1647.
[25]   Art 5 of Act no 5 of 1647.
[26]   Art 6 of Act no 5 of 1647.
[27]   The fact that the property restoration clause needed to be reinforced two years afterwards, in Acts no 10 and 12 of 1649, suggests that the restoration did not go without opposition.
[28]   The records of the 1674 trial are translated and edited in Katalin S Varga, *'Vitetnek ítélőszékre . . . Az 1674-es gályarabper jegyzőkönyve* ('Being taken before

convert to Catholicism were sold as galley slaves. In response to the retaliation, Count Imre Thököly led an uprising of the dismissed soldiers and persecuted Protestants. As a result, in 1681 the terms of the 1608 toleration were re-established to some extent, and persecuted Protestants were allowed to return.[29] Act no 26 of 1681 explicitly listed the places of worship to be returned to Protestants (Calvinists and Lutherans). The terms of this act, however, soon were restricted by a binding interpretation issued by the Royal Court in the form of the so-called *explanatio Leopoldina* (Leopold's interpretation) of 1691. This interpretation introduced a difference between public and private worship, severely restricting public worship for Protestants to those places mentioned expressly in the act, thus going beyond the language of the original statute.[30]

A quick look at developments in the eighteenth century reveals how the legal framework already in place became the established point of reference for further regulation. In 1731 the Emperor Charles VI (III)[31] issued the *Carolina Resolutio* (Charles' decree) that introduced provisions that were unacceptable for Protestants: it maintained the restriction on Protestant worship to those places that had been assigned to Protestants in 1681; it made the performance of marriage rites for those of different denominations the duty of Roman Catholic priests and ordered that all children from such mixed marriages become Catholic;[32] it required Protestants to observe Catholic holy days; and it made public office dependent on an oath mentioning the saints and the Virgin Mary.[33] In 1749 apostasy became a crime for Catholics.

In the spirit of the Enlightenment, the terms of this re-Catholicisation were tamed following requests of Protestants to Joseph II (himself a Catholic). In his decree of toleration of 1781 he allowed Protestants to have their own places of public worship:[34] each community of at least 100

---

judgment . . .' The records of the 1674 galley slave trial) (Bratislava: Kalligram, 2002) (in Latin and in Hungarian).

[29] Act no 25 of 1681.

[30] This restriction of places of worship for Protestants, as well as on private and public worship, was only removed by Act no 26 of 1791.

[31] Charles III, as King of Hungary, was also the Holy Roman Emperor as Charles VI.

[32] From 1768 parents had to make a promise to bring up children from mixed marriages in the Catholic faith.

[33] The terms of the oath were adjusted in 1734 to allow more room for Protestants' convictions.

[34] The original of the decree may be viewed on the website of the National Archives at http://www.mol.gov.hu/a_het_dokumentuma/turelmi_rendelet.html (with Hungarian commentary).

families was allowed to build – at its own expense – a house of prayer that did not have a gate to the main street, and did not have a tower or bells – in other words, features that could attract believers.[35] Rules on the religious affiliation of children from mixed marriages were also revised: while all children of a Catholic father were required to follow their father's faith, only the daughters of a Catholic mother were required to follow hers. The religious oath for public office was also abolished. At the end of his rule, Joseph II – who had strained relations with the Hungarian political elite, in no small part due to his refusal to be crowned with the Hungarian Holy Crown – required all but three of his Acts to be withdrawn. The decree on toleration was among the few to remain in force according to his will.

The thawing of relations between Protestants and the Catholic Royal Court continued with Act no 26 of 1791 restoring the status quo of 1608 and 1647 for the accepted religions, despite the noted opposition of the Catholic Church.[36] Numerous differences were abolished between the accepted religions (for example, concerning the constructions of church buildings). However, the primacy of Roman Catholicism was ensured, for example with the prohibition of proselytism among Catholics (Article 13)[37] and with the retention of the power of the Catholic Church over mixed marriages (Articles 15 and 16).[38] Importantly, the administration of church affairs in the Protestant denominations was placed within their own clerical hierarchy, with the monarch (and not the Catholic Church) as the final arbiter (Article 4). The 1791 Act provides expressly for access of Protestant ministers to their sick and imprisoned, although ensuring the primacy of Catholic priests in such situations, and prohibiting Protestant ministers from making speeches on those occasions (Article 7).

It is significant that the roster of accepted religions was expanded gradually, almost as a sideline to the Reformation/Counter-Reformation struggle. For example, 1791 was the year when the Greek-rite Orthodox faith (essentially meaning the Serbian Orthodox Community) was added to the list of accepted religions.[39] As an achievement of the 1848 revolution, all

---

[35]   In 1786, bells and towers were allowed for Protestants again.

[36]   On this point see Károly Kecskeméti, 'Szabadságjogok a magyar liberálisok reformterveiben (1790–1848)' (Liberties in the reform plans of Hungarian liberals (1790–1848)) (2000) 15(1–2) *Aetas* 301.

[37]   Rules on the conversion of Catholics were established in Act no 4 of 1844, Arts 5–11.

[38]   The rules on mixed marriages were relaxed in Act no 4 of 1844, Articles 2–4, which accepted the validity of mixed marriages officiated by Protestant ministers. The power of the Catholic Church over mixed marriages was finally abolished with the introduction of the civil marriage registry in Act no 32 of 1894.

[39]   Act no 21 of 1791.

accepted religions were declared to enjoy full legal equality.[40] In 1848 the Anti-Trinitarians (Unitarians) were included,[41] and in 1868 the Greek-rite Orthodox community was accepted as including the Romanian Orthodox Church.[42] However Jewish emancipation had to wait until 1895, when Judaism became an accepted religion.[43]

Act no 53 of 1895 introduced a three-tier system of church recognition. Accepted religions remained at the top. Below this the 1895 law introduced the category of 'acknowledged' religions, whilst at the bottom of the hierarchy were those faiths that did not belong to either class, which were simply 'tolerated' (that is, not persecuted). For its time it was a considerable achievement that the 1895 law allowed state recognition of further religious communities and established legal rules for their recognition. The difference between 'accepted' and 'acknowledged' churches was only abolished after World War II, in Act no 33 of 1947. As far as it applied to recognition, however, the 1895 law stayed in force until the currently applicable Act no 4 of 1990 was adopted by the outgoing Communist Parliament. In the 1980s – before transition to democracy began – the Communist government recognised the Hungarian Evangelical Brotherhood, the Congregation of Faith, the New Hungarian Apostolic Church, the Hungarian Community of Jehovah's Witnesses and the Hungarian Community of Krishna Consciousness.[44]

As even such a brief overview suggests, in Hungary the development of the legal framework on church–state relations was gradual, and any movement towards greater toleration was highly dependent on the religious affiliation or personal philosophy of key decision makers. Despite important historic developments (such as the 1568 Diet of Torda or the 1895 Act), it is not an exaggeration to say that before the entry into force of the first democratic constitution, and the 1990 law on religious freedom, the Hungarian legal system did not recognise full legal equality of religious communities, and preserved a prominent position for the Catholic Church

---

[40]   Act no 20 of 1848, Art 2.

[41]   Act no 20 of 1848.

[42]   Act no 9 of 1868.

[43]   See Act no 42 of 1895. The equality of civil and political rights was acknowledged already under Act no 17 of 1867. For a brief account of Jewish emancipation in its nineteenth-century political context in English see István Pogány, 'Poets, revolutionaries and shoemakers: law and the construction of national identity in Central Europe during the long 19th Century', (2007) 16(1) *Social & Legal Studies* 99.

[44]   Here I follow Balázs Schanda, in András Jakab (ed), *A magyar Alkotmány Kommentárja* (*Commentary to the Hungarian Constitution*) (vol 3) (Századvég, 2009) 2244.

throughout much of Hungarian history. Recognition for other religious communities depended on the whims of the political process, and, at least historically, major backlashes were not unusual. In this setting, after each major setback the achievements of 1608 or 1647 became the reference points for what amounts to a minimum level of protection.

3. THE LEGAL FRAMEWORK AFTER TRANSITION TO DEMOCRACY AND ITS BROADER CONTEXT

As mentioned, the Communist regime in Hungary did not prohibit the operation of churches altogether. The legal framework of the 1895 Act continued to exist in Communist Hungary under the supervision of the State Office of Church Affairs,[45] and some churches continued to function under the state-mandated philosophy of atheism.[46] The new democracy's 1990 law on religious freedom and churches was prepared in consultation with the existing churches.[47] This period around the months of transition was a peculiar one, during which 'old' churches were looking for their place, testing the waters with emerging political actors, as well as facing challenges from newcomers in the competition for souls. As Zsolt Enyedi and Joan O'Mahony explain, although churches in Eastern Europe

> were rarely instrumental in shaping the institutional design of the new regimes, the churches gained political significance. Their oppression under communism granted them considerable moral capital, and the dominant churches were obvious allies in the attempts of the new political elites to redefine their national identity, and to accumulate legitimacy behind the new governments. Consequently, churches had access to political elites, a degree of influence on their decisions, and were able to speak with some authority in the early public debates on the post-communist future.[48]

The resulting regime of church registration in Hungary was among the most permissive in Europe. It required 100 members, a charter of

---

[45]   The office was disbanded with the arrival of democracy. It is not a major surprise that the 1990 Act on freedom of religion expressly prohibits the creation of any agency or office the sole purpose of which is the monitoring or management of church affairs (Art 16(1)).

[46]   Péter Paczolay, 'The role of religion in reconstructing politics in Hungary', (1996) 4 *Cardozo Journal of International and Comparative Law* 261, 264–5.

[47]   Schanda (note 44 above), 2245.

[48]   Zsolt Enyedi and Joan O'Mahony, 'Churches and consolidation of democratic culture: difference and convergence in the Czech Republic and Hungary', (2004)11(4) *Democratization* 171, at 173.

operations with a self-governing organisational structure, and a declaration that the founders intended to pursue a religious activity (Article 8(1) and Article 9). The register of churches was kept at the Metropolitan Court in Budapest. Registration was granted as a matter of formal compliance with the language of the 1990 statute, with no further in-depth enquiry. As Balázs Schanda, an eminent Hungarian expert on church–state relations, remarked on the reception of the registration regime of the 1990 act, 'many representatives of the traditional churches felt offended at having been put into the same category as "sects"'.[49] Thus, although the 1990 law did not distinguish between 'proper churches' and 'sects', the distinction clearly existed in the vocabulary of the constituency affected by the 1990 law.

Importantly, the registration of a church is not a precondition for the individual free exercise of religion, as the Constitutional Court has reaffirmed.[50] According to this early decision of the Court, church status confers no additional rights on the community of believers, with the exception of church autonomy. A church registration system does not violate the constitutional right to freedom of religion, unless it is arbitrary, or imposes a disproportionate burden upon free exercise. Using these standards the Constitutional Court has found the 100-member threshold to be constitutional.[51]

It is noteworthy that the registration and prosecutorial supervisory powers did not become a means of governmental control over religious organisations. Church dissolutions were extremely rare under the 1990 law. Over the years, however, Hungarian governments were seen to distinguish in their church relations between 'historic churches' and others without a formal legal definition of historic churches – so-called 'small churches'. However, it is not much of an exaggeration when András Sajó, in his compelling essay, calls the term 'small church' a constitutional nonsense.[52]

Most prominently, the conservative government (1998–2002) attempted to amend the 1990 law in order to make church registration less accessible for dubious sects.[53] The central component of the plan was to introduce a

---

[49]   Balázs Schanda, 'Religion and state in the candidate countries to the European Union: issues concerning religion and state in Hungary', (2003) 64(3) *Sociology of Religion* 333, 342.

[50]   8/1993 (II 27) AB decision.

[51]   Ibid.

[52]   See András Sajó, 'A "kisegyház" mint alkotmányjogi képtelenség' ('Small church' as constitutional nonsense) (1999) 2 *Fundamentum* 87 (showing the discriminatory impact of the distinction between historic churches and small churches).

[53]   For a description of the bill in English see Schanda, 'Religion and state in the candidate countries' (note 49 above) at 343.

definition of religion into the law, along with a list of activities that do not have a religious character and thus could not be the primary activities of churches (such as political representation or psychic healing). The bill to propose this reform provided that a 'world-view can qualify as a religion if it refers to a transcendent entity, has a structured set of beliefs, its doctrines focus on reality as a whole and it encompasses the totality of the personality with its particular behavioural requirements, which do not violate morals and human dignity'.[54] In the end the bill was not passed into law as the conservative government did not have the support of a qualified majority in Parliament for the enactment of this initiative.[55]

The Hungarian government maintains a Concordat-based regime of cooperation with a select few registered churches, while other similarly registered churches fall under the generally applicable legal rules. The Concordat with the Catholic Church was promulgated in an Act of Parliament, and has the status of an international agreement.[56] Other Concordats were subsequently promulgated as agreements between the Cabinet and the respective churches, in a lesser legal norm (a Cabinet decree) and not in an Act of Parliament. The apparent inequality favouring the Catholic Church, even in such a symbolic matter, was explained by the Constitutional Court in its foundational decision on church–state relations in 1993 as legal equality, which allows the social status of individual churches to be taken into account.[57] According to the prevailing scholarly opinion on church–state relations, the concept of state neutrality should be understood in the context of cooperation between the state and the churches, with regard to the nature of the particular instances of such cooperation (for example education and health care).[58]

The Cabinet decree on the army chaplaincy requires that chaplains come from one of four specified denominations (Roman Catholic, Calvinist, Lutheran or Jewish).[59] The preamble of the Cabinet decree explains that

---

[54] Ibid, my translation.

[55] The 'old' Hungarian Constitution in its Art 60(4) prescribed that '[a] majority of two-thirds of the votes of the Members of Parliament present shall be required to pass the statute on the freedom of conscience and religion'.

[56] The Concordat between the Holy See on behalf of the Catholic Church and the Hungarian state was signed in Vatican City on 20 June 1997 (that is, under a Socialist government) and was promulgated in an Act of Parliament (Act no 70 of 1999) during the next, conservative term, as an international agreement. On the status of the Concordat as an international agreement see Constitutional Court decisions 15/2004 (V 14) AB and 99/2008 (VII 3) AB.

[57] 4/1993 (II 12.) AB decision.

[58] Schanda in *A magyar Alkotmány Kommentárja* (note 44 above) 2262.

[59] 61/1994 (IV 20) Korm decree, Art 2(2).

the chaplaincy was established in this particular manner upon agreements concluded by the government and these 'historic churches'. The Constitutional Court upheld the scheme introduced by the Cabinet.[60] The justices were satisfied with seeing that the establishment of the chaplaincy had been preceded by a voluntary opinion poll in the armed forces concerning religious affiliation. Moreover, the Court found that for a group of churches 'historical' is a reference to the actual national history of the formation of churches. Therefore, the designation alone does not constitute 'impermissible discrimination'.[61] It also emphasised that, in the composition of the Army, chaplaincy churches are accounted for according to their 'actual role'.[62] Thereupon the Constitutional Court found that singling out particular denominations does not constitute unconstitutional discrimination or any other violation of freedom of religion. In the aftermath of the decision, a chaplaincy for prisons was established along similar lines.[63]

In the Hungarian church–state regime separation of church and state, or active state neutrality, does not preclude state funding for denominational institutions.[64] The basic terms of the funding are determined in the 1990 law on freedom of religion (Article 17), the 1997 law on the funding of denominational and public interest activities,[65] and the Concordats, where they exist. In addition, sectoral laws also determine the terms of funding – for example, for public education the 1993 law on public education also applies to church-operated schools.[66]

According to its Preamble, the 1997 Act was enacted in the spirit of a Hungarian tradition as embodied by Act no 20 of 1848, the 1895 Act on religious freedom and religious organisations and the 1947 Act, which declared the equality of all 'accepted' and 'acknowledged' religions (discussed above). A less tradition-oriented, yet cooperation-friendly approach would explain state funding for churches as a positive obligation of the government to promote the exercise of religious freedom in community with others, or – as accepted by the Constitutional Court – to compensate churches for their efforts to perform public functions.[67] With regard to

---

[60]   970/B/1994 AB decision, February 20, 1995.

[61]   Ibid; ABH 1995: 739, 743.

[62]   Ibid, 744.

[63]   13/2000 (VII 14) IM decree.

[64]   Churches also received compensation for property that was nationalised from them during the Communist regime. The terms of this compensation scheme will not be discussed here.

[65]   Act no 124 of 1997 on the financial basis of the religious and public interest activities of churches.

[66]   Act no 79 of 1993 on public education, Art 118 (4).

[67]   22/1997 (IV 25) AB decision.

state funding for denominational institutions one may also see a positive obligation attached to the constitutional right of parents to choose an education for their children, according to their own conscience(s) (Article 67(2), Constitution).

Recently, the Constitutional Court reviewed the funding provision of the public education Act of 1993 in the light of the Concordat with the Roman Catholic Church.[68] Applicants were concerned that, while their reading of the Concordat requires equal funding for public and denominational schools, the 1993 law on public education makes denominational schools entitled to lower funding than public schools, since the conditions and procedures for awarding certain types of funding are not specified in the law. The Constitutional Court reaffirmed its existing jurisprudence, and accepted that the Concordat is an international obligation, and thus its terms are included among the applicable norms, and not among the legal rules to be reviewed under the Constitution.[69] The Court explained that the Concordat requires a one-to-one matching of all funding (and not just specific types of funds) that educational institutions receive from the central budget. After the decisions, the manner of calculation of the supplementary funding due on top of regular education funding remains a matter of contention, despite guidance provided by the National Audit Office.

In 2008, a few months before the decision of the Constitutional Court, the first audit of the spending of state funds in denominational schools was conducted by the National Audit Office, and covered the previous three academic years.[70] In the last period the report found over 400 denominational schools that amounted to 5.2 per cent of educational services. On one hand, the report found that the denominational schools used their resources efficiently, and that the state had miscalculated the funding due to them and owed money to those schools. On the other hand, the Audit Office called on denominational schools to keep more transparent books in which the education-related state funding is clearly distinguishable. The newly elected Hungarian government reaffirmed its intention to provide

---

[68] 99/2008 (VII 3) AB decision.

[69] Dissenting Justice Bragyova argued that in its decision based on the Concordat the Constitutional Court relied on an interpretation of the Concordat that was less than compelling under international law, and thus the Constitutional Court had acted *ultra vires*.

[70] The report is available in Hungarian as Report no 0807 on the audit of the efficiency of spending on public education tasks in the chapter on the Ministry of Education and Culture (May 2008) at http://www.asz.hu/ASZ/jeltar.nsf/0/20B085 CE3B98048CC125745E002178B4/$File/0807J000.pdf.

the missing funding in a separate agreement between the government and the Hungarian leadership of the Catholic Church in late 2010.[71]

In addition to direct state funding, the best-known form of support is probably the redirected 1 per cent of personal income tax.[72] Churches have to register to be able to receive this donation. Although the government intends to revise this form of church support, it is still noteworthy that, in 2010, 187 churches were registered with the National Tax and Tariff Authority to receive the redirected 1 per cent of income tax (that is, about half of the total number of registered churches).[73] In addition, charities and NGOs may also receive an additional 1 per cent of redirected tax. Many churches have a charitable arm that qualifies for this second 1 per cent. When in 2009 – upon the request of several churches – the National Audit Office sought to carry out an inquiry into the reasons for the rejection of 1 per cent donations, the National Tax Authority refused to provide data as they pertain to 'tax secrets'.[74] In addition to direct funding and redirected taxes, churches receive considerable tax advantages. When they were exempted from the special tax regime applicable to high-value immovable property by Parliament in 2009, the Constitutional Court – noting that Parliament enjoyed a broad discretion in setting tax regulation – found that the exempted organisations, among them churches, retained a public function and as such qualified for the exemption without need for any further justification.[75]

Although the easy registration system did not result in formal legal equality of churches, it clearly allows access to legal status for communities that struggle elsewhere (notably the Church of Scientology). Despite the permissive regime, the Hungarian government never established a 'sect monitoring regime'. The yearbook of the National Security Services consistently reported for the last decade – without naming anyone – that there is a particular religious organisation that abuses its registered church status

---

[71] 1313/2010 (XII 27) Korm decision, Art 7.

[72] See Art 4 of Act no 124 of 1997. Under this scheme all taxpayers (irrespective of their religious affiliation) may commit 1 per cent of their personal income tax to a church of their choice, and another 1 per cent to a charitable cause. For the second 1 per cent civil society organisations, charities and charitable foundations of churches qualify. Taxpayers select a church and a civic recipient each year from a list approved by the national tax authority.

[73] See the website of the National Tax and Tariff Authority http://www.apeh. hu/magyar_oldalak/nav/szja1_1/kimutat/egyhazak_2010.html (in Hungarian).

[74] The report of the National Audit Office on the execution of the budget for 2009 is available at http://www.asz.hu/ASZ/jeltar.nsf/0/A7AD9B56A77BB957C12 57790004A9B31/$File/1016J000.pdf at 194.

[75] 8/2010 (I 28) AB decision.

to gain political, economic and intelligence advantages. It is understood that the reports refer to the Church of Scientology.

While there is no formal sect monitoring, the legal system appears to offer little protection against intolerant remarks on 'dangerous sects'.[76] For instance, in 1993 Parliament's Committee on Human Rights, Minorities and Religion refused to allocate church funding to four churches (the Society of Krishna Consciousness, Jehovah's Witnesses, the Unification Church and the Church of Scientology) because they were considered destructive (or subversive) sects. The affected churches sought relief against this measure, and the denigrating term used in relation to them, in both ordinary courts and the Constitutional Court, to no avail. In a brief order the Constitutional Court refused to deal with the petition for formal reasons. The constitutional justices held that the Constitutional Court does not have jurisdiction over an individual decision that does not constitute a legal norm, nor can it review the official reasons for a Parliamentary decision.[77] In addition, one church sued the Parliamentary committee for non-pecuniary damages in a civil procedure before the ordinary courts. The Supreme Court dismissed this suit, finding that the claim was filed against the Parliamentary Committee, when the Parliament would have been a proper respondent.[78] Having reached this conclusion, the Supreme Court did not consider the merits of the finding of the lower court, submitting that the Parliamentary Committee had exercised its freedom of expression in a constitutional manner, and that the classification of the plaintiff as a 'destructive sect' was covered by Parliamentary privilege.

This summary of the legal regulation of church–state relations in Hungary is certainly not complete but can only remain exemplary. Nonetheless, it clearly demonstrates that, despite formal legal equality of registered churches and an unusually permissive registration system, 'historic churches' and predominantly the Catholic Church have retained a dominant position in the 20 years following transition. The jurisprudence of the Constitutional Court, promoting the introduction of a cooperation-ist regime (despite strong separationist language in the Constitution) was instrumental in making the legal framework operate in less than neutral ways. Minority, newcomer or non-mainstream religious communities and their churches are not persecuted. Lack of equality at present is mostly

---

[76] R Uitz, 'Aiming for state neutrality in matters of religion: the Hungarian record', (2006) 83(5) *University of Detroit Mercy Law Review*, 761–87 at 771–2.

[77] 439/B/1993 AB order of December 14, 1993 (concerning the use of the term in the reasons attached to the parliamentary decision).

[78] BH 1997: 276.

displayed by severe disparities in funding and a climate favouring 'historic churches', despite the language of equality in the law.

4. CURRENT DEVELOPMENTS: THE EVOLUTION OF A NEW CHURCH REGISTRATION REGIME

The operation of the Hungarian church registration system has not been uncontested in the domestic political arena. The legal regulation, and its most permissive application by the courts together with the refusal of prosecutors to intervene, has continuously given rise to claims in and outside Parliament that several registered churches are facades for lucrative business operations, engaging in 'sect business'. In addition to the Church of Scientology, which easily gets caught in such accusations, the other usual target is the Congregation of Faith, a genuine Hungarian mega-church that emerged in the 1980s with its charismatic leader, the pastor Sándor Németh. With a total of approximately 300 registered churches it certainly should not be a serious challenge to conduct a review of the accounts of registered churches in order to uncover hidden business ventures thriving under the 1990 law. When it comes to reconfiguring church–state relations however, instead of solid data, rumours and suspicions about 'business sects' put the pendulum in motion.

It is not contested that the Congregation of Faith was instrumental in the establishment of one of the opposition parties, the Alliance of Free Democrats. This party was a liberal political force, which had been a participant in the Round Table Talks, and then served in three coalition governments as the junior partner alongside a Socialist majority (in 1994–8, 2002–6, and 2006–10). During the conservative government between 1998 and 2002, the Congregation of Faith – and the Alliance of Free Democrats alongside it, together with the Church of Scientology – were regular subjects of Parliamentary interpellations as business sects. As discussed above, at the time the conservative government did not succeed with its bill to restrain the permissive church registration regime owing to the old Constitution's qualified majority requirement for such a law. Nonetheless, the intensity of the discourse clearly signalled that the church–state regime framed by the 1990 Act on freedom of religion rested on a fragile political status quo, which was preserved by a constitutional requirement for a two-thirds qualified majority, despite the clear disapproval of conservative political forces.

Although the alleged problem of 'business sects', or the divide between 'historic' and 'small churches', has not been a subject of serious discussion during the eight years of the Socialist–Liberal coalition, soon after the sweeping electoral victory of the conservative–Christian Democrat coalition in the spring of 2010, news reports on the spread of sect business increased. While the new Constitution was under discussion in the spring of 2011,[79] news of the outline of a new church law emerged.[80] The new Constitution clearly calls for a law on churches to be adopted by two-thirds qualified majority (Article VII), so such governmental communication must be taken seriously. When introducing the outline of the law, the Secretary of State indicated that the new government was in discussion about the terms of the new law with several churches.[81]

The State Secretary responsible for relations with churches, national minorities and civil society in the Ministry of Public Administration and Justice explained to the press that the government intended to introduce a three-tier system for church registration. The top of the hierarchy would be reserved for 'historic churches,' followed by 'acknowledged churches' under the new church law. The third level would be inhabited by 'ecclesiastical associations' – religious communities that do not merit registration in either of the higher categories under the church law. The latter were envisaged as operating under the legal framework applicable to other associations. This regime was clearly reminiscent of the three-tier framework under the 1895 law on churches.

As disclosed at the press conference in March 2011, the first proposed working definition of 'historic church' would have required 100 years' presence in Hungary, or 25 000 members, and a nationwide network of institutions. For the second level – 'acknowledged churches' – a 20-year presence

---

79   See note 11 and the accompanying text, above.

80   For a description of the new law's approach from the press conference of 17 March 2011 see the website of the government under the title 'Új korszak kezdődik az egyházaknál' (A new era begins for churches) (17 March 2011) (in Hungarian) at http://www.kormany.hu/hu/kozigazgatasi-es-igazsagugyi-miniszterium/egyhazi-nemzetisegi-es-civil-ugyekert-felelos-allamtitkarsag/hirek/uj-korszak-kezdodik-az-egyhazaknal.

81   After coverage by the Hungarian News Service (MTI) news outlets reported the first round of negotiations with the 'four historic churches' on 30 March 2011. Negotiations were confirmed in an interview with Sándor Németh, the lead pastor of the Congregation of Faith in the weekly *Magyar Narancs* (23(18) 5 May 2011) available online at http://www.mancs.hu/index.php?gcPage=/public/hirek/hir.php&id=23646. The chairman of the Calvinist Congregation, Gusztáv Bölcskei, also confirmed to the National News Agency that historic churches had received a 'working draft' from the government, which cannot be regarded as the draft of the bill, yet as reported (in Hungarian) in the Conservative daily *Magyar Nemzet* on 26 May 2011, 'A történelmi egyházakkal is egyeztet a kormány' (The government is also in talks with historic churches) (in Hungarian), available at http://www.mno.hu/portal/786633.

and an undefined, but lower membership requirement were envisaged, while 'ecclesiastical associations' were foreseen as entities under the law on associations with further (undisclosed) special criteria.

It was suggested that there would be little difference under the law between historic churches and acknowledged churches. As to the possible differences, sources indicated that these might relate to levels of state funding, especially for funds other than the 1 per cent income tax redirection.

It was uncontested from the beginning that a new round of registration would have to take place when the new law on churches entered into force, and churches that were registered already would need to be categorised under the new law. Originally, it was suggested that, from among the registered churches, Parliament would choose the ones that were, beyond doubt, 'proper churches'. It has not been clear from the early stages how the membership requirement is to be measured for the purposes of registration, as religious affiliation is sensitive data under Hungarian data protection rules (so the state cannot record a named individual's religious affiliation). Initially, it was expected that the 'four historic churches' (Roman Catholicism, the two Protestant congregations and Judaism) would belong in the first category along with others such as the Unitarian congregation and the Orthodox communities.[82] The government had initially estimated – although they did not make any calculations to this effect – that the number of churches would be 'much, much fewer' than the current 300, an estimate that was subsequently amended to put the number of registered churches 'well below one hundred'.[83]

The government's plan almost instantly came under serious criticism

---

[82] See coverage of the press conference of 17 March 2011 in the printed and electronic press (in Hungarian) following the reporting from the National News Agency without much alteration, such as 'Száz éves múlt szükséges a töténelmi egyházzá váláshoz' (A hundred years of history is required for historic church status) *Magyar Nemzet* (17 March 2011) (in Hungarian) at http://mno.hu/portal/775889 or 'Száz éves működés után járna a történelmi egyház megnevezés' (Historic church nomination due after 100 years of operation) at origo.hu (17 March 2011) at http://www.origo.hu/itthon/20110317-szaszfalvi-laszlo-legalabb-100-eves-multtal-kell-rendelkezniuk-a-tortenelmi.html.

[83] 'Történelmi egyház lehet a HIT gyülekezete' (The Congregation of Faith may become a historic church) (4 April 2011) *Népszabadság online* (in Hungarian) available at http://nol.hu/belfold/tortenelmi_egyhaz_lehet_a_hit_gyulekezete_; also on the news portal index.hu at http://index.hu/belfold/2011/04/04/tortenelmi_egyhaz_lesz_a_hit_gyulekezete/, 'Szászfalvi: Jóval száz alá csökken majd az egyházak száma' (Szászfalvi: Well fewer than a hundred of churches will remain) *Magyar Nemzet* on 5 April 2011 (in Hungarian), at http://mno.hu/portal/775889.

owing to the discriminatory nature of the proposed rules. Discontent resulted from the finding that on reading the membership and presence criteria in the new law in a disjunctive fashion (and not a conjunctive one), the Congregation of Faith would also count as a historic church under the proposed new law. The Catholic Church was reportedly in favour of making the criteria for historic church disjunctive. Sources in the Congregation of Faith signalled that they found the label 'historic' problematic, but would seek recognition in the highest category under the new law.[84]

The Secretary of State explained the need for the new law under the new Constitution stating that the '1990 law on freedom of religion became outdated in international comparison'.[85] Interestingly, this opinion is shared by some legal experts. For example, law Professor Péter Hack, who is a former liberal MP and a prominent member of the Congregation of Faith, said to the press that the mission of the 1990 law on freedom of religion had been fulfilled as it had ensured that church–state relations emerged on a neutral ground in the transition to democracy, so the 1990 law had accomplished its purposes and was ready to be replaced.[86] At a conference the Secretary of State explained that the 1990 law also recognised three distinct classes of religious organisation, and that treating all three classes under the uniform category 'church' in the 1990 law was only a technical matter.[87]

By the time the bill was introduced in Parliament on 14 June 2011, the original plan had undergone serious transformation. Like a previous unsuccessful bill to limit access to registered church status, the bill introduced the same definition of religion (Article 6(1)) as proposed by the conservative government some ten years previously, along with a list of primarily non-religious activities (Article 6(2)).

The criteria for church registration have visibly become more reasonable than was initially indicated to the press. According to the bill, in order to be registered a church has to prove 20 years' existence in Hungary (as a church or association) and has to have at least 1000 members residing

---

[84] Reported on the news portal index.hu at http://index.hu/belfold/2011/04/04/tortenelmi_egyhaz_lesz_a_hit_gyulekezete/.

[85] Secretary Szászfalvi, quoted in the Conservative daily *Magyar Nemzet*, March 17, 2011 at http://www.mno.hu/portal/771990.

[86] See http://index.hu/belfold/2011/04/04/tortenelmi_egyhaz_lesz_a_hit_gyul ekezete/.

[87] 'Új korszak az egyházpolitikában' (New era in church policy) speech delivered at a conference on freedom of religion in the EU on 16 March 2011, available in Hungarian on the website of the Hungarian government at http://www. kormany.hu/hu/emberi-eroforrasok-miniszteriuma/egyhazi-nemzetisegi-es-civil-ug yekert-felelos-allamtitkarsag/az-allamtitkar/beszedek-publikaciok-interjuk/uj-kor szak-az-egyhazpolitikaban.

in Hungary (Article 14(3)(c)). In a long annex, the original bill listed – in three categories – 45 churches that were meant to continue as churches under the new law. Others not included in the annex were expected to seek registration before a court of law (Article 16), turn into religious associations (Article 39(1)), or cease to exist altogether. A roster of experts is proposed to assist courts with the registration criteria (Article 37).

Yet, by the time it was adopted on 11 July 2011 the bill had undergone significant transformation so far as the registration procedure was concerned. The registration criteria, including 20 years' presence and 1000 Hungarian residents as founding members, have been preserved. The most important departure from the original bill was the drastic change in the process of registration, which was included in the final hours of the bill's passage through Parliament. As a result, under the law as adopted, instead of a court of law, Parliament was empowered to decide on church registration with a two-thirds majority (Article 11(2)). There was no judicial review against the rejection of an application by Parliament.

Formerly registered churches that did not appear on the list of churches in the annex should request their registration as a church under the new law (Article 36(1)), or – if they did not meet the statutory criteria – should seek registration as a religious association under the law on associations, otherwise they would be closed down by the forces of the law.[88]

Several churches that were left off the list appended to the 2011 act clearly meet the statutory criteria, such as the Methodists, the oldest Muslim community and the oldest Buddhist community. It is difficult not to read some political symbolism into such Parliamentary omissions. By early December 2011, 72 churches had indicated to the Ministry their intention to file for church status under the new law.[89] Parliament is preparing to handle the applications, while the churches left in doubt about their status are concerned about the conditions they may operate under.[90]

The law adopted in the summer was suddenly withdrawn by Parliament, as the Constitutional Court found it unconstitutional owing to procedural irregularities in Parliament. The bill that was introduced in December 2011, three days after the withdrawal of its short-lived predecessor,

---

[88] Act no 2 of 1989 on associations.

[89] 'Fidesz: 72 egyház megtarthatná státuszát márciusig' (Fidesz: 72 churches could keep their position until May), hvg.hu, 22 December 2011 at http://hvg.hu/itthon/20111222_egyhaz_fidesz (in Hungarian).

[90] See 'Féltik a működésüket az új egyházi törvényből kimaradt egyházak' (Churches left out of the church law are concerned about their operation) origo.hu on 19 July 2011 (in Hungarian) at http://www.origo.hu/itthon/20110719-feltik-a-mukodesuket-az-uj-egyhazi-torvenybol-kimaradt-egyhazak.html.

closely resembled that act. The procedural rigour of Parliamentary super-majority approval was replaced by a somewhat less stringent procedure in Parliament. Interestingly, when the bill was introduced in Parliament the registration criteria were more stringent than in the law adopted in the summer: sponsors of the bill sought to return to the requirement of 100 years' international presence for churches to be registered by Parliament. To this rather demanding requirement an amendment added the less demanding criterion of 20 years' presence in Hungary.

As a result of some clarifications in the law that was finally passed on 30 December 2011 Parliament managed to restore a three-tier church–state regime that clearly resembles the system established under the 1895 law. The effort to return to a status quo from more than a century ago is complete with the requirement that all churches that were registered under the 1990 law have to seek re-registration in the new scheme. This will mean, it is estimated, that at best over 200 religious associations that enjoyed church status under the 1990 law will become religious associations. To invoke the metaphor from the title, we witness the pendulum swinging back. Sadly, as if wishing to live up to the metaphor, when Parliament confirmed the status of 18 churches in February 2012, and rejected the requests of 66 others, it did not follow the new procedure defined in the latest cardinal law. Instead, it passed a simple statutory amendment, emphasising all along that in expanding the list of recognised churches it was exercising its discretion (and not acting out of respect for the rights of religious communities to legal entity).

This state of affairs – leaving one of the most important aspects of religious liberty in the hands of a political majority, together with empowering the same political majority with the means to suppress unwelcome religious teachings and communities – is highly problematic from a human rights perspective. The requirement for pluralism, tolerance and neutrality has emerged in the jurisprudence of the European Court of Human Rights (ECtHR) to describe a minimum standard of state behaviour in matters of religious freedom, under and beyond the confines of Article 9.[91]

It is true that the ECtHR so far has not found that a church registration system violates the Convention per se. Nonetheless, the jurisprudence of the Court clearly indicates that barriers to seeking legal recognition in otherwise available forms of legal entity have consistently merited

---

[91] *Holy Synod of the Bulgarian Orthodox Church (Metropolitan Inokentiy) and Others v Bulgaria* (App nos 412/03 and 35677/04) (ECtHR, 22 January 2009) [119]–[120]. Also see *Kokkinakis v Greece* (App no 14307/88) (ECtHR, 25 May 1993) [33]; *Metropolitan Church of Bessarabia and Others v Moldova* (App no 45701/99) (ECtHR, 13 December 2001) [123]; *Hasan and Chaush v Bulgaria* (App no 30985/96) (ECtHR, 26 October 2000) [78].

condemnation in Strasbourg.[92] It is highly questionable whether the new Hungarian law leaves 'a fair opportunity' for religious groups to apply for church status.[93] A registration regime that is not administered in a neutral and even-handed manner, without discrimination, is clearly in violation of these standards. And so is a regulatory regime that intends to reduce plurality in order to preserve social peace. Doubts about the qualities of the latest cardinal law were also confirmed by the opinion of the Venice Commission in March 2012, which found that the latest Hungarian law on churches violates European human rights norms in several regards.[94]

5. CONCLUSION

This brief analysis of Hungarian church–state relations is intended to show that, despite the operation of a solid legal framework for the first 20 years of Hungarian democracy, the new Constitution together with the new law on churches brought a fundamental change in the Hungarian legal system, with further developments expected in the foreseeable future. Although the exact terms of the regime are not fully known as yet, it is expected that it will set the legal protection of religious organisation back to a pre-World War I level.

This legal change seems to be the outcome of a temporary political compromise and is not evidently mandated by a changed religious landscape. As the chapter sought to demonstrate, such changes were indeed not unprecedented in Hungary during the Reformation and the Counter-Reformation, and throughout the Enlightenment. The new regime clearly seeks to cement the divide between proper and not-so-proper churches, thus determining the terms of governmental behaviour towards communities of believers in a seriously unequal manner. While in practice some inequality persisted under the 1990 law, the doctrine of cooperation in a neutral state did not permit such severe formal inequalities as by now are clearly foreshadowed by the new Constitution, as well as the newly adopted 2011 law and governmental communication introducing it.

It is most regrettable that one of Europe's most progressive laws on freedom of religion – itself an achievement of the 1989–90 process of

---

[92]   In addition to a long line of Russian cases on church registration note also *Religionsgemeinschaft der Zeugen Jehovas and Others v Austria* (App no 40825/98) (ECtHR, 31 July 2008).

[93]   Ibid.

[94]   Opinion 664/2012, of 19 March 2012, as available at http://www.venice.coe.int/docs/2012/CDL-AD%282012%29004-e.pdf.

transition to democracy – will have to give way to yet another wave of government supported re-Catholicisation (or, at best, re-Christianisation) seeking to suppress claims for religious liberty and emerging religious diversity. One may only hope that the pendulum will swing back, as it has many times before.

11. Law, religion and belief in Slovakia, the Czech Republic and Poland

Michaela Moravčíková

1. INTRODUCTION

This chapter will examine the issue of religious freedom in three states in Central and Eastern Europe: Slovakia, the Czech Republic and Poland.[1] While relations are generally good between the peoples and governments of these three nations, there are significant differences between them in terms of religious belief and affiliation. For example, both Slovakia and Poland are often described as being Roman Catholic countries, while the Czech Republic, with which Slovakia formed a single state from 1918 to 1993 (except for a short break during World War II), is generally considered as being one of Europe's most atheistic countries.

In examining these three nations, it is important to bear in mind the impact of Communism in the last century, given that Slovakia, the Czech Republic and Poland were all swallowed up by the USSR in the aftermath of World War II. Such was the impact of Communism that even today, 20 years after its demise, its legacy still continues to haunt these nations, as well as other young democracies in the region. In particular, the fall of Communism generated a wave of national and nationalist feeling that,[2] perhaps most notably in recent decades, has led to allegations of mass murder and genocide in the Balkans.[3]

Under the Communist regimes in Slovakia, the Czech Republic and Poland, the state regulated religious life generally and the role of churches particularly in a way that hardly seems imaginable today. For example, in Czechoslovakia the crime of 'thwarting supervision over the churches' covered a wide range of activities. These included placing restrictions

---

[1]   The independent Slovak Republic and the independent Czech Republic came into being on 1 January 1993.

[2]   See Józef Darski, 'Národnostní konflikty ve střední Evropě', [1990] *Střední Evropa: Revue pro středoevropskou kulturu a politiku* 228.

[3]   See Chapter 12 by Julie Mertus in this volume.

on people wishing to gather together to pray, to partake of religious sacraments, and to meet for the purpose of engaging in communal worship. Certain churches and religious organisations were also subject to legal prohibition (for example the Greek Catholic Church), while worshippers, church leaders, clerics and priests were not merely subject to rigid state control (for example censorship), but were imprisoned or even executed. With religion portrayed by the state in derogatory terms, an avowedly 'scientific' ideology of Communism that embraced atheism became the official state doctrine. This scientific atheism, and the history of the international working class movement, became obligatory subjects at universities in what is now Slovakia, the Czech Republic and Poland, as well as in many other Eastern bloc states.

Those churches and religious societies that survived in Central and Eastern Europe under Communism only did so within the official structure permitted by the state (for example state-sanctioned churches, subject to supervision and control by the state) or beyond its formal remit (for example, independently run 'underground' churches). Whilst in some cases there were people involved in the religious life in both spheres, it may nonetheless be said that, as a general rule, churches and religious organisations in Slovakia, the Czech Republic and Poland were subject to close regulation by the state – with the state's agents and intelligence services keen to isolate non-recognised faith groups and members socially, as well as hoping to influence their decisions as much as possible. Many leaders and members of unapproved churches and faith groups upheld religious faith under tough conditions,[4] a powerful testament to their heroism and loyalty to their ideals. However, on the other hand, there were also cases of religious leaders/members collaborating with the Communist regimes – especially through the various 'peace movements' that the Communist powers organised for clerics.

The Iron Curtain was lifted in 1989, termed by Timothy Garton Ash as the 'year of miracles',[5] which hastened the fall of Communism. For those in Slovakia, the Czech Republic and Poland, as with the rest of the former USSR, a new period began of building democratic institutions and mechanisms to guarantee political, economic and social rights. A natural part of this process was the development of religious institutions that, in the main, tried to find their place in the public space. The metaphysical hunger that

---

[4] Especially in the Czech Republic and Slovakia, these were groups established by the Croatian Jesuit Tomislav Poglajen-Kolakovič. Also note the Czech Academic League, Catholic Action, Catholic Union, etc.

[5] Timothy Garton Ash, *A Year of Miracles. The revolution of '89 witnessed in Warsaw, Budapest, Berlin and Prague* (Paseka, 2009).

often accompanies the fall of an official or obligatory ideology led not only to the revival of interest in traditional religious and cultural facets of life (for example historical churches and religious societies), but also to a fresh interest in non-traditional movements and teachings (for example new religious movements). The period of Communism, synonymous with efforts by the state to marginalise non-sanctioned 'religious' beliefs, has now been replaced by a situation in which both long-established churches and other groups wishing to pursue ethical/life philosophies have been able to enter the public sphere in a way that was previously denied to them.

2. CONSTITUTIONAL PRINCIPLES GOVERNING RELIGION AND BELIEF IN POLAND, SLOVAKIA AND THE CZECH REPUBLIC

Following the momentous changes of 1989, the legal frameworks by which the countries of Central and Eastern Europe regulate their relations with churches and religious societies were established immediately after the creation of the first democratic governments and parliaments. This process was preceded, or rather, was accompanied, by another, arguably more important, process – the creation of new Constitutions for each of these republics. Thus, today Poland has its Constitution of 1997. Similarly, the Slovak and Czech Republics have their own Constitutions, which came into effect following the formal dissolution of the old Czechoslovakia in 1993.

Poland

The Preamble of the Constitution of Poland of 2 April 1997, in stark contrast to those of the Slovak and Czech Republics, contains an *invocatio dei*: 'We, the Polish Nation – all citizens of the Republic, both those who believe in God as the source of truth, justice, good and beauty, and those not sharing such faith but respecting those universal values as arising from other sources.'[6] The Preamble also contains an acknowledgement to the ancestors for (*inter alia*) 'our culture rooted in the Christian heritage of the Nation and in universal human values'.

The Constitution itself contains a number of provisions relevant to religion. For example, Article 25 relates to the legal status of churches and other religious societies; Article 35 guarantees the right of national and

---

[6] The Constitution of the Republic of Poland, Preamble, available at http://www.sejm.gov.pl/prawo/konst/angielski/kon1.htm.

ethnic minorities to the preservation of their religious identities; Article 48 concerns the provision of religious instruction in schools; Article 57 upholds the right to freedom of assembly;[7] and finally, and perhaps most significantly, Article 53 expressly guarantees freedom of religion. Article 53 states that:

(1) Freedom of conscience and religion shall be ensured to everyone.

(2) Freedom of religion shall include the freedom to profess or to accept a religion by personal choice as well as to manifest such religion, either individually or collectively, publicly or privately, by worshipping, praying, participating in ceremonies, performing of rites or teaching. Freedom of religion shall also include possession of sanctuaries and other places of worship for the satisfaction of the needs of believers as well as the right of individuals, wherever they may be, to benefit from religious services.

(3) Parents shall have the right to ensure their children a moral and religious upbringing and teaching in accordance with their convictions. The provisions of Article 48, para. 1 shall apply as appropriate.

(4) The religion of a church or other legally recognized religious organization may be taught in schools, but other peoples' freedom of religion and conscience shall not be infringed thereby.

(5) The freedom to publicly express religion may be limited only by means of statute and only where this is necessary for the defence of State security, public order, health, morals or the freedoms and rights of others.

(6) No one shall be compelled to participate or not participate in religious practices.

(7) No one may be compelled by organs of public authority to disclose his philosophy of life, religious convictions or belief.[8]

The Slovak Republic

The relationship between the Slovak Republic and religion or comparable ideologies is grounded in constitutional principles that serve to frame state–church relations. The 1992 Constitution of the Slovak Republic acknowledges in its Preamble the spiritual heritage of Cyril and Methodius (Christian missionaries to the Slavic people in the ninth century),[9] and

---

[7] Michał Rynkovski, 'State and church in Poland', in G Robbers (ed), *State and Church in the European Union* (Nomos, 2005) 424.

[8] The Constitution of the Republic of Poland (note 6 above).

[9] The Constitution of the Slovak Republic no 460/1992 Zb, as implemented in Constitutional Act no 244/1998 Zz, Constitutional Act no 9/1999 Zz, Constitutional Act no 90/2001 Zz, Constitutional Act no 140/2004 Zz, and Constitutional Act no 323/2004 Zz (Zb and, since 1993, Zz are abbreviations for *Zbierka zákonov* which in effect means 'collection of Acts'; the Czech equivalent is Sb).

the historical legacy of the Great Moravian Empire.[10] In Chapter 1 of the Constitution (General Provisions), the basic principle is to be found in Article 1: 'The Slovak Republic is a sovereign, democratic state governed by the rule of law. It is not bound by any ideology or religion.'[11] Article 24, which guarantees freedom of thought, conscience, religion and faith, states that:

(1) Freedom of thought, conscience, religion and faith shall be guaranteed. This right shall include the right to change religion or faith and the right to refrain from a religious affiliation. Every person shall be entitled to express his or her opinion publicly.

(2) Every person shall have the right to express freely his or her own religious conviction or faith alone or in association with others, privately or publicly, by worship, religious services or ceremonies and participation in religious instruction.

(3) Churches and ecclesiastical communities shall administer their own affairs. All ecclesiastic authorities and appointments, religious instruction, establishment of religious orders and other religious institutions shall be separate from the State authorities.

(4) The rights under sections (1) to (3) of this Article can be legally restricted only as a measure taken in a democratic society for the protection of the public order, health, morality, and rights and freedoms of other people.[12]

The Czech Republic

The Preamble of the Czech Constitution states that its citizens, 'being loyal to all good traditions of the ancient statehood of the Czech Crown's Land and the Czechoslovak state, resolve to build, develop and protect the Czech Republic in the spirit of the inviolable values of human dignity and freedom as the home of equal and free citizens who are conscious of their duties towards others and their responsibilities towards the whole'.[13] The Preamble characterises the Republic as a free and democratic state based on the respect for human rights and the principles of civic society. It also includes the Czech Republic as part of the family of European and world

---

[10] See the Constitution of the Slovak Republic 1992, Preamble. The ancestors of the Czechs and Slovaks inhabited Great Moravia, a Slavic state in Central Europe in the ninth century.

[11] See the Constitution of the Slovak Republic 1992, Preamble.

[12] The Constitution of the Slovak Republic. See Michaela Moravčíková, 'Religion, law, and secular principles in the Slovak Republic', in Javier Martínez-Torrón and Cole W Durham (eds), *Religion and the Secular State/La religion et l'État laïque: Rapports nationaux* (International Centre for Law and Religion Studies, BYU, 2010) 615.

[13] The Constitution of the Czech Republic No 1/1993 Sb, Preamble.

democracies, and emphasises that its citizens resolve jointly to 'protect and develop the inherited natural and cultural, material and spiritual wealth . . . and . . . abide by all time-tried principles of a law-observing state'.[14]

No express mention of religious freedom is found in the Constitution of the Czech Republic. However, Articles 3 and 11 of the Constitution provide that part of the constitutional order of the Czech Republic is the Charter of Fundamental Rights and Freedoms (1991).[15] Article 2(1) of this Charter declares the confessional neutrality of the Czech Republic, while Article 3(3) guarantees fundamental rights to all, and affords freedom to everyone irrespective of religion or belief. Individual and institutional religious freedoms are also recognised in Articles 15 and 16 of the Charter,[16] which are the same as the rights enshrined in Article 24 of the Slovakian Constitution.

It thus follows that, in each of the three nations considered for the purposes of this chapter, the law guarantees freedom of thought, conscience and religion, as well as protecting citizens from the practice of forced belief. Yet in spite of these constitutional provisions the battle for religious freedom in Poland, Slovakia and the Czech Republic has often not been easy, as demonstrated by the recent histories of these nations.

3. THE HISTORICAL DEVELOPMENT OF RELIGIOUS FREEDOM

Poland

Poland, which gained independence in 1918, has long associated with Roman Catholicism and a belief in the Catholic Latin rite.[17] The Polish Constitution of 1921 contained a number of provisions that guaranteed freedom of conscience and belief, although not all religious communities were accorded legal recognition under Polish law at the time. In contrast,

---

[14]   Ibid.

[15]   The Charter of Fundamental Rights and Freedoms No 23/1991. After the dissolution of the Czech and Slovak Federative Republic, this constitutional act had the status of an ordinary act, so it was declared again by resolution of the presidency of the Czech National Council No 2/1993 Sb as a part of the Czech legal order.

[16]   See Antonín Ignác Hrdina, *Náboženská svoboda v právu České republiky* (Eurolex, 2004) 63.

[17]   Neal Pease, 'Poland and the Holy See, 1918–1939', (1991) 50(3) *Slavic Review* 521.

the Roman Catholic Church enjoyed a uniquely privileged legal position, based on a Concordat adopted between the Polish state and the Holy See in 1925.[18]

The fortunes of the Catholic Church in Poland were, however, to take a significant turn for the worse after 1939. With the German occupation of Poland, a number of Catholic churches were damaged or destroyed, priests were expelled from certain territories and bishops were often replaced by Nazi collaborators. The position of the Catholic Church and other religious organisations was further undermined by the incorporation of Poland in 1945 into what was to become the USSR. The birth of a Communist Poland led to the dissolution of the 1925 Concordat with the Holy See, while after 1948 the Polish intelligence services, in emulating the Soviet model, oversaw the creation of a group of clerics that were appointed merely to conform to the dictates of the state authorities.

In the aftermath of World War II Poland's new Communist leaders had 'a well developed plan of anticlerical action', which ultimately resulted in a collective declaration by these newly appointed clerics of their loyalty to the state.[19] The Office for Religious Affairs was established, which was the central governmental body responsible for the regulation of matters pertaining to religion. Thus, for example, between 1950 and 1956, Agreements between the representatives of the People's Republic of Poland and the Polish Episcopal Conference were concluded. Although Article 82 of the Polish Constitution of 1952 guaranteed the separation of church and state, the state gave itself the power to create and abolish ecclesiastical posts, thereby enabling it to remove 'troublesome' priests from their positions. Moreover, in 1961 a law was enacted that prohibited the teaching of religion in Polish public schools.[20] Rather ironically, however, five years later, the Celebration of the Millennium of Polish Christianity was held, an event that helped to reinvigorate the self-confidence of many of the nation's Catholic believers.

Polish Catholic confidence was particularly boosted by the appointment of a Polish Pope in October 1978 – Cardinal Karol Wojtyla who took the name John Paul II.[21] Around this time the Catholic Church in Poland came

---

[18]   Edward D Wynot, Jr, 'The Catholic Church and the Polish State, 1935–1939', (1973) 15 *Journal of Church and State* 223.

[19]   Andrzej Grajewski, *Jidášův komlex. Zraněná církev: Křesťané ve střední Evropě mezi odporem a kolaborací* (Prostor, 2002) 201.

[20]   Piotr Stanizs, 'Poland' (Eurel – Sociological and legal data in Europe); see http://www.eurel.info/EN/index.php?pais=61&rubrique=693.

[21]   Ibid.

to play an important role, alongside trade unions, in campaigning for greater freedom. For example, strikes organised by trade unionists under Lech Walesa in Gdansk shipyard led to an agreement that guaranteed the right to strike and the establishment of independent trade unions. The relationship between the Catholic Church and trade unions was very close. Photos of Pope John Paul II and pictures of the Black Madonna of Czestochova were posted on the gates of the shipyard. The emergence of the independent self-governing trade union Solidarity became a factor that significantly contributed to the collapse of the Communist regime. Moreover, in June 1979, millions of Poles welcomed the Pope on a visit to his homeland. In his speeches the Pope mentioned a close link between the nation and the Catholic Church and called for dialogue between the state and the church. As a result the Polish Catholic Church, led by Cardinal Wyszyńsky, became a sort of mediator between the state and the unions, although (in their public statements) representatives of the Polish Catholic Church would often express support for the unions. However, with tensions growing, the leaders of the Catholic Church became increasingly keen to avoid unnecessary conflict with the state. Following the death of Cardinal Wyszyńsky, his post was taken by Józef Glemp, and on 4 November 1981 Cardinal Glemp, Walesa and the leader of the Communist party Wojciech Jaruzelski met to discuss the possibility of setting up the 'National Understanding Front'. Following their failure to reach agreement on the matter, resulting tensions led to the imposition of martial law on 13 November 1981. Although the measures taken by the state in this regard were aimed primarily at the trade unions, rather than against the Church per se, their introduction led a number of Polish Catholic Church leaders (although not the majority of its ordinary clerics) to be more willing to accept the political status quo in the last years of the Communist administration.[22]

This political status quo was obviously shattered by the demise of Communism and the emergence of a new democratic Poland in 1989. As evidenced by the continued high degree of religious affiliation today in Poland, and the sacrifice of those who resisted totalitarian rule − such as the Catholic priest Jerzy Popieluszko, who was murdered by agents of the state in 1984[23] − the Catholic Church has clearly played an important

[22]   See generally Hank Johnston, 'Toward an explanation of church opposition to authoritarian regimes: religio-oppositional subcultures in Poland and Catalonia', (1989) 28(4) *Journal for the Scientific Study of Religion* 493.

[23]   Ivana Ebelová, Zdeněk Hojda, Jan Kranát, Barbara Köpplová, Jaromír Povejšil, Petr Příhoda and Alice Rahmánová, *Kronika křesťanství* (Fortuna Print, 1998) 435.

role in Poland's transformation in recent decades from Communism to democracy.[24]

Slovakia and the Czech Republic

In the wake of World War II, the nations that today are Slovakia and the Czech Republic both witnessed the imposition of severe restrictions on religious freedom with the advent of Communist rule. In the then Czechoslovakia the postwar Communist regime sought to manipulate churches to serve its own interests. For example, under Act No 217/1949 Zb, a State Office for Church Affairs was created, to serve as a central organ of state administration. Similarly, in 1950, legislation was passed that permitted the state to regulate the funding of churches, as well as creating the institute of 'state approval' for clergy. As a result churches and religious associations ceased to enjoy legal autonomy, and instead became completely dependent economically on the state. With the majority of church property and church schools being nationalised, the state gave itself control over a wide range of 'religious' affairs, such as liturgical, pastoral, social, charitable, educational and economic matters. In addition, the Communist regime established a compulsory registration of churches, while members of the clergy were permitted to undertake their functions only if they had been approved by the state – a state of affairs that was contingent on their taking a vow of loyalty to the state.

Those who objected to the state's attempts to regulate and control religious organisations frequently became the target of persecution by national security forces. In this area the years between 1948 and 1953 were an especially tense and difficult period for state–church relations. However, these tensions in the following years were at least to some extent obviated by an improvement in church–political relations, brought about by the influence of Marxist–Christian dialogue that was popular especially with French and Italian Communists – even though dialogue with Christians was regarded as a specific instrument of the state's ideological battle with religions, aimed at the suppression of religious practice.

It was the Prague Spring in 1968, when Alexander Dubcek became the First Secretary of the Czech Communist Party, that led to new hopes of greater religious freedom, alongside more general democratisation. The

---

[24]   See for example Irena Borowik, 'The Roman Catholic Church in the process of democratic transformation: the case of Poland', (2002) 49(2) *Social Compass* 239; and S Burdziej, 'Religion and politics: religious values in the Polish public square since 1989', (2005) 33(2) *Religion, State & Society* 165.

crushing of the Prague Spring, and the occupation of Czechoslovakia by the armies of five Warsaw Pact states in 1969, dashed these hopes, and put a hold on the wider process of democratisation. As a result, greater restrictions were imposed on personal (including religious) freedom, and it was not until the more general changes that took place in Eastern Europe in 1989 that religious (and other) groups could properly taste freedom.

4. RELIGIOUS AFFILIATION IN THE CZECH REPUBLIC, POLAND AND SLOVAKIA

Poland

In Poland, it has been estimated that 90 per cent of the population are affiliated to the Catholic Church, whereas 7.8 per cent of the population regard themselves as having no religion.[25] Poland's non-Catholic religious minorities represent just 2.2 per cent of the population, and include Orthodox believers, Lutherans, Calvinists, Old Catholics, Jehovah's Witnesses, Baptists, Seventh-Day Adventists and Methodists. The 3 million-strong Jewish population that had lived in Poland prior to World War II was largely destroyed during that conflict, and today it numbers fewer than 10 000. Likewise, the number of Muslims living today in Poland is small. As a result of this religious demographic, the Catholic Church continues to have an important position and is able to exert considerable influence over various elements of Polish public and social life.[26]

The Czech Republic

Today the Czech Republic, traditionally regarded by some as a Protestant country, is generally associated with atheism. Although the Republic has a significant Protestant tradition, its largest faith group today comprises Roman Catholics. Approximately 27 per cent of the nation's population belong to the Catholic Church, which represents more than 80 per cent of Czech citizens with a religious affiliation. This proportion, with some small changes, has been continually maintained since 1918. Other significant religious organisations include the Evangelical Church of Czech Brethren

---

[25] Michał Pietrzak, 'Poľská republika. Právne postavenie náboženských spoločenstiev v Poľsku', in Silvia Jozefčiaková (ed), *Štát a cirkev v postsocialistickej Európe* (Institute for State–Church Relations, 2003) 61.

[26] Ibid.

and the Czechoslovak Hussite Church with membership at 1.2 per cent and 1 per cent of the population respectively. In the census of 2001, 59 per cent of the total Czech population regarded themselves as atheists, while 32.2 per cent were listed as believers and 8.8 per cent professed no religion.[27] The number of Muslims in the Czech Republic is small, as is the case with the nation's Jewish communities. There are, however, some justified concerns that the census of 2001 failed properly to take account of the number of citizens who are affiliated to a religion or equivalent belief, particularly since there was opposition in some quarters to the methodology on which that census was based.[28]

The Slovak Republic

According to a census in 2001, 84.1 per cent of the resident population of Slovakia profess allegiance to a state-recognised church or religious society. Moreover, 68.9 per cent of the nation's approximately 5 million population have declared their affiliation to the Roman Catholic Church; 4.1 per cent to the Byzantine Catholic Church (Greek Catholics); 6.9 per cent to the Evangelical (Lutheran) Church of the Augsburg Confession; 2.0 per cent to the Reformed Christian Church; and 0.9 per cent to the Orthodox Church. In the 2001 census, 12.96 per cent of respondents declared themselves as 'without confession' while 2.98 per cent failed even to answer the religious affiliation question. In the census 6294 persons claimed membership of churches and religious societies that are not recognised by the state and,[29] of this number,[30] 1212 citizens declared their affiliation to Islam, which statistically represents 0.022 per cent of the population of Slovakia. The representatives of the Islamic organisations in Slovakia estimate there to be approximately 5000 Muslims in the country, and this includes about 150 converts of Slovak nationality,[31] with the rest coming from abroad.[32]

---

[27]   Czech Statistical Office (2011), 'Obyvatelstvo hlásící se k jednotlivým církvím a náboženským společnostem', available at http://notes3.czso.cz/csu/2003edicniplan.nsf/o/4110-03--obyvatelstvo_hlasici_se_k_jednotlivym_cirkvim_a_nabozenskym_spolecnostem.

[28]   Jiří Rajmund Tretera, *Stát a církve v České republice* (Karmelitánské nakladatelství, 2002) 9.

[29]   It is 0.11 per cent of the total number of all inhabitants/believers.

[30]   Michaela Moravčíková and Marián Cipár, *Religiozita na Slovensku II* (Institute for State–Church Relations, 2003) 110.

[31]   Radovan Čikeš, 'Registrácia cirkví a náboženských spoločností verzus náboženská sloboda', in Michaela Moravčíková and Miroslav Lojda (eds), *Islam v Európe* (Institute for State–Church Relations, 2005) 15.

[32]   Michaela Moravčíková, 'Religious education and denominational schools

5.   ISLAM AND MUSLIMS IN POLAND, THE CZECH REPUBLIC AND SLOVAKIA

Poland

Islam has been present in Poland since 1392, through the Tatars. Having settled there long ago, many of them later joined and served loyally in the Polish–Lithuanian Army, before gradually becoming Polish citizens. In 1925 Poland's Muslims set up their first religious organisation, the Muslim Religious Union (MRU), which continues to exist today. They also elected the first Polish *mufti*, Jakub Szynkiewicz (1884–1966), who chose Vilnius, the original capital of the Lithuanian Voivodeship, as the MRU's head-quarters. This organisation was subsequently recognised by the Polish state, while Islam was afforded legal recognition by Poland in 1936. Under a Polish law enacted in 1936, the office of *mufti* was recognised as guar-anteeing tenure for life. Moreover, it was stipulated that the *mufti* had to be at least 40 years old, with a theological education, and appointed in an election that had been ratified by the Polish President.[33]

The pre-war rights afforded to Poland's Muslims were lost in the imme-diate aftermath of World War II, however. With the establishment of a Polish Communist regime, the majority of territories inhabited by Tatars were annexed to the Soviet Union. During the period of Communist rule Muslims, like other religious believers, were subject to strict curbs on the extent to which they were free to practise their religion. This changed with the fall of Communism, and in 1989 the MRU became active again, which in turn led, in 2003, to the election of a new *mufti*. With democracy having been reinstated in Poland the composition of the nation's Muslim population(s) has been changing, while the law of 1936 remains in force ensuring that Islam is now an officially recognised religion in Poland.

The Czech Republic and Slovakia

From November 1949 until 1991, there was no formal legal recognition of churches and equivalent religious organisations in Czechoslovakia. The ruling Communist authorities viewed Muslims and other faith groups as

---

in the Slovak Republic', in Ednan Aslan, (ed), *Islamische Erziehung in Europa/ Islamic Education in Europe* (Böhlau Verlag, 2009) 457.
[33]   Agata Nalborczyk, 'Islam in Poland – 600 years of Muslim presence', in Moravčíková and Lojda (eds), *Islam v Európe* (note 31 above) 248.

enemies of the state, with the result that public manifestations of faith were curbed and calls for religious freedom were ignored.[34] Accordingly, during the Communist era the activities of Muslims were limited largely to the holding of personal meetings. In 1968, during the Prague Spring, some Muslims sought, unsuccessfully, to campaign for the protection of their religious beliefs. In what is now the Czech Republic they ultimately were only successful in 2002, when the Czech Government granted them official registration under Act no 3/2002. As a result, the earlier curbs on Muslims were lifted, and the Centre of Muslim Religious Communities was registered in the Czech Republic on 17 September 2004.[35]

In contrast, however, no Muslim organisation has, as yet, been registered as a religious society in Slovakia. To date Muslim groups in Slovakia have not fulfilled the membership criteria necessary for official registration, as stipulated by Slovak law. This state of affairs has led to the representatives of Muslim communities holding meetings with state authorities and institutions, in expressing the wish to be registered as a religious society, which would thereby enable them to receive financial support from the state, like other registered churches and religious societies

As in the Czech Republic, the Muslim community in Slovakia is small. It is mainly composed of foreign students at Slovak universities and of former students who, having been educated in the country, have chosen to settle there. This community is characterised by a high percentage of academically well-qualified people, who often join various Muslim organisations such as the Islam Literature Friends' Association, the Islamic Foundation and the Union of Muslim Students in Slovakia; groups that may, in the future, petition for greater rights for the nation's Muslims.

5. THE FUNDING OF CHURCHES AND RELIGIOUS ORGANISATIONS IN POLAND, THE CZECH REPUBLIC AND SLOVAKIA

Poland

As noted above, there are similarities between Slovakian and Polish people's religious affiliation, for both nations are predominantly Catholic.

---

[34]   Moravčíková, 'Religious education and denominational schools in the Slovak Republic' (note 32 above) 457.
[35]   Jiří Rajmund Tretera, 'Legal status of the Islamic minority in the Czech Republic', in Moravčíková and Lojda (eds), *Islam v Europe* (note 31 above) 300.

However, these similarities do not extend to the financing of churches and religious societies. In particular, Poland does not finance the religious activities of churches and faith communities. For example, Article 4 of the Polish Law (dated 17 May 1989) on Guaranteeing Freedom of Conscience and Belief lays down that the state does not, as a general rule, provide assistance to churches and other religious communities. This article, as well as the constitutional principle of the mutual independence of state and church, should however not be interpreted as a ban on cooperation between the state and churches/religious organisations. After all, the principle of 'collaboration' is respected by the 1989 law (see above), with the result that the state has a duty to collaborate with churches/religious organisations on matters such as the protection and reconstruction of ecclesiastical monuments, museums, archives, libraries and works of religious art that represent an important part of Polish culture. The state will not grant any financial support for the construction of new religious buildings; nor does it contribute to the maintenance costs of existing buildings. However, in contrast, the state is willing to support religious activities that have a wider social remit – such as, for example, religious groups providing care, promoting educational activities or helping to protect public health.[36]

The Slovak and Czech Republics

The Slovak and Czech Republics share the same history with the state agreeing to finance churches, a principle that dates back to the period of Maria Theresa (1741–80) and her son Joseph II (1780–90). Following the demise of Communism in 1989, new legislation was passed in both Republics that enables churches and religious communities to have full internal self-government, but it did not eliminate their direct financial dependence on the state.

At present, in the Czech and Slovak Republics, on the basis of Act no 218/1949 Zb on the financial provision of churches and religious communities and its amendment by Act no 522/1992 Zb, the state must provide churches and religious communities with funds for the payment of their clergy stipends, if churches and religious communities so request. In both states the government also contributes to the operation of the headquarters of registered churches and religious communities. In this regard the

---

[36]　Andrzej Czohara, 'Účasť štátneho rozpočtu pri financovaní činnosti katolíckej cirkvi a iných cirkví v Poľsku', in Peter Mulík (ed), *Modely ekonomického zabezpečenia cirkví a náboženských spoločností* (Institute for Church–State Relations, 1997) 70.

Ministry of Culture is the administrator of the financial support assigned in the national budget by the National Council for churches and religious communities, and the relevant Ministry grants assigned funds to each church on a monthly basis.

In Slovakia since 2000, work has been in progress towards the goal of a new model of financial provision for churches and religious communities. For example, in 2001 the Ministry of Culture submitted a Bill on the financial provision of churches and religious communities. The proposed Bill preserved the principle of the existing model, but suggested that financial provision should take into account the number of members of every church and religious community in accordance with each group's size. The Bill however has not yet been passed, and it has proved difficult to reach agreement with the representatives of the different churches, religious communities, political parties and other vested interests. More recently in Slovakia a new expert committee has been set up, which is expected to address the issue of the funding of churches and religious groups in due course.

6.   THE RECOGNITION OF CHURCHES AND RELIGIOUS ORGANISATIONS BY THE STATE

Poland

In contrast to Slovakia and the Czech Republic, the system by which Polish churches and religious organisations acquire legal personality (that is, gain recognition by the state) is relatively simple. In Poland an application for the official registration of a religious group must be signed by at least 100 of its members. Representatives of a new religious organisation must also attach their Articles of Association (for example, tenets of belief), and, if no objection is raised, the religious group will be recognised by the Ministry of the Interior.

The Polish Constitution (1997) recognises as equal the rights of different religious organisations. Thus, authorities of the state are obliged to grant equal rights and impose equal obligations on all legally recognised religious communities. Poland's judicial and administrative bodies must also respect this principle in addressing any relevant issues or problems. The Polish Constitution recognises the ideological and religious neutrality of the state. This neutrality is evidenced by a separation in the role and functions of the state and the church. In this sense, the Constitution stipulates that the relationship between the state and churches/religious organisations is based on the principle of respect for their autonomy, and the mutual independence of each within its own sphere – as well as on the principle of cooperation for the individual and the common good.[37]

The Czech Republic

In the Czech Republic, following Act no 3/2002 Sb on Churches and Religious Societies, the rules governing the registration of churches/ religious organisations were changed in 2002, so that the number of signatures that was originally needed for a group to be officially registered – 10 000 – was reduced to 300. At the same time however, the 2002 law limited the rights of newly registered communities only to that of gaining legal personality. In other words, it established the notion of 'special rights' that newly registered religious groups may only gain ten years after the date of their initial registration, on the basis that the number of their adult members corresponds to at least 0.1 per cent of the nation's citizens (which is more than 10 000). According to Act 3/202 the application for such registration must be filed with the Ministry by at least three legally competent adults, who are citizens of the Czech Republic, or are foreigners with permanent residence in its territory. The application for registration of the church/religious organisation must contain a basic description of its beliefs, as well as details of its teachings and the period of its establishment.[38]

Slovakia

Slovakia has the strictest system when it comes to the recognition by the state of a church or religious organisation. In Slovakia the state recognises only those churches and religious societies that have been officially registered by law. According to Act no 308/1991 Zb, the registration body is the Slovakian Ministry of Culture. A church or equivalent religious body may submit a proposal for its registration if it can prove that at least 20 000 adults – who are citizens of the Slovakian Republic and are domiciled within its territory – declare their affiliation to it.[39] The application for reg-

---

[37] Michał Pietrzak, 'Poľská republika. Právne postavenie náboženských spoločenstiev v Poľsku', in Silvia Jozefčiaková (ed), *Štát a cirkev v postsocialistickej Európe* (Institute for State–Church Relations, 2003) 64.

[38] §10–12 of Act no 3/2002 Sb, 'Návrh na registraci církve/náboženské společnosti'; see http://www.mkcr.cz/scripts/detail.php?id=372.

[39] §11 of Act no 201/2007 Zz. The majority of registered churches and religious societies evidently do not meet the relatively high membership condition. These churches and religious societies were registered under the provision of the Act stipulating that churches and religious societies, already active either under

istration must contain basic documents that relate to the church/religious organisation that wishes to be registered. In addition, a successful application for registration requires the formal affirmation of at least 20 000 adult members and Slovak citizens, domiciled within Slovakia, pledging that they declare affiliation to the church/religious group; support its application for registration; are its members; are familiar with its tenets of belief; and are aware of their rights and freedoms following from membership of the church/religious organisation.[40] These criteria are more rigorous than those found in Poland and the Czech Republic.

7.   CONCLUSION

It is a truism that nations such as Poland, the Czech Republic and Slovakia, separated from their western European neighbours by the Iron Curtain from the end of World War II until 1989, have been greatly affected by their experiences of the enforced atheism. The effect of this is often compounded by the fact that in some of these (and other) former Soviet satellite states, former 'career communists' continue to exert influence and remain active in public life. This inevitably has an effect, both perceived and real, on the protection of human rights, including religious belief.

A number of issues that generate controversy in the fields of religion and belief in much of Europe have been considered within the three nations considered in this chapter. For example, the often contentious issue of religious symbols has been examined by the Slovak Parliament. On 10 December 2009, the National Assembly of the Slovak Republic adopted the Declaration on Displaying Religious Symbols in Schools and Public Institutions,[41] in which it declared that the judgment of the European Court of Human Rights in *Lautsi v Italy*,[42] in which the Court had held that the display of crosses in Italian schools was a violation of the right of parents to educate their children according to their own beliefs, contradicted the cultural heritage and Christian history of Europe. Doubtless many in the National Assembly will have been pleased with the Grand Chamber's

---

the Act or on the basis of state consent on the date of the Act coming into force, are considered registered. The majority of churches and religious societies in the Slovak Republic work on the basis of deemed registration.

[40]   §11d of Act no 201/2007 Zz.

[41]   Declaration on Displaying Religious Symbols in Schools and Public Institutions available at http://www.nrsr.sk/web/Static/sk-SK/NRSR/Doc/v_nab ozenske-symboly.rtf.

[42]   *Lautsi and Others v Italy*, Application No 30814/06, 3 November 2009.

subsequent ruling that the display of crosses in Italian schools is not contrary to the European Convention on Human Rights (1950).[43]

Poland, the Czech Republic and Slovakia all face a number of challenges today in the fields of religion and belief. In the future particular challenges are likely to arise in areas such as education and the provision of lessons about religion and life philosophies in schools; the public financing of churches or religious organisations; the display of religious symbols; and the legal personality of churches and religious societies. These three nations may now be free from the yoke of Communist domination – but in the fields of religion and belief, many challenges undoubtedly lie ahead.

---

[43]   *Lautsi and Others v Italy*, Application No 30814/06, 18 March 2011 [GC].

12. Human rights and religion in the Balkans

Julie Mertus

1. INTRODUCTION

Eastern Europeans celebrated the end of the Cold War as a great 'opening'. While the Germans had their wall, the opening represented the physical tearing-down of the barrier and the flood of humanity pouring from one side to the other. The Czechs had their bridges and castles; throwing gates wide open, they marched to the castle (*na hrad!*), blasting 1980s dance music from cheap transistor radios. The Poles had their charismatic labour leaders, their poets and their dreamers, many of whom were suddenly set free from their dark jail cells. The people of the south Balkans[1] – in particular those living in what was then Yugoslavia – were less clear about what needed to be opened. To be sure, they had plenty of political prisoners crying for release as well as their own flows of cross-border humanity. Yet they were already considerably 'open'. As the 1984 site of the Winter Olympics, Sarajevo was a jewel in the crown of Yugoslavia, a city neither east nor west, a place where citizens boasted that they 'had the best passport in the world', because it was 'accepted almost everywhere'.[2]

The opening provided both challenges and opportunities for religious leaders in the Balkans. For the leaders of the three main religious groups – Muslim, Catholic and Orthodox – increasing religious freedom provided an opportunity to worship openly and to draw new believers into the fold. The opening, however, also created an incredible challenge. Religious leaders found themselves under international and local scrutiny as politicised figures representing not only their faith, but also their 'ethnic group' (that is, Serb, Croat, Albanian, etc). When conflict did erupt, religion

---

[1] The exact composition of the 'Balkans' is disputed. This chapter does not attempt to cover them all. States that are often discussed as Balkan, but not included here are Serbia, Montenegro, Croatia, Albania and Bulgaria.

[2] From author's interviews.

played a role in demarcating the enemy and religious leaders were under considerable pressure to engage with each other in order to overcome and resolve ethnic conflicts.[3]

Religious leaders who in the past had been persecuted for their faith suddenly witnessed the state refer to them – or at least to some distorted image of their liturgy – as saviours of their nation. The state began to have greater influence on the practice of religion whether as a proponent or an impediment. For example, previously political leaders would not have wanted to be caught wearing religious regalia. Today, a portrait of a political leader would not be considered complete without a religious leader posing nearby. There is a saying in Bosnia illustrating the mutual game of hypocrisy driving the Balkan approach to religious freedom: 'I do not mind if you lie to me, but I do mind if you think I believe you.'[4]

The wars in the Balkans in the 1990s add layers of complexity to any analysis of religious freedom in the region. This chapter examines three countries of the former Yugoslavia affected by the wars and by an internationally sponsored political transition: Bosnia-Herzegovina (Bosnia), Kosova and Macedonia. Each country has been chosen because of its illustrative nature.[5] All had once been part of Yugoslavia, and all have been recipients of foreign aid with additional assistance from foreign non-governmental organisations (NGOs) and faith-based organisations (FBOs). However the first two, Bosnia and Kosova,[6] were sites of protracted bloody conflict, while Macedonia survived a substantial political transition with very little bloodshed. Each case study is divided into two parts – first a very brief demographic section and then an analysis of religious freedom in contemporary times. In all three cases, the ethno-religious demography plays a key role in understanding the current state of religious freedom and prospects for the future.

---

[3] For a contrary argument, contending that religion was important 'in everyday life' in Bosnia, see Neven Andjelic, *Bosnia-Herzegovina: The End of A Legacy* (Frank Cass Publishers, 2003) 146–7.

[4] Dzemal Sokolovic, 'How to conceptualize the tragedy of Bosnia: civil, ethnic, religious war or . . .?', (2005) 1(1) *War Crimes, Genocide, & Crimes against Humanity* 115–30, see http://www.aa.psu.edu/journals/war-crimes/articles/V1/v1n1a4.pdf.

[5] Certainly other important Balkan states are excluded from this line-up due to time constraints.

[6] 'Kosova' is the Albanian term for the area; 'Kosovo' is the Serbian and Bosnian name. This chapter uses the Albanian terminology, because the ruling government is Slavic.

2. BOSNIA-HERZEGOVINA

Demographics[7]

Bosnia and Herzegovina ('Bosnia') is the most ethnically and religiously diverse Balkan state. According to unofficial estimates from the Bosnian State Statistics Agency, Muslims constitute 45 per cent of the population, Serb Orthodox Christians 36 per cent, Roman Catholics 15 per cent, Protestants 1 per cent, and other groups, including the Jewish community, 4 per cent. Relations between Albanian Muslim and Albanian Roman Catholic communities in Bosnia have traditionally been fairly positive.[8] There are 'numerous examples . . . where Muslim and Christian forms of pilgrimage and saint veneration have amalgamated and forms of religious division have become blurred'.[9]

Despite common self-identification with a major ethno-religious group, many people in Bosnia also identify as atheists or agnostics, and a substantial number do not regularly practise any religion. For most Bosnian Muslims 'religion' serves not as a specific system of belief, worship, or conduct, but as a community or ethnic identifier.[10] Bosniaks are generally associated with Islam, Bosnian Croats with the Roman Catholic Church and Bosnian Serbs with the Serb Orthodox Church. For Bosnian Muslims, like most Europeans, religious practice is limited to significant rites of passage, for example birth, marriage and death. Many Muslims view the observance of customary religious practices as compliance with cultural traditions. Bosnia, however, is presently going through a kind of religious revival and it is young Bosnians who are at the helm. Their impetus for greater participation in religious practice most likely stems from a need, common in postwar societies, for identification with their ethnic heritage.

---

[7] US State Department, 'Bosnia Herzegovina, international religious freedom report, 2010', available at http://www.state.gov/g/drl/rls/irf/2010/148920.htm.

[8] Hugh Poulton and Miranda Vickers, 'The Kosovo Albanian', in Hugh Poulton and Suha Taji-Farouki (eds), *Muslim Identity and the Balkan State* (New York University Press, 1997) 168.

[9] Der Duijzings, *Religion and the Politics of Identity in Kosovo* (Columbia University Press, 2000) 2.

[10] See Laurie Johnston, 'Religion in Kosovo and the Balkans: or blessing or curse', in Florian Bieber and Židas Daskalovski (eds), *Understanding the war in Kosova* (Psychology Press, 2003).

Analysis of Religious Freedom

Bosnia provides an excellent example of the importance of state structure and demographics when addressing the question of religious freedom. It also provides an illustration of what happens when religion is used as a symbol for nationhood. Under the Dayton peace agreement which ended Bosnia's 1992–5 war,[11] and under subsequent agreements on government composition,[12] Bosnia was divided into two highly independent entities: the Serb-dominated Republika Srpska (RS) (Serbian Orthodox) and the Croat-Bosniak (Croat-Catholic and Bosnian-Muslim) Federation. These two highly decentralised entities – each with its own government, parliament and presidency – are held together by a weak central body, which has its own set of human rights mechanisms.[13]

This model of government conflates ethnicity with religious faith and creates segregation by ethnicity and, in doing so, segregation by religion as well. This segregation, however, is precisely what advocates searching for a multi-ethnic solution to the Balkan wars had sought to avoid.[14] Under the segregated arrangement, the lines dividing politics, ethnic identity and religion are often blurred. During pre-election periods, for instance, religious sermons and services are sometimes misused for political purposes; furthermore, 'offices of local Bosnian Serb mayors in the RS . . . were often decorated with religious icons, although few officials practiced religion in . . . any meaningful sense'.[15] In this manner, religion is used as a tool in Bosnia, not to illuminate and to bring together populations with similar values, but to distinguish and divide.

Religious freedom in Bosnia does look good on paper. Its 1995 Constitution contains a long list of international human rights documents that are said to exemplify an integral part of the Constitution. Article 2 of the 1995 Constitution of Bosnia and Herzegovina explicitly calls on the government to protect the 'freedom of thought, conscience, and religion' of all citizens of Bosnia. However, the Constitution also explicitly names the

---

11 Freedom House, 'Freedom in the world 2010 – Bosnia-Herzegovina', 3 May 2010, available at http://www.unhcr.org/refworld/docid/4c0ceb0228.html.
12 Ibid.
13 I have written about this in more detail elsewhere. See Julie Mertus, 'Prospects for national minorities under the Dayton Accords', (1997) 23 *Brooklyn Journal of International Law* 793; 'The Dayton Peace Accords: lessons from the past and for the future', in Peter Cumper and Steven Wheatley (eds), *Minority Rights in the 'New' Europe* (Martinus Nijhoff Publishers, 1999).
14 See Sabrina Petra Ramet, *Balkan Babel: The Disintegration of Yugoslavia from the Death of Tito to the War in Bosnia* (3rd edn) (Westview, 1999).
15 US State Department, 'Bosnia Herzegovina' (note 7 above).

three main ethnic groups – Serb, Croat and Bosniak – as 'constituent peoples'.[16] An argument could be made that the Constitution effectively gives greater protection to the three religious groups connected to the ethnic identities – Serbian Orthodox, Croatian Roman Catholic and Bosnian Muslim.[17]

All of these written guarantees of religious freedom are promising.[18] In practice, however, the degree to which an individual or group is able to access their rights in Bosnia depends on the demographics of the area in which they live. While those that live in an area where they belong to the majority religion may have few complaints, those who are of a minority faith in that region could face significant obstacles to declaring their identity and worshipping openly. Religious freedom in Bosnia, therefore, is more complicated than traditional concern for religious minorities. Under current conditions in Bosnia, members of all three of the main religious groups – Muslim, Roman Catholic, and Serb Orthodox – could find themselves in the minority, with significant limitations on their religious freedom depending on where in the country they are located.

All three major ethnic/religious groups face potential human rights abuses through the deliberate targeting of religious structures. During the war in Bosnia, numerous buildings belonging not just to minority communities, but also to Islamic, Serbian Orthodox, and Roman Catholic communities, were damaged or destroyed. Although the state of Bosnia has issued building permits for reconstruction efforts, religious communities often lack the funds and the will to rebuild these facilities because of the fear that rebuilding efforts would only be met with repeated destruction. Religious leaders, therefore, have postponed the reconstruction of more symbolic religious sites in the country, such as the Ferhadija mosque in Banja Luka.[19]

Another issue indicative of progress on religious rights has been the

---

[16] The Constitution refers to 'constituent peoples, along with Others'. 'Others' is not defined.

[17] The Institute on Religion and Policy, 'Religious freedom in Bosnia' (7 October 2008), available at http://www.osce.org/odihr/34244?download=false.

[18] The entity constitutions of the Federation and the RS also specifically grant religious freedom to individuals. 'The RS Constitution, however, differs from the others as it makes no mention of international human rights standards,' Wolfgang Benedek observes. Wolfgang Benedek, 'The role of the international community with regards to human rights and democracy in Bosnia and Herzegovina, Kosova and Macedonia', in Wolfgang Benedek (ed), *Lessons (Not) Learned with regard to Human Rights and Democracy: A Comparison of Bosnia and Herzegovina, Kosova and Macedonia* (European Academic Press, 2009) 14–30, 59.

[19] US State Department, 'Bosnia Herzegovina' (note 7 above).

degree to which Bosnian religious leaders have been willing to tolerate and even support minority religious groups who wish to preach and
proselytise on Bosnian soil. Missionary activity has been limited but is
growing in Bosnia, representing an array of alternative faiths: Seventh-Day
Adventists, Jehovah's Witnesses, Krishna Consciousness and the Baptist
Church. New religious groups find it relatively easy to conduct their activities in Bosnia. The BiH Law on Religious Freedom, enacted in 2004, covers
the licensing and registration of religious groups.[20] Under this law, a new
centre for worship can be built by anyone who can provide a list of 300
adult citizens who are willing to attest that they are members who support
the entity.[21] Once churches and religious communities obtain legal status,
they are given the same privileges as those afforded to NGOs, and very few
restrictions are placed on their operations.[22]

The influx of missionaries has been accompanied by international and
national FBOs.[23] Mojca Leban, a field researcher who has substantial experience with NGOs and FBOs describes their great diversity:

> Some of these organizations are explicitly religious, i.e. they provide religious
> services. Other organizations, which are generally motivated by religious values
> but do not perform religious services, may be termed 'faith-based'. Faith-based
> NGOs engage in a range of activities, including promoting interfaith dialogue,
> providing immediate humanitarian aid, and fostering long-term reconstruction
> and sustainable development.[24]

The FBOs have proved beneficial in many communities. They generally pay
top dollar to the local staff, and they serve anyone in need without regard
to religious affiliation. Aside from offering spiritual guidance, often FBOs
also provide humanitarian relief and, in some cases, interfaith and inter-
religious dialogue towards reconciliation.

Certain FBOs have faced sharp criticism for imposing an outside, conservative religious agenda on a largely secular and more progressive people.
As another scholar with substantial field research, Kristen Ghodsee,
observes:

> 'Faith-based' organizations operate under the same legal framework and
> employ the same methods as most NGOs: social service provision, publish-

---

20   Ibid.
21   Ibid.
22   Ibid. See also The Institute on Religion and Policy, 'Religious freedom in
Bosnia' (note 17 above).
23   Mojca Leban, 'Faith-based NGOs in Bosnia and Herzegovina', (2003) 6(1)
The International Journal of Not-for-Profit Law, available at http://URL.de.
24   Ibid, 1.

ing, sponsoring workshops, etc. The goals of some of these organizations, however, are socially conservative, and their recent proliferation within Eastern European civil society sectors may bode well for democratic pluralism, but could undermine legal and social commitments to gender equality by creating pockets in society where 'religious freedoms' justify the marginalization of women.[25]

One issue that has received considerable attention is FBO encouragement of the wearing of the veil. 'Some women call the veil a return to tradition and a matter of choice,'[26] scholar and activist Vesna Peric Zimonjic explains. 'Those who oppose it call it a hangover of the war days when Bosniak Muslims received support from major Islamic countries, and were asked to respect Islamic laws in return.'[27] Aid organisations from Islamic countries are reported to pay women to wear the veil. While direct cash payments are likely to be an unproven rumour, other forms of incentive – such as high salaries and free private schooling – are documented. The salary offered to a woman worker by Islamic FBOs still generally outweighs that of Bosnian NGOs in general.

Bosnia's policies and practices on religious education are further evidence of significant progress in the area of religious tolerance. In public schools, students are not compelled to take religious courses. Many public schools offer religious instruction, albeit only in the region's majority religion. The treatment of the Holocaust in public schools has been improved in some areas by the involvement of foreign educators in Bosnian reconstruction efforts. The US State Department 2010 report on international religious freedom in Bosnia calls acts of anti-Semitism 'relatively infrequent'.[28] The report noted a 'tendency to mix anti-Israeli sentiment with anti-Semitism, as the general public and the media often failed to distinguish between criticism of Israeli policy and anti-Semitic rhetoric'.[29] The treatment of this issue can be viewed as a barometer of freedom of religion generally in Bosnia.

---

[25] Kristen Ghodsee, 'Religious freedom versus gender equality: faith-based organizations, and Islamic headscarves in the new Europe', (2007) 14(4) *Social Policy* 526.

[26] Vesna Peric Zimonjic, 'BALKANS: the veil comes down, again' (Inter Press Service News Agency, 26 November 2006) at http://www.wunrn.com/news/2006/11_27_06/120106_bosnia_the.htm.

[27] Ibid.

[28] US State Department, 'Bosnia Herzegovina' (note 7 above).

[29] Ibid.

3.   KOSOVA

Demographics

In Kosova, counting membership in religious groups is tremendously difficult. In the 1980s, Albanians who refused to participate in the state-sanctioned census; in the late 1990s and early 2000s, the Serbs in Kosova resisted participation. A stark contrast to Bosnia, Kosova appears to be the least ethnically and religiously diverse Balkan state. The vast majority of people in Kosova − over 90 per cent − are ethnic Albanians who identify as Muslims; an approximate 5–8 per cent are ethnic Serbs who identify as Serb Orthodox Christians, and the rest − 2–5 per cent − are Roman Catholic or Protestant.[30] Closer scrutiny, however, reveals layers of diversity. The 'Muslims' include groups demarcated as 'Turks' (people with a Turkish background, although native to Kosova),[31] 'Bosniaks' (people with a Slavic background, who speak Serbo-Croat),[32] Gorani (a small minority group that speak a particular Slavic dialect)[33] and Roma (who may be either Muslim or Christian).[34] Nearly all Muslims in Kosova are Sunni, although a smaller group of Shi'ites can be found in the countryside.[35]

The interaction of religious groups is further complicated by the phenomenon known as 'crypto-Catholicism', meaning that the population has 'publicly adopted Islam' but also partakes in 'the Catholic sacraments'.[36] In some homes, only the men would publicly go through the procedure for adopting Islam and the women would remain Catholic.[37]

---

[30]   Author's estimate; the last official census was in the 1980s.

[31]   'Turks' live predominately in and around Prizren, southern Kosova. William O'Neil, *Kosovo: An Unfinished Peace* (The International Peace Academy, Lynne Rienner, 2002) 56.

[32]   Ibid. Also known as 'Bosniack.'

[33]   Ibid at 57. Gorani live in the deep south of Kosova. They once dominated the Dragash municipality. Driven out by 'Albanian hardliners' in 1999 and 2000, only half of the Gorani population remains.

[34]   Ibid. The population falls into three groups: Roma, Egyptians and Ashkalia. Albanians accused them of collaborating with Serb forces. After the war with Serbia ended, they needed round-the-clock protection by international peacekeepers.

[35]   See generally Robert Elsie, *A Dictionary of Albanian Religion, Mythology and Folk Culture* (Hurst, 2001).

[36]   Howard Clark, *Civil Resistance in Kosovo* (Pluto Press, 2000) 32.

[37]   Ibid.

Analysis of Religious Freedom

While religion has been a symbol of nationhood in Bosnia and in other break-away states of the former Yugoslavia,[38] 'among Albanians in Kosova, religion has played a far less important role in forming a national identity'.[39] As Albanian poet Pahko Vasa put it, 'the religion of Albanians is Albanianism'.[40]

During the Balkan wars of the 1990s, Serbs and Albanians were particularly adept at using religion as propaganda to support their cause. As a report by the International Crisis Group (ICG) explained:

> The image of Kosova Serbs and their monasteries, usually portrayed as suffering under harassment and persecution by the Albanian majority population, formed a part of the nationalist propaganda that Milosevic and his supporters used to manipulate emotions. The Serbian Orthodox Church, however, was always divided over Milosevic. It supported him in large part to end what it saw as the victimisation of the Serb nation . . .[41]

Today, Kosova society is so firmly divided between Albanians and Serbs that one cannot address religious freedom, or any other social issue, without examining two sets of separate laws and policies: the official law and institutions of the state of Kosova and the law and institution of the pockets of Kosova-ethnic Serbs who refuse to treat Kosova as a state. Taking a line out of Kosova Albanians' own play book,[42] they have created their own parallel social and legal organisations as alternatives to the institutions established by the democratically elected Kosova government and sanctioned by the United Nations and other international players. The 'non-recognition' adherents look to Serbia for law and consistently boycott the new Kosova institutions that have been set up to provide human rights. As the Internal Displacement Monitoring Centre (a European NGO) has observed:

> Kosova Serbs have increasingly boycotted the new Kosova institutions and elections, therefore limiting their opportunities to defend their interests and

---

[38]   See Paul Mojzes (ed), *Religion and the War in Bosnia* (Scholars Press, 1998).

[39]   Johnston (note 10 above) 187.

[40]   Pahko Vasa, quoted in Tim Judah, *Kosova: War and Revenge* (Yale University Press, 2002) 12.

[41]   International Crisis Group, 'Religion in Kosova', 21 January 2001, on file with author.

[42]   For 'parallel structures' see Julie Mertus, *Kosova: How Myths and Truths Started a War* (University of California Press, 1994); Julie Mertus, *Human Rights Matters* (Stanford University Press, 2010).

establish constructive relations with Kosova authorities, which could help them build a future in an independent Kosova. On the other hand, much remains to be done by the Provisional Institutions of Self-Government (PISG) to increase the confidence of minority communities in Kosova institutions.[43]

The confidence of minority groups plummets as assaults directed against the Serbian Orthodox community continue and the police fail to offer protection. Each year there are reports of desecration of Serbian Orthodox graves, rock throwing and other assaults against Serbian Orthodox clergy travelling outside their monasteries, and attacks on Serbian pilgrims travelling by bus from Serbia to attend services at Decani Monastery.[44] Where attacks on Serb property have been particularly acute, clergy requested and received escorts from the NATO-led international peacekeeping force (KFOR).[45] Orthodox Serbs in Kosova also suffer from widespread discrimination and limited freedom of movement, access to property, justice, education, health care and employment.[46]

Kosova is not a case of institutional malfunction or failure. Rather, it is a case of not creating institutions that all residents use uniformly. Kosova was applauded internationally for including human rights prominently in its constitution. The constitution provides for the separation of religious communities from public institutions, stipulates that there is no official religion, and prohibits discrimination based on religion and ethnicity. However, the Commission of the European Communities has observed that the mechanisms for ensuring the implementation of rights are not yet in place. Some municipal human rights units are not operational whilst others, in particular in Kosova Serb majority municipalities, are reluctant to cooperate with the central authorities.[47] Successful prosecutions for attacks on religious minorities are rare in Kosova.[48] Weak administrative and judicial systems compound the problem, posing major obstacles to the realisation of the rights of religious minorities.[49]

---

[43]   Internal Displacement Monitoring Centre, 'Serbia: final status towards Kosova' (17 September 2005), available at http://www.internaldisplacement.org .

[44]   UN Security Council, 'Report of the Secretary-General on the United Nations Interim Administration Mission in Kosova' (1 September 2006) at http://www.unmikonline.org/SGReports/S-2007-707.pdf.

[45]   Ibid.

[46]   Ibid.

[47]   Commission of the European Communities, Brussels, 14 October 2009, SEC(2009) 1340/3, 'Kosova under UNSCR 1244/99 2009 progress report', available at http://vorige.nrc.nl/redactie/Europa/voortgangsrapporten2009/kosovo.pdf.

[48]   US State Department, 'Bosnia Herzegovina' (note 7 above).

[49]   Ibid.

Religious leaders of all faiths have complained of practical challenges resulting from the lack of a mechanism for religious groups to register and obtain legal status.[50] Leaders of various minority faiths make their own allegations. Protestants have a long-standing debate on whether they should be permitted to establish a Protestant cemetery and believe that they should be given a tax exemption for imported charitable donations. As for the dominant religion – Islam – the headscarves issue was heard by both the Ombudsperson's Office and the Kosova Islamic Community (known by its Albanian-language acronym, BIK). Public displays of conservative Islamic dress and culture, although still infrequent, have increased. There have been several cases in which students were expelled from public schools and teachers have also alleged that they were fired or refused jobs for wearing headscarves.[51]

Reports of radical Islamic groups infiltrating Kosova society appear more fanciful than real. One of the targets of fundamentalist missionaries, the youth of Kosova, flatly reject fundamentalism. The ICG argues persuasively that 'Kosova's extremely youthful population is western oriented and looks towards Western Europe and America for cultural influences'.[52] Without the youth on board, fundamentalism is not likely to draw many adherents.

4. MACEDONIA[53]

Demographic [54]

Macedonia has been called a 'mixed fruit salad'.[55] It is multi-ethnic, multi-confessional, multi-lingual and multi-cultural. The population is

---

[50] US State Department, 'Kosovo, international religious freedom report 2009', at http://www.state.gov/j/drl/rls/irf/2009/127318.htm.

[51] Ibid.

[52] Ibid 5.

[53] Because Greece strongly objected to recognising as a sovereign nation a country with the name 'Macedonia' – a name that Greece considers an integral part of Greece's history and territory – many states, including the United States, have recognised the area (which declared its independence from Yugoslavia) as the Former Yugoslav Republic of Macedonia. This territory will frequently be referred to in this chapter and in source documents as Macedonia, simply because the recognised name of the country is unwieldy.

[54] US State Department, 'Bosnia Herzegovina' (note 7 above).

[55] Besa Arifi, 'Lessons (not) learned regarding human rights and democracy in Macedonia', in Benedek (ed), *Lessons (Not) Learned with regard to Human Rights and Democracy* (note 18 above) 164.

overwhelmingly Macedonian Orthodox (65 per cent), while almost one-third of the population describe themselves as Muslim (31 per cent). Muslims in Macedonia receive a double identifier: first, the religious identity (they are Muslims living in Macedonia) and second, the ethnic identity (they are of one particular ethnic group – Albanians, Turks, Roma or Muslim Slavs).[56]

The exact number of Albanians (and of Muslims) is open to debate, as Albanians boycotted the last census in protest at Macedonia's new requirements for citizenship. According to a new law, to qualify one must have proof of one's own birth, evidence of both parents' birth within Macedonia, or proof of 15 continuous years' residence. According to Albanian activists, the onerous requirements are intended to keep Albanians undercounted and, as a result, to ensure that Albanians remain unable to take enough seats in government to veto constitutional change.[57]

The remaining Macedonians identify as Jewish (0.01 per cent), 'other Christian' (that is, Macedonian Catholic and Serbian Orthodox) (4 per cent) and 'unspecified'.[58] Curiously, although Albanians are almost exclusively the congregation of the Macedonian Catholic Church, the church uses the Macedonian language in its worship. Adherents to Serbian Orthodoxy live in northern Macedonia, along the Serbian border.

The demographic picture in Macedonia is perhaps the least likely of all countries in the Balkans to be influenced by inter-marriage. There are simply very few mixed marriages each year. In her review of research on the matter, Natasha Gaber-Damjanovska termed mixed marriages between Muslim Albanians and Turks, on one hand,[59] and Orthodox Macedonians, on the other hand, as 'simply nonexistent'.[60] The research found that Roma were the only group that 'mixed freely with other groups'.[61]

Analysis of Religious Freedom

The debate is open as to why Macedonia was spared the long-term, inter-ethnic, inter-religious violence that affected much of the Balkans

---

[56]   See generally Natasha Gaber, 'The Muslim population in FYROM: public perception', in Poulton and Taji-Farouki (eds), *Muslim Identity and the Balkan State* (note 8 above) 105.

[57]   Interview with author.

[58]   CIA Factbook, 'Macedonia', at https://www.cia.gov/library/publications/the-world-factbook/geos/mk.html.

[59]   At the time of writing the cited book's author, Judge Natasha Gaber-Damjanovska, was Natasha Gaber.

[60]   Gaber (note 56 above) 105.

[61]   Ibid.

following the break-up of Yugoslavia. One explanation is that conditions were relatively good for all residents of Macedonia and, thus, minority groups were more likely to employ civil options over warfare. Another possible explanation is that the communal conflicts simmering in Bosnia and Kosova pitted one ethnic group with a strong religious demarcation against another ethnic group with a strong religious demarcation. A similar conflict can be identified in Macedonia, but the main communal conflict, dating back hundreds of years, involves the Macedonian struggle to establish its own identity.[62] This is a contest within the Slav majority population, pitting Macedonian Orthodox believers against Serb Orthodox, and Slav Macedonians against Greeks and others claiming the Macedonian identity.[63] A quick glance at pro-Macedonian web pages reveals the official government position: 'The Macedonian Orthodox Church has played an important role in the long struggle of the Macedonian people for the preservation of its national identity, as well as in its education and culture. Its roots are ancient.'[64]

The destruction of Yugoslavia presented an opportunity to raise old grievances. Yet the number and percentage of Albanians in Macedonia willing to fight to change the status quo was very small, and other ethnic or religious groups, such as the Turks and Slavic Muslims in Macedonia, did not want to fight at all. In 2001, a band of Albanian rebels in Macedonia did stage an uprising demanding state recognition of their rights. Unlike Bosnia and Kosova, international intervention was quick and decisive, and the two sides could lay down their arms and reach a widely accepted agreement.[65] One of the rights recognised by the Macedonian state is religious freedom.

Article 19 of the Constitution of the Republic of Macedonia clearly states, '[t]he freedom of religious confession is guaranteed. The right to express one's faith freely and publicly, individually or with others, is guaranteed.'[66] Macedonian law protects this right against abuse committed either by governmental or private actors.

---

[62] Wolfgang Höpken, 'From religious identity to ethnic mobilization' in Poulton and Taji-Farouki (eds), *Muslim Identity and the Balkan State* (note 8 above) 74.

[63] See generally Hugh Poulton, 'Changing notions of identity among Muslims in Thrace and Macedonia: Turks, Pomaks and Roma' in Poulton and Taji-Farouki (eds), *Muslim Identity and the Balkan State* (note 8 above).

[64] Mymacedonia.com, on file with the author.

[65] For more detail on the internationally brokered agreement, see generally Arifi (note 55 above) 165–7.

[66] Macedonia Constitution, at http://www.servat.unibe.ch/icl/mk00000_.html.

Officially there is no state religion. However, the first Constitution of Macedonia made the same mistake as several other states breaking away from Yugoslavia: it appeared to favour the Macedonian Orthodox Church (MOC) by mentioning only the MOC 'and other religious communities and groups'.[67] A 2001 amendment to the Constitution tried to rectify the mistake, by including a much longer list: the Macedonian Orthodox Church, the Islamic Community in Macedonia, the Roman Catholic Church, the Jewish community, and the Evangelical Methodist Church. For critics of the state of Macedonia, however, the state had already exposed its true colours: favouritism toward the MOC.

When a law was created for the registration of religious groups, the critics balked at what they viewed as overly onerous requirements. However, the registration process closely resembled that of other Balkan states and all states that registered acquired status as legal entities, equal before the law. More troublesome to critics was the burden placed on individual missionaries. Foreigners entering the country to carry out religious work or to perform religious rites are required to receive letters of invitation and to obtain approval from the State Commission for Relations with Religious Communities; groups must obtain visas.

Another area of concern is education. There are no restrictions on religious education in religious spaces such as churches and mosques; nor are there limitations on private religious schools at the secondary level and above. Under the original plan, when children were to enter the sixth grade, their parents were to choose between a single-faith religious doctrinal course and a secular course on history of religions. The idea quickly changed in 2009, however, when the Constitutional Court ruled that single-faith religious courses were inconsistent with the Constitution's separation of church and state.

Religious training has made some Balkan-watchers nervous. Experts are now seeing an increasing radicalisation in pockets of the country's Islamic community. According to Wolfgang Höpken, a Professor of Balkan History at the University of Leipzig, there has been 'an increase in prestige associated with possession of Islamic knowledge in villages[;] this confers status on older people, as well as the very young, who can now educate themselves in religious matters.'[68] Traditional religious practices, such as praying at prescribed times and abstaining from alcohol and premarital sex, are still not observed to a large extent. On these subjects, young Muslims

---

[67] Ibid.
[68] Höpken (note 62 above) 74.

look to Central Europe for guidance as well as to what could be called a world youth culture.[69]

5. CONCLUSION

A major part of the opening of religious freedom in the Balkans involved not clergy, but lawyers. Lawyers from the USA and western Europe were on hand to offer assistance in making the transition from authoritarian states to human rights-respecting democracies. Religious freedom was a primary beneficiary of this trend. As discussed in this chapter, the new constitutions for the new democracies all include religious freedom. Table 12.1 (see below) unpacks the constitutional provisions in a manner that promotes comparative analysis.

In sum, each of the three Balkan states profiled in this chapter addresses matters of religion, national identity and state–church relation differently. Bosnia conflates religion with national identity: to be Serb is to be Orthodox, to be Bosniak is to be Muslim and to be Croat is to be Catholic. Because peace among these three groups is dependent upon improved relations among both nations and religions, Bosnia has made religious freedom a central component of its new society. It has been only partly successful, however. The degree to which one can enjoy religious freedom in Bosnia is still related to whether one is of an ethnic/religious minority in a particular region. The importance of this observation cannot be overstated. Police escorts are often the difference between life and death for ethno-religious minorities.[70] Although Bosnian religious leaders and refugee advocates have joined together in support of refugees returning to their pre-war homes, very few have actually attempted to return if doing so means becoming part of a minority ethno-religious group.[71] Under the Bosnian scenario then, improving state mechanisms to protect minority rights is essential.

Public perception often paints a dreary picture of Kosova as a region

---

[69]   See eg http://www.youthmesh.org; http://www.slideshare.net/seanmarston/global-youth-culture.

[70]   See US State Department, 'Kosovo' (note 50 above).

[71]   Researchers estimate that out of 1 million returning refugees and internally displaced people, 467 297 are minority returns (people returning to a place where they are now part of a minority group), a remarkable statistic: Huma Haider, 'The politicization of humanitarian assistance: refugee and IDP policy in Bosnia and Herzegovina (The Feinsten International Center) at sites.tufts.edu/jha/archives/700.

Table 12.1 Summary of constitutional provisions

Features Countries	Preamble or sovereignty provision includes ethnic or national groups	Non-discrimination provision includes religion	Citizenship provision mentions religion	Fundamental freedoms section includes religion	Other provisions related to religion
Bosnia and Herzegovina	Bosniaks, Croats and Serbs as 'constituent peoples', among others	All persons within the territory of the Federation shall enjoy the rights to freedom from discrimination based on . . . religion	No persons can be deprived of . . . citizenship [based] on . . . religion . . .	Yes, refers to 'freedom of religion, including public and private worship'	Religion included as 'vital interest of constituent peoples'
Kosovo	The Republic of Kosovo is a multi-ethnic society consisting of Albanian and other communities	No	No	Yes, includes the right to accept and manifest religion . . . and the right to accept or refuse membership in a religious community or group	Provision on 'religious denominations' states: Kosovo ensures and protects religious autonomy and religious monuments . . . religious denominations are free to independently regulate their internal organization, religious activities and religious ceremonies [this

| Macedonia | Macedonia is established as a national state of the Macedonian people; co-existence with Albanians, Turks, Vlachs, Romanies and other nationalities . . . | No | . . . restriction of freedoms and rights cannot be applied to the . . . freedom of personal conviction, conscience, thought and religious confession | Yes, freedom of religious confession is guaranteed | The Macedonian Orthodox Church and other religious communities and groups are free to establish schools and other social and charitable institutions, by ways of a procedure regulated by law |
| | | | | | includes] the right to establish religious schools and charity institutions in accordance with the Constitution and the law |

Sources: Constitution of Bosnia and Herzegovina: www.ohr.int/ohr-dept/legal/oth-legist/doc/fbih-constitution.doc; Constitution of the Republic of Kosovo: http://www.kushtetutakosoves.info/?cid=2,250; Constitution of the Republic of Macedonia: http://www.servat.unibe.ch/icl/mk00000_.html.

plagued by perpetual conflict. Contrary to popular belief, Kosova actually has a long history of 'co-existence with considerable movement across ethnic and religious frontiers, through trade, cultural diffusion, religious exchange and conversion'.[72] Instead of organising political struggles along religious lines, Albanian identity is shaped by national lines. An Albanian Catholic is every bit as Albanian as an Albanian Muslim. But a Serbian Catholic (or a Serbian anything – that is, Serbian Orthodox) is a natural enemy of the Albanian Catholic. In recent times, Albanians and Serbs have taken turns boycotting each other's governments, relying instead on their own 'parallel institutions' that have proved incapable of promoting minority rights. Not until these parallel structures are dismantled will Kosova have any chance at winning back its reputation as an open crossroads in Europe.[73]

The case of Macedonia rests somewhere in between Bosnia and Kosova. To a certain extent, religion is conflated with nationality; religious traditions are used to signify national traditions. Unlike Kosova, where the religion of Albania is Albanianism, the religion of Macedonians is not Macedonianism; rather it is Orthodoxy. A Macedonian is only a true Macedonian when he/she is Orthodox. The debate over Orthodoxy does not pit the state against a minority group (as in Kosova), but rather creates a bilateral struggle of state religion – the Macedonian Orthodox – against its perennial enemy and powerful neighbour: the Serbian Orthodox Church.[74]

States, communities of faith and individual worshippers – east and west – who wish to support religious freedom in the Balkans cannot take a 'cookie-cutter' approach. There is no common and unchanging answer to such questions as 'who wins and who loses under the status quo and under likely changes?', 'what is the relationship between religious and national identity?' and 'what kind of influence do "kin states" or "kin religions" have on the daily practice of religion?' However, understanding the three very different ways in which Bosnia, Kosova and Macedonia address religious freedom is a good start.

---

[72]   Duijzings (note 9 above) 1.
[73]   US State Department, 'Kosovo' (note 50 above).
[74]   US State Department, 'Macedonia, international religious freedom report 2010', available at http://www.state.gov/j/drl/rls/irf/2011/eur/192835.htm.

13. Understanding religion in Europe: a continually evolving mosaic

Grace Davie

1. INTRODUCTION

There are different ways of looking at the religious situation in Europe: the first considers the features that are common to Europe as a whole; the second looks at the differences across the continent. Both are important. This chapter will start by looking at a range of factors that can be found in all 27 member states of the European Union, bearing in mind that their relative strength varies. The second section will develop a series of variations based on the different confessional blocs (Orthodox, Catholic and Protestant) that constitute the Christian churches of Europe. It will also consider the contrasts between what is commonly known as western Europe and the parts of the continent that were under communist domination from 1948 to 1989. In the latter, the religious trajectory is noticeably different. The third section points to the paradox that underlies a great deal of this book: on one hand are the relatively high levels of secularity in most if not all of Europe, but on the other is the marked resurgence of religion in public debate – a combination that was not anticipated in the immediate postwar decades. Two points are central to this discussion. It is important to grasp, firstly, that this combination is indeed a 'paradox' in the sense that the elements in question are not related to each other but have nonetheless occurred at the same time. Secondly, the paradox is best understood in light of the shifting relationship between the public and private. A short discussion of this relationship, and its implications for the study of religion, concludes the chapter.

2.   COMMON FACTORS[1]

There are six very different factors that – taken together – contribute to a better understanding of the place of religion in modern Europe. The crucial point to remember is that these factors are present right across the continent but push and pull in different directions. Currently they are interacting in new ways to produce distinctive formulations of religious life, some of which are unexpected. The six factors are:

1.   The role of the historic churches in shaping European culture;
2.   An awareness that these churches still have a place at particular moments in the lives of modern Europeans, though they are no longer able to discipline the beliefs and behaviour of the great majority of the population;
3.   An observable change in the churchgoing constituencies of the continent, which operate increasingly on a model of choice, rather than a model of obligation or duty;
4.   The arrival in Europe of groups of people from many different parts of the world, and with very different religious aspirations from those seen in the host societies;

---

[1]   The material in this section is largely drawn from two relatively recent publications: Grace Davie, 'Is Europe an exceptional case?' (2006) 8 *The Hedgehog Review* 23–34 (a special issue entitled 'After Secularization') and Grace Davie, 'Religion in Europe in the 21st century: the factors to take into account', (2006) XLVII *Archives européennes de sociologie/European Journal of Sociology/ Europaeisches Archiv für Soziologie* 271–96. What follows is necessarily selective, but additional overviews of religion in Europe can be found in Grace Davie, *Religion in Modern Europe* (Oxford University Press, 2000); Timothy Byrnes and Peter Katzenstein, *Religion in an Expanding Europe* (Cambridge University Press, 2006); Philip Jenkins, *God's Continent: Christianity, Islam, and Europe's Religious Crisis* (Oxford University Press, 2007); Jean-Paul Willaime, *Europe et religions: Les enjeux du XXIe siècle* (Fayard, 2004); *Le retour du religieux dans la sphère publique* (Olivétan, 2008); Effie Fokas, 'Religion: towards a post-secular Europe?', in Chris Rumford (ed), *SAGE Handbook of European Studies* (SAGE, 2009). Political approaches include Philip Schlesinger and François Forêt, 'Political roof and sacred canopy? Religion and the EU Constitution', (2006) 9 *European Journal of Social Theory* 59–81; François Forêt, *Légitimer l'Europe. Pouvoir et symbolique à l'ère de la gouvernance* (Presses de Sciences Po, 2008); François Forêt (ed), *L'Espace public européen à l'épreuve du religieux* (Editions de l'Université de Bruxelles, 2007). More specific discussions of church and state can be found in John Madeley and Zsolt Enyedi (eds), *Church and State in Contemporary Europe: The Chimera of Neutrality* (Frank Cass, 2003); Gerhard Robbers (ed), *State and Church in the European Union* (Nomos Verlagsgesellschaft, 2005).

5. The reactions of Europe's secular elites to the increasing salience of religion in public as well as private life; and
6. A growing realisation that the patterns of religious life in modern Europe should be considered as an 'exceptional case' in global terms – they are not a global prototype.

Each of these factors will be taken in turn in the paragraphs that follow.

Cultural Heritage

The starting point reflects the undisputed role of Christianity in shaping European culture, bearing in mind that other factors (notably Greek rationalism and Roman organisation) must also be kept in mind. One example will suffice to illustrate this fact: the Christian tradition has had an irreversible effect in determining the most basic categories of human existence (time and space) in this part of the world. Both week and year follow the Christian cycle, even though the major festivals of the Christian year are beginning to lose their resonance for large sections of the population. They are nonetheless retained as a framework for public holidays. Sunday, moreover, remains distinctive even though the notion of a 'day of rest' has largely been discarded. The same is true of space. Wherever you look in Europe, Christian churches predominate, some of which retain huge symbolic value for the populations that surround them; and from the largest city to the smallest village, Europeans orient themselves by reference to religious buildings even if they seldom enter them for worship. This is not to deny that in some parts of Europe (notably the larger cities) the skyline is fast becoming an indicator of growing religious diversity. Europe is changing, but the legacies of the past remain deeply embedded in both the physical and cultural environment.

The Historic Churches

Physical and cultural presence is one thing; a hands-on role in the everyday lives of European people quite another. Commentators of all kinds agree that, with very few exceptions, the latter is no longer a realistic aspiration for the historic churches of Europe. That does not mean, however, that these institutions have entirely lost their significance as markers of religious identity. The following terms are useful in understanding these ambiguities: first, the notion of 'believing without belonging' and, second, the concept of 'vicarious religion'.[2]

---

[2] Both ideas come from the work of Grace Davie. See *Religion in Britain*

One of the most striking features of religious life in contemporary Europe is the mismatch between different measurements of religiousness.[3] There exists, first of all, a set of indicators that measure firm commitments to (a) institutional life and (b) *credal* statements of religion (in this case Christianity). These indicators, moreover, are closely related to each other in so far as institutional commitments – in the form of regular religious practice – both reflect and confirm religious belief in its 'orthodox' forms.[4] The believing Christian attends church to express his or her belief and to receive affirmation that this is the right thing to do. Conversely, repeated exposure to the institution and its teaching necessarily disciplines belief.

No observer of the current religious scene disputes that these dimensions of European religion are both interrelated and in serious decline. Fewer Europeans go to church than they used to. As a result, the idea of a common narrative (of Christian liturgy or of Christian language and metaphor) becomes more and more tenuous almost by the day. There is, on the other hand, considerable debate about the consequences of this situation. The complex relationship between belief in a wider sense and practice is central to this discussion, for it is abundantly clear that, in the short term at least, a manifest reduction in the 'hard' indicators of religious life has not had a similar effect on rather less rigorous dimensions of religiousness. For the time being, the latter remain relatively strong (the data are clear on this point). Between two-thirds and three-quarters of Europe assent to 'belief in God', and roughly similar proportions touch base with the institutional churches at some point in their lives, often at times of crisis. It is precisely this state of affairs that is captured by the phrase 'believing without belonging'.

In parenthesis, it is important to remember that many secular institutions have declined similarly, both in Europe and beyond. The most obvious examples are political parties, trades unions and the wide range of leisure activities that require 'gathering' on a regular basis. Following this line of argument, believing without belonging is a pervasive dimension of modern European societies; it is not confined to the religious lives of European people. That said, the connections between emergent patterns of belief and

---

since 1945: Believing without Belonging (Blackwell, 1994), 'Vicarious religion: a methodological challenge' in Nancy Ammerman (ed), *Everyday Religion: Observing Modern Religious Lives* (Oxford University Press, 2007); 'Vicarious religion: a response', (2010) 25 *Journal of Contemporary Religion* 261–7.

[3]   Reliable statistical information at both European and national level can be obtained from the European Values Study (http://www.europeanvaluesstudy.eu/) and the International Social Survey Programme (http://www.issp.org/).

[4]   'Orthodox' in the sense of mainstream doctrine in the church in question.

the institutional churches are complex. Not only do the latter continue to exist; they quite clearly exert an influence, both direct and indirect, on many aspects of individual and collective lives – even in Europe. The notion of 'vicarious religion' is helpful in this context.

By vicarious is meant the notion of religion performed by an active minority but on behalf of a much larger number, who (implicitly at least) not only understand, but appear to approve of what the minority is doing. The first half of the definition is relatively straightforward and reflects the everyday meaning of the term 'vicarious' – that is, to do something on behalf of someone else. The second half captures the legacy of the state churches of Europe and is best explored by means of examples. Religion can operate vicariously in a wide variety of ways. For example, churches and church leaders perform ritual on behalf of others (at the time of a birth or a death for instance); if these services are denied, this causes offence – the more so amongst those who do not attend regularly. Church leaders and churchgoers believe on behalf of others and incur criticism if they do not do this properly. Once again it is, very often, the occasional churchgoer who articulates this disquiet most clearly, and the more senior the church leader, the worse the problem gets.[5] Thirdly, church leaders and churchgoers are expected to embody moral codes on behalf of others, even when those codes have been abandoned by large sections of the populations that they serve. This is true particularly with respect to family life and is one reason for the widespread disgust that many Europeans (and indeed others) felt regarding the disclosures of child abuse among Catholic priests. Churches, finally, can offer space for the vicarious debate of unresolved issues in modern societies. If the latter were not the case, it is hard to understand the persistent scrutiny of their positions on a wide variety of topical issues, from changing views regarding the nature of sexuality to the difficult moral questions surrounding birth and death – which reflect in turn the meaning of life itself.

An alternative way of illustrating the nature of vicarious religion is to consider the place of religion and the continuing role of religious institutions in European societies when they face the unexpected or the tragic. The reactions provoked by the death of Princess Diana in August 1997 offer a revealing illustration: what happened in the week following the car accident in Paris cannot by any stretch of the imagination be described as either

---

[5] The problem is nicely exemplified by the furore that greeted the Archbishop of Canterbury, following a much misinterpreted remark concerning Shari'a law in a lecture given on 7 February 2008. See http://www.archbishopofcanterbury.org/articles.php/1137/archbishops-lecture-civil-and-religious-law-in-england-a-religious-perspective.

rational or secular, but nor was it conventionally religious. So what was it? One point is clear: a great deal of the improvised and markedly heterogeneous rituals that emerged among ordinary people at that time took place in the vicinity of centrally placed churches. It was these churches, moreover, that housed books of condolence and facilities for lighting candles – ordinary people queued for hours to make use of these resources – and it was the established church (the Church of England) that took responsibility for her funeral. Even more important, however, is the fact that the reactions to Princess Diana's death (or any number of more recent equivalents) are simply 'writ-large' versions of what goes on in the everyday lives of individuals and communities all the time. People die, sometimes unexpectedly, and communities suffer, sometimes with little apparent justification. What is to be done on these occasions and who is to do it?

This, of course, is not the whole story. Alternative agencies are emerging all over Europe to respond to such situations, including armies of counsellors and an increasing number of secular officiants trained to undertake the ceremonies that mark the turning points of life.[6] It is equally clear that a sense of vicarious religion remains stronger in some places than others and in some generations than others. It is difficult to establish hard data on a concept as elusive as vicarious religion, but it appears to resonate most strongly among Europeans who reached adulthood before the 1960s and may not, therefore, endure in its present form for very much longer.[7] Regarding regional variations, the notion is most easily articulated in those parts of Europe where it finds financial expression – that is in the Nordic countries and in Germany where church tax, or its equivalent, remains the norm.[8] Paradoxically, on a wide range of other indicators, these are some of the most secular places in Europe. Further south, there are Catholic and Orthodox equivalents of the same idea, some of which relate to national as well as confessional identity. To be Italian, for example, means to be residually Catholic; to be Greek means to be Orthodox, in the sense that active members of minority faiths are considered less 'Greek' than non-practising, or half-believing Orthodox.

---

[6]   See for example the work of the Norwegian Humanist Association in this respect, at http://www.human.no/Servicemeny/English/?index=3 or http://www.human.no/Servicemeny/English/.

[7]   For more details on the nature of vicarious religion, see note 2 above. For an account of the 1960s and its significance for religion, see Hugh McLeod, *The Religious Crisis of the 1960s* (Oxford University Press, 2010).

[8]   That is a system in which contributions to the church are collected through the secular tax system. All members of the population make such a contribution unless they contract out.

From Obligation to Consumption

Where, though, does this leave Europe's diminishing, but still significant churchgoers – those who maintain the tradition on behalf of the people described in the previous section? Here an observable change is clearly taking place, best summarised as a shift from a culture of obligation or duty to a culture of consumption or choice. What was once simply 'imposed' on Europeans (with all the negative connotations of this word), or 'inherited' (which has a rather more positive spin), becomes instead a matter of personal choice. Religiously active Europeans now go to church or to another religious organisation because they choose to, sometimes for a short period and sometimes for longer, sometimes regularly and sometimes occasionally, but they feel no *obligation* either to attend that church in the first place or to continue if they no longer want to do so.

As such, this pattern is entirely compatible with vicariousness: the historic churches need to be there in order that Europeans may attend them if they so choose. Their nature, however, gradually alters, a shift that is discernible in both practice and belief, not to mention the connections between them. There is, for example, an easily documentable change in the patterns of baptism in the Church of England. The overall number of baptisms has dropped dramatically in the postwar period, evidence once again of institutional decline. In England, though not yet in the Nordic countries, or indeed in parts of southern Europe, baptism is no longer seen as a ritual associated with birth, but has become increasingly a sign of membership in a chosen voluntary community. In other words membership of the historic churches is changing in nature. They are becoming more like the growing number of free or independent churches that can be found all over Europe, though more in some places than in others. Voluntarism is beginning to establish itself de facto, regardless of the constitutional legacies of state churches.

A second point follows from this. What are the most popular choices of modern Europeans when it comes to religious attendance? The answers to this question are doubly interesting in the sense that they not only indicate the strengths and weaknesses of the present situation, but reveal that the predictions of an earlier generation (by both scholars and church people) were largely incorrect. Specifically, in the current period Europeans are disproportionately drawn to two kinds of religious organisation: charismatic evangelical churches on one hand and cathedrals or city-centre churches on the other. The former epitomise firm commitments, strong fellowship and conservative teaching, offset by the warmth of the charismatic experience. The latter allow a much more individual (even anonymous) expression of religious commitment: in 'cathedral-type' churches the appeal is often associated with the beauty of the building, the quality of the music and the traditional nature of the liturgy. The important point to grasp is that in both cases there is a noticeable *experiential* element, albeit very differently expressed.

In the middle decades of the period since World War II, something rather different was envisaged. Conservative teaching was out of fashion and cathedrals were often classed as 'dinosaurs' – less and less relevant to the modern world and expensive to maintain. They are still expensive to maintain, but the data indicate that they are increasingly attractive to late-modern populations, whether these come as regular worshippers, less regular worshippers, tourists or pilgrims – noting that the lines between these categories are distinctly porous.[9] Conversely, rather more liberal forms of Protestantism, noticeably fashionable in the 1960s, have not fulfilled their earlier promise. There are, of course, important exceptions to this rule but by and large the purely cerebral has less appeal in the twenty-first century than many people thought would be the case.

New Arrivals

The fourth factor in this sociological 'map' of religion in Europe concerns the growing number of newcomers in many parts of the continent, most notably western Europe. There are three stages in this process. The first was closely linked to the urgent need for labour in the expanding economies of postwar Europe – especially in Britain, France, Germany and the Netherlands. The second wave of immigration occurred in the 1990s and included, in addition to the places listed above, the Nordic countries, Ireland and the countries of Mediterranean Europe (Greece, Italy, Spain and Portugal) – bearing in mind that until very recently many of these had been countries of emigration rather than immigration. Indeed, the shift from one to the other was extraordinarily rapid and took almost everyone by surprise. A third stage can be found in the movement from the east to the west of Europe that mostly took place after 2004 (or in some cases 2007), when the enlargements of the European Union permitted the easy movement of people from the countries formerly under Communist domination to what is conventionally known as 'the west'.

None of these are primarily religious movements, but the implications for

---

[9]   In parenthesis, it is important to note that pilgrimage is an increasingly popular activity all over Europe. The numbers of pilgrims increase year on year and for every type of shrine: medieval (Santiago de Compostela), Marian (Lourdes or Medjugorje) or modern (Taizé).

the religious life of the continent are considerable. The first point to grasp is that the consequences of this process vary from place to place, and depend as much on the host society as on the new arrivals themselves. Britain and France offer an instructive comparison in this respect. In Britain immigration has been much more diverse than in France, both in terms of provenance and in terms of faith communities. Britain is also a country where ethnicity and religion criss-cross each other in a bewildering variety of ways (only Sikhs and Jews claim ethno-religious identities). Thirdly, Britain is more ready than many of her European neighbours to embrace diversity – a tradition that stretches back to a colonial past where rule through local elites was the norm. The situation in France is very different: here immigration has been largely from the Maghreb, as a result of which France has one of the largest Muslim communities in Europe – an almost entirely Arab population. Rightly or wrongly, Arab and Muslim have become interchangeable terms in popular parlance in France. France, moreover, firmly rejects the notion of *communautarisme*, in the sense that French citizens are welcomed as such: their primary identity is to France, not to an intermediate group, be it religious or another.[10] Once again the resonance with colonial policy is clear: French rule in the colonies meant direct rule from Paris.

Beneath these differences, however, lies a common factor: the growing presence of other faith communities in general, and of the Muslim population in particular, is challenging some deeply held European assumptions. The notion that faith is a private matter and should, therefore, be proscribed from public life – notably from the state, from welfare and from the education system – is widespread in Europe. Conversely, many of those who are currently arriving in this part of the world have markedly different convictions, and offer – simply by their presence – a challenge to the European way of doing things. The details of these complex and continuing engagements constitute the subject matter of this volume. The particular question of the public and the private and its implications for social science will be re-opened in the concluding section of this chapter.

Europe's Secular Elites

The interactions described in the previous section raise, however, a further point: that is the extent to which the secular elites of Europe make use of these events to articulate alternatives (ideological, constitutional and institutional) to religion. In order to understand this point fully, it is important to grasp two things: firstly, that such elites have re-emerged in European

---

[10]   See Chapter 8 by Sylvie Bacquet in this volume.

societies as a *reaction* to the renewed presence of religion in public debate (resurgent religion brings with it resurgent secularism); and secondly, that these groups, just like their religious counterparts, vary markedly from place to place. As ever the nature of the religious and the nature of the secular go hand in hand. Key in this respect is an appreciation of the secularisation process – specifically, an awareness that this has taken place differently in different European countries.[11] For example, what in Britain, and indeed in most of northern Europe, occurred gradually (starting with a de-clericalisation of the churches from within at the time of Reformation), became in France a delayed and much more ideological clash between a hegemonic, heavily clerical church and a much more militant, secular state. The result was 'la guerre des deux Frances' (Catholic and *laïque*), which dominated French political life well into the twentieth century. The legacies still remain in the form of a self-consciously secular elite, and a lingering suspicion of religion of all kinds – the more marked when this threatens the public sphere. The fact that these threats are no longer Catholic but Muslim does not alter the underlying reaction.[12]

Norway offers a rather different illustration. Proportionally speaking Norway houses a surprisingly large number of humanists. Many of these are members of the Norwegian Humanist Association, which campaigns for the separation of church and state and the full equality of all religions and life stances in Norway. It actively encourages secular ceremonies for rites of passage, including 'confirmation' (see above). Particular attention is paid to schools (including the place of religious education in the curriculum) and to young people – a separate youth organisation was established in 2007. The Association becomes in fact a parallel institution to the state church and is, in many ways, similar to this. It is, for example, partly financed by the equivalent of 'church' tax (there is also an annual membership fee).[13] Above all the tone of the debate, despite some sharp differences in opinion, is distinctively Norwegian – it is very different from the French case. Both, however, should be considered in the same context: resurgent religion has very largely taken Europe by surprise – hence the vehemence of the secular reaction.

Is Europe an Exceptional Case?

The final factor introduces a rather different perspective. Indeed, it reverses the essential question: instead of asking what Europe is in terms of its

---

[11]   See David Martin, *A General Theory of Secularization* (Blackwell, 1978).
[12]   See Chapter 14 by Jørgen Nielsen in this volume.
[13]   See notes 6 and 8 above.

religious existence, it asks what Europe is not. It is not (yet) a vibrant religious market such as that found in the United States; it is not a part of the world where Christianity is growing exponentially, very often in Pentecostal forms, as is the case in the global south; it is not a part of the world dominated by faiths other than Christian, but is increasingly penetrated by these; and it is not for the most part subject to the violence often associated with religion and religious difference in other parts of the globe – the more so if religion becomes entangled in political conflict. Hence the inevitable, if at times disturbing conclusion: that the patterns of religion in modern Europe, notably its relative secularity, might be an exceptional case in global terms.

This point is all the more crucial if we remember that the paradigms of social science emerge from the European case and are very largely premised on the notion that modern societies are likely to be secular societies. It follows that the traditional, Europe-based understandings of social science might be markedly less suitable for the study of religion in other parts of the world. Indeed, they are not always helpful in Europe itself given the intricacies of religious life in the early years of the twenty-first century.

3. REGIONAL DIFFERENCES

Confessional Blocs

The preceding section has described the factors that are common to Europe as a whole. Central to this story is the mutation in the historic churches of Europe as these once dominant institutions come to terms with a very different situation. As ever, this has happened differently in different places. Common to all Europe's churches, however, are their historic attachments to political power – first in the form of Empire, later in the form of the nation state. An important corollary of this situation is the necessary connection between Europe's state churches and territory, a link expressed at every level of society – supra-national, national and local. This last is important: the whole of Europe, from north to south and east to west, is divided into parishes – a core unit of administration that for centuries had civic as well as ecclesiastical resonance.

This situation dates from the time of Constantine, who in 325 convoked the Council of Nicaea. The Nicene Creed (promulgated by the Council) included the phrase the 'one holy catholic and apostolic Church'. By the end of the fourth century this church – Orthodox Christianity – had become not only the state religion but also a defining institution of the Byzantine Empire. This sharing of power should not be taken for granted; it was a

world away from first-century Palestine and the beginnings of Christianity
as a vulnerable sect. Indeed, the transformation was astonishing. At its
zenith, the Empire stretched from central and eastern Europe, into Asia
and through much of north Africa. It lasted for ten centuries, coming to
an end in the fall of Constantinople (Byzantium) to the Ottoman Turks
in 1453. Even now Orthodox Christianity remains the dominant creed of
much of east Europe: that is, in Greece, Cyprus, Romania, Bulgaria, Serbia
and, of course, Russia.

The first major split in the Christian world occurred in the eleventh
century, the point when the continuing tensions between western (Catholic)
and eastern (Orthodox) Christianity could no longer be contained. The
reasons for such tensions were both doctrinal and ecclesiological: the
former concerned the nature of the Trinity (specifically the *filioque* clause,
which altered the relationship between the three persons of the Trinity);
the latter reflected the pre-eminent role of the Pope in the western church,
which contravened Orthodox teaching that all bishops were essentially
equal – in other words that every bishop is Peter's successor in his own
church. Events came to a head in 1054, the date generally accepted for the
'great schism'.[14]

The western church was centred on Rome and stretched both to the north
and to the west. Until the time of the Reformation, the Roman Catholic
Church and the Holy Roman Empire were the core institutions of western
Europe and were closely interrelated. Such links continued until the sixteenth century (Charles V was the last Emperor to be crowned by the Pope,
in 1530). The relationship was not always peaceful, however, as secular
power vied with the church for dominance, notably over the appointment
of bishops. It was never entirely clear who was dependent on whom. In
the early-modern period, however, *both* these pan-European institutions
suffered as the aspirations of local rulers grew stronger, a movement that
coincided with the growing criticism of the Catholic Church at the time of
the Reformation.[15] The movement took different forms in different parts of
the continent, but a second upheaval in the politico-religious life of Europe
became increasingly inevitable.

The term 'Reformation' is highly ambiguous: does this imply innova-
tion and the breaking of new ground, or does it involve a return to and
rediscovery of primitive excellence? The political implications are equally

---

[14]   See 'Great Schism' in FL Cross and EA Livingstone (eds), *Oxford
Dictionary of the Christian Church* (Oxford University Press, 2005).
[15]   See Diarmaid MacCulloch, *Reformation: Europe's House Divided 1490–
1700* (Penguin, 2004).

hard to define. Were those who endorsed the theological changes taking place at this time looking primarily for radical change or simply for greater independence? It is clear that motives were mixed. The second, rather more conservative option was bound to appeal to political rulers anxious to establish independence from external authority (whether secular or religious), but with a careful eye on stability within. Both were possible within the Lutheran concept of a 'godly prince'. Sometimes the prince had jurisdiction over a whole kingdom or kingdoms. Such was the case in the Nordic countries where Lutheranism became embodied in the state churches of northern Europe. Elsewhere the process was far more local and concerned relatively small patches of land. The German case illustrates the latter, leading to patterns that are not only extant but influential some 400 years later. Both examples embody the principle *cuius regio, eius religio* ('whose realm, his religion'), established at the Peace of Augsburg in 1555 – it was a concept that brought to an end the pre-Reformation notion of a unified Christendom.

The Reformation as such, moreover, was differently understood. In addition to Lutheranism, parts of Europe – notably the Swiss, the Dutch, the Scots, some Germans, some Hungarians and Czechs and a small but significant minority of French people – were attracted first by Zwingli, then by Calvin, towards a more rigorous version of Protestantism. Calvinism was both more radical and more restrained than Lutheranism: radical in the sense of a new kind of theology based on the doctrines of predestination and redemption, but restrained in terms of its stringent moral codes. The effect of this combination on the subsequent economic development of Europe has provided inexhaustible material for continuing debate amongst historians and sociologists alike. The key lies in the influence, or otherwise, of theological changes on the everyday behaviour of men and women.

Broadly speaking, western Europe divided itself into a Catholic south (Spain, Portugal, Italy, France, but including Belgium and Ireland), a Protestant north (the Nordic countries and Scotland) with a range of 'mixed' countries in between (England and Wales, Northern Ireland, the Netherlands and Germany). Central Europe exemplifies similar categories, though the geography is more complicated. Lithuania, Poland, Slovakia, Slovenia and Croatia are firmly Catholic; Estonia and Latvia are predominantly Lutheran and relate closely to their Nordic neighbours (a commonality strongly re-emphasised as the Baltic republics regained their political independence in the early 1990s); Hungary and the Czech Republic, finally, are rather more mixed (primarily Catholic but with significant Protestant minorities). In other words, boundaries gradually emerged all over Europe dividing one nation from another, one region from another and one kind of Christianity from another. Boundaries, moreover, imply dominance as well as difference. Majorities and minorities were, and still are, created depending on the precise location of the line in question.

This, in essence, is the confessional map of western Europe that took shape in the early-modern period and that has remained relatively stable ever since. It would be a mistake, however, to assume that church–state arrangements necessarily follow suit. What emerges in the latter respect is a bewildering variety of arrangements, dictated for the most part by particular historical circumstances, that change over time as political necessity dictates or as economic or social shifts suggest. As we have seen, these very individual histories continue to resonate in the twenty-first century as different European societies come to terms with the changes outlined in the previous section – including the arrival of new and different faiths – but each in their own way. Common to them all, however, are the historic and continuing links between church and territory, a defining feature of religious life in Europe and utterly different, for example, from the situation that pertains in the United States.[16]

Communist and Non-communist Europe

Europe was differently divided following World War II. In the immediate postwar period, not just Germany, but Europe as a whole was carved up by the western allies and the Soviet Union. The Baltic States, Poland, East Germany, Hungary, Czechoslovakia, Albania and (until 1948) Yugoslavia fell under Soviet control. The implications for religion were considerable. The ideology that pervaded the Soviet bloc was aggressively secular – to the point of serious harassment, and in some cases, outright persecution of anyone who displayed almost any form of religion except entirely private belief. Public displays of religiousness were considered a threat to the regime and were rigorously suppressed, more brutally in some cases than others. Exactly what happened in each of the countries listed above varied; equally different were the effects of Soviet policies on religious vitality.

For example, in those countries that had embraced Lutheranism at the time of the Reformation and who found themselves under Soviet control after 1948 (that is, Estonia, Latvia and East Germany), there were undoubtedly countless acts of individual heroism. Institutionally, however, the church was less able to resist, leading to much reduced levels of religious activity in these parts of Europe – a situation that has changed relatively little since the fall of communism. The Catholic Church was in a rather

---

[16]   See Peter Berger, Grace Davie and Effie Fokas, *Religious America, Secular Europe* (Ashgate, 2008).

different position, and became in some places, if not all, a major bulwark against communism. This was particularly true in Poland, a situation that became all the more visible after the election of a Polish Pope (John-Paul II) in 1979. The Soviet authorities found it increasingly difficult to resist the forces of popular Catholicism, galvanised by a charismatic and globally visible Pope. The Orthodox countries display similar contrasts: Bulgaria, for instance, became increasingly secular while Romania did not. Indeed, in the latter religious practice remains particularly high. As ever, the reasons for these different reactions lie in the specifics of each country.[17]

A crucial point, however, is common to all these cases. In all of them, the collusions of religious and political power described in the previous section were necessarily subverted. No longer were the dominant churches of this part of Europe dependent on the state for favours; they were, rather, victims of an aggressively secular ideology. Of course some churches and some individuals were compromised, but in many cases, religious institutions became the natural and very effective carriers of an alternative ideology – providing space for gathering and for increasingly public debate. As we have seen, this was particularly true in Poland, where the protest was highly visible. Interestingly, an equally effective example can be found in East Germany, where – at the critical moment – a tiny, infiltrated and seriously weakened Lutheran church became the focus of resistance. In the Nicolaikirche in Leipzig, meetings for religious discussion became more and more political and gradually spilled out into the streets. Such protests constitute one factor among many in the collapse of the Soviet bloc, which becomes a pivotal moment not only in the history of Europe but in the entire global order. The implications for religion are difficult to overestimate.

The future, however, is hard to predict as the post-communist countries continue to work out their new-found freedoms. In this part of Europe, the religious indicators remain volatile and are not always easy to interpret. They are, moreover, closely bound up with national identities, sometime benignly, sometimes less so. Equally important are the movements of population from one part of the continent to another. Poles, for example, are moving west (to the United Kingdom and to Ireland in particular) and Romanians are moving to Italy – a trend, however, that is beginning to diminish as the whole of Europe confronts the current (2008) economic

---

[17]   Though outside the European Union as such, it is important to note the Uniate (or Greek Catholic) churches, which follow the Orthodox rite but remain in full communion with Rome. They are found on the eastern border of Europe, notably in Belarus and the Ukraine. The fact that they are more west-facing than either the Russian or the Ukrainian Orthodox churches is of significance in the political alignments of their members.

crisis.[18] In short, the patterns of religion in Europe continue to make and remake themselves as old boundaries dissolve and new ones arise, and as economic opportunities continue to ebb and flow.

Levels of Religious Activity

It is important, finally, to look at the different levels of religious activity in different parts of Europe.[19] The first and most obvious contrast lies between the notably more religious countries of southern Europe (both Orthodox and Catholic) and the less religious countries of the Protestant north. This variation holds across almost every indicator; indeed, they are interrelated. Levels of practice are markedly higher in Romania, Greece, Poland, Lithuania, Italy, Spain and Ireland (closer in its religious life to continental Europe than to Britain) than they are elsewhere. Unsurprisingly, one effect of regular attendance is a corresponding strength in traditional belief in both Orthodox and Catholic Europe – confirming a point already made.

There are, however, exceptions to this rule. France, for example, displays a very different profile from the other Catholic countries, a contrast that cannot be explained without reference to French history. Belgium and Spain, moreover, look likely to follow this pattern, in contrast to Italy where practice remains relatively high. Other exceptions to a European pattern, or patterns, should be looked at in a similar light. Conspicuous here are the two Irelands where high levels of religious practice endured for longer than they did elsewhere. Once again, the particular nature of Irish history accounts for this: religion has become entangled with questions of Irish politics on both sides of the border. The persistence until very recently of religious practice as well as belief in both the Republic and Northern Ireland is both cause and consequence of this situation.

One final variation within the overall framework should also be noted. In France, Belgium, the Netherlands and, possibly, Britain (more especially England) and Norway, there is a higher than average incidence of those claiming no religion, or at least no denominational affiliation. It is quite possible that this may become the norm in other European societies, but it might not. The continuing and marked secularisation of much of Europe is most certainly a persuasive factor but it is not the whole story.

---

[18]   Ireland, for example, has resumed its traditional status as a country of emigration.

[19]   See note 3 for sources of statistical material.

4.   A PERSISTENT PARADOX

Indeed, it is the unpredictability of the present situation that is most striking. As already indicated, two things are happening at once in twenty-first-
century Europe. On one hand are the increasing levels of secularity, which
lead in turn to an inevitable decline in religious knowledge as well as in
religious belief. On the other is a series of increasingly urgent debates about
religion in the public square. This largely unexpected combination is difficult to manage, both across the continent as a whole and in its constituent
nations. This is hardly surprising in that European populations are losing
their knowledge of religion (that is, of vocabulary, concept and narrative)
just when they need these most – given the requirement, on an increasingly
regular basis, to pass judgement on the rights and obligations of the very
varied religious actors, individual and corporate, that currently cohabit in
Europe. The consequent debates are both ill-informed and ill-mannered
as Europeans re-open questions that they had considered closed, and are
doing this largely on the basis of ignorance.

Much of this book has been dealing with these issues, for the simple reason
that many of them have legal implications. In terms of the social-scientific
understanding of religion in Europe, the emphasis – in terms of the questions asked – is rather different. Two themes, however, are of particular
importance in the context of this chapter: first, the ambiguous distinction
between the public and the private, and second, the significance of this
question not only for the secular but the *post*-secular – asking specifically
whether the latter is a helpful term in current analysis. One point is already
clear: simply deeming religion to be a private rather than a public matter does
not get to grips with the issues at stake. Quite the reverse in fact, given that it
is more likely to hide the problem that requires attention than to resolve it.

Initial (for the sake of argument, mid-twentieth-century) interpretations of the European situation went more or less as follows: scholars of
many disciplines very largely agreed that religion was disappearing from
the public sphere in Europe, but that it continued to endure in the private
lives of many Europeans. This moreover was a normative position: most
Europeans, notably the political class and a wide range of intellectuals, considered the privatisation of religion to be a good thing. The point should
not be exaggerated: until very recently religion remained an important
marker of identity, of political allegiance and of voting behaviour right
across Europe – indeed in many places, it still is. As an institution, however,
religion should be independent of the state (de facto if not de jure), and
neither entity (state nor church) has the right to impose a belief system or
specified forms of liturgy on its citizens. The state, in other words, should
be strictly neutral in matters of faith.

The privatisation of religion can also be approached in terms of religious practice. Hence the discussion above that related to both 'believing without belonging' and 'vicarious religion', recognising that the latter (amongst other things) constituted a step back from privatisation in the sense that it partially reinstated the role of the religious institution – bearing in mind that for many Europeans institutional commitment is passive rather than active. Much more radical, however, have been the very visible changes that made themselves felt in the final decades of the twentieth century and which are, if anything, intensifying at the present time. The point can be exemplified in a whole series of events that have brought the question of religion to the forefront of debate in Europe. A by no means exhaustive list would include the heated discussions surrounding the preamble to the European Constitution, the Rushdie controversy in Britain, the *affaire du foulard* in France, the murders of Pim Fortuyn and Theo van Gogh in the Netherlands (together with the subsequent defection of Hirsi Ali to the United States), the furore over the Danish cartoons of Mohammed, and the bombings in the transport systems of both Madrid and London in 2004 and 2005 respectively. More recently, the debate about representations of Mohammed has spread to Sweden, the legality of minarets has been challenged in a Swiss referendum, and in some parts of Europe the *niqab* has been banned altogether.

Each episode is different but they share a common feature: in each case minority voices, from whatever faith, have challenged the values of the host society – including the notion that religion is primarily a private matter. A burgeoning literature in this field, both academic and other, is in itself an index of growing concern.[20] Equally revealing is the lively discussion that has emerged in the social sciences regarding the *post*-secular as a cogent idea in intellectual analysis, and as a possible framework within which to approach the issues at stake.

Broadly speaking there are two approaches to the post-secular. On one hand are those who argue that, since the 1970s, there has been a marked change in the nature and forms of religion in the modern world – a trend that peaked, at least in terms of its visibility, in the attack on the twin towers in New York in September 2001. On the other are scholars who emphasise not so much a change in religious situation as such as a shift in the attitudes of western scholars to this. Both are instructive.

The shorthand for the first position is 'God is back'[21] – a phrase that

---

[20] An up-to-date bibliography of this exponentially growing field can be found at http://www.euro-islam.info.

[21] 'God is back' is the title of an important, though controversial book by two

indicates that something *substantive* has changed regarding the place of religion in the modern world, a shift that requires the attention of scholars from many different disciplines (the economic and social sciences, international relations, development studies and so on). This situation moreover has penetrated Europe in the sense that even this 'most secular' continent can no longer isolate itself from what is happening elsewhere. Europeans react accordingly, though not all in the same way. Some wish to preserve the distinctiveness of Europe as a relatively secular enclave. Others emphasise two millennia of Christian history and resent the intrusions of other faiths. (Interestingly, each of these reactions depends very largely on the other.) Yet others are more open to the modern world in the sense that they are ready to embrace change and to live in an increasingly diverse environment. The reactions of social scientists are equally varied and range from rigorous reaffirmations of the secular nature of their disciplines to new forms of thinking that make every endeavour to accommodate the religious factor.

The recent work of Jürgen Habermas has become a touchstone in this respect.[22] In a key statement, Habermas takes as his starting point the increasing visibility of religion in the modern world. He addresses the issue in terms of John Rawls's celebrated concept, the 'public use of reason'. The challenge that emerges is provocative: Habermas invites of secular citizens, including Europeans, 'a self-reflective transcending of the secularist self-understanding of Modernity'[23] – an attitude that quite clearly goes beyond 'mere tolerance' in that it necessarily engenders feelings of respect for the world view of the religious person. There is in fact a growing reciprocity in the argument. Historically, religious citizens had to adapt to an increasingly secular environment in order to survive at all. Secular citizens were better placed in that they avoided, almost by definition, 'cognitive dissonances' in the modern secular state. This might not be the case for much longer, however, as religion and religious issues increasingly pervade the agenda.

An additional question follows from this. Are these issues simply to be regarded as relics of a pre-modern era, or is it the duty of the more secular citizen to overcome his or her narrowly secularist consciousness in order to engage with religion in terms of *'reasonably expected disagreement'*,[24] assuming in other words a degree of rationality on both sides? The latter

---

senior editors from *The Economist*: John Micklethwait and Adrian Wooldridge, *God is Back: How the Global Rise of Faith is Changing the World* (Allen Lane, 2009).

[22] Jürgen Habermas, 'Religion in the public sphere' (2006) 14 *European Journal of Philosophy* 1–25.

[23] Ibid, 15.

[24] Ibid.

appears to be the case. Habermas's argument is challenging in every sense of the term and merits very careful reflection; it constitutes an interesting response to a changing *global* environment – one moreover in which the relative secularity of Europe is increasingly seen as an exceptional case.

There is, however, an alternative point of view – the second of the approaches set out above. Protagonists of this position are less ready to say that 'God is back' for the simple reason that God never went away. The real shift that has taken place in recent decades is not so much a return of religion to the modern world, and indeed to Europe, as a return of religion to the consciousness of western social science. Hans Joas, for example, challenges Habermas on precisely this point, arguing that the latter's earlier approaches to the key activities of modern societies were insufficiently sensitive to the religious factor, which was nonetheless present.[25] In other words, it is the perceptions of Habermas (and indeed many others) that have changed rather than the religious situation as such. In his own contributions to the debate, Joas himself moves in a different direction. He is more inclined to scrutinise the different understandings of the 'secular' and the very varied processes of secularisation, distinguishing up to seven different meanings in the latter. It is in working through these complexities that we will find the keys to a better understanding of modernity, not in an exaggerated contrast between unitary, and thus distorting, concepts of secular and post-secular. In a more theological response to this discussion, Ola Sigurdson takes a median position.[26] He argues that something substantive has changed, not least in Europe where what he calls 'the Westphalian paradigm' is no longer viable. It follows that neither the state church, nor its *alter ego* the radical privatisation of religion (believing without belonging) offer an adequate frame for the understanding of religion in this part of the world. For want of a better word, Sigurdson labels this situation post-secular.

Whatever we choose to call it, it is clear that the place of religion in modern Europe merits the close and continuing attention of scholars from a wide variety of disciplines. This is so in terms of the features that are common to the continent and in terms of those that divide it, bearing in mind that both are likely to mutate in the course of the twenty-first century. Precisely how is harder to say and must remain an empirical question.

---

[25]   Hans Joas, *Do We Need Religion? On the Experience of Self-Transcendance* (Paradigm Publishers, 2002).

[26]   Ole Sigurdson, 'Beyond secularism? Towards a post-secular political theology' (2010) 26 *Modern Theology* 177–96.

14. Islam and secular values in Europe: from canon to chaos?

Jørgen S Nielsen

1. INTRODUCTION: UNDEFINING 'MUSLIM'

As politicians and the media constantly remind us, Islam and the presence of sometimes long-established Muslim communities in the countries of the European Union (and its immediate neighbours)[1] often seem to be one of the main drivers in debates about the interaction of law, religion and the public space. The public profile of issues identified with Islam and Muslims gradually rose during the 1990s, taking on a marked security dimension towards the end of the decade that was strikingly confirmed by the events of 11 September 2001 and subsequent terror attacks in Europe. The centrality of the challenge has been emphasised by other 'crises': the Danish cartoons affair over the winter of 2005–6, the rise of anti-Islamic voices on the political right both within existing political parties and acting as the mobilising factor for new parties, such as that led by Geert Wilders in the Netherlands. Most recently, female dress, especially the wide range of fashion covered by what has become the generic term *burqa*, has become a focal point – the French debate leading to the banning of face covering in public, which came into force in April 2011, started a trend that has been copied in other countries, mostly at the local government level, although Belgium has also passed a law.

A core dimension of this whole process has been a strengthening of the tendency to treat Islam and Muslims in Europe as if they constitute an undifferentiated community. When challenged, most exponents of this approach (though not all) will quickly acknowledge the many differences of an ethnic nature, and sometimes also of a class or educational character.[2]

---

[1] By this I refer not only to Norway and Switzerland (take, for example, the minaret ban voted for in the latter in late 2009) but also the countries of former Yugoslavia (where Kosova, for example, had its own 'headscarf crisis' during 2010.

[2] The main reference work providing an introduction to these aspects is

However, the differentiation goes rather deeper and is much more complex than this. There is not only a question of what kind of Islam (defined as theological, legal or political as well as cultural, national and linguistic) Muslims relate to, but also a question of how they relate to whatever it is they relate to. A study of mosques in Denmark has suggested that by a very broad and inclusive reckoning at the most 50 per cent of the roughly 220 000 people of a Muslim cultural background have any kind of active relationship to Islam in any visible manifestation.[3] But anthropological research working with the concepts 'implicit religion'[4] and 'everyday religion'[5] has further diffused the question. As increasingly with questions of identity in general, it is clear that it is contextual and relational. In his study of the London district of Southall, Gerd Baumann showed in the mid-1990s that as a communal identity component religion was very closely related to local conditions both social and political.[6]

All this takes place in a context, that of Europe, where the process of secularisation, in its broadest sense, has been under way for two centuries or more. The disappearance of shared authoritative references and discourses, which this development has led to, provides an environment in which Muslims, especially those who have arrived since 1945, find scope for reviewing what it means to be Muslim on a scale that is quite unfamiliar historically or in their countries of origin. The motivation for exploring this open – secular – space can be found in a variety of factors but primary among them is the mix of cultural and religious traditions that have come together in the same urban spaces as a result of the migration. I recall the experience of a research student who, in the late 1970s, visited the Birmingham Central Mosque at Friday prayer to find out what young men there felt the community needed from the local authority. When the questioning turned to burial, there was a heated argument between two groups about how a burial should be conducted, both groups claiming authority in the Qur'an, which says nothing about how to bury. It turned out that the young men originated from villages in two different parts of

Jørgen S Nielsen, Samim Akgönül, Brigitte Maréchal and Christian Moe (eds), *Yearbook of Muslims in Europe*, vol 2 (EJ Brill, 2010).

[3]   Lene Kühle, *Moskeer i Danmark – islam og muslimske bedesteder* (Mosques in Denmark: Islam and Muslim places of prayer) (Univers, 2006).

[4]   Grace Davie, 'Believing without belonging: is this the future of religion in Britain?', (1990) 37 *Social Compass* 455.

[5]   Nancy Ammerman, *Everyday Religion: Observing Modern Religious Lives* (Oxford University Press, 2007).

[6]   Gerd Baumann, *Contesting Cultures: Discourses of Identity in Multi-ethnic London* (Cambridge University Press, 1996).

Pakistan and were both claiming their tradition as the correct Islamic one. Repeated innumerable times, that kind of experience has forced Muslims to reconsider the link between religion and its cultural expressions, and those Muslims who have grown up in Europe have acquired the intellectual tools to conduct that analysis.

The main part of this chapter looks at the various processes that are taking place within this environment, looking at how the resources of the Islamic tradition – theology, jurisprudence, institutions, etc – are being mobilised and adapted in the European context. A shorter concluding section then looks briefly at the discussion specifically on secularism, before a brief 'afterthought' considers some implications for the European legal constitutional models of recognition.

2.   DE-CENTERING ISLAM: THE FRAGMENTATION OF TRADITIONS

Probably the most critical point of interaction between Muslims and the European environment is the issue of Shari'a. The problem is exacerbated by the fact that there is really no agreement among Muslims themselves, nor among European observers, on what Shari'a means or stands for. To the extent that Shari'a has become a point of conflict it is more as a symbol than a matter of substance.

Some Muslims will immediately protest that there is no argument over what is meant by Shari'a: it is God's will as revealed in the Qur'an and modelled by the prophet Muhammad in the Sunna. The medieval North African scholar Abu Ishaq al-Shatibi (died 1388) stated it even more simply: the Qur'an is the Shari'a.[7] But this presentation begs the question of interpretation. The more puritan traditions of the present, as witnessed in those trends usually conflated under the term Salafi, insist that the Qur'anic revelation must be understood literally and cannot be subjected to human interpretation – which is, of course, itself a human interpretation. Not far distant from such views is one representative of Hizb al-Tahrir, a radical offshoot of the Muslim Brotherhood tradition:[8]

---

[7]   MK Masud, *Shatibi's Philosophy of Islamic Law* (Kitab Bhavan, 1997) 247ff.

[8]   See Suha Taji-Farouki, *A Fundamental Quest: Hizb al-Tahrir and the Search for the Islamic Caliphate* (Grey Seal, 1996).

Islam obliges us to accept the Sovereignty of Allah (*Salla Allahu Alaihi Wasallam*) in all of life's affairs from the individual to social, economic and political affairs.[9]

In this statement one sees a reflection of the often presented view that Islam is all-encompassing, that it governs all aspects of life.

It has traditionally been taught in western academia that Islamic law, after an initial period lasting some 400–500 years, during which it emerged, developed and took on its classic form, then stagnated and underwent a process of repetition and confirmation rather than renewal. This view is expressed in the concept of the 'closing of the gate of *ijtihad*', which describes how independent reasoning (*ijtihad*) was replaced by adherence to existing authority or 'copying' (*taqlid*): the Shari'a is immutable, we are told. This view of Shari'a has taken hold in the European public mind, supplemented with regular reminders of harsh punishments and suppression of women and non-Muslim minorities. It has also infiltrated some corners of European law. The European Court of Human Rights seems to have adopted this view of Shari'a. For example, in 2003, when it upheld the Turkish Supreme Court's banning of the Refah party, it said 'that sharia, which faithfully reflects the dogma and divine rules laid down by religion, is stable and invariable'.[10]

However, over the last few decades scholarship has convincingly shown that this has been only one tendency. There has always been a practice of *ijtihad* at various times in various regions. In the Indian subcontinent during the sixteenth and seventeenth centuries there were significant new developments both spiritual and legal that have become the foundations of characteristic dimensions of South Asian Islam. In a rather technical 1988 study on land tax and rent in the late Mamluk and early Ottoman period, Baber Johansen showed that, through much of Islamic history, the key to legitimacy was not the particular ruling or regulation, but rather whether it had been arrived at by legitimate lines of reasoning.[11] More recently Knut Vikør points out succinctly that 'the central factor was that the law was common and had the proper authority, not necessarily what it said'.[12]

---

[9] See http://www.khilafah.com/home/category.php?DocumentID=6454&Tag ID=2 (accessed 13 May 2005).

[10] *Refah Partisi (The Welfare Party) and others v Turkey* (App nos 41340/98, 41342/98 and 41344/98) (ECtHR, 13 February 2003) (GC) para 123.

[11] Baber Johansen, *The Islamic Law on Land Tax and Rent* (Croom Helm, 1988).

[12] Knut Vikør, *Between God and the Sultan: A History of Islamic Law* (Hurst, 2005) 30.

From this perspective, Shari'a takes on the character of a discourse rather than a code of the Napoleonic style.

Historically the significance of the Shari'a – whatever it may have meant at any given time or place – is reflected in the central role in the structures of public life that those institutions that have carried the Shari'a have often played.[13] Some of the most critical moments in the development of early and classical Islamic state formation have been contests over the control of either the substance of the Shari'a as a legal corpus, of the training and disposition of the professional groups, the *ulama*, who implemented the Shari'a, or of the courts and their processes. Put succinctly, the result of these developments before the modern period was that the manpower and institutions of Shari'a achieved and regularly confirmed their independence from political power. Rulers did retain ways of influencing the religious institutions as the most essential factor in preserving their legitimacy. They could bribe or browbeat, and often did, but throughout Islamic history the *ulama* who associated too closely with the ruler risked losing both respect and authority. The rulers could attempt to sponsor the colleges that trained the *ulama*, and establishing and endowing such *madrasa*s could be a successful way of assuring at least the acquiescence of most of them.[14] Or the rulers could support rival power centres, most commonly either (or both) in the shape of the Sufi orders and their endowments or in alternative legal jurisdictions, most famously in the Ottoman *qanuni* courts.

As political power has changed under the impact of European expansion from the eighteenth century, some quite radical alterations have taken place. First and foremost has been the prolonged weakening of the institutional expressions of the Shari'a. A traditional Islamic training has ceased to be the entry visa to government or professional employment as European-style schools and universities have been developed to serve the new bureaucracies and independent professions of modernising states. And the law has come under direct state control in a manner that was unprecedented in Islamic history, both in that the state has now established and managed the court system with state-appointed judges, and in that the state has taken control of legislation. This has been the case even in the field of family law, the one area of the traditional Shari'a that had

---

[13] See Emile Tyan, *Histoire de l'organisation judiciaire en pays d'islam* (EJ Brill, 1960).

[14] This technique was used with a great deal of success in consolidating Sunni preponderance in Egypt, Syria and Mesopotamia after the collapse of the Shi'te Buyid rulers of Baghdad in 1058 and the Fatimids of Egypt a century later; see Ira M Lapidus, *A History of Islamic Societies* (2nd edn) (Cambridge University Press, 2002) 291.

remained the preserve of the *ulama* until the late nineteenth century, while all other areas had gradually been taken away over the previous centuries. In the context of contemporary state organisation in much of the Muslim world, especially in the Arab world, what amounts to a contract has been established between authoritarian states, often founded on professions of secularism, and the Islamic teaching structures in the form of Islamic Studies Faculties at numerous old and new universities. Both sides of this contract are riding tigers, which requires constant adjustments and renegotiations.

In the meantime forms of Islam, more or less organised, have been appearing in the interstices, where the state finds it difficult to impose its will, spaces that occasionally are sponsored by foreign states with their own interests. So beside these various forms of official Islam, one has seen a growing variety of new ideas finding traction. They experiment with concepts of community and society, of nation and family, of rights and obligations, and with the theological implications of those questions, especially when so often the state seems unable to provide the minimum of social, health, educational and economic infrastructure and at a time when high-speed and mass-capacity electronic communications provide almost unlimited access to the broad range of ideas around the Muslim world and outside.[15] While the recent upheavals in the Arab world are not primarily religious in character, they illustrate the impact of electronic communications in raising awareness of alternatives to those ideas and systems currently dominant.

This not-quite-free 'market' of ideas finds a much more open environment in Europe, so much so that one can almost talk of a fragmentation of Islamic tradition. An opinion poll in early 2006 in Denmark indicated that of those Muslims surveyed less than 20 per cent attached themselves to any of the prominent Islamic personalities and their mosques or organisations, and the highest any one of these scored was 6 per cent. A similar fragmentation showed up in a survey published in 2007 by the right-of-centre UK think tank Policy Exchange.[16] It suggested that, likewise, the largest national Muslim federation, the Muslim Council of Britain, could only raise 6 per cent support. In France since 1990 there have been three attempts on the part of the government to sponsor a Muslim federation

---

[15]　See Ibrahim M Abu-Rabi', *Contemporary Arab Thought: Studies in post-1967 Arab Intellectual History* (Pluto Press, 2004); Asef Bayat, *Making Islam Democratic: Social Movements and the Post-Islamist Turn* (Stanford University Press, 2007).

[16]　Munira Mirza, Abi Sernthilkumaran and Zein Ja'far, 'Living apart together: British Muslims and the paradox of multiculturalism' (Policy Exchange, 2007) 79–83.

with which it can negotiate. Currently the third such attempt, the Conseil Français du Culte Musulman (CFCM), has been in existence since 2002. Since its foundation there have constantly been assertions from one or other party about the 'representativeness' of rivals.[17]

Of course, such rivalries are often primarily of a political character as organisations seek standing in public and among Muslims, as well as access to resources both in the countries of the Muslim world and in the country of settlement. But they are also more than that since the organisations often represent not only a political standpoint, often with national and ethnic foundations, but also an ideological stance. Since the Turkish government first sought greater control over its émigrés through its religious structure, the Diyanet (the Directorate of Religious Affairs located in the office of the prime minister), after the military coup of September 1980, Turkish Islamic organisations in Europe have tended to keep their communications with the representatives of this official structure open, even when they are not formally sponsored by the Diyanet. But the Diyanet also has a theological stance, a broad and inclusive one, granted, but one that has at times set it against more radical groups, especially of a Shi'ite nature. The hold of the Moroccan government over the major Moroccan groupings in western Europe has also been quite pervasive, but this has not prevented the activities of more Sufi-oriented groups that either do not recognise the Moroccan monarchy's claim to descent from the Prophet or, at least, regard it as of little significance. The weakness of Pakistani government structures is reflected in the fragmentation of Islamic groupings of Pakistani origin in Europe, something that applies also to Muslim groupings of Indian and Bangladeshi origin.

A different kind of diffuseness, if not fragmentation, is to be found in Sufi networks. Traditionally they illustrate well the absence of sacral hierarchical structures in Islam (at least in Sunni Islam) while at the same time incorporating a form of priest-like function in the form of the Sufi Shaykh. At the height of their activity historically, Sufi *tariqa*s were deeply integrated in the social and economic structures with a significant degree of overlap with craft and professional guilds and, occasionally, elite military regiments, such as the close links between the Bektashi order and the Janissaries in the seventeenth and eighteenth centuries in the Ottoman empire. Following a decline associated with the great changes driven by expanding European influence, Sufism has experienced something of a

---

[17] For references to data from individual European countries throughout this chapter, see Nielsen and others (eds), *Yearbook of Muslims in Europe*, vol 2 (note 2 above).

revival in recent decades, now more often related to ethnic migration patterns and, most recently, as a counterbalance to the ethical puritanism of Salafi-style groups or the political activism of Islamist tendencies.

An example of such a movement is that of Shaykh Nazim al-Haqqani al-Qubrusi.[18] Based in Northern Cyprus, Shaykh Nazim traces his spiritual lineage to the Naqshbandi *tariqa* via a Syrian Shaykh originating in Dagestan. In the 1970s he directed his attention to western Europe and then to the USA, attracting a number of followers including a significant number of converts to Islam. Access to the *tariqa* is open and informal, and numbers who are said to have declared their loyalty (offered *bay'a*) to the Shaykh are large only because they seem to include anyone who has shown an interest at public meetings. The centre of the *tariqa* seldom seeks to set a centrally directed course to follow, either in belief or practice. Local groups remain quite small in practice and only swell when the Shaykh visits. The *tariqa* core membership locally has little in the way of shared teaching beyond veneration of the Shaykh, which has led them to be attacked (often virulently) by groups holding to a more explicit doctrinal discipline of belief and practice. Nor does it hold closely to traditional Naqshbandi forms of meditation, *dhikr*. There have been several instances of Shaykh Nazim's local groups organising open *dhikr* that practise the Mevlevi form, known from the so-called 'whirling dervishes'. In essence each local group appears to be engaged in a process of constant and fluid reinvention or re-imagination of what it means to be an adherent of the Shaykh. The diffuse and fluid character of the *tariqa* was neatly reflected by the informant who told the researchers on this project that only where the Shaykh was present did the *tariqa* really exist.

But Islam in Europe is not just that found in immigrant communities, primarily in the west. There are long-standing Muslim communities in central and eastern Europe, where communist regimes dominated till the end of the Cold War in 1989–91. A common pattern there, with the exception of Albania, was of an officially recognised religious authority, in the Muslim case usually the office of a *mufti*, which also had the exclusive right to represent the religion in the public space. After the fall of the communist system new legislation governing religion in the public space gradually came into effect. The existing Islamic authorities continued to exist but in

---

[18]   The research for this was carried out between 1998 and 2001 in a project entitled 'Ethnicity, politics and transnational Islam: a study of an international Sufi order' funded by the UK Economic and Social Research Council. See Jørgen S Nielsen, Mustafa Draper and Galina Yemelianova, 'Transnational Sufism: the *Haqqaniyya*', in Jamal Malik and John Hinnells (eds), *Sufism in the West* (Routledge, 2006).

some countries, such as Bulgaria, there have been disputes between groups who have wanted the communist-era *mufti* to be dismissed and those who have supported the status quo. Perhaps more significant has been a new ease of organisation that has allowed other groups to establish a public profile in competition with the old recognised authority. In Kosova a large number of Islamic NGOs appeared under the UN Interim Administration in Kosovo but many have subsequently disappeared, probably a reflection of the growth and subsequent decline of the activities of aid and development agencies from the Muslim world. In Albania as in a number of other countries in the region there has been a resurgence of the Bektashi movement, a Sufi tradition that goes a long way back in the Ottoman period.[19] Today there are major Bektashi monasteries in Tetovo (Macedonia), Prishtina (Kosova) and Tirana (Albania). Additionally, in Albania a number of Sufi orders have re-established themselves and formed a loose union, called the 'Divine Light'.

A distinct issue is that of the Alevis of Turkey (not to be confused with the Alawis of Syria).[20] Where there are Turkish communities in Europe a part is usually Alevi. This community is in a rapid process of forming an identity distinct from the majority Turkish Sunni Islam, but the extent to which the separation is taking place is contingent on the country in which the community is located.[21] For some years the Alevi community in Austria has been seeking recognition on a par with the 'Sunni Hanefi' that in 1979 achieved a revival of the earlier recognition of 1912. Towards the end of

---

[19] Western scholarship on this has been ambivalent. The article 'Bektashiyya' in the 2nd edition of the *Encyclopaedia of Islam* makes no mention of either Alevis or Kizilbash (sometimes written Qizilbaş). However, one of the classic works on the Bektashis (John K Birge, *The Bektashi Order of Dervishes* (Luzac, 1937)) identifies a very close connection, describing the Alevis as the broader, popular form of the Bektashi movement, as distinct from the more formal and 'regularised' order. The Kizilbash are one particular trend among the 'village groups' of the Alevi 'sect', he says. The article on 'Alevis' in the newest edition of the *Encyclopedia of Islam* describes them as 'a number of heterogeneous socio-religious communities in Turkey and the Balkans, historically referred to as Qizilbaş . . .' (Markus Dressler, 'Alevis', *Encyclopaedia of Islam* (3rd edn) (Brill Online, 2009). See also Yuri Stoyanov, 'Early and recent formulations of theories for a formative Christian heterodox impact on Alevism' (2010) 37 *British Journal of Middle Eastern Studies* 261.

[20] For sources see note 19 above. See also Antonina Zhelyazkova and Jørgen Nielsen (eds), *Ethnology of Sufi Orders* (IMIR, 2001) available at http://www.imir-bg.org/imir/books/Sufism1.zip.

[21] Elise Massicard, 'Alevi communities in Western Europe: identity and religious strategies' in Nielsen and others (eds), *Yearbook of Muslims in Europe*, vol 2 (note 2 above).

2010, the Austrian Constitutional Court determined that the government had to consider such recognition, as to refuse it was a breach of the community's human rights.[22] But in itself this process will potentially contribute to further fragmentation. Recognition in Austria gives the right to publicly funded religious education in schools as well as publicly funded training of teachers of the subject. There is very little agreement today among Alevis about their belief and practice, and the process will require that they be delineated and developed, a process that invariably will lead to internal disagreements.

Separate from particular instances of this kind, although not unrelated, is a much more diffuse development of ideas. In part this is driven by the transition of initiative from the immigrant generation to their children and grandchildren. These young people's links with the countries of origin remained significant but they have increasingly had to share attention with other priorities, both domestic and international. In some quarters, especially where there have been large concentrations of particular ethnic communities, it has been possible to recreate elements of traditional community in one form or another. Over ten years ago, in an attempt to develop a typology of routes of integration, I identified a process of 'collective isolation, in which communities find protection in collective retrenchment', of which this is an example.[23] Elsewhere there has been a process of weakening inherited ethnic belonging linked to a strengthening of identification with other developments and priorities shared with other Muslims. This is a process that can place young people in a relationship of conflict both with their more traditional parents and with elements of the surrounding European society. At the same time, the extended family relations often continue, maintaining links with the country of origin, including regular return visits: emigration no longer means a permanent break with the original home.[24]

Through the ease of travel, large numbers of young Muslims get access to experiences of other ways of thinking about Islam and of being Muslim. Maintaining contacts with the family home or charitable or political engagement with regions of conflict can suggest options for a personal way forward through the conflicted space of identity formation. Gill Cressey describes how British Kashmiri and Pakistani youth respond to the expe-

---

[22]   Entscheidung des Verfassungsgerichtshofs B 1214/09–35, 1 December 2010.

[23]   Jørgen S Nielsen, 'Muslims in Europe: history revisited or a way forward?' (1997) 8 *Islam and Christian-Muslim Relations* 135.

[24]   Not much research has been done on the consequences of this process, but worth mentioning is Gill Cressey, *Diaspora Youth and Ancestral Homeland: British Pakistani/Kashmiri Youth Visiting Kin in Pakistan and Kashmir* (EJ Brill, 2006).

rience of visiting kin in the ancestral homelands.[25] While they carry with them some vague and diffuse view of being Muslims and part of the *umma* their experiences challenge them to put some flesh on these ideas. Some end up distancing themselves from the cultural mores of their kin, especially as regards gender patterns, while others are attracted to dimensions of what can feel like more 'authentic' expressions than what is on offer in Britain. These experiences are then placed back into a British context that, especially after the terrorist actions of September 2001 in New York and July 2005 in London, has tended to put greater pressure on communities of Muslim background to decide on their 'Muslimness' and its relationship to their Britishness.

But return visits can be a dangerous path if the options suggested are among those on offer in regions subjected to war or violent instability. In extreme cases, visits to family in Pakistan, Somalia or Algeria have been a route through which individuals have been radicalised. At the same time, the phenomena of 'home grown terrorism' and the increasingly decentralised nature of Al-Qa'ida indicate also a process of fragmentation in this extreme sector.[26]

Despite all the headlines, radicalisation is a small minority activity, although no less dangerous for that. More common is the way in which so-called Salafi tendencies have attracted especially younger people. They could also be located in the group denoted 'collective isolation' in the typology mentioned previously, except that the community that is isolating itself here has a much more voluntary character. It is a community of shared theological commitment rather than one of shared cultural heritage. Salafism as a term has its origins in the concept of the *salaf*, namely the Muslims of the time of the Prophet Muhammad and immediately after: the founder generations. The term was resurrected in the late nineteenth century by early reformers and is particularly associated with Muhammad Abduh, the Egyptian scholar who became the first reforming rector of Al-Azhar University.[27] More recently it has come to be associated more closely with more puritanical forms of Islam often identified with the Wahhabi tendencies of Saudi Arabia.[28] The tendency, at least as it manifests itself in

---

[25] Ibid.

[26] Marc Sageman, *Leaderless Jihad: Terror Networks in the Twenty-First Century* (University of Pennsylvania Press, 2008).

[27] W Ende, 'Salafiyya', *Encyclopedia of Islam Online* (EJ Brill, 2008). See also Albert Hourani, *Arabic Thought in the Liberal Age, 1798–1939* (Oxford University Press, 1962) ch 6.

[28] See the report 'Understanding Islamism' (Cairo and Brussels: International Crisis Group, Middle East/North Africa Report no 37, 2 March 2005).

Europe, focuses on study of the Qur'an and the Hadith and particularly encourages pious and correct personal behaviour emphasising the Prophet as a model to be emulated.

Salafi mosques and study groups are attractive because they offer a supportive environment for young people who, theologically self-taught, have become disenchanted with their parents' customs while finding insecurity and rejection in wider European society. They are particularly attractive to young families who fear for their children's upbringing in an environment lacking coherent values and authority. Because of the way their members dress they often become the focus of attention when there is a terrorism scare, but all the evidence suggests that the European Salafi groups abjure violence. In this they have something in common with the well-known and in many quarters notorious Party of Liberation, Hizb al-Tahrir, which otherwise bears little resemblance to the Salafiyya.[29] The problem with both of these, as well as with other, similar tendencies, is that they have a strong focus on what they see as the injustices of the politics of the Muslim world. It is therefore not surprising that they can function as feeder routes into the more radical activist groupings and occasionally slip over the line into violent activism.[30]

On the other hand, the process of political engagement that may arise out of a growing identification with headline issues in the Muslim world can play an important integrative role, when the issue in question is one that has activated broader sections of society as a whole. One prime example of this in Europe (as well as the United States) is the movement opposing the 2003 invasion of Iraq. Here there has been a cause where often very angry Muslims have found common ground and shared in common political activity with a wide spectrum of trends in society as a whole. Here they have discovered a route of integration and inclusion in the European public space. I would suggest that, similarly, the controversies provoked by the Muhammad cartoons in *Jyllands-Posten* a couple of years ago have encouraged an increase in cross-cultural and cross-religious activities in Denmark. This crisis may thus in the future also come to be seen as an integrative event.

Throughout these various developments, participation in the public space has become an essential tool to facilitate integration, and the very

---

[29]   Taji-Farouki (note 8 above); M Grøndahl, TR Rasmussen and K Sinclair, *Hizb ut-Tahrir I Danmark: farlig fundamentalisme eller uskyldigt ungdomsoprør?* (Aarhus Universitetsforlag, 2003).

[30]   For aspects of this see Ed Hussein, *The Islamist* (Penguin, 2007); Ian Buruma, *Murder in Amsterdam: the Death of Theo van Gogh and the Limits of Tolerance* (Atlantic Books, 2006).

process of participation requires the development of mechanisms and forms of expression that can persuade the target audience, be it local or central government, or various civil society institutions. Equally, the process of participation itself favours those trends within the Muslim communities that wish to move away from attitudes to, for example, social and human relations that are commonly identified with traditional Islam, and to which anti-Islam polemicists choose to devote their undivided attention. In 2007 there was a particularly absurd example of this process, when a German judge notoriously refused to grant a woman of Moroccan origin a divorce on the grounds that the Qur'an permitted a husband to beat his wife – so she had to live with it. In the uproar that followed, the decision was presented as proof of the medieval character of Islam. Apparently it was of no importance in the polemic that not only was the judge suspended and the case retried to the advantage of the wife but, more interestingly from my point of view, German and Austrian Muslim organisations also vehemently condemned the judgment. The Zentralrat deutscher Muslime not only insisted that intra-marital violence was grounds for divorce in the Muslim world but also stated that '[t]he judge should have made a decision based on the German constitution not on the Qur'an' that, it went on to stress, could not in any case be interpreted in the way it had been by the judge.[31] The Islamische Gemeinschaft in Österreich issued an official statement condemning the judgment based on reference to both the Qur'an and the prophetic Sunna.[32]

This takes us full circle to the question of Shari'a with which this part of the discussion started. The opinions expressed by these German and Austrian Islamic organisations could cynically be interpreted as an opportunistic and politic adjustment to prevailing public pressures. They may have been, but that is hardly important in this context. More significant is that such opinions reflect some deeper discussions that are taking place among European Muslims, discussions that are reflections of the broader discussions taking place in the majority Muslim world. I will just take two examples. In Sarajevo, Professor Fikret Karčić talks of an exploration of the 'norms' of the Shari'a, stating that historically there is a detailed experience of the strictly legal aspects of Shari'a, as traditionally developed in the detailed corpus of jurisprudence (*fiqh*), functioning in partnership with legal rules and norms developed by government – in the Ottoman Empire a system known as *qanun* (the origin in the Greek concept of 'canon' is obvious). The basic criterion for the legitimacy of such a practice

---

[31] Report by Agence France Presse (circulated by email 28 March 2007).
[32] Statement 'Kein Freibrief für prügelnde Ehemänner' (23 March 2007).

is the welfare of the community in general (*maslaha*), a concept that was already central to the Hanafi law school to which the Ottomans adhered. Reviewing the spread of secular government in the twentieth century and then the revival of interest in Shari'a among Muslims in the last generation, he reflects on the situation of Muslims in secular states, such as his own Bosnia, and in minority situations. He considers Shari'a, in its traditionally developed form, to consist of religious, ethical and legal norms. As legal norms the Shari'a depends on the existence of an Islamic state. In a secular state, as in a minority situation, the Shari'a can function for Muslims individually and collectively as the basis for religious and ethical norms.[33]

Such an approach is echoed in some quarters among Muslim thinkers in France. Tareq Oubrou is *imam* of the main mosque in Bordeaux and a leading figure in the Union des Organisations Islamiques en France (UOIF), which has its roots in the Muslim Brotherhood. He is active in a movement seeking to develop a Shari'a for the minority, *fiqh al-aqalliyat*.[34] His perception of 'minority' is not primarily quantitative but an acknowledgement that, in Islamic terms, the situation is exceptional and therefore requires an exceptional approach, accepting that the situation of being a minority in Europe is a permanent condition. Basing himself in the Islamic intellectual tradition, Oubrou also reaches a conclusion that distinguishes the three facets of Shari'a, the religious, the ethical and the legal, where the legal is essentially laid aside.

Some Islamic scholars have taken this dimension further in the development of a '*fiqh* of minorities', *fiqh al-aqalliyyat*. This has found its most formal expression in the circle around the European Council for Fatwa and Research (ECFR).[35] This is chaired by the renowned Yusuf al-Qaradawi and has particularly sound roots in France and to a lesser extent in Britain, although the majority of its scholar members are from outside Europe.

While many are sceptical about the viability of *fiqh al-aqalliyyat* as a

---

[33] F Karčić, 'Administration of Islamic affairs in Bosnia and Hercegovina', (1999) 38 *Islamic Studies* 535; F Karčić, 'Applying the Shari'ah in modern societies: main developments and issues', (2001) 40 *Islamic Studies* 207.

[34] See Manni Crone, 'Shari'a and secularism in France', in JS Nielsen and L Christoffersen (eds), *Shari'a as Discourse and the Encounter with Europe* (Ashgate, 2010) 141; John R Bowen, *Can Islam be French? Pluralism and Pragmatism in a Secular State* (Princeton University Press, 2010) 144. The legacy of the Muslim Brotherhood in France is dealt with by Brigitte Maréchal, *The Muslim Brothers in Europe: Roots and Discourse* (EJ Brill, 2008).

[35] See A Caeiro, 'Transnational 'Ulama, European fatwas, and Islamic authority: a case study of the European Council for Fatwa and Research', in Martin van Bruinessen and Stefano Allievi (eds), *Producing Islamic Knowledge: Transmission and Dissemination in Europe* (Routledge, 2010) 121.

way forward, there is more broadly a trend of reaching solutions to the problems of individual Muslims seeking to find ways of living a Muslim life in a modern, non-Muslim, urban environment. Depending on where one stands, such solutions can be regarded as compromises or evidence of the inherent adaptability of the Islamic *fiqh* tradition. The instrument by which much of this flexibility is expressed is the *fatwa*. Traced back to the very earliest period after the death of Muhammad, a *fatwa* is an opinion in any field of religious faith and practice given by a qualified person (a *mufti*) in response to the question of an individual (*mustafti*) – the whole process is called *ifta'*.[36] Over time theorists formalised the process and from around the fourteenth century the official post of *mufti* became widespread.[37] Today the chief Islamic official in a number of states holds the title *Mufti*.

Some of the debates provoked by the *fatwa* pronounced in February 1990 by Ayatollah Khomeini against Salman Rushdie showed, however, that *ifta'* remains a contested field. It is not uncommon for people issuing *fatwa*s to be condemned by opponents for being unqualified, or for *fatwa*s to be dismissed for not meeting formal criteria as laid down in the classical texts. Thus the *fatwa* against Salman Rushdie was dismissed in many quarters as not meeting the required criteria because it was not issued as an opinion in response to a question put by a *mustafti*. Its character also of being a decree of punishment placed it at odds with a proper *fatwa*. However, this kind of unrequested *fatwa* is far from unusual: the sometimes quite vicious polemics between the Deobandi and Barelvi movements of the Indian subcontinent since the late nineteenth century have often taken the form of '*fatwa* wars'.

In the contemporary European situation *fatwa*s have shown themselves to be a useful tool. In her recent PhD thesis Lena Larsen documents a variety of types of *fatwa*.[38] She cites Shaykh Sayyid Darsh, who died in London in 1995, as an example of the traditional format, where an individual brings a question to the authority. In this case, the process took place in a regular *fatwa* column in the pages of the London-based Islamic

---

[36] See E Tyan and JR Walsh, 'Fatwā' in P Bearman, T Bianquis, CE Bosworth, E van Donzel and WP Heinrichs (eds), *Encyclopaedia of Islam*, vol 2 (2nd edn) (EJ Brill, 1991).

[37] Jørgen S Nielsen, *Secular Justice in an Islamic state: Mazalim under the Bahri Mamluks, 662/1264–789/1387* (Netherlands Institute for the Near East, 1985) 91ff.

[38] Lena Larsen, *Islamisk rettstenkning i møte med dagliglivets utfordringer: Fatwaer som løsningsforslag for muslimske kvinner i Vest-Europa* (Islamic jurisprudence in the encounter with the challenges of daily life: Fatwas offering solutions for Muslim women in Western Europe) (PhD thesis, University of Oslo, Faculty of Humanities, 2011).

magazine *Q-News.*[39] The feature was not unlike an 'agony aunt' column
to be found in many of the popular weekly magazines. In his responses
Darsh offers solutions that combine reference to traditional Islamic norms
and consideration for both the minority setting and the context of gen-
erational conflict.[40] He consistently avoids the terms 'forbidden' (*haram*)
and 'obligatory' (*wajib* or *fard*) in favour of 'reprehensible' (*makruh*) and
'recommended' (*mandub*).

A more formal process has been adopted by the ECFR. The Council has
a procedure under which questions are dealt with by a permanent officer
unless they raise a matter of some principle. In this case it is forwarded to
the annual session of the Council, which may work out a response or del-
egate it for study by a sub-committee before a response is finally published.
This represents a bureaucratisation of *ifta'* that is a radical break with tradition but which has become common in the last couple of generations. A
related example of this structure is the *Dar al-Fatwa* set up by the UOIF.[41]
This is closely related to the ECFR with several individuals being on both
groups. One of their main methods for providing *fatwa*s has been a regular
telephone service, in addition to the more common approaches by letter,
fax or email.

Around the margins of these organisations in France the status of
Islamic marriages is sharply contested and a source of some confusion.
John Bowen recounts how some *imams* insist that the French law be
obeyed, under which a religious marriage can only be celebrated after a
civil marriage has been conducted.[42] The term 'halal' marriage is often used
for the Islamic form, and the question in some quarters is whether this is
'corrupted' by being associated with forms of marriage authorised by a
non-Islamic state. Some Muslims in France insist that it is the nature of
the state granting the authority to the civil marriage that is the determining element, so therefore no such marriage can be halal. Others argue that
there is nothing in the substance of the civil marriage that contradicts the
substance of an Islamic one, and that therefore there can be no objection.

This question of the significance of the substance of the law/*fiqh* relative
to the religious legitimacy of the state authorising the law had arisen earlier
in the United Kingdom in connection with a claim raised as early as 1975
by the Union of Muslim Organisations of the UK and Eire (UMO) for the

---

[39] The magazine last appeared in 2006 but many of its issues are still accessible
at http://www.q-news.com.
[40] Larsen (note 38 above) 172ff.
[41] See Maréchal, *The Muslim Brothers in Europe* (note 34 above).
[42] Bowen (note 34 above) 157.

implementation of Islamic family law for Muslims.[43] In the mid-1980s I was involved in arranging two seminars in Birmingham as part of a wider European project under the title 'Islamic law and its significance for the situation of Muslim minorities in Europe'. The participants, lawyers and Islamic scholars, discussed the substance of marriage, divorce, inheritance and child custody in Islamic and English law. The conclusion was that the vast majority of Islamic expectations could be met within the existing English law, and the rest required only minor legislation.[44] But the major argument among a minority of the Muslim participants, who found it difficult to go along with this conclusion, was precisely this question of whence the authority for the law emanated.

Underlying this issue is an argument about whether the traditional distinction between the territory of Islam (*dar al-islam*) and that of 'the enemy' (*dar al-harb*) remains valid today. Tariq Ramadan is a figure who has provoked sometimes heated debate both among Muslims, some of whom regard him as a leading European Islamic reformer and moderniser, and among European politicians and commentators, some of whom (especially in France and the Netherlands) regard him as a closet fundamentalist.[45] He makes the point that this traditional territorial division, which is a core element of classical Islamic international political theory and jurisprudence, was devised by the scholars some time after the period of revelation – it does not appear in the Qur'an or the Sunna. Even at this formative stage some prominent scholars, notably al-Shafi'i (died 820), suggested a middle status of *dar al-'ahd*, or the territory of treaty, which some later scholars termed *dar al-aman*, or territory of safety. Arguing that in many western countries Muslims are safer and have greater freedom of religion than they do in some Muslim states, Ramadan suggests that the two traditional terms can equally apply more or less across the whole world.[46] They have therefore become meaningless. Instead, he puts forward

---

43   See Jørgen S Nielsen, 'Il diritto familiare nelle rivendicazioni dell'inserimento nei paesi europe', in J Waardenburg (ed), *I musulmani nella societa europea* (Fondazione Giovanni Agnelli, 1994) 79.

44   Jørgen S Nielsen, 'Islamic law and its significance for the situation of Muslim minorities in Europe: Report of a study project', *Research Papers: Muslims in Europe*, 35 (September 1987).

45   See Aziz Zemouri, *Faut-il taire Tariq Ramadan?* (Paris: l-Archipel, 2005), and Jørgen S Nielsen, 'New centres and peripheries in European Islam?' (2002) 7(3) *Mediterranean Politics* 64.

46   In a lecture in Tunis in April 2003, at which I was present, the Director-General of the Islamic Educational, Scientific and Cultural Organization (ISESCO), Dr Abdul Aziz Othman Altwaijri suggested that wherever there are Muslims, there is *dar al-islam*.

the concept of *dar al-da'wa*, the land of testimony, the spaces in which Muslims as fully integrated participants have a responsibility to contribute to the public sphere on the basis of Islamic social and moral teaching.[47] While many more conservative Muslim intellectuals are unhappy with this way forward, it is attractive to many younger intellectuals providing, as it does, a legitimate space in which to engage fully with the European context.

3.   THE QUESTION OF SECULARISM

A standard characterisation of Islam (and thence of Muslims and Muslim cultures) is that it is incompatible with secularism. In this last section I intend briefly to indicate the problematic nature of this view. Firstly, the question must not be confused with discussions about the private and public spheres, although in European discussions about the secular nature of the state the two questions are closely interrelated. Islam does have a conception of the private and the public; it is just rather different from the ones we are used to in Europe.[48] Secondly, the term secularism is often used carelessly, and has led and continues to lead to misunderstanding, especially in relation to the Islamic world. It must be distinguished from secularisation, a process whereby religion (or at least traditional religious institutions) has lost its dominance as the measure by which everything else is assessed, and from secularity, meaning culture in which religion and its institutions are but one contributor among many and with no *a priori* claim on precedence. Secularism is most appropriately used to denote a political system in which church/religion and state are in some form or other separated. 'In some form or other' reflects the fact that in the west the secular state has many incarnations. Veit Bader distinguishes as many as twelve distinct types, of which 'secularity of the state or the relational autonomy of state from (organised) religion' is only one.[49]

   In Islam the matter is far from being as clear-cut as is commonly assumed – and as is commonly stated by Islamist political movements with their slogans 'Islam is the solution' and 'no distinction between religion and

---

[47]   Tariq Ramadan, *Western Muslims and the Future of Islam* (Oxford University Press, 2004) 62–77.

[48]   Of course, the distinction between public and private is not really as obvious as we commonly think; rather, it is under constant renegotiation. See Raymond Geuss, *Public Goods, Private Goods* (Princeton University Press, 2003).

[49]   Veit Bader, 'Constitutionalizing secularism, alternative secularisms or liberal-democratic constitutionalism? A critical reading of some Turkish, ECtHR and Indian Supreme Court cases on "secularism"', (2010) 6 *Utrecht Law Review* 8.

state'. The repetitive Islamist insistence on this point suggests that the need is felt to hammer the point home, that is, that there is no consensus among Muslim thinkers, let alone general Muslim public opinion. Opinion polls conducted among European Muslims have indicated that this common Islamist agenda is not shared by the majority. A Gallup poll published in 2009 showed that Muslims in Germany and Britain were more supportive of government, the judiciary, financial institutions and the honesty of elections than were the overall population. The Muslims of France, however, appeared to be more hesitant.[50] The same survey also sought to discover Muslims' sense of national identity compared to their religious identity. Remarkably, British Muslims identified almost equally with Islam and with Britain at levels above 70 per cent, French Muslims were slightly more uncertain with 58 per cent identifying strongly with Islam and 52 per cent with France, while German Muslims reported 59 per cent identifying with Islam and only 40 per cent with Germany.[51] This does not suggest an environment in which the view that religion and politics are one has much traction.

In fact, if one looks at the question historically the contemporary Islamist slogan has a significantly ahistorical character. As with a number of other concepts in modern political discourse, secularism in the Muslim world has been absorbed into Islamic discourse as a symbol of the overmighty and ungodly West. In some Muslim languages 'secularism' has been translated as 'non-religion' if not explicitly atheism. In Arabic the most commonly used terms are *'ilmaniyya* or *'almaniyya* with the slightly artificial distinction being that the former refers to knowledge or science, and thus a rationally based outlook, while the latter refers to the world, and thus a this-worldly outlook – but in some Islamic circles these meanings amount to atheism.

However, Islamic history provides ample resources for those who would argue for some form of distinction between religion and state/politics. In 1925 a scholar at Al-Azhar University in Cairo, 'Ali 'Abd al-Raziq caused a scandal when he published a book entitled *Al-islam wa-usul al-hukm* ('Islam and the foundations of government'), in which he argued that the roles of Muhammad as prophet and as statesman were distinct and separate, a principle that Islam has since ignored but needs again to take seriously.[52] This whole field is encompassed in the Islamic discourse by the statement

---

[50] *The Gallup Coexist Index 2009: A Global Study of Interfaith Relations*, 23ff, available at http://www.gallup.com/se/ms/153578/REPORT-Gallup-Coexist-Index-2009.aspx.
[51] Ibid, 19ff.
[52] See Hourani (note 27 above) 183–92.

that Islam is *din wa-dunya* – 'faith and this world' would be one reasonable translation. Firstly, it is worthy of note that the phrase itself recognises a distinction between the two, *din* and *dunya*. Historical experience suggests that the distinction has consistently been more than just conceptual. Even in the early post-Muhammadan period the proto-governmental structures of the newly conquered provinces were led by a pair of governors, one responsible for 'religion' (*amir 'ala al-salah*) and the other for financial administration (*amir 'ala al-kharaj*). This distinction soon fell away as leadership was merged under a single governor, but it continued to exist within the government administration in the distinction between religious and civil divisions that are recorded in the great administrative handbook *Subh al-A'sha* of al-Qalqashandi (died 1418). It is reflected also in institutional form in the establishment in the Ottoman Empire of the *Qanun*, a legal system with its own professionals and its own laws, separate from that of the Shari'a and its *qadis*.[53]

More fundamentally, as the reference earlier to the thinking of people like Tareq Oubrou and Fikret Karčić indicates, the conception that Shari'a consists of *'aqida* (faith), *'ibadat* (worship) and *mu'amalat* (works) is one that also clearly recognises a distinction in which the thinking about *mu'amalat* is a human responsibility subject to interpretation according to time and place (*makan wa-zaman*). What we have here is a complex and deep-rooted intellectual resource that is available for a time when circumstances, such as those of contemporary Europe, encourage if not require that they be re-mobilised.

In contemporary Europe, argues Tariq Ramadan, Muslims like all other communities of faith or shared social and political commitment, religious or not, have as their starting point the principles of their faith and its scriptural sources. But, like everyone else, it is the derived moral, social and political commitments that are brought into the public debate and with which one negotiates with others towards common goals for the interests and wellbeing of the broader community, *maslaha* in the Islamic terminology. Here he refers to the theory of the 'intentions of the Shari'a' (*maqasid al-*

---

[53] See my reflections on secularism and contemporary challenges, 'Al-'ilmaniyya wa'l-tahaddiyyat al-jadida' (Secularism and the new challenges), in Luai Husayn (ed), *Al-'Ilmaniyya fi al-Mashriq al-'Arabi* (Secularism in the Arab East) (Dar Atlas and Dar Petra, 2007) 76. At the same conference the Lebanese scholar 'Atif Atiyya presented a good case for using the term *dunyawiyyah* both because it reflects better the substance of the concept of secularism in a Muslim context as well as avoiding what has become the inflammatory character of the term *'ilmaniyya*; ibid 59.

shari'a), a line of thinking that can be traced back to the eleventh century.[54] For all the various groups in the plural societies of the modern world (and Ramadan is explicit in suggesting that western Muslims are developing ideas and experiences that the Muslim world can learn from), it is secularism that creates the necessary space for participation and negotiation. But this requires that secularism be conceived of and function as a framework. The moment secularism becomes a participating ideology it threatens to close off that space – one suspects an implied critique of more hard-line forms of French-style *laïcité*.

4. CONCLUSION: WHAT OF LAWS OF RECOGNITION?

While this chapter is not about Islam and European laws of recognition, it does, in my view, suggest some implications. These centre around the very fluid and increasingly fragmentary nature of Islam on the continent – and, for that matter, of every other religious tradition, old or new, in the region. The inherited forms of recognition grew out of a particular set of historical circumstances, circumstances that to a great extent no longer apply. As the distance grows between these legal regimes and the realities on the ground, it seems clear that the law is losing its ability to manage the situation.

The Austrian Supreme Court decision (considered earlier) to allow the recognition of an Alevi community also involved a decision not to allow the recognition of a rival Alevi group.[55] This recognition is likely to lead to further fragmentation within the Alevi group that has been recognised, because it will now have to start thinking about what Alevism is as a religion in preparation for the time when it seeks the higher grade of recognition already granted to the main churches and the Sunni Islamic community under a law of 1874. This form of full recognition will entitle the community to teach its children Alevi religion in school at public expense as well as to train teachers to teach the subject. But, as we have seen, there is no agreement for the time being on what the teachings and practices of Alevism are; they will have to be worked out.

The Danish constitution has made provision for the status of 'recognised faith communities', which since the first democratic constitution of 1849 covered those small religious communities, Christian and Jewish, that existed at the time. When in the 1970s the question arose of adding new

---

54 Ramadan (note 47 above) 144–51.
55 See text accompanying note 22, above.

communities to the list (first and foremost Islam), the authorities insisted that the list was closed. Instead, and after some pressure, they invented the category 'authorised faith communities', which brought with it the authority to formalise recognised marriages and some tax advantages.

Silvio Ferrari has pointed to the inadequacy of traditional classifications of church–state relations in Europe.[56] He suggests that the centrality of the individual, as it is being developed by European human rights law, is making the traditional recognition regimes irrelevant. On the other hand, English law, where the highly institutionalised church–state structures of mainland Europe are generally absent, seems to be moving from a highly individualistic position to a position between establishment and secularism, at least according to a recent analysis by Julian Rivers.[57]

At least to the present observer, the experience of an increasingly fragmented Islam – fascinating as it may be to students of Islam in particular and religion in general – suggests that the recognition regimes of mainland Europe, evinced by the stubborn refusal of the French public administration to recognise religion as a public phenomenon (at least theoretically), have become unsustainably brittle and will have to give way to something that makes space for the fluidity that this chapter identifies.

---

[56]   Silvio Ferrari, 'The legal dimension', in Brigitte Maréchal, Stefano Allievi, Felice Dassetto and Jørgen Nielsen (eds), *Muslims in the Enlarged Europe: Religion and Society* (EJ Brill, 2003) 219.

[57]   Julian Rivers, *The Law of Organized Religion: Between Establishment and Secularism* (Oxford University Press, 2010).

15. Legal considerations concerning new religious movements in the 'new Europe'

James T Richardson and Valerie A Lykes

1. INTRODUCTION

New religious movements (NRMs) have been controversial throughout history, as they are often viewed as challenging extant societal values and authorities. Also, more recent NRMs have been accused of aggressive proselytising and 'stealing children', given that many have tended to attract young people, sometimes from relatively affluent families. This concern has fed the moral panic about so-called 'cult brainwashing' that has spread around the world.[1] The ongoing controversy over NRMs has been amply demonstrated in recent decades within western societies, particularly the United States[2] but also in Europe.[3] Many times this controversy has resulted in legal actions of various kinds, as societal agents attempt to exert control over new religions or private parties (sometimes parents of young people involved) take 'self-help' actions to extricate their children that might involve or result in legal actions. And on occasion NRMs have attempted to make use of the legal system in defensive actions against those who would attack or criticise them, be they politicians and governments,

---

[1] See J Richardson, '"Brainwashing" claims and minority religions outside the United States: cultural diffusion of a questionable concept in the legal arena', [1996] *Brigham Young University Law Review* 873; J Richardson and M Introvigne, '"Brainwashing" theories in European parliamentary and administrative reports on cults and sects', (2001) 40 *Journal for the Scientific Study of Religion* 143.

[2] See A Shupe and D Bromley, *The New Vigilantes: Anti-Cultists and the New Religions* (SAGE, 1980); D Bromley and J Richardson, *The Brainwashing/ Deprogramming Controversy* (Edwin Mellen, 1983).

[3] See J Beckford, *Cult Controversies: The Societal Response to New Religious Movements* (Tavistock, 1985); E Barker, *New Religious Movements* (HMSO, 1984); A Shupe and D Bromley (eds), *Anti-Cult Movements in Cross-Cultural Perspective* (Garland, 1994).

journalists, deprogrammers, representatives of dominant religions, or even academics.[4]

This chapter presents an overview of the legal status of NRMs in the European context, focusing on policies and statutes that have been enacted or enforced against NRMs, and on court cases from national courts, but also (and more importantly) from the European Court of Human Rights (ECtHR), which has jurisdiction over the 47 member states of the Council of Europe (COE). We will begin our analysis with an overview of the situation concerning NRMs in selected individual nations in Europe, grouped into 'old' (original members of the Council of Europe) and newer nations that have joined the COE since the fall of the Soviet Union. Included in this analysis will be some attention to the actions of constitutional courts in specific nations or regions where such entities have taken noteworthy actions. This focus on categories of individual nations will be followed by an examination of selected decisions by the ECtHR that affect the 47 COE nations and set precedents for the entire area over which the Court has jurisdiction.

Before proceeding, a word on definitions is needed. Cumper's analysis of the status of NRMs in Europe focused exclusively on the set of newer religions that have come to the attention of the public and governments over the past few decades.[5] This includes groups such as Scientology, the Unification Church, the Children of God and the Order of the Solar Temple, all groups that have attracted much attention and engendered controversy in various European countries and elsewhere. However, Cumper explicitly excluded from his coverage minority religions such as the Jehovah's Witnesses and other religious groups, including Islamic groups, that have been present in Europe for longer periods of time. For the purposes of this examination such groups will be included, because in Europe the legal status of both types of group have become intertwined to a considerable extent, especially over the past decade. The jurisprudence that has developed in Europe concerning religious groups and religious freedom, particularly with the ECtHR, seems to treat minority faiths (whether 'new' or 'old') similarly, at least in some circumstances. Our analysis will take a

---

[4]   J Richardson, 'Legal status of minority religions in the United States', (1995) 42 *Social Compass* 249; J Richardson, 'Law and minority religions: "positive" and "negative" uses of the legal system', (1998) 2 *Nova Religio* 93; P Cumper 'The rights of religious minorities: the legal regulation of new religious movements', in P Cumper and S Wheatley (eds), *Minority Rights in the 'New Europe'* (Kluwer, 1999) 165–83.

[5]   Cumper (note 4 above).

similar approach, and will sometimes use the more general term 'minority religion' in this chapter.

2. MINORITY FAITHS IN SELECTED EUROPEAN NATIONS

For purposes of illustration, three member states from the original COE western European nations will be selected for more detailed examination: Germany, France and the Netherlands.[6] The newer COE members from Central and Eastern Europe that will be discussed are Russia, Poland and Hungary. The selection of three nations from each region is somewhat arbitrary, but demonstrates the tremendous variety in how nations in these two regions of Europe deal with minority faiths. There is no monolithic approach in either region, as will be amply demonstrated, and each nation responds to the growth of interest in minority religions in a way that relates to its historical situation and cultural values. First we will attend to our sample of original COE members, all three of which have taken different paths in their response to minority faiths.

Western Europe

Germany

In recent decades, Germany has had a very complex relationship with minority faiths, including NRMs from the United States, especially Scientology. Early in the controversy surrounding NRMs the German government took a firm stance in opposition to such new groups, and even produced voluminous literature for distribution in schools and in other forums, warning German youth about becoming involved in 'dangerous sects'.[7] This posture by the government was in keeping with its historically paternalistic approach to its citizens, even concerning religious matters.[8]

---

[6] For a broader coverage of nations and groups see J Richardson (ed), *Regulating Religion: Case Studies from Around the Globe* (Kluwer, 2004) and P Lucas and T Robbins, *New Religious Movements in the 21st Century* (Routledge, 2004).

[7] See Beckford (note 3 above); B Schoen, 'New religions in Germany: the publicity of the public square', (2001) 4 *Nova Religio* 266; J Richardson and B van Driel, 'New religions in Europe: a comparison of developments and reactions in England, France, Germany, and The Netherlands', in Shupe and Bromley, *Anti-Cult Movements* (note 3 above).

[8] See G Besier, 'Current problems of religious minorities in Germany', in D Davis and G Besier (eds), *International Perspectives on Freedom and Equality of*

The concern about sects led to the establishment by the German Bundestag in 1996 of a high-level Enquete Commission on 'So-called Sects and Psychogroups'.[9] This Commission was set up to review available information on NRMs and even sponsor research on such groups operating in Germany. The Commission, the work of which is described by Hubert Seiwert, a Religious Studies scholar who served on the Commission, ended up concluding that there was little danger associated with such groups.[10] However, a majority of the Commission nonetheless recommended the enactment of legislation designed to curtail the activities of 'sects and psychogroups'. Seiwert and some other members of the Commission filed a minority report dissenting from the majority's recommendations for further legislation, which is included in the Final report, and which cited research done by the Commission to support their position.

The Commission took special note of Scientology, and treated it somewhat differently in its recommendations, illustrating the special concerns about Scientology that are rampant in Germany.[11]

A 15-year-long judicial battle over the legal status of the Jehovah's Witnesses has been taking place in Germany, and it was only in 2006 that the Witness organisation gained the type of status that they had been seeking – that of a 'religious corporation', enabling them to be treated somewhat similarly to Catholic and Lutheran religious organisations in terms of rights and privileges. The Witness victory had been long in coming, and occurred after a long series of court cases: a Federal Constitutional Court case in

---

Religious Belief (Baylor University Press, 2002) 125, who discusses the '. . . paternalism that pervades German culture'. Also see the lengthy discussion of German paternalism in operation against 'cults' in Beckford (note 3 above) 251–62 and note especially such statements as '. . . the ministry (Ministry for Youth, Family, and Health) supports anti-cultism, not in order to infringe religious liberty, but in order to discharge its constitutional responsibility to protect citizens from potential or actual harm' (at 257).

[9]   Deutscher Bundestag, *Final Report of the Enquete Commission on 'So-called Sects and Psychogroups': New Religions and Ideological Communities and Psychogroups in the Federal Republic of Germany* (Deutscher Bundestag Referat Offentlichkeitsarbeit, 1998).

[10]   H Seiwert, 'The German Enquete Commission on Sects: political conflicts and compromises', in Richardson, *Regulating Religion* (note 6 above) 85–101.

[11]   See G Melton, 'Scientology in Europe: testing the faith of a new religion', in Davis and Besier (note 8 above) 69–84; Schoen (note 7 above). One recommendation of the Enquete Commission was to amend the Associations Act making it easier to dissolve associations, including religious ones. This proposal was resisted strongly by some minority religions in Germany, particularly Scientology, but it was approved in the aftermath of the attack on the Twin Towers on 11 September 2001.

2000 forced reconsideration of earlier rejections, but it was not until 2005 that a *Land* (State) decision finally acknowledged that the Witnesses should gain the long-sought status. And that decision was somewhat limited, for only *Land* Berlin was initially forced to grant the status, and even that victory twice required the intervention of the German Constitutional Court before it was actually accomplished. It has taken years and more legal actions to get other German states to also recognise the Witnesses as a legal corporation, and some are still refusing to do so at time of writing.[12]

Another minority religious population currently sometimes at odds with the German government is the growing Muslim population.[13] Currently there are over 3 million Muslims in Germany (about 4 per cent of the population), and they are exerting themselves on various fronts. Particularly controversial has been the issue of building mosques to serve the growing Muslim population, as well as the matter of public support for Muslim schools. Also, issues have arisen concerning how the community relates to the governmental structures, as there is no one Muslim organisation that can speak for all Muslims in the country. This lack of similarity between how Muslims are organised and organisational structures for other major religious groups has hindered the development of relationships between Muslims and governments, and has perhaps been used as an excuse for granting fewer privileges to Muslims in Germany.

France

France has also experienced great controversy over NRMs and other minority religions, although the underpinning logic is considerably different, and is based on France's philosophy of *laïcité*, which roughly translates into a view that all of society should be secularised.[14] That the Catholic Church occupies a place of some prominence both formally and informally is ignored, and instead the focus is on other groups that are smaller, newer

---

[12] See G Besier and R Besier, 'Jehovah's Witness request for recognition as a corporation under public law in Germany', (2000) 42 *Journal of Church and State* 35; and G Besier, 'How to understand religious freedom in Germany', (2009) 10 *Religion-Staat-Gesellschaft* 325–36. Key decisions include: Federal Constitutional Court s BDV 1500/97, decision announced 19 December 2000; Higher Administrative Court Berlin Decision OVG 2 B 12.01, VG 27 A 214.93, decreed 24 March 2005.

[13] See W Aires, 'Germany's Islamic minority: some remarks on historical and legal developments', in Richardson, *Regulating Religion* (note 6 above).

[14] See J Beckford, '"*Laïcité*", "dystopia" and the reaction to new religious movements in France', in Richardson, *Regulating Religion* (note 6 above); J Willaime, 'The paradoxes of *laïcité* in France', in E Barker, *The Centrality of Religion in Social Life: Essays in Honour of James A Beckford* (Ashgate, 2010).

and less politically powerful. This has resulted in some severe repercussions for minority religious groups in France,[15] including especially the Aumists,[16] the Twelve Tribes,[17] Scientology[18] and The Family (formerly the Children of God).[19]

As in Germany, the Jehovah's Witnesses have experienced considerable difficulty in gaining acceptance in France, even though the organisation has existed in France for over 100 years and is the third largest non-Catholic denomination in the country. The Witnesses have been fighting a battle on taxes allegedly due the government for over five years, and have yet to gain any redress from the government. This has led the Witnesses to apply to the ECtHR, in a case that languished for years, as it seemed that the Court was trying to avoid dealing with religion cases from France or others of the original COE members (see below for fuller discussion of this case).

The concern about NRMs and other minority faiths in France led to the establishment in 1996 of a Parliamentary Commission to examine the perceived problems with such groups.[20] Unlike the German Enquete Commission, the French Commission met behind closed doors, taking testimony only from critics and detractors, while not allowing any input from groups that were being discussed. The Commission then issued a report that included a list of some 173 groups that were allegedly not real or acceptable religions.[21] The list was very inclusive, including most of the well-publicised NRMs, as well as many other groups that were accepted in other countries or that had been operating in France for many years.

---

[15]   See S Palmer, 'The *secte* response to religious discrimination: subversives, martyrs, or freedom fighters in the French sect wars?', in Lucas and Robbins (note 6 above); C Duvert, 'Anti-cultism in the French Parliament: desperate last stand or opportune leap forward: a critical analysis of the 12 June, 2001 Act', in Richardson, *Regulating Religion* (note 6 above), and N Luca, 'Is there a unique French policy on cults? A European perspective', in ibid.

[16]   See M Introvigne, 'Holy mountains and anti-cult ecology: the campaign against the Aumist religion in France', in Richardson, *Regulating Religion* (note 6 above).

[17]   J Swantko, 'The Twelve Tribes messianic communities, the anti-cult movement, and governmental response', in Richardson, *Regulating Religion* (note 6 above).

[18]   Palmer (note 15 above).

[19]   See J Richardson, 'Social control of new religions: from "brainwashing" claims to child sex abuse accusation', in S Palmer and C Hardman, *Children in New Religions* (Rutgers University Press, 1999).

[20]   Richardson and Introvigne (note 1 above).

[21]   See ibid for discussion of this list and various official reports prepared in France.

Included in this list were the Jehovah's Witnesses, as well as the Aumist group located in southeastern France at Mandarom.

One outcome of the French Parliament's focus on minority religions has been the passage of new laws such as the one passed on 12 June 2001.[22] Included in early discussions was a proposal that would make it easier to dissolve religious groups that are 'regarded as trouble for public order or a major danger to human personality'.[23] The phrase 'danger to human personality' reminds one of the pseudo-scientific term 'brainwashing' that has been used in the United States and elsewhere as a weapon against NRMs.[24] The statute that was eventually passed did not use that phrase, nor another that was proposed to make illegal 'mental manipulation'. These proposals caused an international protest and thus were dropped from what actually was enacted. However, the statute that was passed makes it much easier to dissolve religious groups than was the case before.[25]

Many groups on the list of 173 developed in the first Parliamentary report have been subjected to discriminatory treatment by government agencies as well as private individuals, and many claims of such actions have been made since by groups included on the list.[26] Following the publication of the list by the Commission, the French tax authorities used it to force listed groups to submit detailed information about their finances, including the names of their donors and the amounts given.[27] Following submission of this required information, a report was issued stating that no major violations were found, but that regulation of such groups was to be called for anyway. Then, based on information furnished by the Witnesses and the Aumist group, the French tax authorities sent communications demanding large amounts of past taxes due on contributions

---

[22] See Duvert (note 15 above).

[23] See Richardson and Introvigne (note 1 above) 161.

[24] See D Anthony and T Robbins, 'Pseudoscience versus minority religions: an evaluation of the brainwashing theories of Jean-Marie Abgrall', in Richardson, *Regulating Religion* (note 6 above); J Richardson, 'A social psychological critique of "brainwashing" claims about recruitment to new religions', in J Hadden and D Bromley, *Handbook of Cults and Sects in America* (JAI Press, 1993); Richardson, '"Brainwashing" claims and minority religions outside the United States' (note 1 above).

[25] See Richardson and Introvigne (note 1 above) and Duvert (note 15 above).

[26] See V Altglas, 'French cult controversy at the turn of the new millennium', in Barker, *The Centrality of Religion in Social Life* (note 14 above) for a discussion of the consequences of being placed on the list, some of which have been quite severe. See also Luca (note 15 above) 60–62, showing how various state agencies in France implemented the list, and Introvigne (note 16 above) and Swantko (note 17 above) for discussions of direct impacts on two different specific NRMs in France.

[27] Richardson and Introvigne (note 1 above).

given to the two organisations. The tax bills were based on the conclusion that, since the groups were on the list of unacceptable groups, they were not religious or charitable groups deserving of tax breaks usually afforded to such entities.

In the case of the Witnesses the demand was that they pay the equivalent of over $50 million, which, with penalties, meant that the group was being asked to pay over 100 per cent of what had been given by members in support of the organisation.[28] Also, if any funds were raised to help pay the large tax bill, then those funds were also to be taxed at the high rate set for both groups. The Aumist group was treated similarly, but, as far as can be ascertained, these are the only two groups treated in this manner by the tax authorities. It is also worth noting that since this action was taken no other of the 173 groups on the list developed by the Parliamentary study have been charged with violating the same tax code provisions.

Both the Witnesses and the Aumists have made efforts to seek redress in the French courts, but to no avail, as all cases have been dealt with in a summary fashion, and dismissed, leaving the groups with little recourse within France. To compound the situation, the French tax authorities have taken action to compel payment of the taxes that are being claimed, and this includes attempting to foreclose on property owned by the groups. Due to the lack of domestic remedies both the Witnesses and the Aumists have sought relief from the ECtHR.[29] As indicated above, the Court has not dealt with these cases with any speed, and, as a consequence, both cases remained undecided for many years. However, the Court did admit the JW case on 29 September 2010 on the Article 9 claim,[30] and on 30 June 2011 the Court rendered a decision favouring the Witnesses, unanimously

---

[28] J Richardson and J Shoemaker, 'The European Court of Human Rights, minority religions, and the social construction of religious freedom', in Barker, *The Centrality of Religion in Social Life* (note 14 above).

[29] The JW case application number is 8916/05 and the Aumist case application is 50471/07. See J Richardson and V Lykes, 'Aumism and the European Court of Human Rights: political and procedural impediments to justice' (presented at Conference on Religious Freedom for Minority Religions, Paris, April, 2010). The first author has been in regular contact over the past two decades with officials of the Aumists and the Jehovah's Witnesses in France, and has documentation on various cases carried to the ECtHR. That documentation clearly shows that the groups exhausted internal remedies within France before they submitted to the ECtHR.

[30] See J Richardson and A Garay, 'The European Court of Human Rights and former Communist states', in D Jerolimov, S Zrinscak and I Borowik, *Religion and Patterns of Religious Transformation* (Institute of Social Research, 2004); Richardson and Shoemaker (note 28 above).

finding a violation of Article 9 of the Convention.[31] The imposition of limitations on the 'margin of appreciation' of original members in cases involving minority religions, as was done with this recent decision, is quite new for the Court, and may represent something of a 'sea change' in how the Court treats original members of the COE in such cases. (Later in this chapter the ECtHR situation *vis-à-vis* NRMs and minority religions will be discussed in more detail.)

France has been having great difficulty finding a way to deal with the large Muslim population within its borders. It has the largest Muslim population of any European country, with over 5 million, or 10 per cent of its population being Muslim, mainly of North African origin. Most of the Muslims live in less affluent circumstances, and they represent something of an underclass in French society. The problems associated with integrating this group into French society are immense, not the least reason being that secular French society is based on the principle of *laïcité* that is not desired by a significant number of Muslims. For most French Muslims, their identity as Muslims is important, and there is a desire to act out their religion, something that flies in the face of official efforts to promote secular values and erase religion from all aspects of public life in France. This conflict is well illustrated by the number of 'headscarf cases' from France that will be discussed below in the section dealing with the ECtHR.[32]

The Netherlands

The situation in the Netherlands concerning NRMs and other minority religions is considerably different.[33] In 1980, because of media concerns about the development and importing of NRMs the Dutch government sponsored a study of the issue, and concluded in a quite sophisticated 320-page report, issued in 1984, that NRMs were not a serious problem

---

[31] *Association Les Témoins de Jehovah v France* (App no 8916/05) (ECtHR, 30 June 2011).

[32] See also Chapter 8 by Sylvie Bacquet in this volume.

[33] See R Kranenborg, 'The anti-cult movement in the Netherlands: an unsuccessful affair', in Shupe and Bromley, *Anti-Cult Movements* (note 3 above) and R Singelenberg, 'Foredoomed to failure: the anti-cult movement in the Netherlands', in J Richardson, *Regulating Religion* (note 6 above). The situation in Italy concerning NRMs is also quite muted. See M Introvigne, 'Anti-cult movement in Italy', in Shupe and Bromley, *Anti-Cult Movements* (note 3 above) and L Homer, 'New religions in the republic of Italy', in Richardson, *Regulating Religion* (note 6 above). On religious freedom in the Netherlands generally see Chapter 2 by Marjolein van den Brink and Titia Loenen in this volume.

requiring attention from the government.[34] Thus, the controversy in the Netherlands was very muted, and did not have official sanction, although efforts have been made over the years to call public and governmental attention to the issue. Such efforts have failed, and Dutch representatives in the Council of Europe have expressed opposition to some efforts in that body to exert control over NRMs.[35]

This more tolerant attitude in the Netherlands has allowed NRMs to operate with considerable impunity in that society, and few legal or political issues developed in the years after the initial report. However, as Singelenberg notes,[36] there has been a growing concern about what to do about the growing Muslim population in the Netherlands, which is now over 5 per cent of the total population. Issues similar to those faced within Germany and France have arisen, and no easy ways have been found to resolve tensions as to how to best treat Muslim groups. This issue has become quite volatile in the Netherlands, with right-wing politicians using it to make significant political gains in elections and influence public policy.[37]

Central and Eastern Europe

Russia

Russia is a very special case regarding NRMs and other minority faiths. For over 70 years all religions were stifled by the official policy of the Soviet Union. Hundreds of Russian Orthodox priests were killed and thousands of churches and other Russian Orthodox Church (ROC) institutions were destroyed in the decades after the Bolshevik revolution, while other religions were also persecuted.[38] Only during World War II, as Joseph Stalin sought support from the ROC in the effort to defeat the Nazis, was there any kind of *rapprochement*, and that was quite limited.[39]

The collapse of the Soviet Union opened up many possibilities for

---

[34] See Richardson and van Driel (note 7 above) and Singelenberg (note 33 above) for a discussion of this government report.

[35] Singelenberg, ibid, 217.

[36] Ibid.

[37] See Vanessa Mock, 'Wilders makes shock gains in Dutch elections', *The Independent* (London, 11 June 2010) available at http://www.independent.co.uk/news/world/europe/wilders-makes-shock-gains-in-dutch-elections-1997293.html; see also Chapter 2 by Van den Brink and Loenen in this volume.

[38] See A Dickinson, 'Quantifying religious oppression: Russian Orthodox church closures and repression of priests 1917–41', (2009) 28 *Religion, State, and Society* 327.

[39] See B Bociurkiw, 'The formulation of religious policy in the Soviet Union', in J Wood, *Reading on Church & State* (Baylor University, 1989).

religious groups, and this opening was exploited by NRMs and other religious groups from the west, endemic religious groups within Russia, and especially by the ROC, which sought to reassert itself as the major purveyor of Russian values and nationalism. As Russia dealt with the collapse of the Soviet Union it chose in the early 1990s to adopt some quite western concepts of religious freedom, and passed statutes in 1990 recognising these ideas, even enshrining them in a new 1993 constitution. However, the bloom came off the rose of religious freedom quickly, and traditional Russian values were reasserted that severely limited newer religious movements from gaining a foothold in Russia.[40] The ROC sought to develop and maintain a monopolistic position *vis-à-vis* other religious groups, and politicians opportunistically made use of the alleged 'invasion' of western religious groups to foment concern about Russian nationalism. It is noteworthy that western anti-cult groups played a major role in the shift of sentiment that occurred in Russia over a short period.[41]

Thus the liberal laws passed in the early 1990s were replaced with a much more rigorous and limiting new statute in 1997, that was clearly designed to force a number of religious groups to limit their activities or even leave the country.[42] Religious organisations that had found it easy to register and enjoy privileges under the initial law were forced to re-register, a process that was very onerous and seldom successful, as the Russian bureaucracy responsible for registration simply refused to allow a number of groups to do this, even though they had been functioning with legal sanction since the early 1990s. The new 1997 law also contained a provision that a religion could not be registered as such unless it could prove that it had been operating in Russia for at least 15 years, a provision obviously designed to disallow the new groups that had arrived or developed since the fall of the Soviet Union. A number of Protestant groups, the Jehovah's Witnesses, Catholic groups such as the Society of Jesus, as well as Scientology, the Hare Krishna and even the Salvation Army were all precluded from re-registration under the new law, and thus sought redress in the courts.[43] The

---

[40] M Shterin and J Richardson, 'Local laws on religion in Russia: precursors of Russia's national law', (1998) 40 *Journal of Church and State* 319; W Daniel and C Marsh, 'Russia's 1997 Law on Freedom of Conscience in context and retrospect', (2007) 49 *Journal of Church and State* 5.

[41] M Shterin and J Richardson, 'Effects of the western anti-cult movement on development of laws concerning religion in post-Communist Russia', (2000) 42 *Journal of Church and State* 247.

[42] See W Cole Durham, Jr and L Homer, 'Russia's 1997 Law on Freedom of Conscience and on Religious Associations: an analytical appraisal', (1998) 12 *Emory International Law Review* 101.

[43] J Richardson, G Krylova and M Shterin, 'Legal regulation of religions in

Russian Constitutional Court ruled in favour of the Salvation Army, the Jesuits, at least one Protestant group and the Witnesses, but refrained from finding for the applicants in the Scientology case. However, various governmental authorities refused to honour those rulings, and groups, including Scientology, filed cases with the ECtHR with considerable success, to be discussed further in this chapter.

The ROC used minority groups as part of a massive campaign to regain its prominence in Russian public life. The Church sponsored conferences to which western anti-cultists were invited,[44] and it published very derogatory materials attacking the so-called 'totalitarian sects'. One such publication led to a major libel action against the ROC, brought by a former liberal member of the Russian Duma on behalf of several religious groups that had been defamed in it. This widely publicised case, which demonstrated the power of the ROC and the lack of autonomy of the judicial system of Russia, has been analysed by this author and Marat Shterin.[45] Since that time the court system in Russia, with the occasional exception of rulings by the Constitutional Court, has regularly found against minority religions of all kinds. More recently, this has been demonstrated by rulings upholding the application of anti-terrorism laws against the Jehovah's Witnesses in a number of Russian regions.[46]

Poland

Poland presents a very different situation, albeit one with some important similarities. Poland has had a traditionally dominant Catholic Church, and the Church's role in the fall of Communism was quite significant.[47] The Communists were never able to suppress the Catholic Church in Poland, as they were with the ROC in Russia. On the contrary, the Catholic Church

---

Russia: new developments', in Richardson, *Regulating Religion* (note 6 above); J Richardson, 'Protection of religious minorities in former Communist states with dominant religions', in I Murzaku, *Quo Vadis Eastern Europe? Religion, State and Society after Communism* (Longo Editore Ravenna, 2009), and Richardson and Shoemaker (note 28 above).

[44] Shterin and Richardson, 'Local laws on religion in Russia' (note 40 above).

[45] J Richardson and M Shterin, 'The *Yakunin v Dworkin* trial and the emerging religious pluralism in Russia', (2002) 22 *Religion in Eastern Europe* 1.

[46] See the Human Rights without Frontiers report outlining the use of anti-terrorism laws in Russia against the Jehovah's Witnesses, at http://www.hrwf.net/images/forbnews/2011/russia%202011.pdf.

[47] See J Casanova, *Public Religions in the Modern World* (University of Chicago Press, 1994) and J Richardson 'Religion, constitutional courts, and democracy in former Communist countries' (2006) 603 *The Annals of the American Academy of Political and Social Science* 129.

grew in membership and political power through the post-World War II occupation, and served as a not-so-loyal opposition to the Communist-dominated Polish government. The selection of the Bishop of Krakow as Pope John Paul II, and his subsequent visit to Poland where some 17 million people participated in mass meetings at which he spoke and administered the sacraments, were major catalytic events in the sea change that occurred with the fall of Communism. The Church also openly supported the Solidarity movement led by Lech Walesa, and supported his election. Thus, when the Soviet Union collapsed, the Church was in a dominant position, and it chose to exercise power in a number of ways.[48] However, Poland was not ready to have a society completely dominated by the Catholic Church, as many citizens had responded positively to less religious education in the schools, to easier divorce and access to abortions, to a more flexible approach to sexuality and to a more 'free market' approach to the economy. Thus conflicts developed, even though the Catholic Church was usually able to work its will within the political arena.[49]

One area of special interest for this chapter concerns the regulation of NRMs and other minority faiths within Poland. As in Russia with the ROC, the Catholic Church in Poland sought to exert control over other religions seeking to operate in Poland. However, it has not been as successful as the ROC in Russia. In this regard Richardson has offered a sociological assessment of the religious situation in Poland after the fall of Communism, and Tadeuz Doktor and Agnieszka Koscianska have both discussed efforts by the Church and political authorities working with the Church to limit the activities of NRMs and other faiths within Poland.[50]

---

[48]   The Church has promoted limits on abortion and on divorce, strict controls over mass media coverage of itself, required religious instruction in schools, and more control over NRMs, among other things. See I Borowik, 'Religion and civil society in Poland in the process of democratic transformation', in D Marinovic Jerolimov, S Zrinscak and I Borowik, *Religion and Patterns of Social Transformation* (Institute for Social Research, 2003); T Doktor, 'New religious movements and the state in Poland', in J Richardson, *Regulating Religion* (note 6 above); A Koscianska, 'Anti-cult movements and governmental reports on "Sects and Cults": the case of Poland', in ibid.

[49]   J Richardson, 'New religious movements and religious freedom in Eastern and Central Europe: a sociological analysis', in I Borowik and G Babinski, *New Religious Phenomena in Central and Eastern Europe* (Nomos, 1995); and Richardson, 'Religion, constitutional courts, and democracy' (note 47 above).

[50]   Richardson, 'New religious movements and religious freedom in Eastern and Central Europe' (note 49 above), A Koscianska (note 48 above) and T Doktor (note 48 above). Also see G Goldberger, D Hall, L Greskova and R Smoczynski, 'Societal reactions to new religious movements in Poland, Croatia, and Slovenia',

Noteworthy in these discussions is the role that France attempted to play, which has vigorously promoted its approach to minority faiths in Poland and around the world. However, the political climate in post-Soviet Poland was different to that of the officially secular French government. In Poland, with the Church attempting to achieve a dominant position in virtually all areas of public and private life, more liberal political forces were less inclined to back Church-supported efforts to enact legislation similar to that passed in France. Instead, there was some public preparedness to allow minority religions greater participation in public life in Poland.[51] Thus, something of a stalemate developed over this issue, which meant that minority religions could still operate in Poland, whether or not they were officially registered.

Hungary

Hungary is yet another unique situation for NRMs, other minority faiths, and religion in general.[52] Hungary was never fully subjected to Soviet rule, and remained more westernised than most other countries in the region. It also has a long history of accommodating different religious traditions,[53] and that was reasserted as the hold of the Soviet Union diminished. In the late 1980s the Communist government in Hungary was forced to negotiate and share power with opposition forces, and that negotiation resulted in more openness towards religion, including minority faiths. A 1989 law made it easier for minority groups to register with the government and gain official recognition, and many groups took advantage of this reform.[54] Major protections for religious freedom were also written into a

---

in D Hall and R Smoczynski , *New Religious Movements and Conflict in Selected Countries of Central Europe* (IFIS Publishers, 2010).

[51]   See Koscianska's (note 48 above) discussion of a major effort mounted by anti-cult and government entities that resulted in a report in 2000 to the Polish Parliament pointing out the many alleged dangers of sects operating in Poland, and recommending new criminal legislation to deal with the issue. However, she notes that the effort failed to result in any new laws. Doktor (note 48 above) 261, offers this analysis of the differences between the reaction towards sects in France and in Poland: 'In contrast to France, where the anti-sect policy is promoted by the left-oriented government on the basis of *'laïcité actif,'* in Poland it is supported by the political right and opposed by the left of the political spectrum, which is critical of current policy as going too far and being too sensitive to the informal pressure of the Church.'

[52]   On religious freedom in Hungary generally see Chapter 10 by Renata Uitz in this volume.

[53]   B Schanda, 'Freedom of religion and minority religions in Hungary', in Richardson, *Regulating Religion* (note 6 above).

[54]   Ibid, 282.

new Hungarian Constitution, including quite importantly a provision that changing the law on 'the freedom of religion and conscience requires the two-thirds vote of the MPs present'.[55]

These changes were not without controversy, however, as western anti-cultism also spread to Hungary. For example, in 1992 efforts were made to change the liberal registration law. Four groups that had been properly registered (the Unification Church, Hare Krishna, Scientology and the Jehovah's Witnesses) were referred to as 'destructive cults' and all were to be refused any state financial support that would have been due them under the recently reinstituted state funding mechanism for registered churches. The proposal also contained other, more rigorous, requirements for registration, such as requiring them to have existed for 100 years in Hungary, and having at least 10000 adherents. However, this effort to make significant changes to the registration law eventually failed, due in part to a very effective campaign by the Hare Krishna against it,[56] as well as the constitutional requirement for a two-thirds vote of Parliament.[57] The Hare Krishna became something of a 'poster child' for liberal political forces that were fearful of conservative political values promoted by the Catholic Church. However, the other three groups that were designated as 'destructive cults' were not allowed to receive funding for a time.

The law granting financial support for religious groups was modified significantly in 1997, shifting to a voluntary system under which individuals could redirect 1 per cent of their personal income taxes to the religious group of their choice.[58] This was in lieu of the direct subsidy that occurred under the older law. Under the new law nearly 70 religious groups received some funding, including a number of minority ones. For example, the Hare Krishna have been consistently shown to have received funds from a much larger number of citizens than their actual membership. Likewise, Scientology received designations from nearly a thousand citizens, which may approximate to its actual membership in Hungary.

The courts also have played a role in determining the place of minority religions and NRMs in Hungary. One early case brought by the Hare

---

[55] Ibid. These provisions are under considerable duress at the time of this writing, however. See posting by Human Rights Without Frontiers, 15 July 2011, 'The Hungarian Civil Liberties Union's first assessment of the new law on religion'.

[56] I Kamanas, 'Devotees of Krishna in Hungary', in Borowik and Babinski (note 49 above); Richardson, 'New religious movements and religious freedom in Eastern and Central Europe' (note 49 above); P Torok, 'New religious movements and social conflict in Hungary', in Hall and Smoczynski (note 50 above).

[57] Schanda (note 53 above) 284.

[58] Ibid.

Krishna had quite an unusual outcome, in that they won a libel suit against a prominent Reformed Church minister who had led an anti-cult effort against NRMs in the early 1990s, and their victory was affirmed by an appeal court.[59] The Hungarian Constitutional Court also has issued decisions that have affirmed the public role of religion in Hungary, and those decisions, which will be briefly discussed later, have offered protection to minority faiths as well.[60]

3. CONSTITUTIONAL COURTS

The role of constitutional courts has grown over the years, and the spread of such courts through former Soviet-dominated nations in Eastern and Central Europe represents the latest 'wave' of such expansion. This movement is worldwide in scope and is a major reason why scholars talk about the dramatic growth of 'constitutionalism' as a key aspect of modern political culture.[61]

Most of the 47 members of the COE have constitutional courts, and establishing a constitutional court was almost a prerequisite for COE membership for nations that were previously part of the Soviet bloc.[62] However, constitutional courts operate in considerably different ways, particularly in terms of access. For instance, in Germany ordinary citizens can petition the Constitutional Court, and thousands do so, whereas in France the Constitutional Council can be accessed only by political officials and the Parliament so as to seek advisory opinions on proposed legislation. Most constitutional courts in the 'new Europe' follow the German model, but there are a few exceptions.[63]

---

[59] Kamanas (note 56 above) and Richardson, 'New religious movements and religious freedom in Eastern and Central Europe' (note 49 above).

[60] Richardson, 'Religion, constitutional courts, and democracy' (note 47 above).

[61] See S Arjomand, 'Law political reconstruction and constitutional politics', (2003) 18 *International Sociology* 7; K Scheppele, 'Constitutional negotiations: political contexts of judicial activism in post-Soviet Europe', (2003) 18 *International Sociology* 219; J Go, 'A globalizing constitutionalism: views from the postcolony', 1945–2000', (2003) 18 *International Sociology* 71.

[62] See K Scheppele, 'Declarations of independence: judicial responses to political pressure', in S Burbank and B Friedman, *Judicial Independence at a Crossroads* (SAGE, 2002).

[63] G Brunner, 'Structure and proceedings of the Hungarian Constitutional Judiciary', in L Solyom and G Brunner, *Constitutional Judiciary in the New Democracy: The Hungarian Constitutional Court* (University of Michigan Press, 2000).

Constitutional courts also vary greatly in powers and autonomy, with some exerting tremendous authority for at least a time as was the case in Hungary during the 1990s,[64] and in Germany, where the Constitutional Court is perhaps the most powerful such court in the region if not the world.[65] Such courts in other nations were even disbanded for a time, as happened in Russia during the Yeltsin regime in the early 1990s,[66] or have not been able to exercise much power, as in Belarus, Azerbaijan and the Ukraine. The full history of constitutional courts and explanations of why these non-democratically selected institutions are so popular cannot be recounted here.[67] Instead we will focus on selected decisions from the countries that have been briefly discussed (except the Netherlands), focusing on how those courts deal with issues of religious freedom.

Constitutional Courts in Western Europe

Germany

As noted above, Germany has perhaps the most respected and autonomous constitutional court in the world. This court, established in 1951, has developed a huge body of jurisprudence focused on monitoring and maintaining democracy in Germany. In this time it has decided over 150 000 cases, 144 000 of which have been complaints brought by individual citizens, and it has published 2700 full opinions.[68] As might be expected, some of those cases involve religious issues.

Besier and Besier have described the long battle over the official status of the Jehovah's Witnesses in Germany, a battle that saw several rulings by the Constitutional Court, in which it overturned decisions by other courts within the German judicial system.[69] Eventually the administration of the *Land* Berlin (the Federal State of Berlin) was forced to accede to the

---

[64]   See Scheppele, 'Constitutional negotiations' (note 61 above); J Richardson and M Shterin, 'Constitutional courts in postcommunist Russia and Hungary', (2008) 36 *Religion, State, and Society* 251.

[65]   D Kommers, 'The Federal Constitutional Court: guardian of German democracy', (2006) 603 *The Annals of the American Academy of Political and Social Science* 111.

[66]   See Scheppele, 'Constitutional negotiations' (note 61 above); Richardson and Shterin, 'Constitutional courts in postcommunist Russia and Hungary' (note 64 above).

[67]   See W Sadurski, A Czamota and M Krygier (eds), *Spreading Democracy and the Rule of Law? The Impact of EU Enlargement for the Rule of Law, Democracy and Constitutionalism in Post-Communist Legal Orders* (Springer, 2010).

[68]   See Kommers (note 65 above) 115.

[69]   Besier and Besier (note 12 above).

Constitutional Court's ruling and grant the status of a religious corporation to the Witnesses.

Besier describes another case brought by a minority religious group, Universal Life, which claimed that the religious corporate status of the dominant churches in Germany should be revoked because they were no longer serving the public interest as shown by their attacks on minority faiths in publications, the mass media (to which they had access because of their status) and in their schools.[70] In short, the claim was that the dominant churches were using their legal position to limit religious freedom. The Constitutional Court rejected the case, but noted in its ruling that the churches holding corporate status have 'special instruments of power' at their disposal,[71] a special responsibility to uphold the rights of third parties, and that the effects of attacks on other groups could be cumulative. Thus, the Court sent a message that has apparently resulted, according to Besier, in fewer attacks by the major churches on minority religious groups.[72]

France

France's Constitutional Court has not dealt with many cases involving minority religions.[73] The Constitutional Court's jurisdiction is extremely limited, and the Court is able to hear only those matters that are specifically referred to it by the President, the Prime Minister, or combinations

---

[70]   Besier, 'Current problems of religious minorities in Germany' (note 8 above).

[71]   Ibid, 124.

[72]   The Church subsequently made an application to the (now defunct) European Commission of Human Rights, which rejected the application as 'manifestly ill-founded' since there had been no interference with the applicant's rights to freedom of religion under Art 9 ECHR: *Universelles Leben e V v Germany* (App no 29745/96) (ECommHR, 27 November 1996).

[73]   Jeremy Gunn, in a personal communication to the author (30 January 2011) wrote:

> The Constitutional Court's jurisdiction is extremely limited. They are able to hear only those cases that are specifically referred to them by the President, Prime Minister, or combinations of parliamentary representatives while bills are pending. After the bill is adopted into law, there can be no further constitutional challenges. So no French court or administrative body can question the constitutionality of a law once adopted. Most decisions interpreting laws involving religion have been made by the administrative court system – but even they cannot question a law's constitutionality.

Also see M Rogoff, *French Constitutional Law: Cases and Materials* (Carolina Academic Press, 2011).

of Parliamentary representatives while bills are pending. No French court or administrative body can question the constitutionality of a law once it has been adopted. Most decisions interpreting laws involving religion have been made by the administrative court system, and such courts cannot question a law's constitutionality.

However, one recent case that has attracted considerable attention was when the Constitutional Court upheld the constitutionality of the well-publicised French law banning the wearing of a *burqa* or any face covering in public.[74] The law, which has been justified in part on the ground of gender equality, passed the French Parliament by a vote of 240–1. It imposes a €150 fine on any woman wearing a face covering in public, and that term is defined broadly. If a man is found to have forced a woman to wear a *burqa* he can be fined €30 000 and sent to prison. This law, which came into force in April 2011, has been criticised as violative of the French and European human rights legislation and values,[75] but it passed muster with the highest court in France and has been approved by the French Parliament. The Constitutional Court did however rule that an exception must be made to the law for women who are attending a public place of worship, indicating that forcing women not to wear the *burqa* in such places would violate their freedom of religion.

Constitutional Courts in Eastern and Central Europe

Russia

As indicated above, in the past decade the Russian Constitutional Court has attempted to exert itself in the area of religious freedom. It has shied away from cases dealing with the separation of powers ever since the famous conflict between President Yeltsin and the Supreme Soviet (the Parliament), during which it sided with the Supreme Soviet and, after Yeltsin prevailed, was temporarily disbanded by him.[76] Instead, the Court has focused on cases involving individual rights and concerns.[77] As an example of its more recent thrust, the Court has ruled in favour of four religious groups appealing refusals by the state to re-register them after the 1997 law. While the Court did not explicitly say that the new law or aspects

---

[74] See Decision 2010–613, 7 October 2010. See further Chapter 8 by Sylvie Bacquet in this volume.

[75] See criticism by Amnesty International at http://english.ntdtv.com/ntdtv_en/ns_europe/2010-07-15/685875583705.html.

[76] Richardson and Shterin, 'Constitutional courts in postcommunist Russia and Hungary' (note 64 above) 257.

[77] Scheppele, 'Constitutional negotiations' (note 61 above) 263.

of it were unconstitutional, it did assert in its rulings that the 15-year presence criterion could not be imposed on groups that had already been properly registered under the previous statute.[78] Although the Russian bureaucracy chose to ignore those rulings, they perhaps had some effect and may illustrate Sadurski's claim that the ECtHR works in concert with national legal systems (including constitutional courts) to promote human and civil rights in countries where such values are not fully respected.[79]

Poland

In Poland the Constitutional Court has exerted considerable influence, and has been referred to as a strong constitutional court.[80] Several major decisions by it have had the effect of allowing greater involvement by the Catholic Church in the affairs of the state, and affirming the right of the government to regulate the media and enforce laws disallowing criticism of the Catholic Church in the mass media. It has also upheld decisions of the executive branch to reimpose through an executive order religious education in the schools, a long-standing tradition in Poland prior to World War II. These decisions, affirming a prominent place in public life for the Church, have had the indirect effect of discouraging minority faiths from exerting rights. However, to date the Court has not rendered any decisions that explicitly limit the activities of minority religions.

Hungary

Kim Scheppele has focused considerable attention on Hungary and the role of the Hungarian Constitutional Court during the decade after the fall of Communism.[81] She has noted that the Court, which was the first constitutional court established in a Soviet-dominated nation, was the most popular institution in Hungary in that period, and that it exerted itself in many areas of public life, operating as something of a 'courtocracy'. As has been noted by its former Chief Justice,[82] most appointees to the Court during this crucial first decade had been trained in Germany, working with that nation's strong constitutional court. The Hungarian Court could be

---

[78] Richardson, Krylova and Shterin (note 43 above).

[79] W Sadurski, 'Partnering with Strasbourg: constitutionalisation of the European Court of Human Rights, the accession of central and east European states to the Council of Europe, and the idea of pilot judgments', (2009) 9 *Human Rights Law Review* 397.

[80] Scheppele, 'Constitutional negotiations' (note 61 above).

[81] Ibid.

[82] L Solyom, 'The role of Constitutional Court in transition to democracy, with special reference to Hungary', (2003) 18 *International Sociology* 133.

accessed by ordinary citizens during this early period, but it also advised Parliament on proposed legislation, and for a time was regularly declaring unconstitutional laws passed by Parliament.[83]

The Hungarian Court adopted a position that is quite protective of 'fundamental rights' and includes religious freedom, enshrined in the Hungarian Constitution that was heavily revised in 1989. The revision, worked out between Communist authorities and opposition leaders, rejected Socialism and embraced a market-based economy and more human and civil rights, as well as establishing the Constitutional Court and granting it considerable power.[84] The Court, using an approach that we would designate 'positive neutrality',[85] has upheld the liberal laws concerning religion that were enacted after 1989, and has taken a position that the state should be neutral in how it deals with various religious groups, and should even support efforts to help them succeed as actors in the public sphere. While some decisions have granted a special place in the public arena to the Catholic Church,[86] a number of decisions have had the direct effect of allowing minority religions and NRMs to function openly.[87] More recently, however, conservative Hungarian governments have sought to limit the powers of the Constitutional Court severely, as well as those of other institutions in that country. Kim Scheppele writes about the most recent turn of events, and makes the following dramatic statement: 'Since the national elections of April 2010, the constitutional underpinnings of the Hungarian regime are being radically dismantled to the point (that) it is now doubtful that Hungary has a viable constitutional government anymore.'[88] Perhaps the early decisions it made concerning religion are now part of the landscape in Hungary, and might not be easily dismissed, but that is not clear at this time as the current conservative government has a

---

[83]   Scheppele, 'Constitutional negotiations' (note 61 above).

[84]   Richardson and Shterin, 'Constitutional courts in postcommunist Russia and Hungary' (note 64 above).

[85]   In the decade after the fall of Communism Hungary was quite supportive of religious involvement in public life. Schanda (note 53 above) 285 comments: 'It is to be noted that neutrality has to be distinguished from indifference, which is not meant by the Constitution . . . Neutrality is not "laicism"; the state may have an active role in providing an institutional legal framework, as well as funds for the churches to ensure the free exercise of religion in practice.'

[86]   Ibid, 286–90.

[87]   Richardson and Shterin, 'Constitutional courts in postcommunist Russia and Hungary' (note 64 above).

[88]   K Scheppele, 'Hungary in constitutional crisis' (Invisible Constitutions Conference, Princeton University, 10 December 2010) 1. See also Chapter 10 by Renata Uitz in this volume.

majority in the Parliament of more than two-thirds, which means it can change constitutional provisions much more easily.

4.   THE EUROPEAN COURT OF HUMAN RIGHTS

The European Court of Human Rights (ECtHR) has a variable history concerning NRMs and other minority religions. The European Convention right that underpins the Court's jurisprudence concerning religion is Article 9, which states:

1.   Everyone has the right to freedom of thought, conscience, and religion; this right includes freedom to change his religion and belief, and freedom, either alone or in community with others and in public and private, to manifest his religion or belief, teaching, practice, and observance.
2.   Freedom to manifest one's religion or belief shall be subject only to such limitations as are prescribed by law and are necessary in a democratic society in the interests of public safety, for protection of the public order, health or morals, or for the protection of the rights and freedoms of others.

For decades after the Court was established in 1959 this article was largely neglected and, in those cases that were brought, the Strasbourg bodies deferred to the member states in matters of religion, granting them a wide 'margin of appreciation'.[89] Not until 1993 did the Court find a violation of Article 9, in the famous *Kokkinakis* case involving a Jehovah's Witness who had been found guilty of violating a criminal Greek statute against proselytising.[90] The Court, in what might be termed a very early 'pilot

---

[89]   See C Evans, *Freedom of Religion under the European Convention on Human Rights* (Oxford University Press, 2001). See also L Garlicki, 'Collective aspects of the religious freedoms: recent developments in the case law of the European Court of Human Rights', in A Sajó, *Censorial Sensitivities: Free Speech and Religion in a Fundamentalist World* (Eleven International Publishing, 2007) 218, who discusses the margin of appreciation granted member states, and even makes the comment that '. . . in some respects that margin (in Article 9 matters) may be wider than under other provisions of the Convention'.

[90]   *Kokkinakis v Greece* (App no 13407/88) (25 May 1993); (1993) 17 EHRR 397. J Richardson, 'Minority religions, religious freedom, and the new pan-European political and judicial institutions' (1995) 37 *Journal of Church and* State 39; Evans, ibid; P Danchin, 'The evolving jurisprudence of the European Court of Human Rights and the protection of religious minorities', in P Danchin and E Cole, *Protecting the Human rights of Religious Minorities in Eastern Europe* (Columbia University Press, 2002).

judgment',[91] ruled (6–3) against Greece and in favour of the claimant.[92] Since 1993 the Court has found a number of violations of Article 9, although nearly all of those decisions have come from Greece or eastern and central European nations that joined the COE after the demise of the Soviet Union.

This major apparent disparity in origin and outcome of cases brought to the Court has raised questions about the possibility of a double standard that might be operating in its jurisprudence concerning religion. Some have claimed that the disparate pattern of decisions has favoured original members of the COE, while disfavouring newer member states.[93] Carolyn Evans[94] and Lech Garlicki[95] have suggested that the Court's decisions are explicable by focusing on the distinction between group or collective rights and individual rights. Many of the decisions from former Soviet-dominated areas have dealt with registration and even the right of minority faiths to exist and operate, while Garlicki and Evans claim that cases from all regions of the COE that involve individual rights have been dealt with summarily, with a wide margin of appreciation given to the nations involved.[96] Several 'headscarf cases' from France and Turkey seem to illustrate the Court's apparent lack of concern for individual religious freedom. However, other scholars who have focused on *Refah Partisi,* a case in which the Court endorsed the Turkish government's decision to abolish a major political party,[97] have reached a different conclusion. The European Court's ruling contained some strong language concerning Islam, leading Meerschaut and Gutwirth to claim that the Court is simply exhibiting a bias toward secularism and neutrality that has the effect of favouring traditional Christian values and denigrating Islam.[98] This point has also been discussed by Cumper, who offers several reasons why a pro-Christian bias might exist in the jurisprudence of the Court, and suggests that the

---

[91] Sadurski (note 79 above).

[92] Richardson, 'Minority religions, religious freedom' (note 90 above).

[93] Richardson and Garay (note 30 above); Richardson and Shoemaker (note 28 above).

[94] C Evans, 'Individual and group religious freedom in the European Court of Human Rights: cracks in the intellectual architecture' (2010) 26 *Journal of Law and Religion* 321.

[95] Garlicki (note 89 above).

[96] See also Danchin (note 90 above).

[97] *Refah Partisi (the Welfare Party) and others v Turkey* (Apps no 41340/98, 41342/98, 41343/98 and 41344/98) (13 February 2003); (2003) 37 EHRR 1.

[98] K Meerschaut and S Gutwirth, 'Legal pluralism and Islam in the scales of the European Court of Human Rights: the limits of categorical balancing', in E Brems, *Conflicts between Fundamental Rights* (Intersentia, 2009).

bias might work against NRMs being treated fairly by the Court.[99] This brief treatment cannot resolve this controversy over the meaning of recent ECtHR jurisprudence involving minority religious groups and religious freedom. However, some relevant evidence can be garnered from an examination of selected recent cases from France, Germany, the Netherlands, Russia, and Poland.[100]

Cases from Newer Council of Europe Member States

Russia
Strikingly, Russia has developed a losing record before the ECtHR in the area of minority religions. Richardson and Shoemaker have summarised some of these cases, pointing out, by way of contrast, the success of the Salvation Army at the Court.[101] This religious group won its case at the Russian Constitutional Court, because the Moscow authorities had failed to afford it legal recognition as a religious organisation, but it received no redress from government authorities in Russia, prompting it to submit an application to the ECtHR. There, the Salvation Army won a unanimous ruling on 5 October 2006, with a finding that Article 11 (freedom of association) had been violated in conjunction with Article 9.[102] The Jehovah's Witnesses also won a case involving efforts by some local authorities to shut down the operation of a congregation of deaf Witnesses who were meeting in Chelyabinsk.[103] The group had also been refused re-registration by the authorities, but on 11 January 2007 ended up with a unanimous ruling that its Article 6 (right to a fair hearing) and Article 9 rights had been violated. In *Barankevich v Russia,* an evangelical Christian group had been refused permission to hold an outdoor meeting because to do so might result in 'discontent' and 'public disorder' since most citizens were not members of the group, but the ECtHR ruled unanimously that there had been a violation of Article 11 'interpreted in light of article 9'.[104]

Perhaps most surprising was a strongly worded, unanimous ruling by

---

[99]   Cumper (note 4 above) 174–5.
[100]   A preliminary examination of ECtHR cases dealing with minority religions reveals few if any cases from Hungary that have been dealt with by the Court.
[101]   Richardson and Shoemaker (note 28 above).
[102]   *Moscow Branch of the Salvation Army v Russia* (App no 72881/01) (ECtHR, 5 October 2006); (2007) 44 EHRR 46.
[103]   *Kuznetsov and Others v Russia* (App no 184/02) (ECtHR, 11 January 2007); (2009) 49 EHRR 15.
[104]   *Barankevich v Russia* (App no 10519/03 (ECtHR, 26 July 2007).

the ECtHR in April 2007 in favour of Scientology,[105] which had been denied re-registration ten times by the Moscow authorities. The ECtHR, in condemning the Moscow authorities for their handling of this case,[106] held that '. . . it can be inferred that, in denying registration to the Church of Scientology of Moscow, the Moscow authorities did not act in good faith and neglected their duty of neutrality and impartiality *vis à-vis* the applicant's religious community . . .'.[107]

In September 2009,[108] the ECHR issued a unanimous Chamber ruling in favour of the Scientology branches in Surgut and Nizhnekamsk, holding that Russia could not ban the Church of Scientology simply because it did not have a long history in the country. Two cases from different regions of Russia were joined in this decision, which hinged on the 1997 law's requirement that a group could not be registered as a religious organisation unless it had existed for at least 15 years in Russia. The ECtHR stated that such a restriction, which would leave Scientology and other newer faiths without a legal personality and therefore greatly hinder their functioning, was not necessary in a democratic society. In a similar case that concerned the forced expulsion from Russia of a member of the Unification Church and thus separated the applicant (Nolan, a missionary for the Church) from his 3-year-old son, the ECtHR ruled unanimously that there had been violations of Article 5 (right to liberty and security), Article 8 (right to respect family and private life) and Article 9.[109] And finally, in a case where the applicants complained about severe problems encountered by Jehovah's Witnesses in re-registering after the 1997 Russian law was passed, the ECtHR held that there had been violations of Article 11 (freedom of association) read in the light of Article 9, and a violation of Article 9 read in the light of Article 11, as well as a violation of Article 6 (right to fair trial).[110]

These ECtHR cases from Russia have all resulted in the Court offering quite critical comments on Russia's treatment of minority faiths. Russia

---

[105] I call this and the Jehovah's Witness case surprising because of the strong animus that has been generated against these two groups in a number of countries. For the Court to support their efforts against a major power such as Russia is noteworthy. See Richardson and Shoemaker (note 28 above).

[106] *The Church of Scientology v Russia* (App no 18147/02) (ECtHR, 5 April 2007).

[107] Ibid [97]. See the judgment in this case for details on this long legal battle within Russia.

[108] *Kimlya and Others v Russia* (Apps no 76836/01 and 32782/03) (ECtHR, 1 October 2009).

[109] *Nolan and K v Russia* (App no 2512/04) (ECtHR, 12 February 2009).

[110] *Jehovah's Witnesses of Moscow v Russia* (App no 302/02) (ECtHR, 10 June 2010).

has responded slowly, usually paying whatever damages have been awarded by the Court, but making few other concessions. This is particularly so with this last decision – that went in favour of the Jehovah's Witnesses – which seems completely at odds with the current practice in Russia of attempting to define the Witnesses as a terrorist organisation.[111]

Poland

Poland has seen a few cases brought before the ECtHR deriving from some of the recent Catholic-supported strictures that have been implemented on schools, as well as a prison case. For example, in a case in which the applicants complained that the school authorities had failed to offer an ethics class for their son in place of the required class in religious instruction, give the boy a grade in the place reserved for 'religion/ethics' in his school report, and stop harassment of the boy by fellow students, the Court found a violation of Article 14 (prohibition of discrimination) in conjunction with Article 9.[112] Another successful application involved a Buddhist prisoner (Jakóbski) who had repeatedly unsuccessfully asked for a meat-free diet; the ECtHR found a violation of Article 14 (prohibition of discrimination) in conjunction with Article 9.[113] The Court concluded that prison authorities had failed to strike a balance between Jakóbski's Article 9 rights and the prison's interests in operating an efficient and economical food service in the prison.

Cases from Original Council of Europe Member States

Germany

In a major case from Germany, a group of organisations involved with religious or meditation groups belonging to the Osho movement (formerly known as the Bhagwan movement) brought an action against the government for publishing official pamphlets and other documents accusing them of being 'sects', 'youth sects', 'psycho sects', and issuing warnings that the groups were 'destructive', 'pseudo-religious' and that they 'manipulated their members'. In 2002 the German Constitutional Court had ruled that the government could not use the terms 'destructive', 'pseudo-religious', or

---

[111]   See R Griffin, 'More raids and trials, pressure on lawyers, defendant forced to resign from job', Human Rights Without Frontiers, 18 April 2011 and Office of General Counsel for Jehovah's Witnesses, 'Jehovah's Witnesses in Russia: state sponsored campaign on harassment and mistreatment' (Patterson, NY, March 2011).

[112]   *Grzelak v Poland* (App no 7710/02) (ECtHR, 15 June 2010).

[113]   *Jakóbski v Poland* (App no 18429/06) (ECtHR, 7 December 2006).

say that they 'manipulated their members', but it allowed the other terms to be used. This case was taken to the ECtHR, which ruled against the group's claims (5–2), stating that the government was within its rights to use the authorised terms when referring to non-mainstream religions.[114]

France

France, with its long standing constitutional principle of *laïcité*, is a special and much-criticised case,[115] so it should not be surprising that a number of cases dealing with the rights of minority religions and their French members have been brought to the ECtHR. However, the Court has been very reluctant to accept cases from France, as the record clearly shows. Richardson and Shoemaker point out that France has only lost two cases involving minority faiths, in both cases the Jehovah's Witnesses, and neither of those cases resulted in a ruling that Article 9 had been violated.[116] One was a custody dispute in which a violation of Article 14 (prohibition of discrimination) was found.[117] The other loss was a case brought by a lawyer who was a Jehovah's Witness, who had written a book about the severe discrimination he experienced within the legal profession because of his faith. The plaintiff was disbarred after publishing the book, and also subjected to a tax audit by government tax authorities. The Court accepted his submission and ruled that there had been a violation of Article 10 (freedom of expression).[118]

Richardson and Shoemaker have discussed another major ECtHR case over the decision of tax authorities (discussed in section 2 above) to submit a very large tax bill to the Witness organisation on the grounds that they were not a true religion, and therefore did not have any kind of exemption from revenues collected. This case, with claims that Articles 6, 9, 14, 18 and some Protocols have been violated, languished for years with no decision being made on whether to accept it for adjudication.[119] This case was finally declared admissible in 2010 under Article 9, and a judgment was rendered in favour of the Witnesses on 30 June 2011.[120] The decision undercuts to

---

[114] *Leela Förderkreis EV and Others v Germany* (App no 58911/00) (ECtHR, 6 November 2008).

[115] See Richardson and Introvigne (note 1 above); Beckford (note 14 above); Introvigne (note 16 above); Swantko (note 17 above); Luca (note 15 above); Duvert (note 15 above).

[116] Richardson and Shoemaker (note 28 above).

[117] *Palau-Martinez v France* (App no 64927/01) (ECtHR, 16 December 2003).

[118] *Paturel v France* (App no 54968/00) (ECtHR, 22 December 2005).

[119] *Association les Témoins de Jéhovah v France* (App No 8916/05) (ECtHR, 21 September 2010).

[120] Ibid (ECtHR, judgment 30 June 2011).

some extent the 'double standard' argument mentioned above, and may support Evans's thesis (discussed earlier), since having to pay the tax bill (or lose their property) would effectively put the Witnesses out of business in France.

The Aumist group has filed 15 cases against France with the ECtHR over a number of difficulties they have had with the French government, including a situation similar to that of the Witnesses concerning taxes that the French government is claiming are owed on contributions made to the organisation. All but one of those cases has been summarily rejected with no explanation. One case has resulted in the Court seeking more information from the French government, but that case is still pending and remains unresolved.[121] However, the recent decision in the Jehovah's Witness case (above) suggests that the Court may be taking a different view of France's exertion of control over minority faiths via unusual application of tax laws.

France has been successful in a number of other cases that have been submitted to the ECtHR dealing with the religious attire of Muslim and Sikh students who have been expelled from school for violating a policy against conspicuous religious symbols.[122] In cases brought by Muslim girls/women dealing with veils and head coverings there have been findings either of no breach of Article 9,[123] or of inadmissibility.[124] Similarly, there have been findings of inadmissibility in cases brought by male members of the Sikh religion.[125] The Court dismissed all of these cases, declaring, amongst other things, that the pupils could continue their schooling via correspondence courses.

The Netherlands
In one case from the Netherlands a Muslim foreign national applied in 2003 for a work permit to serve as *imam* of a local Moroccan community. The permit was refused, citing that the mosque had not posted any adver-

---

[121] *Association Cultuelle du Temple Pyramide v France* (App no 50471/07) (ECtHR, 14 November 2007).

[122] See also Chapter 8 by Sylvie Bacquet in this volume.

[123] *Dogru v France* (App no 27058) (ECtHR, 4 December 2008).

[124] See for example *Aktas v France* (App no 43563/08) (ECtHR, 30 June 2009); *Bayrak v France* (App no 14308/08) (ECtHR, 30 June 2009); *Gamaleddyn v France* (App no 18527/08) (ECtHR, 30 June 2009); *Ghazal v France* (App no 29134/08) (ECtHR, 30 June 2009). Similarly, the Court has upheld Turkey's decision to ban face and head coverings in a university setting, granting a considerable 'margin of appreciation' to Turkey, a secular state. See *Leyla Şahin v Turkey* (2007) 44 EHRR 5 which was decided by a 16–1 Grand Chamber vote on 10 November 2005.

[125] *J Singh v France* App No 25463/08 (ECtHR, 30 June 2008) and *R Singh v France* App no 27561/08 (ECtHR, 30 June 2009).

tisements seeking other potentially qualified candidates that were Dutch citizens or EU members prior to offering the post to the applicant. After further attempts to have this decision overturned at various state levels, the applicant and applicant foundation brought their case to the ECtHR, arguing that a violation of Article 9 and of Article 18 had occurred. During the proceedings, in 2006, the applicant received a work permit to serve as an *imam* after the mosque resubmitted the paperwork for employment of foreign nationals. This being the case, the Court decided (by 14 votes to 3) to strike the application from their list.[126]

5. CONCLUSIONS

This brief overview reveals tremendous variance in the legal status of NRMs and other minority faiths in the 'new Europe'. Some nations such as Hungary and the Netherlands have seemed more solicitous of minority faiths, while others, such as France and more recently Russia, seem quite hostile to such entities.[127] Also, the pattern of legal protections and opportunities afforded such groups varies by location and time, with great changes sometimes occurring in a short period, as has been the case with Russia.

This chapter also reveals a pattern of rulings from the ECtHR that demands more examination. There has been some evidence from the case law of the Court that a double standard might be operating, as Richardson and his colleagues posit.[128] However, there also is some evidence for Evans's theory and that of Garlicki that the major focus of the Court is on protecting the right of religious organisations to exist, and that the Court is not nearly as solicitous of individual religious freedom concerns.[129] And, as Meerschaut and Gutwirth and Cumper suggest, the European Court's jurisprudence also seems to demonstrate a pro-Christian (and anti-Muslim, anti-NRM bias).[130] Thus no general conclusion about the legal status of

---

[126]   *El Majjaoui & Stichting Touba Moskee v The Netherlands*, App no 25525/03, decided on 20 December 2007.

[127]   However, there has been a very recent development in Hungary with efforts to pass what some call the most restrictive law in Europe concerning minority religions. See note 55 above.

[128]   Richardson and Garay (note 30 above) and Richardson and Shoemaker (note 28 above).

[129]   Evans, *Freedom of Religion under the ECHR* (note 89 above) and Garlicki (note 89 above). The recent decision favouring the Witnesses in France (note 119 above) would seem to offer especial support for this view.

[130]   Meerschaut and Gutwirth (note 98 above) and Cumper (note 4 above).

NRMs and other minority religions can be drawn from this review, except to say that when examining this issue the history and cultural values of the nation being studied need to be taken into account. Political changes such as occurred in the mid-1990s in Russia, and which might be occurring in Hungary, can result in dramatic modifications of the legal status of religious groups.

Index